THE TRAINING TECHNOLOGY PROGRAMME

Volume 7

THE MANAGEMENT OF TRAINING

Produced by the North West Consortium

Volume 7

THE MANAGEMENT OF TRAINING

Andy Davies, John Macleod, Chris Williams, Aidan Hughes, Mike Cross, John Stock and Jim Garbett

Supported by OPEN TECH

Parthenon Publishing

THE PARTHENON PUBLISHING GROUP LIMITED

The Training Technology Programme is published on behalf of the North West Consortium by:

In the U.K. and Europe

The Parthenon Publishing Group Ltd
Casterton Hall
Carnforth
Lancashire LA6 2LA
England

ISBN 1-85070-164-4

In the U.S.A.

The Parthenon Publishing Group Inc
120 Mill Road
Park Ridge
NJ 07656
U.S.A.

ISBN 0-940813-36-X

Editorial Note

The male pronoun has been used throughout the Training Technology Programme for stylistic reasons only. It covers both masculine and feminine genders.

© Crown Copyright 1987

Published by permission of the Controller of Her Majesty's Stationery Office.

This work was produced under an Open Tech contract with the Manpower Services Commission. The views expressed are those of the authors and do not necessarily reflect those of the MSC or any other Government Department.

This work may not be reproduced in any form without the permission from the publishers except for the quotation of brief passages for the purpose of reviews.

Printed in Great Britain

THE TRAINING TECHNOLOGY PROGRAMME

The Training Technology Programme (TTP) aims to provide materials which will help improve training and learning.
The Programme is presented by the North West Consortium, consisting of Lancashire Polytechnic, S. Martin's College and Lancashire College.
TTP is a set of distance learning materials in two versions. There is a choice between a hard-back Volume edition and a soft-back Package edition.

Volume/Package 1	The Systematic Design of Training Courses *Bob Wilson*
Volume/Package 2	Methods of Training: Groupwork *Bob Wilson*
Volume/Package 3	Methods of Training: Individualised Instruction *Bob Wilson*
Volume/Package 4	Methods of Training: Resource-Based and Open Learning; Study Skills *Bob Wilson*
Volume/Package 5	Learner Psychology in Training *Melissa Towner et al*
Volume/Package 6	Assessment and Evaluation in Training *John Stock et al*
Volume/Package 7	The Management of Training *Andy Davies et al*
Volume/Package 8	Graphics in Training *Peter Osborne et al*
Volume/Package 9	Audio Techniques in Training *Peter Darnton*
Volume/Package 10	Projected Still Images in Training *Roy Thorpe*
Volume/Package 11	Using Video in Training *Fred Fawbert*
Volume/Package 12	Computer Based Training *Bob Lewis et al*
Volume/Package 13	Interactive Video in Training *Gerard O'Neill*

PROGRAMME PRODUCTION

Project Manager .... *Bob Wilson*
Co-ordinator .... *John Stock*
Programme Co-ordinator .... *Kath Litherland*
Video Advisor .... *Fred Fawbert*
Audio Advisor .... *Peter Darnton*
Main Illustrators .... *Angela Pour-Rahnema*
David Hill & Lesley Sumner
Editors .... *Andy Davies & Derek Oliver*
Production Team Members .... *Lynne Hamer, Judith Hindle*
Caroline Nesfield (Programme Secretary)
Susan Western, Bobby Whittaker

ACKNOWLEDGEMENTS

With gratitude and appreciation to the many who have supported the Programme including the Directorate, Principals and mangement of Lancashire Polytechnic, S. Martin's College and Lancashire College; David Bloomer, Norma Brennan, Cyril Cavies, Ryland Clendon, Noel Goulsbra, Stanley Henig, Tony James, Peter Knight, Joe Lee, Ken Phillips, Alan Sharples, Ross Simpson; The Director and members of MSC Open Tech, especially Steve Emms, Les Goodman, Fiona Jordan; last, but certainly not least, The Authors' Families.

FOR FURTHER INFORMATION

Write to Bob Wilson, Programme Director,
Training Technology Programme, Lancashire Polytechnic,
PRESTON, PR1 2TQ. Tel. (0772) 22141

Foreword
to the Training Technology Programme

Today we see technology being applied to every department of civilised living. It comes in many forms and its applications are virtually limitless. What we see today, although it is transforming society, is but the beginning, and the extent and pace of change is likely to increase many times.

It is most fitting and timely therefore that a systematic effort is being made to apply technology to training. The techniques available are very varied ranging from computers to audio visual equipment. It will enable training to be undertaken privately at home or at the work place in a group, in the remote croft or in the city.

Technology is revolutionising training; I welcome therefore this Training Technology Programme developed by the North West Consortium and Parthenon Publishing, supported by the Manpower Services Commission. It brings training in technology, through the medium of technology, to more people than ever before.

I commend it and I am delighted to have been invited to contribute this foreword.

John Banham
Director General CBI

Contents

Study Unit Five:

ANALYSING TRAINING MATERIALS

Study Unit Six:

DESIGN AND IMPLEMENTING TRAINING PROGRAMMES

Study Unit 1:

Establishing the overall need for training

Component 1:

Analysing your Organisation

Key Words

 **Analysis; aims and objectives; authority, power and decision making; organisational activities; formal preference; simple/complex; primary/secondary.**

The main aim of this Unit is to help you to analyse your organisation, so that you can form a good idea of the training needs of its personnel.

To do this you will need:

1. to have some introductory or background information;
2. to have some idea (or definition) of what an organisation is;
3. to decide what kind of an organisation yours is (i.e. to classify it);
4. to set out what the objectives of your organisation are, and to see how these relate to the personal objectives (outlooks, aims, ambitions, preferences) of those who work in it.

We begin with some background material.

1. Background

It would be hard (? impossible) to imagine life in our society without organisations. This has always been true for civilised humans, but it is particularly true of the late twentieth century. We are born in organisations, and are laid to rest by organisations. We spend our leisure time paying, playing and praying in a variety of consumer, service, and voluntary organisations. In an advanced economy, organisations (rather than individuals or families) provide the goods and services on which we depend.

Think of a goods-producing organisation (car factory; building firm; bakery). Think of a service-giving organisation (bank, dry cleaners; hotel). What do they have in common? Employees — of many grades, and having many skills.

Some would say that it is employees that are the most important element in any organisation. Without them, nothing at all. But employees without the necessary competence or commitment severely restrict what an organisation can do.

Is this a new idea? No, but industrial and commercial organisations have come to face:

— a new and rapidly changing technology;
— changed social attitudes;
— shifts in the expectations of consumers and buyers,

as they have had to work out much more positive and systematic approaches to the training and development of their employees. Training can make a major contribution to the success with which an organisation can meet its objectives. Training is **needed** from time to time, by all members of the organisation — from shop-floor, or counter staff, to board room directors.

Training is important. But what sort of training? If we want to go somewhere, we must know where we are starting from. We need a careful, objective, analysis of the organisation's overall training requirements. We also need a commitment to act on the analysis we make, but we cannot do without a patient, careful analysis. Draw on your own experience. You can no doubt recall occasions where action was taken to put a matter 'right' before a proper diagnosis was made. How disastrous was the result, in wasted money, time and effort?

Proceed with caution. Do not plan training without a diagnosis of training needs. To make a diagnosis of teaching needs is not easy without first of all establishing what **kind** of organisation you are working in. And to do this, you need to know what an organisation is.

It may help to think of training as a course of medicine. You cannot prescribe without diagnosing what is wrong with the patient. To do this you need to know what kind of body you are dealing with (old, young, male, female, ill for a long time etc.). To make sense of any of this, you have to know some physiology i.e. what is a body and how does it work? This will apply whether you are working in an organisation which is part of a much larger one as a branch etc., or an organisation which has only one offer of place of work etc.

2. Organisations — what are they?

Let us suppose you were asked to describe your organisation in not more that **two** short sentences. Try it, it's not very easy is it? Now try and write down one sentence which might describe all organisations you know. This is even more difficult. Before you give up in disgust, let's try another way.

Write down at least **five** facts which you think are common to **all** organisations.

I don't know what you have written down but compare them with the following:

(a) organisations always include people;
(b) all these people are involved with both one another in some way, i.e. they interact with each other;
(c) all these interactions are not random ones but can be ordered in some way;
(d) everybody working in the organisation will have some personal reasons for being in the organisation, which guides his behaviour;
(e) some of these reasons may be shared with others within the organisation.

Now try again to define your organisation; I hope you found it easier this time.

Can I mention two problems which **you** may have already met. The first is that you may end up with a statement that has to cover too much and become meaningless. The other is that your statement is too narrow and from your own point of view. Try it out on somebody else in the organisation. Does it have any meaning for them? If it does then you are on the right track.

I am now going to set out a definition of organisations which I have found useful as a starting point. I hope you find it useful too.

I have taken this definition from "The Management of Organisations" by H. G. Hicks, published by Open University Press (1972).

> "Organisations are social units (or human groupings) deliberately constructed and reconstructed to seek specific goals. Corporations, armies, schools, hospitals, churches and prisons are included. Tribes, classes, friendship groups and families are excluded. Organisations are characterised by:
>
> 1. divisions of labour, power and communication responsibilities, divisions which are not random or traditionally patterned but deliberately planned to enhance the realisation of specific goals;
> 2. the presence of one or more power centres which control the concerted efforts of the organisation and direct them towards its goal. These power centres must also review continuously, the organisation's performance and reputation and its structure where necessary to increase its efficiency;
> 3. Substitution of personnel through transfer and promotion."

In your research for a suitable definition for your organisation will probably have made you aware of other organisations which you or your own organisation deals with. You will also have realised that they are all very different. As a general step in the process of analysing your own organisation it would be useful to try to find out if different organisations have anything in common so that it may be possible to set out a more detailed classification.

Checkpoint

Take any **four** organisations you have knowledge of, including your own and compare and contrast their main activities. I hope you did not find the task difficult. I do not know what you decided, but you can compare your answer with the examples I am now going to set out.

The first approach is to label organisations **formal** *or* **informal** *according to the way in which the different individuals, groups, etc. relate to each other. We can show it like this:*

FORMAL ◄————————————————► INFORMAL

It would probably be impossible to find a good example of either of these types of organisations and most would fall somewhere in between.

A formal organisation *will be very clear in the way it defines its authority, power and other responsibilities. It clearly sets out its channels of communication and all the jobs will be clearly specified. What the organisation does will be clearly set out as will be the pay and status of jobs. These organisations are usually shown by an organisations chart. Has yours got one?*

This is a chart showing exactly what the chain of authority etc. in the organisation is **supposed** *to be — it does not mean that this is the way in which the organisation actually functions!*

E.g. Large companies, B.B.C., Government departments.

E.g.

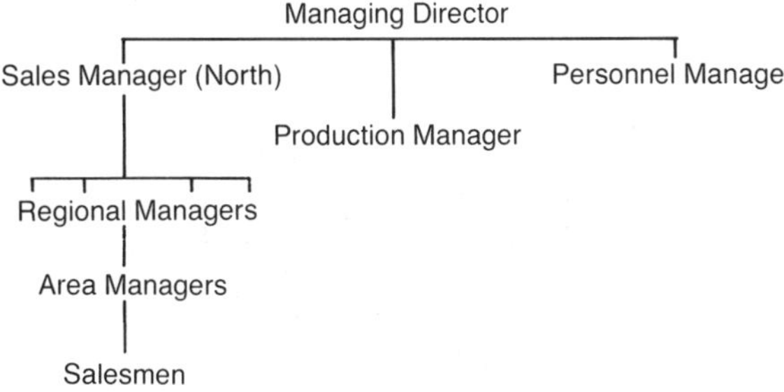

At the other end of the scale are **informal organisations** *which are loosely organised and not nearly so well defined. What the organisation does is not too clear and the jobs of the people involved are not specified in a straight-forward way.*

A second approach to classifying organisations is to just call them **simple** *and* **complex. Simple** *organisations can vary from just two people meeting in the street to the small corner shop or small firm. Most of the people working in them usually do more than one job.* **Complex** *organisations are usually very large and usually much more formal.*

A third way to classify organisations is to label them **primary** *or* **secondary** *according to how involved in the organisation each individual is. Primary organisations are usually characterised by the way in which the members work together. They are usually professional people who do not have clearly set out contracts and deal with each other in a personal face to face manner. Examples of these include lawyers, accountants etc. Secondary organisations are made up of people with well defined job specifications and involve themselves in the organisation, only to the extent of what is set out for their job. Loyalty to the organisation only goes as deep as the job they do. Of course any organisation can have members for whom the organisation is primary and other members who may regard the organisation as a secondary one. How do you classify yourself?*

How do you classify yourself in relation to your commitment to your organisation? Are you primary or secondary?

A fourth way to classify organisations is according to the most important part of the work they do. Every organisation is formed for some important reason and they can be grouped on this basis. I will give some examples for you:

(a) Service organisations — local authorities
(b) Economic organisations — business firms
(c) Religious organisations
(d) Protective organisations — police force
(e) Government organisations — DHSS
(f) Social organisations — clubs etc.

Now go back and compare your classifications in the first Checkpoint with these so far. I don't suppose they are the same but I am sure some of them may be similar. Can you fit any of the organisations you used into any classification? I doubt if you can exactly; and some of the organisations will contain pieces of all these classifications. This does not matter; the important point is for you to have a much clearer idea of what your organisation does.

---

3. Analysis

I hope you now have a few ideas of what your organisation looks like but this is only a start. If you want to make sure you have enough information to see if you need a training programme then we must take a closer look at your organisation.

There are a number of ways of doing this. One way is to divide the organisation into its most important areas and look at each of these in turn. It would be impossible for me to set out the most important areas of all organisations. What I am going to do is to set out **three** examples of the most important areas which I think are common to **all** organisations and are very important for information to be able to make decisions on training policy. I will explain them and set out some key questions. Your job will be to build on these and to be able to do the same exercise for the other important areas of your organisation.

(a) Aims & Objectives

The first area to look at is what is called by the technical terms: **aims** and **objectives**. What is the **organisation** supposed to be doing and what are the **individual members** of the organisation supposed to be doing.

What the organisation is supposed to be doing may be set out in an information booklet about your organisation or you may have to find out for yourself if they are not written down somewhere. These organisational objectives should serve as reference points for what the organisation does and are also supposed to detail such things as organisation policy, proceeding rules etc. when you find out what the organisational objectives are, see if they actually describe what the organisation does now and what it hopes to be doing in the near future. If your organisation is a profit making one then the organisational objectives may be set out under different headings like profits, level of investment, product development etc. If your organisation is a non profit making one, the aims and objectives will be set out by reference to the areas in which the services are provided e.g. developing and maintaining high professional standards.

Now although **all** organisations may have aims and objectives, most organisations are created and maintained by the members as a means of satisfying their **personal** aims and objectives. "Should I stay with this company or should I go and look for another job?" "Should I join this club or not?" Such questions are always part of a person's decisions to go into, remain, or leave an organisation. Any individual supports an organisation if he believes that through the organisation his own personal objectives are being met. If not it won't be long before he loses interest. It is therefore very important to try and find out what the personal objectives of the members are and the extent to which **they** think they are being satisfied. The effectiveness of a member's input into the organisation is directly related to his own idea of how the organisation helps him to satisfy his own objectives. If he thinks they are, then he will be a useful member, if he thinks they are not then the organisation may have a problem, where a course of training **may** help. Let me explain this a bit more fully. Each member of the organisation has **two** ideas about himself and his organisation; let's call them A. and B. A. is his idea of the objectives that he expects to achieve by being a member of the organisation. B. is his idea of the objectives of the organisation. Of course the member will not think of them as A. and B. He may not even be conscious of them at all. What usually happens is something like this: "This firm builds good houses and pays its work force quite well." "I need the money and I think I am a good brick layer". Thus A. and B. appear to coincide for him. He, therefore, joins the firm, so that by helping the organisation he is helping himself. Probably the most successful organisations are those for which A. and B. coincide for **all** its members and where all the ideas about B. are the same for all its members.

Before we leave the topic it is important to recognise the main points about objectives:

1. All organisations and individuals have them — whether they know it or not.
2. In any organisation (or indeed in the case of an individual generally-speaking) the overall objectives are usually fairly general but as one moves down the structure, as it were, they become more and more specific and limited. For example, the industrial company with the development of new markets as a main objective will have more specific ones set out as one goes into departmental objectives. Such specific ones might include expansion into European markets — thus limiting the original objective — and you can no doubt see that additional limits or terms of reference may be produced as the objectives become more specific still. Another example will illustrate this — the expansion into European markets might become 'starting with West Germany in 198- and concentrating on our four main lines only for the first year'.
3. All objectives must change or be modified as circumstances demand; they are not set for all time! They relate to a living organism (either you as the

individual, or an organisation made up of people) hence they must adapt.

4. Objectives need not be written — but it is better if they are so argument can be avoided, so they can be read by all concerned, so they can be crystallised. Many organisations and most individuals do not have written ones; do you?
5. Objectives can only be achieved if they are realistic; highflown and unattainable ones are of little value. They must relate to the circumstances in which the organisation or the person finds itself (himself) and they must link with resources available.
6. All objectives must link with a policy or policies — that is, a statement of intent showing how the objective(s) are to be achieved. Objectives without policy are just so much hot air — impractical probably.
7. Departmental objectives cannot be set in isolation; they must fit in with objectives from other departments otherwise the organisation will collapse. The same goes for policies as we will see later.

At this point take five or ten minutes to consider and list:

(a) the objectives of the organisation with which you are familiar;
(b) the objectives of your own department within that organisation;

and

(c) your own objectives for the next twelve months. I suggest you list them using these three headings.

(a) Organisational
(b) Departmental
(c) Personal

I don't know what your answers will be but they could include some like these:

(a) Organisational
To consolidate our share of the market over the next year, to improve profitability by X% over the next Y months.
To devote £XYZ to the development of the proposed
....
To develop W new retail outlets in the East of England by......
To provide a superduper BMX track for geriatrics in the ...... area of the city.

(b) Departmental
To place X% of our sales promotion budget in the development in West Germany by means of exhibitions and locating one senior salesperson in Bonn.
To reduce transport costs by 10% by December 19..
To allocate Y staff for the development of the new engine within a budget of £ABC.
To negotiate the rental of Z new sites below £W per square foot.
To restructure staffing levels in the existing BMX tracks to allow for the new track without increasing staff in the department.

(c) Personal
To improve my game so I will be picked to play for my country.
To learn how to drive a car.
To decorate the lounge and kitchen before August.
To learn elementary German before going on holiday to the Rhine.
To improve my work performance in the hope of promotion.

I have spent some time on this section because I think it is very important that you establish the aims and objectives of the organisation and the aims and objectives of its members. If the gap between these for a lot of the members is big then something has to be done about the situation very quickly. This will probably involve you in asking a lot of questions and some interviewing. You will find some examples of questions at the end of this component. They are only examples and I hope you will change them and add to them as you analyse your own organisation.

(b) Achieving objectives
A second example of an area to look at in your organisation is what the organisation is doing to achieve the objectives it has set out. You must look at what work is being done and what work needs to be done if all the objectives both of the members and of the organisation are to be achieved. Establish exactly what the organisation is doing. For example, is your organisation producing some product or is it a service one or is it a selling organisation? Does the organisation rely on a lot of human labour and/or does it use a lot of technical equipment? The analysis of the organisation's activities should establish what is and what is not being done? Who is doing it? Where is it being done and how much is being done? You should establish the extent to which everything is being done that needs to be done and that nothing is being done that does not need to be done and the extent to which all activities are being done in the right place at the right time and by the right people. Again you will find some specimen questions at the end of this component.

(c) Decisions! Decisions!

A third area to look at is the way in which decisions are being taken in the organisation. This will, for example, show how work is being delegated and how and where decisions are being taken. The main aim here is to establish who has the final say in making decisions in the different areas of the organisation, who is responsible for setting out questions for decision making and who contributes information and advice. Analysis of the decision making process within your organisation should concentrate on the extent to which the decisions are being made in the right place and the extent to which there is adequate information, communication and consultations during the process of decision making.

I have now set out **three** key areas of any organisation be it a large organisation, or a branch of one, which must be analysed in order to understand how the organisation works and help you towards making decisions on what the training needs of the organisation are.

You look at your own organisation — **what** are the **other** main areas in it? **What information** do you think you need? **Which questions** do you need to ask in order to get this information and **who** do you ask? You need to **observe what is** going on and ask a lot of questions. If you do this thoroughly you should have enough information about your organisation to start sorting out its training needs.

Specimen questions

(a) Aims and objectives

1. *What are the overall aims of the organisation?*
2. *Are these aims clearly defined?*
3. *Are they appropriate?*
4. *What is the general nature of the work carried out by your organisation?*
5. *List the specific objectives of the organisation in terms of the main sections of its work e.g. profits, market share, services etc.*
6. *How clearly are the organisation's objectives understood by its members?*
7. *Are the members' objectives clear?*
8. *Are all the members quite clear as to what is expected of them?*
9. *Are these expectations consistent with the overall objectives of the organisation?*
10. *How much job flexibility is there in the main sections of the organisation?*
11. *Do all the jobs done by the members given them satisfaction?*
12. *Are the organisation's job specifications quite clear?*

(b) Activities

1. *What are the main activities carried out by your organisation? Classify these in terms of the main sections.*
2. *Are all the activities of the organisation consistent with the objectives of:*
   (a) the organisation
   (b) the members.
3. *How much unnecessary work is being carried out?*

(c) Decisions

1. *What key decisions have to be made by your organisation in any time period (a) day, (b) week?*
2. *Who has the authority to make these decisions?*
3. *What other members contribute to the key decisions?*
4. *Are the guidelines for decision making clearly laid out?*
5. *Can those who have to make the decisions in your organisation obtain information easily?*
6. *Are* **all** *the decisions being made by the* **right** *people in the* **right** *place at the* **right** *time?*
7. *What evidence can you get to show that the* **proper** *decisions are* **not** *being taken?*

May I remind you again that these questions are only for your guidance. **You** *know* **your** *organisation. Decide what information you want and design your own questions.*

Component 2:

Reasons for Training

Key Words

 **Change; environment; policies; technology; economics.**

1. Introduction

We will start off this Component with a short story: Fred Smith was a small coach operator running advertised tours from a small town in the north to various places of interest throughout the country. Sometimes he would hire one of his coaches out to a private party but as he thought this type of business was unpredictable he did not do much of it.

Trying to earn as much as possible Fred decided on a policy of not changing anything except his prices, which he increased in line with inflation. He kept the same coaches, the same old drivers and his main tour contracts; after some years the business declined and the inevitable headlines appeared in the local paper, "Fred's buses go bust".

Checkpoint

Attempt to list **five** reasons why poor Fred's business went broke.

See if you can group your answers according to the following questions:

1. How many were directly Fred's fault? — he could have prevented them.
2. How many could he do nothing to prevent?
3. How many could he have avoided by taking earlier action?

Fred could probably have stopped wasteful spending of cash, the old coaches breaking down, the lack of efficient booking arrangements etc. On the other hand he could do nothing to prevent another company moving in with its new coaches and new tours, the number of people who were put on the dole due to closing of local industry or the changing tastes of his former customers. By taking earlier action he could have avoided having his coaches off the road and he could have had some trained relief drivers to take over when the regular ones went sick.

Look at Fred's problems again. What were the **reasons** for his problems?

Group your reasons under the following headings:

1. Changes that came about outside the firm and therefore largely out of Fred's control.
2. Changes that came about inside the firm and therefore under his control.

Changes outside the organisation have been recognised for a long time and have become popularly known as Murphy's Law. The most common version of Murphy's Law is "Whatever can go wrong, will". No matter how carefully you plan something happens over which you have "no control" and affects your plans. These are the events that take place in the outside world or to give it its technical term "the environment". Organisations wouldn't have any problems if its environment were stable and did not change. Unfortunately it does change and also the ***rate*** *of change also changes to make things more interesting. You may know things are going to change but what you do not know is:*

(a) when the change is going to take place and
(b) what the change is going to be.

Looking at your own organisation, what do you think is its main environment?

Take a few minutes to think about this question.

Changes can also occur **inside** the organisation. Some occur naturally and while they cannot be controlled they can be planned for. People, machinery and buildings get older day by day and while this process cannot be prevented, it can be foreseen. Some changes can be controlled to a greater or lesser extent, such as the rate at which people leave the organisation or the frequency with which equipment is to be replaced. Other changes occurring inside the organisation are those that are deliberately planned. For example, someone in authority may not be happy at the way in which some part of the organisation is working and will introduce changes to try and improve the situation.

I have spent so much time over the introduction for a number of reasons. All organisations are faced with changes both inside and outside. If the organisation is to survive, all these changes have to be anticipated as far as possible and planned for. This fact of industrial and commercial life is not very new, but it is only comparatively recently that these changes have forced employers to pay a particular attention to the **manpower** policies and practices. More and more companies have become aware of the need to adopt a systematic approach to the training and development of its employees. Training is now seen as making a major contribution to company achievement and survival.

I shall now go on to take a closer look at these external and internal reasons why it is so important for an organisation to have a positive and systematic training programme. However before we leave this section two last questions. In your organisation:

1. Who has been trained to take over from your immediate boss if that individual gets promotion or leaves?
2. Who will take over from you if you leave?

Take 10-15 minutes for this task.

---

2. What external factors does an organisation have to take into account?

(a) The political environment

Every country has to have a government of some sort and all governments have to engage in certain activities which will cost a lot of money — defence, social services, education, etc. In order to raise this money the Government has to tax individuals and organisations. At any one time a government, because of the need to finance its activities, may be using up at least one third of the wealth of the country for this purpose. In addition our governments use other regulations as well as taxes to regulate the economy and these all affect organisations. All organisations have to live with this and always have to take into account whatever the government is doing. Some governments try to leave firms alone while others seem to take a delight in creating new laws that increase the number of forms that have to be filled. If that is not enough, all organisations also have to deal with local councils whose actions may also affect the way in which an organisation is run.

GOVERNMENT PLANS FOR NATIONALISATION

Take a look in your daily or local newspapers and find the biggest story involving a national or local political decision (passing a new law or a statement by a minister or local councillor). Ask yourself how much the decision affects:
(a) your own organisation;
(b) your local shop;
(c) a local housebuilder.
Take 5-10 minutes to complete this task.

(b) The Economic Environment
Probably the most important sector which our organisations have to take into account is the economic environment. Every year in late March or early April the whole country eagerly awaits what the Chancellor of the Exchequer has to say in his budget speech and the effects this may have on individuals in firms.

These could be immediate, as for example, a rise in petrol prices would set up queues at pumps. The state of the economy is always changing and the organisation that succeeds is usually the one which is able to keep ahead of the main trends.

Probably the **two** main areas of the economy which have the most effect on organisations are first of all **the inflation rate**. Everyone knows about the rate of inflation and what the effects are, as prices rise in the shops. Everyone has to pay more for what they buy. Organisations, also in inflationary terms, have to pay more for their raw materials, wages, electricity bills etc. For a time the organisation may be able to overcome these problems by raising its own prices but there comes a point when people will resist these rises and stop buying the organisation's goods and services. Then there are **interest rates**. If you have money in a Building Society or a bank then you know that you will receive interest on your money but if you are buying your house on a mortgage or have a loan from a bank you will have to pay interest and the higher the interest rate, the more you will have to pay. Organisations sometimes have to borrow a lot of money to expand or finance a new product and if the interest rate rises, it will cost them a lot of money.

Try this simple sum: calculate the amount of extra money that your organisation would have to pay in a year, if the interest rate on their loan of £1 million were to rise from 10% to 12.1%.

Again, the successful organisation will be the one which is able, by this efficiency, to overcome these sudden changes and a well informed labour force will pay a major part in this.

(c) The Technological Environment
In 1960 the USA had the largest tape recorder industry in the world but by 1970 not a single magnetic tape was manufactured there. In ten years a major industry had vanished. Changes in technology have had immense effects everywhere in the last thirty years. Space-age technology, as it is popularly called, has taken over everywhere — look around your house and count how many examples of new goods you have. Organisations must be aware of all these changes. For example they have to beware of those competitors who may achieve some technological development and undercut them. This is what happened to the American tape recorder industry in the face of Japanese competition. If the organisation does not build the latest technological development into its own products then they will soon be left behind and go out of business. Also all organisations have a lot of equipment of one kind or another, from very computerised production equipment to office machines, typewriters, telephones etc. These are being updated all the time and all organisations are faced with the problem of how much to spend on the latest equipment for office or workshop. The organisation that fails to keep up-to-date will not succeed for very long.

Then....

Now...

Look round your place of work and identify the most up-to-date piece of equipment you can see. How soon do you think it will be out of date?

In the face of all these technological changes it is the firm which has a systematic training programme to enable the work force to come to terms with all the latest equipment that will survive. If not, the only answer is the laying off of its employees as machines take over their work. This may be inevitable in some cases but at least the workers will have had the benefit of a training programme and may get another job as a result.

I have now set out **three** important areas of an organisation's **external** environment where it has to take careful notice if it is going to survive. You should now try to set out at least another **three** areas of your organisation's external environment which you think are important. Take about 15 minutes for this task.

Having now read all of this section you should have a few ideas of how the external environment is affecting your organisation. The increasing rate of change and the difficulty of making accurate predictions of what is going to happen means that the organisation which is going to survive is the one which adapts most quickly to these changes. This is very important in the area with which we are concerned, namely, the labour force. It does not take much intelligence to see that a well trained and flexible labour force in an organisation that is fully geared to systematic training and realises the need for retraining will go a long way to help the organisation to survive in the very competitive world of today.

3. What are the internal benefits of a training programme?

It would be impossible to list all the internal benefits that a systematic training programme will bring to every organisation, as they are all very different and will all emphasise different aspects of training in different ways. What I shall do is list several types of training that can be identified in all organisations.

(a) Training for the immediate job to be done, e.g. helping a new sales assistant to deal with customers.
(b) Training to understand more about the company and how it operates.
(c) Training to prepare for promotion.
(d) Training for general all round efficiency and understanding, e.g. training in computer skills.

Take a look at your own organisation and either using my headings or some of your own, make a list of the benefits which you think a good training programme will bring to your organisation. Take about 15 minutes to do this task and try not to look at the examples that follow.

Again I do not know what you have written but see if they include some of the following:

1. *Training helps employees to learn their jobs quickly and effectively and thus minimise the costs to the firm while they are learning.*
2. *Staff who are given help by efficient training to learn their jobs quickly will probably get more job satisfaction and will lead to remain longer with the firm.*
3. *Training to improve job performance will help the company to achieve its standard of work.*
4. *A good retraining programme will enable new abilities to replace out of date skills.*
5. *Employees will stay with the firm longer if they can see that the firm has a systematic training and development programme.*
6. *A company with a reputation for providing good training tends to attract better applicants.*
7. *A well trained staff will make less mistakes and on the whole produce more goods in an efficient manner.*
8. *Training will probably reduce accidents and enforced lay offs which will cost the company money.*

This is just a general list and I hope yours contains all these and more.

I think you are now in a position to do one or two important jobs for your organisation. If it has not got a training programme, you are now able to set out a clear case of why it should have one. If it already has a training programme you can supply a lot of information to those involved in the programme on how to improve it. I wish you a lot of success.

To recap; what we have done in this Component was first of all to show the importance to an organisation of a systematic training programme to maintain staff development. Secondly, the rapidly changing environment and the important internal benefits means that no organisation can survive long without a training programme.

Component 3:

The Training Policy in the Organisation

Key Words

Policy; a course of action; reasons for a policy; realism; relationships; contents; implementation; implications; revision.

Objectives

By the end of this Component you will:—

1. understand and appreciate the purpose and importance of designing a training policy
2. appreciate the inter-relationships between the training policy and the other policies within the organisation
3. have established the main features of an effective training policy
4. be able to design a relevant training policy for your own section/department/organisation and take into account the implications arising
5. be able to consider its application in practice and the need for regular examination and revision.

1. Introduction

In this Component the aim is to allow you to develop your understanding and appreciation of the training policy in either your own organisation or one with which you are familiar and, indeed, to be able to consider and evaluate those of other organisations if you so wish.

We shall be looking at a number of important aspects starting with defining what a policy is and then going on to consider the relationships any particular policy has with, and its possible effects upon, other policies in that organisation. We shall, too, consider the possible implications of fulfilling the training policy in particular on, for instance, the people, time, finance and other resources.

Unless we know and understand what the training policy is there is little point in going further and devising any training schemes or programmes; such schemes or programmes will run the risk of being 'hit-or-miss', or like the proverbial curate's egg they will be good in parts! However, many organisations train for a variety of reasons such as 'it's a good thing', 'well, if it's good enough for . . . . . . it's good enough for us'. (**N.B.** fill in the name of some well known organisation here). You might be able to produce a number of similar statements from your own experience - all indicating that the organisation's training policy is not its own but really from another organisation. A little thought will show that such a 'policy' is likely to be somewhat irrelevant as all policies, whether training ones or others, must relate to the needs and aims of the specific organisation.

However, the purpose of this introduction is not to develop your knowledge of excuses and rationalisations but to set the scene for what follows.

Anyway, enough of that — let's start by examining this word 'policy' and trying to define it;

Here you can look in a dictionary to see how it is defined – you will find a series of definitions depending on the size and type of dictionary.

Most include something such as 'a course of action'; in other words, **how** the objectives are to be reached. In any organisation there will be overall policies and more precise ones covering departmental activities; whatever number there is they will cover all aspects of the organisation's operations — and the same applies to individual policies, of course. For example, there will be a financial policy dealing with such points as how money can be raised, from what sources, over what periods, with what security, on whose authority, via the stock market or a commercial bank, a secondary bank or by borrowing from great-aunt Hilda, to name but a few. There will be a policy covering research, perhaps stating what lines are to be followed, how much money is to be allocated annually, if the research is to be original or more in the way of development, if it is to be limited to lines capable of being in production within a year, if it is to be in-company or in association with other organisations or via a research organisation (such as W.I.R.A. — the Wool Industry Research Association) or university or polytechnic. These are just two areas of policy within an organisation; you can multiply them greatly — consider, for instance, distribution, transport, industrial relations, welfare production, marketing, selling, sales, promotion, property development and many others. You will, of course, have noticed we have omitted training — so far.

Checkpoint

You have read one hint at a definition of training policy and you may have read others; take five minutes — and no more — to produce your own definition of what a training policy is — not its contents (we'll come to them later). Try to produce something understandable and acceptable; you are not trying to produce the all-time definition but really to clear your mind. Write your definition on a separate sheet of paper or in your notebook.

Now you have produced your own definition remember that there is no one set and standard version; however, here is a fairly common one:—

A policy *is a statement of intent showing how the objectives of an organisation are to be fulfilled bearing in mind the resources available and any possible constraints.*

Check how yours measures up against this one; it is highly unlikely that they will be identical — that is not necessary so long as the three points of 'objectives', 'resources' and 'constraints' are included in one form or another.

Now we have seen what 'policy' is, let us look at a training policy from an organisation and see what it contains; here it is — incidentally the organisation is a large national one; identification features have been removed:—

Statement of Training Policy

The Organisation recognises that training and development of management and staff is a major priority if it is to create and maintain satisfied customers and expand as a profitable concern.

The aims of training are to ensure that all employees are given the necessary help to develop the knowledge, skills and attitudes that they require to carry out their jobs efficiently and to provide every opportunity for career development. The Organisation trains both to satisfy its requirements as identified by management and to fulfil the needs of the individual.

It is recognised that the responsibility for training lies with all members of the management and supervisory team who will be given appropriate training in instructional techniques. They will be supported in this role by Regional and National training specialists.

The specific commitments of the training policy are as follows:

1. Induction training will be given to all new employees, to familiarise them with the Organisation and to illustrate their place within it.
2. During the early weeks of employment, or following transfer, all employees will receive thorough training in the basic skills of their jobs, including off-the-job instruction where relevant.
3. Training will be provided on a regular basis to reinforce and update an understanding of the Organisation's objectives, policies and procedures.
4. Where practicable, to encourage job satisfaction and maintain efficiency, staff will be trained in a variety of skills to achieve flexibility within units.
5. All employees will be trained in health, safety and hygiene for the protection of the individual and to meet both the needs of the business and legal requirements, in accordance with the Organisation's Policy Statement.
6. Job-related further education is considered an important element of career development and staff will be encouraged to make full use of external facilities which could include colleges of further education and correspondence courses.
7. All managers and supervisors will coach and counsel their subordinates appropriately as a regular feature of the relationship.
8. Regular, formal appraisals will be conducted at least once a year to assess performance and potential for promotion and to identify training needs. Each such appraisal will involve a face-to-face interview and discussion with manager or supervisor.
9. Job succession planning will be carried out and appropriate training given to develop potential before or immediately following promotion.
10. Training records will be maintained, to indicate the achievement of objectives and to assist in the identification of further training needs.

Finally the Organisation recognises that adequate resources and facilities must be provided to ensure that the commitments described above can be met.

This is just one example of a modern training policy; it comes from a successful organisation but it does not follow that all policies must be like this one. Some may be longer, some shorter, some very precise, some much more general; this is not particularly important so long as certain factors apply. However, before we look at some of the factors let's have another activity.

Take ten minutes to produce from the policy quoted what you think are the main points of interest which we can apply to every effective training policy. For starters, here is one point:—
All employees are covered
Now you go ahead and add as many others as you can find:—

You could well have added some or all of these:
Training and development go hand-in-hand
Training is a major priority
The aims are to develop knowledge, skills and attitudes
Another aim is to satisfy both the organisation and the person
ALL *new employees get induction training*
Training applies to transfers as well as new employees
Training is on-job and off-job
Managers and supervisors have the responsibility for training
Advice and assistance is available from regional and national resources
Training is regular
Job flexibility is encouraged
Further education is approved so long as it relates to the job
Coaching is an essential part of development and will be done by managers
Appraisal is part of development
Job succession is part of development
Records will be kept
Resources to match the policy will be available.

This is one example only of a successful training policy; as you will know, there will be countless others — some clearly expressed, some rather woolly, some written, some unwritten, some assumed, some simply copied from another organisation. However, if any training policy is to be successful it must contain major features and these include:—

1. The organisation must recognise the role of training at the highest level; in other words, like any other policy covering its operations, there must be active support at board and senior management levels.
2. The policy must be realistic; it must relate to the identified needs of the organisation and not just be so many words, fanciful, incapable of being achieved.
3. The policy should be spelt out in terms all can recognise and understand — and related to themselves.
4. The policy must state responsibilities clearly; it is especially important to define the role of management.
5. The policy should state how — in broad terms — it is to be carried out; more specific terms are developed departmentally. This includes resources and facilities.
6. The policy should state the role and responsibilities of the professional training services.

If it is possible, get a copy of your own organisation's training policy; if there is none written see if you can write down what you think it is. Having done that then take ten minutes to check against the features listed above and decide how closely your policy matches them, noting the differences:

As we do not know your policy, we can only suggest here that you then decide where, if anywhere, there is need for improvement. It may be in the area of managerial responsibility — quite a common area; it may be in support from the top of the organisation or in the provision of resources. The purpose of this Checkpoint is to get you to examine your own situation against the suggestions made here and see for yourself what action, if any, ought to be taken.

---

2. Why Have a Training Policy?

Now we have spent a fair amount of time looking at what a training (or indeed, in general terms, what any) policy is, let us consider why we need a policy.

Let's start by considering a policy — not just training, but any policy. If you are in operation for any purpose what-so-ever then you are trying to achieve some objectives — that we already know — and it is impossible to do that unless you have a policy stating how you propose to reach those objectives. We know that this means we have a statement of intent but it is necessary to have a policy because:—

1. All concerned in the organisation know how the objectives are going to be achieved.
2. We can translate the overall policy into departmental or sectional policy showing exactly how we, in our own corner as it were, will achieve our own departmental objectives, what roles will we ourselves play, when we will train, who we will train, where we will train, what resources and facilities we can use, what support we can expect from elsewhere in or outside the organisation.
3. We can see possible relationships with other policies in the organisation so we can co-operate and avoid conflict.
4. The people in the organisation know where they stand with, for instance, limits of responsibility being stated.

Take five minutes again and write down the reasons why **you** think **your** organisation has a training policy; it may well be that you will come up with other reasons in addition to the four listed above:—

You might have discovered that one reason for your policy is so that your organisation keeps up-to-date with what is happening in the whole field in which it operates, another might be of continually changing products with consequent changes in operations, another might be so that you produce all your own supervisors and managers, another that your organisation is so specialsed it must breed its own future supervisors and managers, another might be because your organisation has always placed emphasis on training as part of its overall to enable people to develop their own abilities and personalities.

---

3. Relationships with Other Policies

THE INTER-PLAY

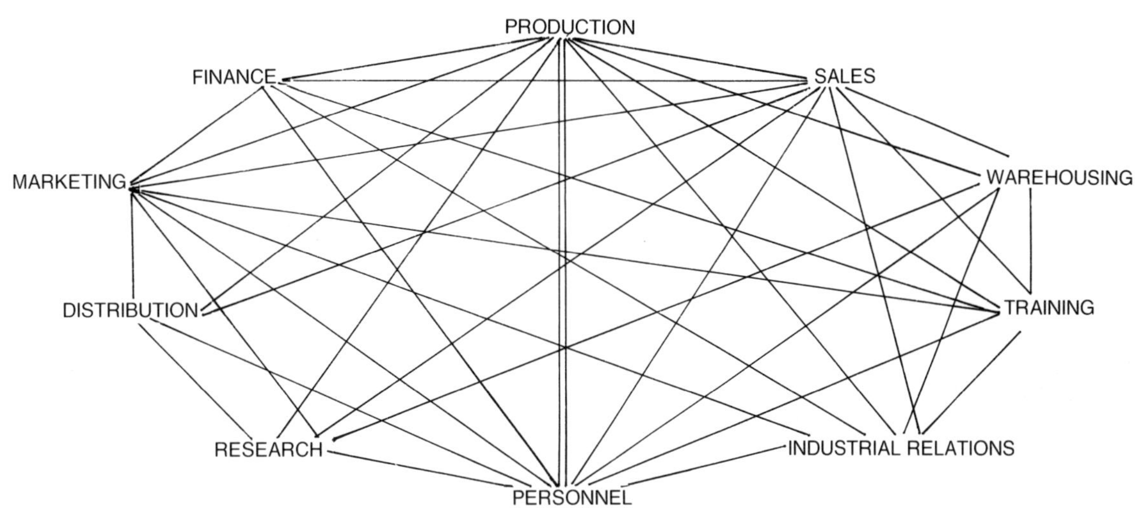

No policy in any organisation can exist in isolation; every organisation, as we know, has a series of objectives and therefore a series of policies. They start off in fairly broad terms covering the major functions and, as they come down the line, as it were, they become more specific and more departmentalised. This increase in precision is quite right and proper — we could not possibly work without having the policy spelt out to suit our own situation. Unfortunately sometimes problems arise when you consider the effect of one policy on another or others. Let us take a couple of examples, one general and the other from training.

Suppose in an organisation it is decided that major effort and resources will be put into the research and development of a new engine; this means a decrease in the provision of resources for other areas and it might also mean that that particular department assumes the major importance and the major sway in any decisions to be taken in the organisation. This can produce disillusionment in other departments or functions, it can mean the deployment of too many resources (people, materials, finance — to name but a few) into one area and it can mean the starving of other departments or functions which might then become almost subordinate to the R and D function and department. In common parlance it's called putting all your eggs in one basket! The results of failure can be catastrophic and you can no doubt think of many examples from British industry and commerce which illustrate this.

Let's come nearer home now and consider the effects of **one aspect only** of a training policy on other policies. Take that aspect which states that all employees will be allowed to take such further education or training as may further their development in the organisation; then think of the possible points emerging:

(a) Who decides if an employee shall receive such training? Is it the employee, the training department or the departmental manager?
(b) Who decides what is meant by 'development in the organisation'?
(c) Who pays for the further education — the employee, the training department or the department where he works?
(d) Who recompenses the department for loss of production while the employee is away on training?
(e) Who arbitrates if there is any dispute among the three interested parties (employee, training department and employee's department)?
(f) What part do other organisations (such as trade unions, professional associations) play in the implementation of training policy?

Here we have just two examples of the potential problems which might surround the establishing of a training policy — or of any policy, come to that! When establishing a policy, therefore, it is essential that full consideration be given to the effect of that policy on others in the organisation otherwise conflict will result or the policy will become ineffective or it will not achieve its original objectives — or a combination of these.

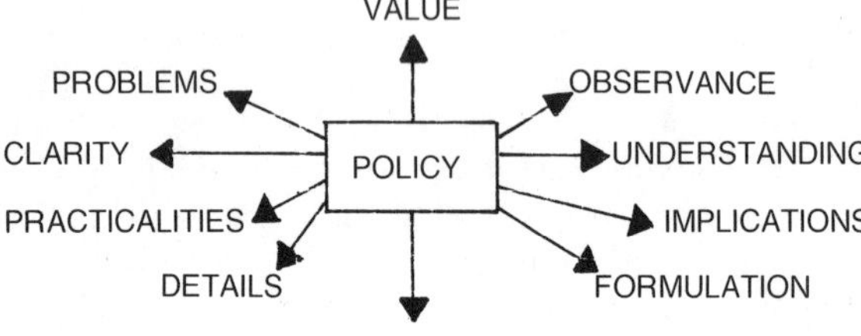

4. Implications of a Training Policy

As with the previous four sections the points made here apply to all policies in general terms. Let's look at some of the implications of establishing a training policy; here they are:

1. People

Will the organisation need to employ extra people to run the training function?

How much time will managers and supervisors have to spend on training each week or month or year? How will they find the time?

Who decides to whom training will be given — the employee, the specialist training department or the manager of the employee?

What is the training for?

If an employee is away being trained will he be replaced and, if so, by whom?

If the training involves working away from home what compensations are to be available?

If training involves being posted to another outlet of the organisation what compensation will be allowed? And what about the possible effect on the trainee's family?

2. Time

How much time is available for training per year? How much time per employee is allowed for training? Per year/month – or what?

How long will specific amounts of training take?

How will you, as the trainer, plan the time allowed?

How will you plan your own time?

Over what period of time do you expect to see results?

3. Finance

What amount of finance is needed to do the training?

What is included in the finance required? Training salaries, expenses, replacement costs for employees away from the work area, training room(s), rent and occupancy costs, etc?

Will you work to a budget?

What will be included in the budget?

How is it to be monitored — and by whom?

Will employees wishing to take further education linked to the job (e.g. professional training) have to pay the fees or have to pay them originally to be reimbursed later on grounds of success — or what?

4. Resources

What room(s) are available?

Equipment? Furniture? Audio-visual aids?

Books? Stationery?

Are all tutors to be from within the organisation or can we hire outsiders?

Take a few minutes to list any other possible implications apart from the four listed above:

You might have added one or more of these:
Appraisal
Promotion
Job rotation
Use of machinery
Use of systems
Analysis of systems and methods
Legislation
Management development
Training for retirement
Job succession
Creating ambition
Training for other organisations.

---

5. Summary

In this Component we set out to examine in detail the business of the training policy starting with defining it — essential so that we know where we are! We looked at an example of a training policy and we suggested you compared it with one with which you are familiar bearing in mind that no two policies are identical as all organisations differ (though they may appear alike on the surface) because they are composed of people. It is people who make organisations — not things!

We then established the essential features of an effective training policy before looking at the links with other policies in the organisation and the possible effects one has on the others and finally we have considered the potential implications of the policy.

By this time you should have a very clear idea of what a successful training policy is, why it is important to have one and how it can be vital to the growth of the organisation.

Tutor Seen Work

Now you have gone through this Component you should be able to devise and produce a training policy of your own. As you know, your organisation will have a training policy — though you may have to search for it a bit! Regardless of that you can, if you wish, now look at your own department or section and write out what you think ought to be the training policy as you see it. It does not need to be as long or as detailed as the one quoted earlier but it certainly should be more specific — as we know. When you have done it send it to your tutor for his comments.

Component 4:

Responsibility for Training

Key Words

Responsibilities; organisation, employee, manager, specialist; objectives agreed and clear; managerial support and encouragement; role of specialist; relationship between line and specialist; action.

Objectives

By the end of this Component you will:—

1. understand the differing roles and responsibilities of the organisation, the employee, the employee's manager and the training specialist in the training field
2. have extablished the details of the responsibilities for the four parties and seen how they inter-link
3. have reconciled the responsibilities of the line manager and the training specialist and seen how they must work together if the learner is to benefit
4. have produced a realistic survey of the training situation in your own organisation with recommendations for changes (where necessary).

Introduction

In this Component we shall be considering in some depth the responsibility for training within an organisation; aspects to be covered include the roles and responsibilities of the organisation as a whole, the individual employee (the learner), the manager of the learner and the training specialist. By the end of the component you should be able to assess how those various roles and responsibilities are fulfilled in your own organisation or in some other with which you are familiar. 'Organisation' here means any body of people who have come together either in work or in leisure activities for a common purpose. Training, in one form or another, affects them all whether the group is a large sophisticated one or a local social or sports one in which you are involved. As you will realise, the range, depth, pattern and methods used will vary with the organisation and the demands for training **but** the principles remain the same.

Responsibilities

As we know, there are four main parties involved in training; they are the organisation, the employee, the employee's manager and the training specialist. Let us take each in turn.

1. The Organisation

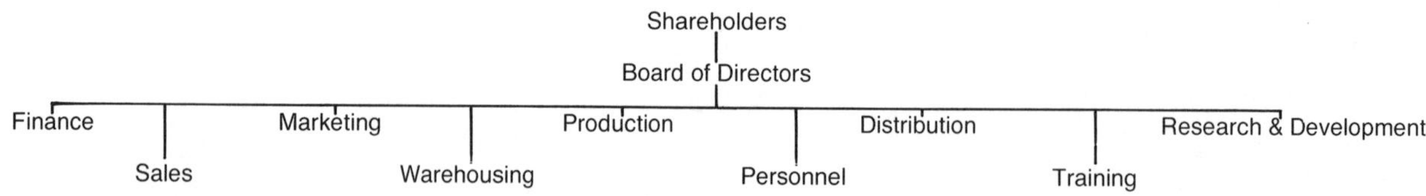

By 'organisation' is meant the board of directors (or its equivalent in other areas of operation) — that is, the top management. From its point of view training is one of a number of necessary functions without which it cannot operate; other functions include, for instance, finance, production, research, development, marketing, sales, distribution, transport, maintenance, personnel, industrial relations — to name the principal ones. Not every organisation has need of all of these, of course, but the responsibility of one to each is generally-speaking the same so, in regard to training, it is responsible for:—

A deciding the overall objective(s) and ensuring that they fit in with the organisational objectives.
B deciding the training policy taking suitable advice as necessary.
C providing the people, facilities, time and resources to run the function.
D periodically evaluating the effectiveness of training in relation to its original objectives.
E modifying the objectives and policies to suit changing circumstances.

Let us look at these five points in a little more detail. First, it is essential that the objectives of the training function tie in with those of the whole organisation; it is no use simply establishing training objectives and failing to examine them regularly as they will often quite quickly move more and more away from the organisation's. For instance, if one of the organisation's objectives is to expand its overseas business by developing export markets in the Far East but not developing any further in Scandinavia then it is a futile training objective to continue providing courses at the same intensity in Swedish, Norwegian, etc. Yet we have all come across examples where the training department has only woken up to the fact of a new development too late and expertise has had to be bought in. It is the major responsibility of the overall organisation to see that the training objectives are part and parcel of its own.

The top management must then, after taking advice from the specialists, decide what the final training policy is to be — again, in broad form only. If you want to know more about this aspect see Component Three, 'Training Policy in the Organisation'.

Too many organisations produce good sounding objectives and attractive policies — on paper — but baulk when it comes to providing the proper people to carry out the function and making the people available for whom the training is designed. Also, the organisation must see that the proper facilities (e.g. rooms, equipment, aids) are provided and that time is allocated for training.

Above all, the organisation must see that the training is effective; in other words, it meets the aims set out for it. If it is not effective, then the organisation must make the changes necessary; after all, it is the organisation which has allocated finance, set the objectives and it should not then sit back and forget.

Checkpoint

Now take a few minutes to revise what we have covered and perhaps you could use your own organisation to check. The question you are asked to answer is:—

What should be the main features of organisational responsibility in the area of training? Don't requote what is in the text; think for yourself and use your own experience.

Among the points you might have considered are:—
Clarity of objectives
Policy spelt out and relating to objectives
A budget provided and used
Policy written
Support (active) from top management
Training objectives in line with company objectives
Provision of time for training
Provision of effective trainers
Results evaluated
Policy achievable

---

2. The Individual

Often it can appear that once training has been accepted as an integral part of an organisation it becomes an activity undertaken by a specialist, in association with the departmental head (we'll use the term 'manager' as the commonest form of departmental 'boss' from now on). A little thought will, however, show that if any training is to be effective it can only be achieved by the improved performance of the actual learner — the employee. It is necessary at this stage to distinguish between the responsibility **for** training and the responsibility associated **in** training. The organisation, the manager and the trainer all have responsibility **for** training — that is, for seeing that training is done in accordance with policy and objectives. The trainee or learner has no real responsibility for seeing that training is done but, notwithstanding that, he does have some responsibilities in regard to what is actually done — after all he is the person being trained — the person round whom it all revolves!

With no further preamble, take ten minutes and list what you think a learner might be responsible for; remember that you ought to have one great advantage — you are a learner yourself so — what do you think you are responsible for in the field of training?

Here are some suggestions you might have included:—
a) to ensure that the training is relevant to:—
i) your specific needs
ii) your own experience and background
iii) your abilities (that is, what you are able to do)
iv) your capabilities (that is, what you ought to be able to do)
v) your personal development
b) showing and maintaining interest
c) participating as necessary — and willingly
d) raising queries if you do not understand a point
e) telling the trainer if and where the training does not satisfy the needs
f) consolidating what you have been taught by practice
g) perhaps doing some self-training as a follow-up
h) at a later stage evaluating the training given to see if it actually was suitable
i) giving feedback to indicate where training might be modified to give better results
You will not have produced all these and doubtless there will be some you have thought of which are not included here.

---

3. The Manager

The manager in most organisations has two major responsibilities. He is responsible for his own performance and also for that of the people who work in his department; this pattern of shared responsibility exists throughout the organisation. It is also clear that many factors may affect performance; for example, location, physical conditions, lack of finance, lack of understanding, lack of motivation — to name but a few. Training, or the lack of it, is also a possible factor. If we improve any of the first set of factors we ought to be able to achieve improved performance; similarly training, or better training, can do so. However, there sometimes exists a danger in organisations of thinking that an improvement in one particular factor can of itself produce improvements; in common with such techniques as work study, budgetary control, job enrichment, etc., training is seen as a cure-all — a panacea — yet experience shows that rarely does the improvement in one factor produce lasting improvement all round. As a result, that particular factor falls into disrepute — and not because of its inherent virtues or faults but because we often expect far too much from it. If you think of situations in your own experience you will probably be able to find plenty of examples to support this point. It particularly applies where the factor is a comparatively new one or one which has been subject to vast changes or where it appears to be the fashion – the flavour of the month, so to speak!

In the area of training all managers need to see it as **one** of the many functions which might help in any given situation where there is a problem or a potential problem but it must not be automatically assumed that it is the answer.

As we know, the manager is responsible for the most effective use of all the resources at his command such as finance, materials, methods, systems, space, time, equipment, layout, communications and, of course, for that most important of them all — people. Hence training is a real responsibility for any manager. This does not mean that he must be a financial wizard, a super methods study engineer, the most effective communicator ever — a specialist, in fact. Indeed there can be danger if a line manager is a specialist in one particular aspect of the organisation's business. What is necessary is that the manager must know enough about each particular resource (in this case, training) to ensure that it is used where applicable and where it can produce results.

The normal line manager is the person charged in his job with **getting things done** whether it be production or sales or distribution or patients cared for — it is he who is in a key operational role and therefore he is ultimately responsible for the most effective use of each resource. In our case that means training.

There can, however, often exist a tendency for a manager to take the view that, for instance, finance is the responsibility of the accountant or that similarly training is the responsibility of the training specialist. Such a manager is in reality withdrawing from his main objective — to make the most effective use of all the resources at his command. Of course we need the specialist — we all know that — but fundamentally the specialist should be seen as rendering a service to the whole organisation based on the needs and policies it has and the line or operational manager should know enough about each specialisation (training in our case) to see that it is properly used. If he passes responsibility over to the training specialist that he may wake up one morning to find that training has indeed been done but it is not capable of being applied in his department. Take some of the specialisations in your own organisation and ask yourself just how much you know about their purpose, their operations, their language, their responsibilities; perhaps you may then decide that you would benefit — and so would the organisation in the long run — by knowing more (not by knowing all the specialist knows but knowing enough).

As with the previous Checkpoint, take a few minutes to write down what **you** think are the main responsibilities of the manager. We shall not produce any suggestions at the end of this activity but you will find them at the end of the next.

You ought, from your own experience, to have been able to produce a reasonable list; we have not produced our own because we want to link it in with the specialist's responsibilities — hence we have left it to the end of the next Checkpoint.

4. The Training Specialist

Here 'specialist' means the person who has the overall responsibility for the training function, who decides on the detailed allocation of resources to achieve the aims of the function; he does not, of course, decide on the overall allocation — that is the responsibility of the ultimate authority — the board or its equivalent.

Every organisation has a training specialist (though the degree of specialisation varies greatly depending on the size and policy of the organisation) and among his responsibilities is an element of persuasion in the overall allocation of resources and the establishment of objectives but the main purpose of the specialist's job is to make those decisions, within the resources available, which determine how effectively they are used. In this he is like the manager referred to in 3 above, as you will appreciate. He will need to understand the essentials of the other specialisations — and in this context general management becomes a specialisation (we do not mean the General Manager but the generalist manager — the line manager as he is often called).

Take a few minutes to list what you think, from your own experience and thoughts are the main responsibilities of the training specialist.

It is best if you consider them in a form of cycle covering seven stages with the seventh linking back in to the first — here they are:—

1. *To define the problems*
2. *To arrange problems in priority order*
3. *To analyse each problem*
4. *Produce the analysis*
5. *Design the process; produce the plan*
6. *Assemble resources; implement*
7. *Evaluate*

As you will see there is a logical progression through these seven factors with the last leading back into the first (though with a different set of problems). In greater depth here they are again:—

1. To define the problems. Problems may be fed in by line management or the training manager may be invited by line to investigate and recommend. The training manager may persuade line to let him tackle a problem of which both are aware. Very often these problems are not what they appear to be at first sight. Investigation is needed and may well produce a different problem. Each problem must be clearly stated; many problems, when dealt with thus, become half-solved because the solution begins to emerge as the analysis proceeds and definitions are made. The training manager should beware of setting his own problems without reference to line. This tends to isolate training from reality in the same way as with other functions.

2. To arrange problems in priority order. An important but difficult step. Line may indicate which are crucial problems and which are not but the trainer may often have to assess for himself what are the benefits, long term and short term, to the organisation. He therefore needs to be in close and constant touch with line management. In this way he can build up, and modify as the company proceeds, a list of priorities. As a manager the trainer has his own responsibilities and his own expertise and must make decisions within his competence. His view of priorities will not always coincide with that of line but it should always be related to the objectives of the organisation.

3. To analyse each problem. In the order of priority he has established he should analyse each problem to determine the change in organisation or selection or training (or any combination) which will give the best results. This is the vital step. Problems should be looked at as performance and not training problems; in some cases training may not be needed and a system change may give the result wanted, in others the people may be unable, from some cause or other, to perform satisfactorily and no amount of training will benefit things. A major error may occur through pressure from line or from himself; this is where the situation put forward is accepted blindly and training is administered rather like a patent medicine. This is training for training's sake and usually will not produce the real solution. Not every problem can be dealt with by training.

4. Produce the analysis. The job here is to decide who needs to be trained, how many people there are, location and time of training plus their existing knowledge, skill, etc., to prevent waste of time and money in actual training. Having analysed the people (known as defining the target population) the next substep is to analyse what is to be learned by breaking down the job into tasks and subtasks which comprise that job. This substep operates on a need-to-know basis — a statement of what is necessary to the relevant detail level. This is followed by a performance analysis where one examines how the task is done and determines the skills, etc., needed. In this step skills analysis is done (if relevant) where the perceptual-motor performance is analysed as developed by W. D. Seymour and others. Producing these analyses avoids the vagueness which often accompanies training and the apparent irrelevancies which arise. Not all training can achieve this stage as not all training can be as easily defined as that associated with definite skills.

5. Design the process; produce the plan. The process may or may not be a recognised course — an old familiar solution was to "send him on a course". The process may involve sitting by Nellie, extending carefully an area of responsibility, assigning tasks, encouraging controlled reading, taking a specific or a specially designed course. Having designed a process then a plan is needed so that all concerned — person, line manager, and specialist — know what is going on and to avoid the never-ending elasticity which accompanies some training where the aim is never reached. On this aspect it is important that the line manager realises the possible consequences of the training; for instance, extending a man's responsibilities means surrendering some on the part of the boss.

6. Assemble resources; implement. In this stage equipment and premises, tools, books, films, etc., have to be procured after due evaluation. Instructors need training and retraining, time needs to be allocated, outside facilities investigated and used. If the preceding stages have been well done then this should be easy by comparison. It often can be the area where too much training time is wasted.

7. Evaluate. The training should be evaluated immediately it has ended or, if it is lengthy, at stages throughout and the results discussed with line. It should also be assessed on the actual job. The trainer then returns to the first stage to see if problems and priorities have changed and start the process again. Of course, many problems and priorities may well be tackled simultaneously.

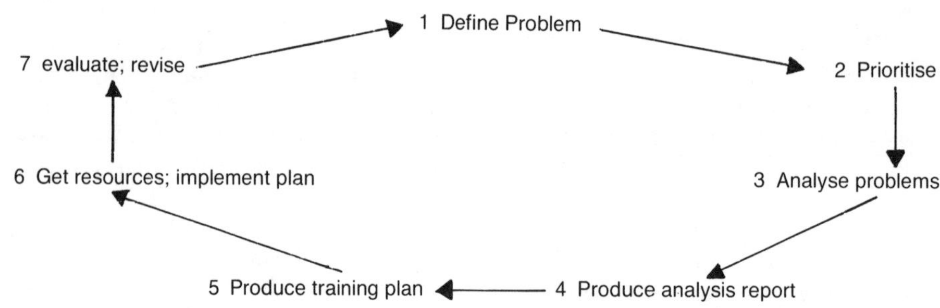

5. Relationship between the line manager and the training specialist.

In section 3 we stated that we would look at your findings on the responsibilities of the line manager; in section 4 we looked at the responsibilities of the specialist and in this section we consider how the two inter-act — how they fit together in the training area. It is essential that they do otherwise either no training is done or that which is done is not necessarily appropriate to the needs identified.

Because it is the line manager who actually uses the people trained by the specialist then it is the line manager who has the initial task of identifying areas of need, informing the specialist, maintaining liaison, ensuring that the training done is relevant and necessary and, finally, evaluating the results — that is, did the training achieve what it set out to achieve?

Listed here are the steps taken to ensure effective training is carried out — the ACTION. List the responsibilities of the line manager and specialist in relation to each step then check your reply with our suggestions below.

Action

1. *Identify needs*
2. *Devise methods*
3. *Implement*
4. *Check results*
5. *Communicate*
6. *Research and develop*

THIS IS A BROAD GUIDE TO THE DIVISION OF RESPONSIBILITY BETWEEN THE LINE MANAGER AND THE TRAINING SPECIALIST AND INDICATES THE LIAISON NECESSARY BETWEEN THE TWO TO ENSURE SATISFACTORY BENEFITS TO THE ORGANISATION. REMEMBER THAT CONDITIONS WILL CHANGE FROM ORGANISATION TO ORGANISATION THUS THE ACTUAL RESPONSIBILITIES MAY VARY.

Responsibility for Training

Action	Line Management	Training Officer
Identify needs	Analyse present/future objectives, assess present performance against agreed targets. Identify training needs by analysis.	Assist in identifying and analysing training needs. Agree order of priority.
Devise methods	Decide upon most suitable methods of meeting training needs. Draw up individual training programmes in broad terms. Review and approve Training Officer's plans. Provide technical information and instructor-staff needed to prepare programmes, ensure programme meets need of organisation.	Advise and assist. Draw up programmes to fit where training needs appear to be common. Prepare to assist in preparing detailed group training programmes. Run trial scheme, revise and prepare final programme.
Implementation	Implement individual training plans. Approve finished plan. Provide facilities needed; time, space, equipment, etc. Provide instructors. Commence programme. See that skills, knowledge and attitudes learned are **effectively** used on the job.	Advise and assist. Prepare detailed plan for implementation of group programme including advice on materials, facilities and equipment required. Train instructors, use Further Education, other organisations, etc. As programme proceeds ensure that required standards in skills, knowledge and attitudes are being reached; adjust as required. Check that skills, knowledge and attitudes **are** being used on the job and that there is no return to old habits.
Check results	Job performance must be continuously judged and measured against targets. Plan and provide for supplementary training as needed (further education etc.).	Assist in drawing up methods of appraisal to facilitate the measuring of training results. Assist management to understand training appraisal data and advise and plan any further education training needed.

Responsibility for Training

Action	Line Management	Training Officer
Communication	Ensure, at all times, that everyone involved is kept informed on current and proposed training activities. Establish information network on training matters. Ensure information understood by using adequate feed-back systems.	Ensure management keep abreast of all developments and results, also responsibilities. Report, and inform management at regular intervals. Consistently endeavour to improve dissemination of information.
	Keep training staff informed of targets of performance required and any changes which may indicate new training needs.	Keep management briefed on management training, plans of competitors, also new techniques worth trying. Be a source of advice/ information on all matters appertaining to training/education.
Research and development	Continuously encourage research into methods of development.	Study continuously new methods of improving and developing people. Recommend to management specific areas of change (and maybe experiment) in training methods and techniques. Control study of results in knowledge, skills and attitudes.

6. Summary

In this Component we set out to discover the real responsibilities of the various people involved in training. Most of us tend to think that it involves only the learner and the trainer with a slight involvement (usually inconvenience!) from the manager. You should by now appreciate that there are four main parties actively concerned — this does not take into account the other parties such as colleagues, customers and the public at large. You should also have discovered that training in isolation is of little value and that there needs to exist a very close liaison between the operational manager and the training specialist — one which needs constant nurturing and keeping up-to-date with current requirements.

Tutor Seen Work

Having completed this Component now stand back, conduct a survey of your own organisation from the training point of view and produce a brief report. In your survey you should examine critically four things:—

1. The organisation's overall objectives
2. The training objectives
3. Training policy
4. Roles and responsibilities of the four main parties

Consider and report on:—

1. The existing situation
2. Your assessment of the current strengths and weaknesses
3. Need for any changes (with reasons and evidence)
4. Your recommendations (in outline)

REMEMBER to keep the report brief and to the point; then, having completed it, send it to your tutor.

Component 5:

What are your Resources?

Key Words

 **Resources; policy; attitudes; needs.**

1. To the reader beginning this Component

Before you begin this Component, you should take stock of your situation. To do this well, you may need to ask a number of prior questions: and only when you are satisfied with the answers, will it be worth your while to proceed.

Checkpoint

Give yourself time to answer the following questions:

1. Do you have a clear picture of the structure of your organisation — or at least of that part of it with which you are most concerned? Can you identify the managers in charge of the various sections? Have you information about its plans for the future? What does it have as its marks of success? (Component One of this unit on 'Analysing your Organisation' may help to answer these questions.)
2. Are you clear about the idea of training? What is its nature and its purpose? What do you want out of a training operation?
   (You might find it useful to look at Component Two of this unit on 'Why Train?').

Give yourself ten minutes to answer these questions. There is no need to give a lot of detail at this stage. The main purpose of these two questions is to link the idea of **resources for training** — first, to the organisation and your understanding of it, and second, to your understanding of what training is and what it is for. The diagram may make this clearer.

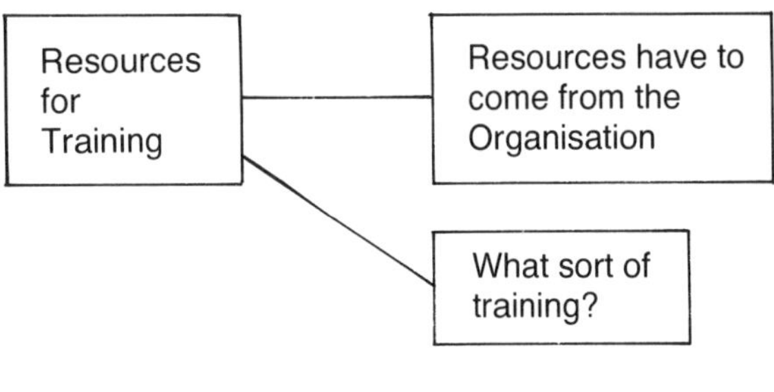

2. Objectives

When you have completed this Component, you should be clearer about a number of matters.

1. The word 'resources' itself: you may be surprised at the range of possibilities picked up by the word.
2. You should be able to decide what types of resources you need — human resources; time; money; facilities or equipment or materials.
3. You should be much clearer about a number of matters which have a bearing: matters such as organisation policy, people's attitudes; distinctions between long-term needs and short-term needs.

Before you read on, you should try to focus your interest in resources for training as sharply as possible. The clearer you are, the more effectively you will be able to select from the available resources. The questions below may help you to focus. Allow about 10 minutes for this task.

Some suggested questions

Is your problem narrow and specific e.g. are some employees unable to use a new item of machinery adequately?

Is the problem wide and not easy to define e.g. do attitudes held by many people seem to be unsatisfactory? Are relationships poor?

Does the problem affect not just people inside the organisation, but also their relationship with people outside it? E.g. have there been difficulties when employees have attended off-site training courses?

---

3. What do we mean by 'resources'?

Like many words we use about our work, the word 'resources' can be used in a variety of ways to denote several different things. It is very important not to get trapped into considering only one of these different aspects of resources.

When we talk about resources, we can be thinking of at least four aspects:

Money — obvious enough, but not always the most important.

Equipment and facilities — again very important, but these alone will not solve all the problems a firm may face.

Time — a major matter, and one the importance of which is often underestimated.

Human resources — people who, even in an automated world, are the foundation of a firm's success.

Let us now have a look at each of them in turn.

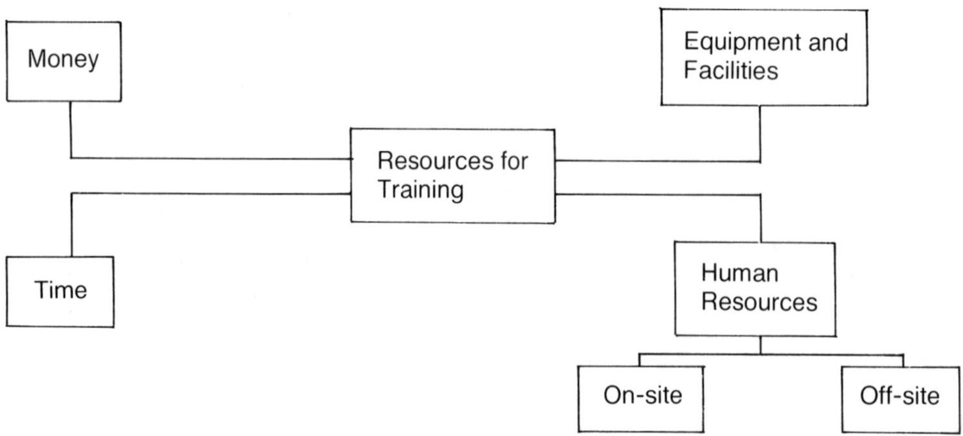

Human Resources

Training has to be done **for** people **by** people. Who in your organisation can be called on to provide training? (Then people may not actually have the label 'trainer', but will probably be described as manager.) Let us take some typical situations.

Line managers and personnel managers will have been given designated responsibilities for certain types of training. Within the various departments, there will be departmental training officers.

(The Component on 'Who is responsible for training?' will give you help in finding your way through this problem.)

These managers and training officers may be able to give you a list of people who have the necessary knowledge and skill and the right temperament to provide the training that will meet your problems. If so, then the training can be provided **on-site** (assuming that time, money and suitable equipment can be found).

They may tell you that people with these qualifications and qualities do not exist inside the organisation. If this is the situation, and if it is vital that the training problem you have identified is solved, then the training may have to be provided **off-site** by another **agency**. This being the situation, you have then to check-out the procedures used in your firm for obtaining off-site training.

The approaches outlined above all take for granted one assumption: that there is a general commitment to the principle that training is a good thing. Employees generally are likely therefore to be keen to take training when it is offered.

But this may not be the case. Employees may show suspicion about the firm's motives. ("They train you for this wonderful new job, and then they tell you that you'll have to transfer to their other factory seventy miles away." "They start training you on this new machine, and it's not long before you realise it's going to make half of your mates redundant.")

Or they may be cynical about training. ("It's no good bothering, because foreign competition will get the trade anyway.")

Employees may show suspicion and cynicism.

We can now summarise several points about the human resources on which an organisation can draw:

(i) If the human resources are inadequate, then this problem has to be given high priority.

(ii) This inadequacy may be the result of poor planning: there exists no proper allocation of responsibilities or no machinery for making and carrying out a plan.

(iii) There may be a more widespread problem of attitudes — of suspicion and distrust.

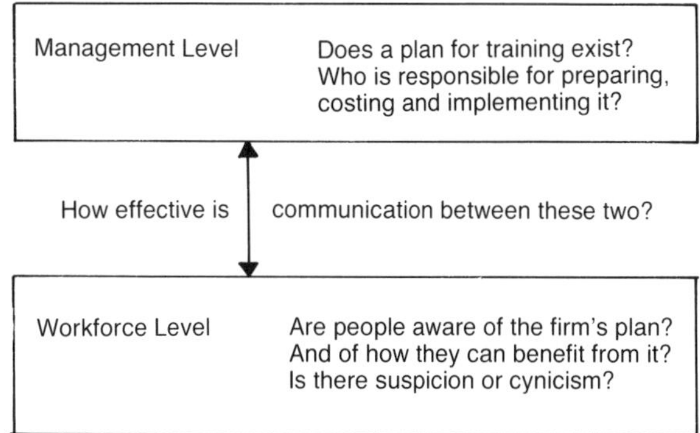

(i) Identify a/the line manager and/or personnel manager and/or training officer. Can he give you the information you seek about meeting the need for training that you have discovered?

(ii) As you seek this information, you may reach the conclusion that there is a low level of active support at management level for the idea of training at all. If your supposition is correct, then a shift of policy is needed. (More is said about this problem in Section 4 of this Component).

(iii) Check also whether you are receiving the message that there is widespread distrust of the idea of formal training among the workforce. If this distrust is also deep-seated, then it is likely that time and effort spent on training will be wasted unless this distrust is tackled as a matter of organisational policy. You will need to raise this with the personnel management, or with departmental training officers, in the first instance.

(iv) If you decide that the training cannot be met inside the organisation, then consider what is said in section 5, about training off-site.

Time

Time is a major resource in all organisations. If time is used badly, then the organisation is bound sooner or later to decline because both money and effort will have been misused. Training requires time; if the organisation is committed to training, then training must be built into the overall planning of time. This is easy to say, but for success a variety of factors must be taken into account.

HOW IS TIME FOUND FOR TRAINING?		
ON-SITE		OFF-SITE
ON-JOB	Employee does not stop work, but is guided into a new method or approach. Time not a major problem.	Can the flow of employees be organised so that they complete their training within the time required but without upsetting production or the service offered to the public.
OFF-JOB	Does the training affect everyone? Can schedules easily be altered? Can the training be staggered?	

Several questions have to be faced here.

(i) Can the training need you are concerned with be met by **on-job** training? If it can, then work schedules may need little modification and time is not a great problem. But it is vital that the trainers are available at precisely the time and place where the trainees/learners are working.

(ii) If the training has to be done **off-the-job**, but on-site then how is time to be found for it? The answers to this question will vary a great deal according to the type of organisation and the numbers of people who require training.

Let us take one or two examples.

If most of the work force need short bursts of regular refresher off-job training, then it may be quite practicable to make same alterations to the services provided or the public. A store may be opened for trading a few minutes later on one day in each week. Few people are inconvenienced, and the training programme can be easily organised (provided that the skills or knowledge to be acquired can be learned in regular few-minute bursts).

This approach will not work where continuous production or service is required. A power station cannot be shut-down for fifteen minutes while the whole staff have some training. Bus time-tables cannot be changed so that drivers can receive instruction. The training programme must therefore be staggered.

Up to now in talking about off-the-job training, we have focussed on situations where all or most employees need training. But there will also be many situations in which only a small proportion of the work force require it. This is, in many ways, an easier situation, but there are still problems, such as the finding of substitutes or the alteration of times, if this does not give difficulty.

We can now summarise the answers we might give to the questions; what is the optimum way of organising the time for training? The possibilities which follow may not directly meet your need, but they may help you to decide on your best course of action.

(a) Short, weekly periods of off-job training for all or most of the workforce.

(b) Pre-specified, but variable, periods of off-job training, the work of some employees being covered by substitutes.

(c) As (b), but with the work not covered by substitutes.

(d) Off-job training of a non-regular kind provided to enable some of the workforce to meet a new or non-regular demand.

(iii) If the training requires specialist facilities, we must ensure that these are available at appropriate times (see 3.3).

(iv) Finally, the question has to be raised: how will we know whether the time allocated for training is adequate? This is not a simple matter, and there is no scope to face it in detail in this component. You need to consider carefully how you will **assess** training given. For further guidance on this, consult Volume 4, **Assessment and Evaluation in Training.**

Facilities/Equipment/Materials

If we go back to a definition of training, we remind ourselves that it is the learning of knowledge and/or of skills and/or of attitudes, all three related to work needs. A moment's pause for reflection brings the realisation that these learning objectives are unlikely to be met well unless the correct equipment, or materials or facilities are available.

For **on-job** training, we can assume that the necessary equipment or machinery is already available. It is important to discover, however, what additional materials will help. Books, pamphlets, diagrams, models may help the learner to develop the knowledge and skills much more quickly. If they are to be useful, they must be purchased beforehand, with time for trainers to become familiar with them.

If the training is to be **on-site** but **off-job**, then it is even more important to build the correct range of resources into the planning. Some suggestions now follow.

A separate room or rooms may be needed for the training. The rooms may need equipment such as film projector, video display unit, overhead projector; photocopying and/or duplicating equipment (or access to these); a flexible seating arrangement to allow for varied activities; black-out; black or white-board; tables or benches for practical work; space for specialist equipment.

(If a training room is being planned, the last item is of great importance. Ease of access and a capacity to support a heavy weight may turn out to be crucially important for some types of training.)

The timetabling of a training room or block needs also to be thought through carefully. Can trainers, trainees (and those covering their normal work) and the facilities all be available simultaneously? How much notice needs to be given for the booking of the room? Does this amount of notice fit comfortably with the planning of a training schedule?

Resource of Money

This aspect of resources for training has been left to this point, since each of the previous three topics (trainers, time, facilities) has financial implications. It hardly needs to be stated that if the organisation has no satisfactory budget for training, then training will be neglected.

A member of an organisation who wishes to use or develop a training programme needs to establish clear answers to questions such as the following:

(i) Who has authority over the preparation and approval of a budget for training?

(ii) How does this person or group relate to those who have training needs or responsibilities? You can seek answers to this question from personnel or line managers or training officers.

(iii) What is the amount of money available for training? Can this be varied? How? What are the priorities over spending the budget? Can these be varied?

(iv) How does the sequence of dates for the preparation of a training budget relate to the sequence for the preparation of other budgets in the organisation?

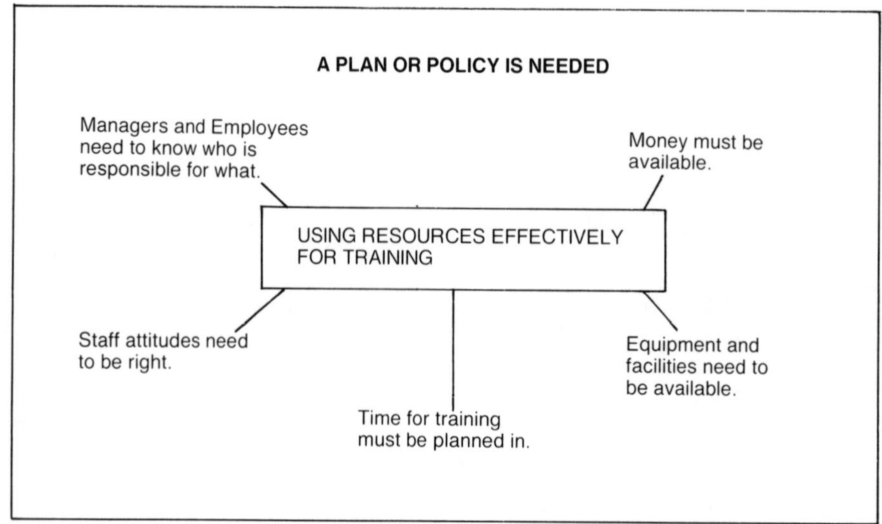

4. General Policy on Training

We have seen that the successful deployment of resources for training requires:

1. a clear idea of what training will be required (off-job, on-job) for what purposes?;
2. the availability of the necessary training personnel;
3. the careful planning of time;
4. the availability of appropriate facilities;
5. the existence of a training budget which reflects these requirements.

We can bring all of these aspects together by stressing that the organisation needs a **policy** on training. (The topic of organisational policies is dealt with in Component Three.) A policy is a planned and definite course of action, designed to meet the objectives seen by the organisation as important. Such a policy on training should be clear, written down, and available for change as problems and possibilities change. If the organisation has no policy, then the question has to be asked: why not?

Up to now in this component, we have spoken as though training can always be achieved on site. This is not necessarily so, and the organisational policy and budget may well include the use of **off-site training** also.

5. Training provided off-site or organised through off-site agencies

A variety of agencies outside the employing organisation has come to be recognised as a vital training resource, not least by H.M. Government, particularly since the Industrial Training Act of 1964. (Note also the Employment and Training Act of 1973, since there have been modifications to the original Act.) The various resources can best be divided into three groups.

1. The Manpower Services Commission (MSC)

The work of MSC in directing and co-ordinating a national policy on training has now become so complex that it is difficult to summarise. The scheme which has attracted public attention most is the Youth Training Scheme (YTS), but MSC takes a number of other initiatives also.

Given the rapid rate of change in MSC provision, this component merely makes the point that any organisation with a training need should seek contact with current MSC literature to check what is available.

2. Local Further Education or Tertiary Colleges
These colleges are funded by Local Education Authorities, and provide a wide range of short and long, full-time and part-time courses, some of which lead to national qualifications recognised by the Business and Technical Education Council, or by other examination boards.

The field is too complex to summarise. What is important is for an organisation to have good contacts with such colleges and accurate, up-to-date information about what training opportunities they can provide.

Addresses of these colleges are easily found through a Local Education Authority office or through a telephone book.

3. Courses for Managers and Supervisors
A number of universities and polytechnics provide substantial courses leading into diplomas or degrees in the field of management. Information about these can be obtained from the handbooks and prospectuses issued by these establishments.

Component 6:

Is your Training Worthwhile?

Key Words

Worthwhileness; reactions to training; job behaviour; training and the organisation.

Is Your Training Worthwhile?

As you consider working through this Component, you should ask yourself two questions. If you can answer 'yes' to both of them, then you are likely to bring useful ideas and experience to this topic. If you find yourself answering 'no', then it would be as well to have a look first at Component 1, which will help you to analyse your organisation, or Component 2 which tells you about the reasons why training programmes are provided.

Question 1

Consider the organisation that you are concerned with. Do you have a clear idea of its main attributes (structure, size etc.), its purposes (what is it trying to achieve, and how does it judge success?), and also some idea of what is wrong with it (and along with this some thoughts about how it might be improved)?

Question 2

Consider the question of training. Do you have a clear idea of what opportunities your organisation has on this topic? Is there a policy, or not? Is this policy widely understood and adhered to? Does the organisation rely on its own resources for training, or does it use outside agencies?

These are not the only aspects of training you might consider; there are other important ones. But these suggestions may start you thinking.

Checkpoint

Take about 10 minutes for this activity. Try to answer both of the above questions. Look at your answers. If the task bewildered you, look at earlier Components in this unit. If you have, on the other hand, concluded that you have a reasonable grasp of organisation and training policy, then you will probably have sharpened up some specific questions which you can keep in mind as you work through this Component.

Objectives of this Component

(i) It helps you to ask some basic questions about the usefulness of a training programme.

(ii) Because it is introductory, the Component confines itself to suggesting ways you can appraise the training that is currently on offer in your organisation. It does not raise much broader questions of how you might change company policy, or what broad future plans for training might be.

(iii) Because this Component deals with Training Contexts, some matters will be raised about links between your organisation and other agencies which provide training.

(iv) It will suggest some ways of judging what is worthwhile.

When you have completed the Component, you should:

(v) be able to frame useful questions to ask about your organisation's current training opportunities; and

(vi) about the training it takes in from other organisations;

(vii) be in a position to gain more benefit from Volume Six on **Assessment and Evaluation.**

The word 'worthwhile'

One of the problems we often run into in our working life is that of using words which are vague and lead to misunderstanding. The word 'worthwhile' is a good example, and we risk muddle if we do not make an attempt to analyse it. It is not as straightforward as it seems.

Look at the sentences below. Each contains the word 'worthwhile'. See if you can tell whether the word is used with the same intentions by each of the three speakers.

(a) 'It isn't worthwhile investing in new equipment at this stage'.
(b) 'It isn't worthwhile for English-speaking salesmen to learn foreign languages: all our customers speak English anyway.'
(c) 'Taking part in tiddleywink competitions just isn't a worthwhile activity for a grown man!'

Did you notice any differences as you moved from (a) to (c)?

Do these three have the same idea of 'worthwhile'?

Here is one suggested way of sorting the question out. Compare what is said in this next section with your own ideas. We use the word 'worthwhile' to denote something that repays the effort, the time, the money, the resources, the commitment that we put into something. The idea of 'repayment' is built into the judgements that we make about a course of action.

What sort of 'repayments' might we be looking for?

In sentence (a), we are probably looking at the idea in **cash** *terms. Will projected increased profits more than cover the capital outlay on the new equipment? This is important, crucially important; but it may not be the only idea in our minds when we use the word.*

In sentence (b), the financial idea is still there. It will cost money for training salesmen in, say, Portuguese. And this will bring no obvious return if our Brazilian customers all speak English. But there may be wider questions here. We might not just be concerned about cash but image: does the company look as if it has to rely all the time on other people's willingness to learn a foreign language? Or are we uncovering a wider worry? To learn a foreign language takes time, and effort and commitment. Are we perhaps exposing the worry that it might be difficult to overcome British resistance to learning foreign languages?

In sentence (c), the cash element has more or less disappeared. We seem to be making a **personal** *or* **moral** *judgement about this man — implying he is squandering his time and talents. This aspect of 'worthwhile' is one that often crops up, simply because we are all human beings. Human beings want some sort of satisfaction from their lives, and when they judge the training provided for them, they may be influenced by negative feelings that they were being 'pushed around' or 'talked down to' or 'being got at'.*

So, in talking about training, it will be useful to concentrate on (a), but we must not forget (b) and (c). These other aspects will not go away.

Judging worthwhileness of training: how might we go about it?

If we wish to do this well, we should try to draw on the work of the many researchers who have made earlier attempts. The system to be set out here is based on the work of A. Hamblin, whose book *Evaluation and Control and Training*, published in 1975, has been influential. You are likely to find others who are also familiar with it.

He suggests that we can ask **five** important questions about any scheme of training. The headings for the questions are: Reactions; Learning; Job Behaviour; Organisation; Ultimate Level.

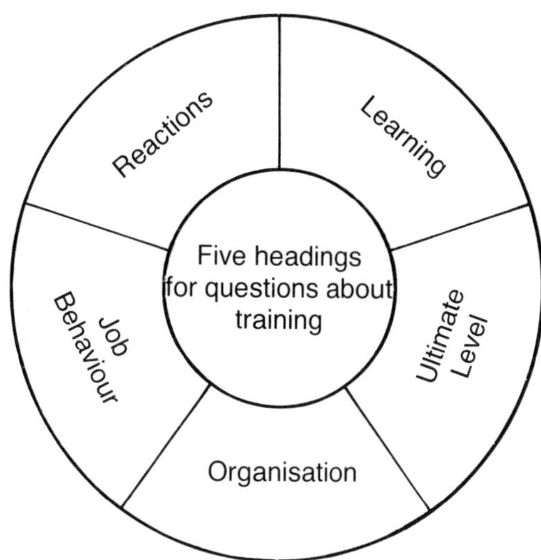

Reactions

Employees who have experienced training are often asked to give their impressions of it. This approach can clearly be tried in relation to pretty well any mode of training e.g. on-site/off-site; short/long; on-job/off-job.

To ask for trainees' reactions to their training is important, even though, of itself, it may not tell us all we need to know. For one thing it **may** tell us if trainees have the negative feelings we have just been speaking about.

Let us take one or two examples. An employee who has experienced some short on-job training may say, "I could have worked it out for myself. It seemed to be too childish", etc. etc. He may be telling us a good deal here about his own insecurity, or his own difficulties in accepting any advice or criticism. The training as such may have been perfectly sound, and what is more, this employee's on-job skill and knowledge may actually have benefited. It is worth noting also that to have information about an employee's attitude to training may be just as important as knowing about the training itself.

Here is another example. An employee has been sent one day a week on a six-month course organised at an F.E. college. The employee's reactions may be dominated by practical annoyances such as difficult transport to the college, or poor canteen facilities. Mixed with these practical issues, however, may be useful criticisms also about the course itself, such as, 'not really about my job' or 'too many other people there who knew nothing about it, and the standard was very low'.

Take a training programme (of any sort, short or long) with which you are familiar. Try this first question on reactions in relation to it. Write down the skills and the knowledge that you think the training was intended to give you. Using just your own personal powers of judgement, how successful do you think it was? Next, and more important, write down any attitudes that you formed to it, irrespective of these skills and knowledge. Were you pleased, encouraged, made more confident? Or were you annoyed, frustrated, or even made to look silly?

It is useful at this point to stop and reflect for a moment on this question of attitudes. All trainees are human beings, and as such have attitudes i.e. feelings of loyalty, hostility, trust, commitment, jealousy, anxiety, towards the organisation that employs them. Negative attitudes are clearly going to depress the level of commitment and willingness shown by employees. This aspect of work has received a good deal of attention in recent years from researchers in industry, and it should not be forgotten. The training may be much less worthwhile than we think if it increases bad attitudes, or does not even allow for this possibility.

EMPLOYEES ARE HUMAN BEINGS. THEY HAVE GOOD AND BAD FEELINGS ABOUT WHAT HAPPENS TO THEM

Learning

The next question is about learning: what exactly have employees learned through training? To carry out this work of enquiry is a complex business, and may require specialised help. If we take the job seriously, we have to produce schedules, carefully worked out, of precise skills and items of knowledge which can be tested before the training and re-tested afterwards.

More about such questions is said in Package Four on Evaluation and Assessment. However, there are some useful and fairly straightforward activities under this heading that can be undertaken by any organisation and which are not likely to be too demanding of time and resources.

At this common-sense level, it is possible to look at training manuals, course programmes, or other schemes of training produced within your organisation, and to make judgements about them. Are the objectives of the scheme carefully spelled out? Is it clear what trainees will learn by way of skills and knowledge? Does the scheme provide some method of testing both skill and knowledge, at the beginning and end of the programme?

From evidence that you can fairly quickly gather in this way it will be possible to make a first judgement about whether the training programme is a **valuable** one, i.e. whether the knowledge and skill developed are clearly related to your needs.

Example. Imagine you are concerned with a service industry where good relationships with customers/ clients are vital. You wish to introduce some general training for all employees. The schemes you review are very good on developing an understanding of specific aspects of the organisation (such as stock control procedures, hygiene routines, invoicing procedures). You may, nevertheless, decide **not** to proceed with the scheme since little or nothing appears about topics such as routine courtesies, the tactics for dealing with difficult customers, or how to make customers feel welcome.

Analyses like these may take comparatively little time to undertake (and they are not a complete substitute for more technically sophisticated approaches), but they may rule out many unsuitable schemes. They will certainly make you think twice, before you rush into or continue with a scheme that does not give benefits right across the areas that you think important.

Job Behaviour

Readers will be aware that one very important question was left unasked and unanswered in section 4.2. That question is: no matter how valid the training is, have the trainees **applied** it in the job they do in the organisation? How good is the transfer? As well as having learned something, have they also put it to good use?

This question is again a complex one, and it is possible very quickly to become involved in many technical questions about how best to carry out the necessary checks.

Nevertheless, even though many difficulties exist the task of checking on employees' changes in behaviour after training, the task is based on a principle which is, in itself, straightforward. Think of it this way.

Why were employees selected for training in the first place? Presumably for one of two reasons.

(i) The employees are judged to be performing a task inadequately. If so, someone must have observed and noted these inadequacies.

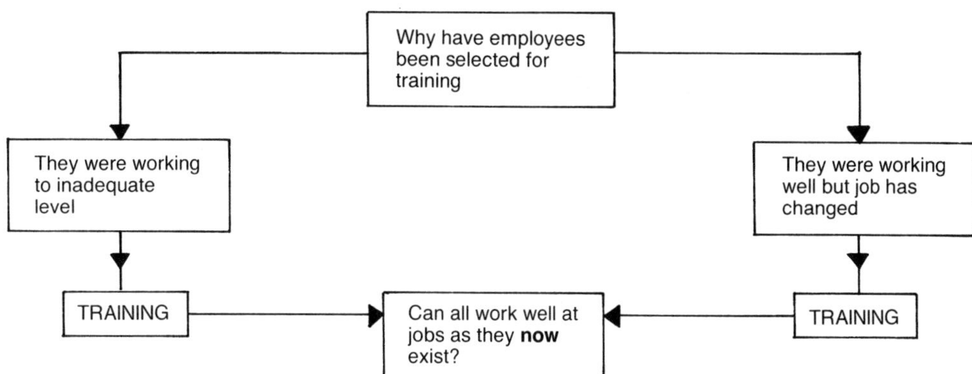

(ii) The tasks required of employees are changing, and it is likely that performance will fall off when the new tasks arrive.

When the training is finished, the same employees are monitored once more to judge their new level of performance. This monitoring might be done in two ways.

First method: **observation**. Those responsible can check, by observation, whether the work level is better than before or (if the work has changed) whether the expected difficulties have been avoided.

Second method: **interview**. The employee's view of both job and training can be identified, and ways over these obstacles found.

For an aspect of working life with which you are familiar, attempt to write down those features of job performance which merit employee training. Be as specific as you can. Try to list alongside these features the improvements you look for, and how you would find out how well the expected improvements had been met. Decide how far you need further (possible expert) guidance.

Before you start on this task, have a look at the example which follows. Perhaps it will help you.

You work for a bus company. Most of the buses are one-man operated.

This fact gives the drivers a full day, since as well as driving, they have to collect fares.

There is a problem. Passengers have been complaining that, when they ask drivers for information about times and other routes, they often receive no help or worse, rude answers. There is clearly a training problem.

First, drivers might be observed at a variety of times (peak, off peak), and their responses to passengers noted.

Next, a training programme might be worked out for updating drivers (off-job) on new schedules and routes.

Third, they would be monitored through observation after training. (And any future passenger complaints investigated.)

Fourth, drivers might be interviewed about their opportunity to apply what they had learned.

After all of these operations, a variety of outcomes can be foreseen.

(1) The drivers cope easily with the new commitments (performance is improved).

(2) Drivers are not able to apply their new knowledge, because they are so busy, but at least they are no longer rude (performance is improved).
(3) The company places notices asking passengers not to involve the drivers in any such requests. The company draws the conclusion that the training was to no purpose, but at least knows that the drivers are working effectively and to full capability. The safety of the passengers is seen to be more important than the minor convenience of having information about services.

The Organisation
So far, we have concentrated on aspects of worthwhileness that are very closely related to specific work tasks and employees. However, the context of training is, in one sense, the whole organisation. And it is useful to ask the question: in what ways will specific training programmes affect the overall organisation — for good, it is hoped.

Again, this is a very wide topic, but it is still possible to ask a number of questions to which even impressionistic answers will be useful, in particular for discussion with your colleagues.

Identify a number of features of working life in your organisation where you suspect that the situation may be less healthy than you wish. Here are some aspects that you might consider.

Absenteeism
Running costs
Productivity
Employee turnover
Amount of waste material.

For any one of these it may be relatively easy to obtain national or international figures. Through the help of colleagues, or through the public library service, or through a nearby college, figures of lost days through absenteeism as a percentage of the total of days worked for a particular industry can be found. These can be compared with figures for your own organisation. (Ensure that you are comparing like with like!) Comparisons of this sort can become very complicated, but the intention of this exercise is to get a rough impression, and so to form an idea of how your organisation compares.

It may be that you discover that your organisation carries, for instance, no figures on employee turnover. If this is the case, this discovery in itself may lead to an improvement in company record keeping.

What does this have to do with training? Comparisons of this kind may suggest a number of possibilities.
(i) Training is not provided in some aspect of company affairs which, if provided, would lead to an improvement in performance.
(ii) Training is provided, but is ineffective in some respect or another. (Example. Is poor training linked to high employee turnover?)
(iii) It may be that high absenteeism or high employee turnover is linked to employees' holding negative attitudes to the company. Why is this? Can training be devised that leads to a change in **attitude**, as well as to a gain in skill and knowledge.

This activity has opened up some very wide questions. But the possibility of improving the general health of the organisation through training for specific purposes is always keeping on your agenda.

Ultimate Level
All of the aspects looked at above can be brought together to look at their implications for the organisation as a whole. It is important not to omit this, even though your attempts to deal with it will almost certainly be impressionistic. What we are discussing here is the 'feel' of one organisation as against the 'feel' of another. In Organisation A, the feeling is widespread that the organisation knows where it is going, that employees are well fitted to their work, that relationships are good, that people take a pride in what they do. In Organisation B the reverse is true. The place 'feels' wrong to all sorts of people. An enquiry into the overall plan for training in the organisation may give some important clues about the differences.

End-note on this aspect. Does a programme of this kind exist in the organisation? Who is responsible for it? Is the 'remit' of the programme organisers written down.

Practical issues related to the above

Inside the organisation
Nearly everything that we have discussed in this component is potentially 'explosive'. To talk about what is worthwhile is to raise matters about which people may feel very strongly, or about which they may differ when it is not easy to see how agreement can be found. Or to talk about 'worthwhile' practices may very quickly lead to judgements that people find threatening; such people may rapidly become defensive and try to cover up evidence, or may not co-operate with those who are trying to find out what is really happening.

It is important to remember that problems of this kind will certainly occur during the process of trying to decide whether training has been worthwhile. Be prepared for them. Remember that these processes are undertaken so that your organisation may become like Organisation A mentioned above.

Relations with other organisations
The point has been made elsewhere in this Unit (e.g. in Component 5) that training is carried out not only internally within the organisation, but also by a variety of agencies outside it. In Component Five, these were listed as universities and polytechnics; as colleges of further education or tertiary colleges; as various other agencies organised, say, through Manpower Services Commission. When training has been undertaken for your organisation by another agency, **it is important that the same processes are undertaken as listed in**

section 2. There is this time, however, a further problem, a 'diplomatic' one. Criticisms about a programme (or praises of it) have now to be conveyed to a third party, which is probably also trying to meet the demands of other organisations than your own.

How can an effective relationship with external agencies be developed and maintained? A number of possibilities should be looked at.

(i) Flow of information from your organisation to the agency e.g. College. It is important to see that comments of whatever level (see 2.1, 2.2, 2.3) reaches the training agency — perhaps edited so that irrelevant information is filtered out.

(ii) Flow of information from the agency to your organisation. It is important to ensure:
   (a) that the information is clear (e.g. does it have details of course changes?) and
   (b) that it reaches those who may need to act on it.

(iii) Consultation. It is important to ensure that, if at all possible, the views of your organisation reach the training agency at the time when it is **planning** what to do. This is obviously likely to prevent complaints about irrelevance. It is also vital to see that complaints about courses etc. are faced quickly and honestly. Does the training agency have any sort of consultative machinery to deal with these matters? If it does not, it is highly likely to be willing to introduce it.

Study Unit 2:

Identifying Training Needs

Component 1:

Training Needs and How to Assess Them

Key Words

Training need; performance gap; task; skill; knowledge; duty; responsibility; job; standard.

Objectives

By the end of this Component you will:—

1. be able to identify cause for the gaps between desired and achieved performance
2. be able to identify if the gap can be plugged by training
3. be able to separate out the four varieties of task (skill, knowledge, duty, responsibility) and produce examples of each from your own organisation
4. be able to analyse a job into the four categories listed in 3
5. be able to determine where training needs arise in each of those categories within your own organisation

Introduction

Training, as we know, is one of the functions of an organisation and, like all the others, exists to serve the aims and objectives of that organisation. If the function is properly run and efficient it will be effective in serving those aims. However, it is easier in some functions than in others to identify precise roles, targets and results; in general it is not always possible to show the results of training either immediately or in tangible and precise terms. Much of the problem arises due to the fact that too often training is haphazard - on a hit-or-miss basis. You will have seen situations where the same training is given to all the learners without any regard to their actual standards of achievement, ability, understanding and interest. You may also have seen situations where the training given is old hat or out of date but it's given because 'we've always done it that way'.

The result is that though we may well end up with a person apparently trained we may in reality have produced an undertrained, an incorrectly trained or, worse, an overtrained one — with all sorts of unexpected results. You can probably think of people who would have fitted into one or other of these categories!

We start by considering what we mean by the term 'training need' and how a gap between the standard of performance you want and what you actually get can arise. We shall cover aspects such as tasks, skill and knowledge in a little depth both in principle and by giving examples. Finally we shall look at methods of assessing training needs — remember that there is no one set pattern of approach — so much depends on circumstances, the resources you have available (money, time and materials - to state three only). However, there is a set of principles you can follow or you can adapt to suit your own organisation; they are well-proven principles and are practical. During each Component you will be asked to undertake what are called Checkpoints — these are short practical exercises in which you have to draw on your own experience and knowledge — the main objective is not just to get you to recall what has been covered but to think for yourself about your own situation. This Component does not go into depth about standards of performance — you will need to go through

Component Three for that and Component Four for more information about the performance gap.

What is a Training Need?

Like most other concepts the idea of a training need is basically simple — it's when you start to think more deeply about it that the possible implications begin to arise. Here is one definition which covers all the essential features (and at the same time indicates the implications) — the key words are in bold:—

A **training need** is the **gap** which exists between the **required** and the **actual standards** of **performance** of a **person** in a **task** which can be **bridged** by **training**.

Sounds quite good but, as mentioned earlier, it's the implications which really matter!

There are four main ones:—

GAP STANDARD TASK JOB

Let's take each separately though not in precisely the order in which they appear in the definition (and we shall leave the detail about standards to Component Three) and examine each more closely.

The Gap

In our definition of a training need we mentioned the gap between the expected and the actual standards of performance and we added an important qualification — 'which can be bridged by training' — remember that! Gaps in performance cannot always be bridged by training; you can no doubt think of many cases in your own experience where no amount of training would have improved performance and yet training was prescribed as the bridge. We all have a tendency at times to feel that, for instance, what worked once will work in the current problem regardless of the fact that the situation is different — we like cure-alls so we often prescribe training as the magic medicine! When you identify a gap in performance and immediately try to bridge it by training (or by any other 'immediate' solution, come to that) you will stand a good chance of failing. You can waste time and money and, worse, produce a disillusioned learner — all very costly. Of course, if you're human you'll probably cast the blame on someone or something else — we all tend to do when really we should have put on our thinking caps for a while.

Checkpoint

Now take five or ten minutes and, using your own experience, list some possible causes for the gap apart from lack of training. We'll start you off:—

Lack of training (easy, that!)
Task not clearly defined

Now have a look at our list; you will probably have some of these possible causes on yours — some will be new to you and you will probably have produced some which don't figure on ours. In fact, if you spend a lot of time on this short exercise you can produce a list as long as your arm.

Anyway, here goes with out list:—

- *Directions not clear*
- *Directions not understood*
- *Directions ambiguous*
- *Person not suitable for task — physically, mentally, emotionally, etc.*
- *Poor supervision*
- *Clash of personalities*
- *Inability to get on with colleagues*
- *Too many bosses*
- *Lack of resources (money, materials, machinery, time, space, etc.)*
- *Poor system of operation*
- *Poor method of work*
- *Poor layout of department, shop, office*
- *Too much time spend walking for stock and stores, signatures, etc.*
- *Machine breakdown (total or partial)*
- *Wrong machine*
- *Lack of training*
- *Task not clearly defined*
- *No incentives*
- *No job satisfaction*
- *Fear (e.g. of asking, of looking a fool)*
- *Erratic deliveries*
- *Shortage of suitable people*
- *Poor inter-departmental liaison*
- *Frequent changes of standard*
- *Demarcation problems*

This is a pretty long list but, even so, we have not exhausted the possible causes of a performance gap.

What Now?

We suggest that having found the gap you stand back from it as it were and think of the possible causes; the best way is to produce your own checklist of possible causes for any gap — you will probably end up with a fairly long one. So what? Well, make this checklist — and add to it as you come upon new experiences, new causes — and then use it whenever you have the problem of a person failing to meet the level of performance the task requires. In other words, **use** the list, go through it eliminating one possible cause after another. You will probably have to go through your checklist a number of times eliminating at the first attempt those causes which obviously do not apply — then, at the second attempt, perhaps thinking a little more deeply about the list you have left and eliminating some more possible causes. Soon you will be left with a hard core of causes and from this core you should be able to select those which actually apply. Sounds like hard work? Of course it is — it's like most detective work — working from a list of known and proved factors and slowly eliminating until you are left with the likeliest factors. As you will no doubt have heard before — most analytical work (for that is what this is) is 95% perspiration and 5% inspiration! When you reach this stage go through the few you have remaining carefully and you should end up with those which actually apply. Remember also that only rarely is there one cause only — usually there are a few with one or two maybe more important than the rest. All will be worth following up. Let's take an example to show what we mean.

The XYZ company operates a nationwide distribution service based on a large central warehouse and offices with twenty four depots throughout the U.K. Recently it installed a computer and amongst the first set of operations to be transferred to it was the wages system. For years, each depot maintained records of its own employees, based on hours worked (including overtime, bonuses and absenteeism) sending details to Head Office weekly on Mondays covering the previous week. Head Office worked out all the wage details and sent out wageslips to each depot on the Thursday of the same week. Depot employees were paid during Friday — they thus worked a week in hand (as it is said).

When the computer was installed the hope was that the costs of the wages office could be reduced by about 25% and two out of the eight staff employed there could be placed elsewhere.

At the same time the wages system was revised; henceforth each depot manager would submit details of hours worked, bonuses, etc., to arrive at Head Office by first post on the Monday succeeding the week concerned. The Wages Office would then work out all the details for feeding to the computer by midday on Tuesday; wageslips would then be sent out to the depots to arrive on Friday morning.

All the depot managers were given a half day training session of three hours at which the Chief Accountant made his presentation — that lasted about two and a half hours with a short period for questions and a break for a cup of tea. At the session each manager was given a sheaf of instructions for the new system; this consisted of ten typed pages of A4 size (the same as this sheet).

The sessions all occurred in one week and the system was to start from the following week. The existing manual system was withdrawn at the same time. After four weeks it was obvious that the system was not working; the Wages office were now working twelve hours overtime — always on Mondays — and the Supervisor had asked for two extra girls to 'tide things over' as she put it.

Other information

Depot opening hours — 0800-1730 daily plus 0800-1200 on Saturdays.

Security system in operation which necessitated depots closing at latest by 1230 Saturdays.

Saturdays were optional overtime for depot staff and often manager did not know who would be in until Thursday or Friday.

Saturday morning often very busy in depot with last minute demands for deliveries.

Depot manager worked alternative Saturdays.

Only eighteen depots had deputy managers.

New instructions — ten pages of closely typed information mainly written in accountant's language and terminology; old instructions occupied three sheets.

Depot managers complained to Wages Office Supervisor who had said 'send it all to me and my girls will sort things for you'.

The Chief Accountant blamed the depot managers.

Always there is some conflict between a Head Office and the outposts (in most organisations this applies).

Well, there is much, much more — but you should have enough here to identify some of the factors which caused the gap between the expected and the actual levels of performance. List them — take five minutes to do so:—

Here are our suggestions:—

1. *Complicated instructions.*
2. *Insufficient time for absorption of new system.*
3. *System written from wrong viewpoint — Chief Accountant's — whereas it should be from the user's angle.*
4. *Cancellation of manual system too rapid.*
5. *Training session wrongly planned.*
6. *Depot managers had no previous opportunity to read instructions and make notes for questions.*
7. *Antagonism between depots and Head Office.*
8. *Poor practical training and guidance.*
9. *Attitude of Wages Office Supervisor.*
10. *Attitude of Chief Accountant and depot managers.*
11. *System written in too detailed a form for quick and easy understanding.*
12. *Lack of proper training.*

Well, here are twelve factors; you will probably have found many others — good! This example, by the way, is true and incidentally no one in Head Office (including the Chief Accountant) could see the causes. The general tendency was to suggest that the depot managers were bloody-minded and should be changed. It took an outsider (a training manager from another firm) to see the root causes. We expect you may have seen something like this example from your own background.

This example points the need for the trainer to stand back and try to look at the problem dispassionately, to use a checklist and to eliminate potential causes but not to rush in with one cause or solution! The example also shows that though there might be a lack of training it is not always in the area which appears most obvious; in this case the depot managers needed further training but so did the Wages Office Supervisor and the Chief Accountant — more about the provision of training in a later Component and Study Unit.

How You Can Tell If Training Can Bridge the Gap

As we know, we train people and not things; one problem a trainer can encounter is being able to tell if the gap between actual and expected performance standards can be bridged by training or if it is due to some other cause such as lack of equipment, time, suitable materials, etc., i.e. some cause which training cannot deal with. It can help you if you check to see if one or more of these three conditions applies — they all concern people, as you will see:—

1. People are involved in the undertaking of the task(s) (not just as performers of the task but as clients, customers, colleagues, supervisors, etc.)
2. Change has occurred or is about to do so — or is on the horizon (for example, changes in policies, methods, structures of management, markets, materials, machinery, methods, manpower — to name but a few).
3. The performance of a person varies under standard conditions, that is, it varies from the performance of colleagues operating under identical conditions.

Just go back to the example we have recently examined; do any of these three conditions apply? This should only take you a couple of minutes. Write down your answer on a separate sheet.

Certainly conditions one and two apply and probably three also although we don't know enough to establish that fully.

Under condition 1 we know that people were involved — the Chief Accountant, the Wages Office Supervisor, the depot managers and, of course, the drivers. The first had produced the new system but felt that a straightforward presentation would suffice forgetting that he had spent many hours devising and modifying the new system whereas the depot managers had no previous knowledge.

Under condition 2 — well, obviously change occurred — and rapidly, too — too rapidly for the managers to cope with as well as doing their daily jobs. We would need to have information about a deeper investigation to enable us to determine if condition 3 applied although there is a strong chance that it did.

Task, Job, Occupation

The definition we gave for a training need was:—

A training need is the gap which exists between the required and the actual standard of performance of a person in a task and which can be bridged by training and we underlined several words in it. Pretty obviously you cannot assess a gap or even identify if there is one unless you have established the standards of performance you require from that task. We shall consider standards very much more deeply on Component 3 after we have thought about who sets the standards. Here we want to look at three elements which are the foundations from which standards are established. In ascending order, as it were, they are TASK, JOB and OCCUPATION. We shall spend most time on the first because a series of tasks forms a job and a number of similar if not identical jobs form an occupation. Also, it is in the area of tasks that most training is done, after all, if task standards are not met then the job will not be satisfactorily performed. We will leave methods of assessing gaps in performance until the end of this Component.

Let's start by defining the three elements:—

A TASK is a major element of work intended to achieve a specific result involving skill or knowledge or the exercise of a duty or the exercise of a responsibility or any combination of these four factors.

A JOB is a collection of tasks which together constitute the work of one person.

AN OCCUPATION is the term given where a number of jobs which are sufficiently similar in their main tasks can be grouped together for the purpose of identification and classification.

Task

Picking up the definition of a task let's take each factor in turn and consider its use.

A) Use of **skill** where a joiner planes a piece of wood to pre-set dimensions. The joiner has to be able to measure the timber, lay out the finished dimensions, select the right plane, adjust the blade, clamp the timber securely, plane smoothly and accurately and check at intervals to ensure the specification is being met.

B) Use of **knowledge** where a dairy farmer recognises a cow which has aborted in the herd and identifies brucellosis as the likely cause, knows it is an identifiable disease and knows the procedures to be followed with the vet, the Ministry of Agriculture and his insurance company, etc.

C) Exercise of a **duty** where a security guard patrols a factory (as one of a range of duties) regularly following a set routine, noting the times at which he passes checkpoints and either signing a book or clocking on (or some other similar system) and reporting any untoward occurrences according to instructions.

D) Exercise of a **responsibility** where a pilot is responsible for making a decision about an emergency landing (one he never has to exercise, we hope) against some established criteria.

We will see in Component 3 how standards can be determined but for now let's ask you to do a bit of work.

Take five minutes or so and from your own background list at least one example of each of the four factors.

a) Skill
b) Knowledge
c) Duty
d) Responsibility

Remember, most of us have several tasks to achieve in our daily lives at work and at home. Some we do repeatedly throughout the day (such as answering the telephone, driving, walking through the department as part of supervisory duties to name but three) and all have standards of performance. Other tasks we may do rarely or never at all although we hold them as part of our overall jobs (examples of such tasks include responsibility for evacuation in case of fire, for negotiation in the event of an industrial dispute and for motivating the people who work for us). Again, these will have standards of performance — some standards will be precise (as in the case of the joiner) while others will be somewhat subjective (as in the case of the motivation of others).

Job

We know that a job is a collection of tasks which together form the work of one person. The tasks may be similar, they may be linked or they may be diverse; that does not matter so long as they are the work of one person. It also does not matter if the work of that one person fills a normal working day — the important aspect is that the tasks are performed by one person. Let's just look at these three categories:—

A) **Similar** As, for instance, where a sewing machinist may be able to use different machines for straight work, overlocking, buttonholing, etc. Or the machinist may be able to use different attachments on the same machine.

B) **Linked** As, for instance, the joiner using his knowledge to identify a piece of timber, his skills to cut, plane, dovetail, assemble, etc., and his knowledge again to see that the finished article is 'true'.

C) **Diverse** As, for instance, an office supervisor who may have to deal with incoming post, allocate daily tasks to the staff, occasionally select a new employee, hold discussions with other departments, attend meetings, be responsible for safety, etc.

Take another five or ten minutes and briefly list the contents — the tasks — which make up a job with which you are familiar. If possible use your own job; don't take all day about it – a quick run through will suffice at this stage. Here are the four categories for you to use:—

a) Skill
b) Knowledge
c) Duty
d) Responsibility

As an example here are some of the tasks associated with the job of a branch manager in a TV Rental Company:—

a) **Skill**
Operating electronic cash register
Operating telephone with conference facility attached
Lifting large TV sets

b) **Knowledge**
Branch ordering system
Stock control system
Local market
Staff abilities and performances

c) **Duty**
Check security daily
Make daily banking report
Plan service calls and routes

d) **Responsibility**
Ensure deliveries made on time
Ensure complaints promptly dealt with in accordance with company regulations
Health and Safety of staff

This is part of the list of tasks of the manager of the branch; as you go through it you will realise that each task has standards attached to it based on company policies, company practices and customs, local conditions, etc.

Before you can start training, therefore, you must find out what the job contains - the tasks in their various forms — and you must establish the standards of performance those tasks demand. Only then can you begin to consider how much training to give — and in what form.

Occupation

You have the definition of an occupation and we do not propose to go further than that as we are only concerned with the training of individuals or small groups and not with the training and development of whole occupations. However, we included the definition as it completes the development from 'task'.

As an example consider the occupation "driver". He can drive a taxi, a small delivery van, a lorry (HGV), a bus, etc. — all different but all in the same occupation.

Methods of Assessing

Here we shall only outline some common methods of assessing training needs; for more about sources of information see Component 5 and for more about measuring gaps see Component 4. We need to conduct an analysis so that we can determine the standards required and reached and thus, if necessary, the training needed to bring the person up to standard. As a result of making an assessment of training needs we can then set out a training programme covering the content, level of treatment, methods to be used, evaluation systems and timespan.

Let's start by saying that there is no magical way of assessing nor is there only one sure way! Here is a list of common methods with a bit of additional information to each:—

1. LOOK! Use your eyes, look around you, watch the operation being undertaken and check against the correct method. Most of us can see — very few LOOK! Looking is a difficult thing to do — it demands concentration and also knowing what you are looking at or for.
2. LISTEN! Not secretly or as a spy but in the normal course of work. Like looking it demands concentration — and knowing what to listen to.

Bet you thought you'd finished with these; well, this is the last. Take five minutes to produce a list of other methods you could use.

You could have added one or more of these; you may have produced some we haven't got here — if so, that's great! Our list:–
Charting
Filming
Doing task yourself
Surveys
Customer surveys
Records
Questionnaires
Interviews (jobholder, boss, etc.)
Market Research
Discussions
Inter-departmental or inter-firm comparisons

Summary

In this Component we set out to define what we mean by a training need; we then showed that a gap between the desired and the achieved performances may be due to one or more of a range of reasons and **it is up to the trainer to ascertain what they are.** We then went on to consider some of the fundamentals such as deciding what a task is (and a job, too, of course) and we ended with a brief run through the possible methods you can use to see where the gaps are and what the potential causes might be.

Tutor Seen Work

Now you should try your hand at assessing where there are gaps in some situation with which you are very familiar — at work, at home or in some leisure activity. Start by selecting some area of interest to you (at work, home/or in leisure); you can take more than one, of course. Then set down the required standards of performance as far as you can establish them and alongside set down, in your own words, the actual standards you (or the person you are observing) have achieved. Finally note the gaps; decide if they can be bridged by training. Having done this send your report to your tutor for comments. Remember to keep the assessment and report fairly broad. At this stage you are only beginning to develop the skills and methods of analysis; you can go on to greater depths in your study of Components 3 and 4 of this study unit.

Component 2:

Who Identifies Training Needs?

Key Words

Needs; types of organisation; senior management; personnel management; line management.

When you have worked through this Component you should

i) be clearer about what this deceptive question implies, and

ii) have some guidelines to help you understand better the situation in your own organisation - in particular about how to identify who you should contact in order to find out what your firm's policies are, and

iii) have a framework into which you can place the problems that concern you directly.

Checkpoint

Taking the organisation you work for, try to write down the names of people who have responsibility for identifying training needs. Take about ten minutes.

Look at what you have written, and try to analyse any difficulties you ran into. (a) Was the difficulty **simply** *that you did not know names? (b) Or did you find yourself puzzled by what the question implies? Did you find, for example, that you simply did not understand clearly how your firm was organised for training?*

You will probably have found that the question 'Who identifies training needs?' demands an answer that is more than just writing down a list of names. Let us now look at some of the issues that arise.

Issue Number One: the word 'needs'

When we use the word 'needs' we have to remember that it has two features, each of which is worth a closer look. The first feature is that a 'need' is different from a 'want'. We use the word 'need', not so much when we are talking about what people feel like doing, as when we are talking about what people may be required to do in order to fulfil some aim. For example, we may say that an employee 'needs' training in keyboard skills. This only makes sense if we know that the firm has introduced microcomputers and requires staff who can use them efficiently. So, when we talk about needs, we imply that some plan or aim exists.

The second feature of the word 'need' is that we may not be aware that we have one. We always know when we have a 'want'. When we want food, or want money, or want promotion we can somehow feel these wants. But, quite often, we do not know that we have a need until someone tells us. For example, someone may tell us that we 'need' to be more punctual, or more accurate, or more polite; and it is when we are told that the realisation hits us. Even so, we may put up an emotional resistance to accepting the truth of what we have been told. To be told that we have a need may sound like being told that we are inadequate. It takes a lot of honesty and courage to face such an idea.

So, we can see that the question, 'Who identifies training needs?' is not as simple as it looks. There are two clear implications. First, a person with responsibility for identifying needs cannot work without an aim or plan. Second, this person may have to say some unpopular things to colleagues — of which they were unaware, and to which they might put up resistance. Whoever has the job of identifying training needs is likely to be someone who carries authority in the organisation. Without that, such a person is probably wasting his time.

Issue Number Two: Types of Organisation

What we have said so far will probably apply to any organisation. However, there will obviously be variations, from organisation to organisation, in the way tasks are allocated and carried out. These variations may be the result of size. Or they may reflect the views taken by management about how best the organisation will operate i.e. about what is often called 'management style'. Or they may reflect the nature of the work itself.

An example may make this clear. Take the case of a small garage, with a work force of six or so, which undertakes mechanical, electrical and bodywork repairs on cars. With a work-force of this size, and with a readily defined range of work, training needs can be established without much difficulty. For example, a big switch to the ownership of diesel cars would be obvious enough from the vehicles brought in for repair. And the topic of diesel cars probably features in the magazines and house journals that the work force sees. The manager, and all six in the garage, can quickly work out the options. Refuse to accept diesel cars (and risk ever-decreasing business). Or get the training necessary to cope with diesel engines. By self-help? Can the work-force learn from manuals? Are there courses on diesel maintenance? Can staff be spared, or paid for? On what scale? How rapidly?

When the work-force is small, and the options look straightforward, there is little need for analysis of the structure of the organisation. Even differences of managerial style are not likely to be of great importance. It is where the work-force is large, the jobs to be done are very varied, or are rapidly changing, or require a high level of technical understanding that we need to take the analysis further.

Before we look more closely at the ways in which larger organisations allocate the tasks of identifying training needs, it will be useful to have a reminder of the main aims or purposes of training.

Reminder: why do organisations provide training? Training may be provided for any or all of the following purposes.

1. It increases the employability of the work-force, by securing a better match between employees' knowledge and skills, and the tasks required by the organisation.
2. It helps to improve output or — to be more precise — productivity.
3. It helps an organisation to make best use of its plant, equipment and processes.
4. It helps employees to see more point in their jobs.
5. It helps all employees to co-operate in the standard ways of working that the organisation requires.

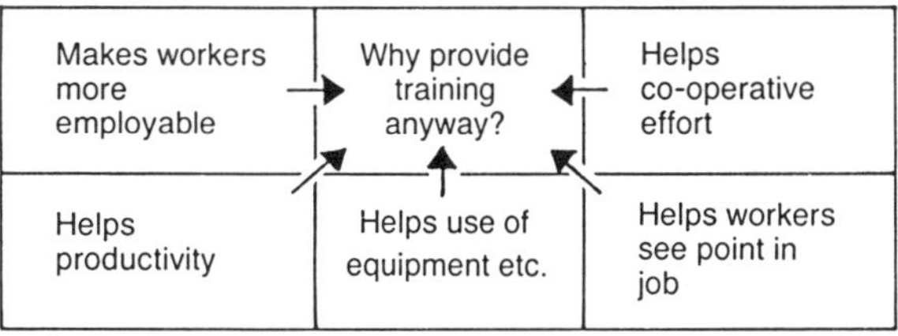

Identifying Training Needs in Large and/or Complex Organisations

Several different groups can be identified: senior management, personnel management, line management, departmental management, the work-force generally.

Senior Management.

One of the tasks of senior management is to produce a general or corporate plan for the organisation. This will set out the basic strategy for the continuance and development of the organisation. What is the organisation trying to produce or offer? What are the various tasks or jobs that are required to produce the product or service? Who is to identify and specify these varied tasks or jobs? What kinds of employees will it need in order to carry out this plan? What equipment? What investment has to be planned?

If such a plan does not exist, it is impossible for anyone to identify training needs systematically. In such a bad situation, all an organisation can do is

- to carry on as it has done in the past (with a risk of collapse in the future);
- to discover that particular training needs exist, only when a crisis is on the way.

Assuming that a corporate plan exists, and that it is realistically updated in the light of changing market preferences and changing technical possibilities, it now becomes worthwhile to ask the question: who, other than senior management, has responsibility for diagnosing training needs in relation to this plan? We can now go on to look at the work of the other groups already mentioned.

Personnel Management

Managers in charge have responsibilities as follows.

(A) They have to ensure that new employees are placed adequately in the firm. This means that they need to have a clear idea of what the various job specifications are within the firm, and how they relate to the corporate plan. As part of the task of ensuring good initial placement, they also need to ensure that new employees have good pre-job or on-the-job training. In other words they need to diagnose the precise needs that arise from the particular processes and ways of doing things found in the firm.

(B) They have a responsibility for the internal movement of employees from job to job — perhaps as vacancies become available, or as they decide that particular employees merit a chance for promotion or widening experience.

(C) They have a responsibility for seeing that good records are kept of employees' experience, and of ensuring that employees' abilities are examined (or 'appraised', a word often used in this context), particularly when employees are likely to be promoted. Personnel managers, therefore, form a group with a very clear responsibility for identifying training needs.

Managers of this type are not, however, the only kinds of managers found in organisations. Another type is the line-manager.

Line Management

What do line managers do? It is easiest to understand their work by going back to the corporate plan produced by senior management. This plan provides a framework of aims or targets. It is the task of the line manager to ensure that these aims or targets are met. For example, if the corporate plan contains the aim of increasing production (say of a particular range of garden furniture) and of cutting down the unit cost (so that the firm can underprice its competitors), then it is the task of the line manager to organise production methods to achieve this goal.

Having this responsibility, they have to make decisions which have strong implications for their colleagues in the personnel department. It may be found that men and women involved in producing the goods or delivering the service need different skills or knowledge, or that employees are needed in different numbers and proportions. Judgements of this kind have strong implications for training. So, although line managers may have as a first duty to liaise with the personnel department, we can see that they have a clear role in identifying training needs.

Training within the various departments of the organisation.

Up to now, we have used the word 'organisation' as though it referred to something that is not subdivided. Managers responsible for the corporate plan may find it useful to think in this way, since by definition the corporate plan is about the **whole** organisation. But, for many, who are managers at the middle level or who make up the majority of the work-force, their daily work is concerned with only one or two departments. For example, an employee in the accounts department may know little about the work of those in the quality control department.

This separation is quite understandable. The range of jobs being so wide and varied, the training needs are likely to be equally divergent. What is more, someone working in one department may not even **understand** the training needs of another, particularly if the work is specialised.

So we can now name a third group of people who, in a large organisation, have a hand in identifying training needs: the staff responsible for training within a particular department. Departmental staff bring specialist knowledge and experience to bear on the problems faced by that department in meeting the requirements of the corporate plan. Departmental training managers, working closely with personnel and line managers, have to ensure that their particular and specialised needs are fully co-ordinated into the firm's overall training programme.

Look at the block diagram. The cube represents the total of the firm's training requirements. The three faces shown (B, C, D) give the responsibilities of three groups of people for identifying training needs. Side A is not shown: we can take this to be senior management and the corporate plan. Can you identify any groups missing? Who might be shown on side E?

Up to now, we have been speaking as though all training needs are identified only by people called managers. People with titles of this sort may make up less than 10% of the total work-force. What about all the others? Do none of these have a part in identifying training needs?

Look back now at the beginning of Section 2.2. We made suggestions there about ways in which organisations might differ. One way was in size and complexity. The other way was in managerial style.

There are many types of managerial style, but two clearly distinctive ones can be contrasted. Examine the two diagrams.

In Style One, most members of the work force will feel that they have little to do with the policies, plans or development of the company. They simply carry out instructions.

Style Two, however, implies a much wider role for employees generally. They form the group that could be shown on face E of our block diagram. In a firm where there is a good deal of interaction between management and work-force, then individual employees (or groups of them) become people who can offer advice about training needs. They might do this through consultative meetings, suggestions boxes, day to day contact with managers etc.

Conclusion We can now summarise.
The responsibility of defining training needs will vary greatly according to the size, complexity and managerial style of the firm. In large, complex organisations, it is possible to see how four groups of people share this responsibility: senior management, line management, personnel management, departmental management. In all organisations it is possible (some would say desirable) for the work force as a whole to be associated with this task.

The diagram below may help to clarify the relations between the various groups.

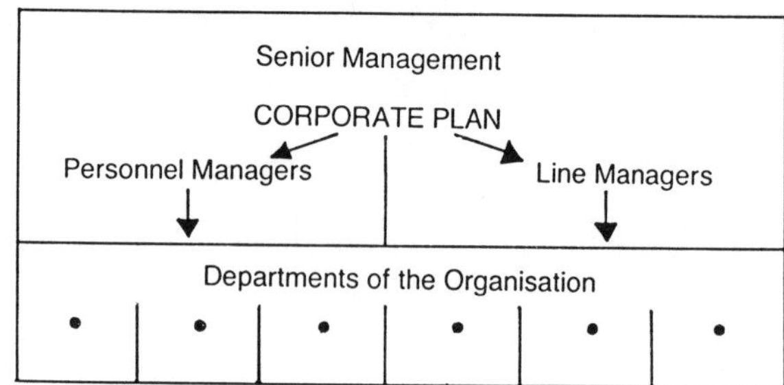

Component 3:

Standards of Performance

Key Ideas

 **The meaning of 'standard performance'; need to set standards; common features; factors appropriate to the setting of standards; people involved; establishing and producing standards.**

Objectives

After working through this Component you will be able to:—

1. determine standards of performance for those tasks, duties and responsibilities within your control
2. use the factors appropriate to the tasks, etc
3. check that the standards established are realistic and relevant to the needs of the parties concerned
4. produce written standards capable of being measured or assessed effectively

Introduction

Unless you have had experience of assessing gaps in the performance of a person in work you will need to have studied Component One of this Study Unit before attempting this Component. This is because you need to know how to identify those gaps and, just as important, determine that they can be bridged by training or that they are due to some other cause which training is unlikely to be able to remedy.

If you return to our earlier definition of a training need (in Component One) we stated there this definition:—

A training need is the gap which exists between the required and the actual standards of performance of a person in a task (duty or responsibility) **and which can be bridged by training.**

In Component One we went into some depth in defining 'task', 'job' and 'occupation' and showed that the basis of all jobs is the **task.** Central to 'gap', 'task' and 'job' is one essential feature — STANDARD OF PERFORMANCE. No matter what task you do there will be a standard of performance attached to it. You may find it difficult to uncover or it may be glaringly obvious; you may find it to be precise or perhaps rather vague (for example, '. . . . to within 0.001″. . .' as compared with '. . . as smooth as possible . . .'). A standard, too, may have been relevant once upon a time but, with changing technologies or methods has become outdated — hence the need for regular reviews of standards with, in some cases, consequent revision. Finally, you may know the standard required before you start a task or you may only find out during or afterwards! No doubt you can think of examples to suit each of these situations.

Whatever the situation the fact remains that every task (and here we include 'duty', 'responsibility' and 'job' to avoid continual repetition of these other terms) has a standard of performance as an essential part of it. The establishment of a standard of performance is central to the whole business of training. As you will appreciate, you cannot really train a person to perform a task effectively unless you (and preferably the learner also) know clearly the standard required.

Standard of Performance

So, let's start by producing an acceptable definition of this phrase 'Standard of Performance'.

Checkpoint

Before looking at **our** definition try producing your own; keep it fairly short and produce it from your own thoughts — leave the dictionaries alone!

It's somewhat unlikely that we shall have produced identical definitions but here is ours:—

The standard of performance is that which a qualified worker will achieve naturally when undertaking a clearly defined task and following the required method of work.

Compare your definition with ours and look for the key words and phrases; here they are:—

a) qualified — that is, trained to the level the task demands
b) achieve naturally — without undue strain — either physical or mental — and without undue constraints (such as insufficient time, excessive travelling, lack of correctly cut or prepared materials — to name a few only!)
c) clearly defined — so the worker knows exactly what has to be done, the method(s) to be used, the time available, etc.
d) required method of work — again, so the worker knows exactly what is required and **will have had practice** in following that method.

Why Set Standards?

Sometimes you can come across a person who says something like this — "Why bother spending time defining things? Let's get on with the job; it'll sort itself out" or words to that effect. For all we know, you may have uttered sentiments of a similar nature yourself especially when perhaps time is pressing or you are feeling out of sorts with the world in general! It is not as bad a comment as might appear; too often we take things for granted without questioning them — possibly because they have always been done in one particular way or to one long-established pattern. So let's take the opportunity to think about reasons for the setting of standards and, as previously, use a Checkpoint to do so.

What might the reasons be for setting and defining standards? Take a few minutes to make a list on a separate sheet of paper of the reasons you can think of and then check with ours. As previously, it is unlikely we shall produce identical lists though there will be some common to both. To start you off here is one possible reason:—

So that the learner and the trainer both know exactly what has to be achieved.

Now you produce your list and compare with ours.

This is our list; you will appreciate that it is not exhaustive but it does contain a number of common reasons:—

a) to ensure that products match customer requirements
b) to ensure most efficient use of materials
c) to keep wastage and other losses to a minimum
d) to maintain proper safety standards
e) to ensure effective cost control
f) to ensure maximum return on capital invested
g) to use time to the best effect
h) to ensure conformity to specifications throughout the organisation
i) to ensure conformity to organisational procedures
j) to allow the transfer of people doing the same task/job with minimum disturbance
k) to conform to legal, statutory and similar requirements

There can be many other reasons but these will do to cover the main ones for our purpose — that is, to make us think about why we set standards. Just one more point — periodically it can be to your advantage to check the reasons for setting standards in your own organisation. You can then determine if those reasons are still valid, if new ones have arisen and if there has been any change in the relative importances of the relevant reasons.

Standards — Main Features

Whatever forms standards of performance may take (for example, exacting measurements, adherence to procedure) there are certain essential common features. One obvious feature is that the standard set must relate directly to the actual task as it is to be done and not to some hypothetical or idealistic situation. When we are considering features we are not concerned with precise measurement, for example, but with those aspects which establish whether or not the standard is 'real'. As with reasons for setting standards, too often we simply take the common features for granted and it is possible to ignore them in the enthusiasm involved in setting the standard. To give an example, consider the case of a company where trainees spent their initial training period in a specially built training centre in a quiet atmosphere with no disturbance yet when they entered the areas in which they were to work they found things to the contrary — noisy, some interference, stocks of materials not close to hand. Performances did not match those produced in the training centre.

Of course, we can produce a long list of common features but, as you will know, you learn better if you have to do some activity connected with what you are learning so we shall use another checkpoint here.

Using your own experience write down on a separate sheet of paper what you think are the essential features of standards in general. You need not bother with precise measurements or even the forms of measurement but concentrate on the common features. You already have one common feature mentioned in the first paragraph above and here is another — Standards must be attainable.

You may have included some of these from our list and no doubt you have included some we do not have here; if so, congratulations — keep up the good work!

Our list:—

a) realistic
b) acceptable by the learner
c) acceptable to the organisation (e.g. boss, department)

d) understandable
e) related to the real task and not a simulated task
f) related to the real work situation and not a simulated one
g) capable of being self-monitored
h) achievable in stages with self-monitoring
i) relevant to **today's** *needs*
j) measurable
k) assessable if not measureable
l) straightforward
m) acceptable to the client/customer
n) correct
o) not over-precise
p) should contain interest
q) could contain reward
r) can be altered or amended as circumstances change (e.g. change in materials, specifications, style)

These features apply in general terms though not all apply to each individual standard. For instance, there are many tasks where it is not possible to lay down a precise and measureable standard (as in answering the telephone); instead you will have to produce a clear and acceptable definition so 'measureable' will not apply but 'assessable' will. Again many tasks cannot be self-monitored but must be monitored by others. Take the checkpoint a little further and just spend a few minutes thinking of tasks within your own experience where some of these features apply yet others do not.

Setting Standards — Factors

Having considered the meaning of 'standard of performance', established the necessity to set standards and thought about the common features we now come to the factors to be taken into account when setting standards. Here we are going to consider in some depth those factors which can help you to ascertain and set the specific standards required in a task. We can divide these factors into three broad categories:—

1. TASK-RELATED
2. INTERNAL TO THE ORGANISATION
3. EXTERNAL TO THE ORGANISATION

Task-related factors, as the term implies, are very much related to the performance of the task as it stands at the time and in the very short-term future. As you will appreciate such performances must follow strictly the methods and systems laid down otherwise there would be no overall control and a totally haphazard form would ensue. It is probable that task-related performances are those with which you are most likely to be concerned but you neglect the others at your peril even though, at first sight, they might appear to be of minor importance.

Factors internal to the organisation do not, of course, include task-related as these are dealt with separately. They do include aspects such as organisational policies which may well ultimately affect standards but are generally unlikely to do so immediately. They are on what we might call the 'middle horizon'.

Factors external to the organisation are those which are, as it were, on the far horizon and only slowly affect your own organisation's standards; a typical one would be a change of government in a major supplying country.

Initially we shall concentrate on the task-related factors and then go on to deal with the other two groups.

A. Task-Related Factors

These can be divided into four main subdivisions:—
a) Quantity
b) Time
c) Frequency
d) Opinion

As with all such divisions there is a degree of artificiality about them and there is in some cases overlapping (e.g. between time and frequency). Further, one subdivision may affect another (e.g. quantity and time).

a) Quantity

Quantity can be defined as:—

The amount of work done which meets the specifications laid down.

Here are some examples of quantity:—
output
sales volume
amount of scrap
gross or net profit
return on capital invested in an organisation
share of a market held by an organisation

All can be measured in finite terms as indicated; for example, output in number of items produced to specification or sales volume measured in amount of turnover produced in cash terms. However, if they are to be used in establishing a standard each must be measured against a commonly accepted yardstick so that effective comparisons can be made.

Here are some examples of commonly accepted yardsticks appropriate to the examples quoted above:—

Output
— number of items produced, value in £ of those items, per unit of production, per worker;

Sales volume
— number of items sold, value in £, per worker, per company, per £ of costs, per square foot;

Amount of scrap
— in volume or value, per worker, per machine, per process, per unit of production, per £ of sales turnover;

Gross or net profit
— in £ or percentage, per unit of production, per item manufactured or sold, per worker, per £ of capital invested, against turnover;

Return on capital employed
— in £ or as percentage per £ of capital,

Share of market
— against total market, per factory in the

organisation, per branch or subsidiary, in percentage terms.

You should note that the yardstick may vary — your own experience should tell you that different types of organisation (even in the same field of operations) will use different yardsticks — but it must be common for the area of work you are examining and with which you are comparing. For instance, there is no point in setting standards in imperial measures and comparing with metric or a standard per linear foot when you need square feet as the base.

Let's stop here and bring in another checkpoint.

Using your own experience make a short list of examples where quantity is a main factor in the establishment of standards of performance. Include yardsticks, of course.

You might have included some of these:—
finished parts produced per eight-hour shift
coal produced per man/hour by weight
hectares sown per day
peas harvested per twelve hour shift by weight
parcels wrapped per employee per week
deliveries per driver per day
calls per TV engineer per day

The list is endless! Quantity is one of the important bases from which standards of performance can be produced.

---

b) Time

As with quantity the definition is quite straightforward:—

The time taken to perform the task under consideration and to produce the desired result to the specifications laid down.

Here are some examples of time:—

Time taken to:—
produce fully sewn shirt collar
complete document
drill one hectare of winter wheat
'pick' a range of merchandise in Mail Order retailing
deliver set quantity of goods
make an omelette
remove old exhaust system and replace with new one

As with quantity it is necessary also to include a commonly accepted standard — so one can make comparisons either within or outside the organisation. Common measures include one second, one minute, one hour, one eight-hour shift.

As with the previous subdivision of quantity let's have another checkpoint here.

Using your own experience list as many illustrations of time as you can in no more than five minutes.

You might have included some of these — or you might not, as the case may be; the list of possible examples is enormous.

The time taken to:—
produce one complete tin
type a standard letter
paint standard internal door with one coat of gloss
assemble wardrobe
remove old tyre and fit new one to rim
deal with telephone enquiry
enter cash statement
dig grave
etc., etc.

---

c) Frequency

May be defined as:—

The number of times an event is required to occur per unit of time, such as an hour or a day.

Here are some examples of frequency:—

Customer transactions per hour
collars sewn per shift
number of people leaving voluntarily per year
calls out to service machines
delivery drops per day

And another checkpoint to consolidate what we have just covered.

Again, take not more than five minutes (and that's not a figure of speech) and make a list of other examples from your own experience.

Here are some other examples which might coincide with your contents:—
standard letters typed per hour
customers for shampoo and set dealt with per day
yards of carpet sewn per eight hour shift
stitches per inch
stock turned over per four week period
absenteeism rate

---

d) Opinion

At first sight this may seem out of step with the previous three as it cannot include precise measurements but, as you will know, there are many tasks where it is just not possible to lay down precise standards in a strict sense. An example of a common task where precise measurement is not possible is in the handling of a telephone caller; it is foolish to set a standard of, say, three minutes per caller as you do not know what the caller may require, how detailed the conversation might become, how much information you have to hand — and there are many other aspects to be considered in this one case alone.

Yet we all know that it is important to set standards for such cases and therefore we should set what might be termed a considered standard — one produced after careful thought, as objectively as possible. Another difference between 'opinion' and the other three factors is that they can be defined in commonly accepted terms which most of us understand easily. In the case of 'opinion' we have to use rather more words (and possibly examples) to describe what we mean and even then we can enter into argument about the exact meaning of what we stated! It might be advantageous to use the term 'assessment' though this again can cause confusion as it often includes the more accurate measures listed above.

Opinion, then, in this context is:—
The considered and objective determination of standards which cannot be determined in any other way.

Here are some examples:—
a good telephone manner
close supervision
impartiality
courteous approach

All of these demand expansion and explanation with examples to help illustrate what is meant but let us have another checkpoint here to enable you to produce your own work.

Take five minutes to produce a list, from your own experience, of examples where 'opinion' is a vital factor.

Here are some examples which may include some of yours but, as with the previous subdivisions, the potential list is long!:—

clear communication *using normal English and avoiding jargon, abbreviations and technical terminology, speaking fairly slowly and allowing the caller to interject as necessary . . . . . .*

having a pleasant manner, *keeping temper under control, listening carefully, looking at the other party without staring, not interrupting but if not clear about a point raising it at a suitable point in the conversation — e.g. at a pause for breath — avoiding argument . . . . . .*

We have given two examples only; partly to save space but mainly to show that it is not easy to produce a clear definition of what is meant by, for instance, 'clear communication'.

Well, you can probably drive a horse and cart through some of these examples — what, for instance, does 'close supervision' mean? Watching through a telescope? Sitting on the person's back? Being in the immediate background? Doing frequent spot checks? Or what?

As we know, in many areas of work, especially in what are called the service areas of work, it is not possible to lay down hard and fast standards but the tasks undertaken are important and therefore there must be some standard. You, and your organisation, must try to define as clearly as possible what you and the organisation really expect as the correct standard. You should also bear in mind that standards in this context may well vary from one person to another and from one organisation to another — to say nothing about local attitudes, behaviour patterns, etc. You get the best results by (a) spelling out the standards required in clear and unambiguous English and (b) giving examples.

B. Internal to the Organisation

There are factors which can affect the standard of performance — either the current one or a future standard — in a task. In this respect they are task-related though any changes in them may take some time to be felt in the completion of many tasks, especially routine or similar types. We shall give two examples of internal factors which directly affect and may well determine standards of performance.

1. Policy

If, for instance, the policy regarding depreciation of assets is one of rapid depreciation and replacement with more modern machinery then the standards of performance will change with the introduction of that new machinery. The same can apply where there are changes in system consequent upon the change in machinery — a new machine bringing in new methods and systems may well demand higher standards than previously. If the policy towards the customer is one of complete and detailed concern to give the maximum customer service then that policy will determine standards of performance throughout the company so that **every** product goes out in A1 condition to the customer's satisfaction.

2. Structure

The management and supervisory structure of an organisation will play a part in setting standards of performance by dictating the responsibilities (with the associated authority) of the various grades of job. If among those responsibilities is one concerned with, for example, tight cost control then this will form a major aspect of the job of the manager and will affect the standards of performance of jobs responsible to that manager.

Let us see how this applies in your own circumstances or experience; here is a further checkpoint.

Make a list of factors within the organisation which may determine and probably will affect standards of performance — not just in the job of the person directly affected but also in the jobs of those indirectly affected.

Your list is probably fairly substantial; ours should coincide with yours in many respects — here it is:—
Organisational objectives
Attitudes to the product, the business, the job
Current methods and systems
Influence of trade unions in-plant
Finance available
Type of activity the organisation is involved in
Time
Space and layout
Location of workplace, associated departments
Changes in job descriptions, management, style, product (which have occurred or are likely to)
Changes in the workforce (e.g. redundancies)

The important thing to recognise is that standards of performance are set and affected not only by the actual task demands but also by other factors within the organisation; you can probably think of many examples where standards have been set or amended by something which has happened in the organisation (or which is to occur). One example, in addition to those given earlier in this section, is where a distribution network is changed and fewer people cover the same area as the original larger number — the standards will be affected. The changes may include less visits, more travelling, discarding of small customers, introduction of a computer-controlled system, less freedom for the employee in choice of route, etc. Standards will then change.

C. External to the Organisation

As with the internal factors these are many; at first sight it may seem that they do not affect standards in your own organisation but a little thought will show that they can — and do — although, in general, their effect takes time to work through. We all know of companies which have gone out of business through ignoring all except those factors directly related to the producing of the product or the sale; we need to get our eyes up from the ground and look outside our own organisation to see how our standards may have to change. We have split them, for convenience, into three areas though there is a fourth one (attitudes) running right through them and you ignore that at your ultimate peril!
Here are the three with examples:—

a) International

Bodies such as the E.E.C. with its legislation on, for example, the import of milk, live animals, producing a change in the standard of performance of environmental health inspectors.

Legislation in the U.S.A. concerning car exhaust emissions (less lead in petrol) producing a need for raising standards of performance in design and finish.

Cultural attitudes (as in the Middle East) affecting the standards required of export sales staff or installation engineers.

b) National

Legislation covering employment, rights of employees, Health and Safety, etc., demanding higher standards of performance among relevant workers.

National attitudes to some forms of work (e.g. the leanings many people have against engineering which is in turn viewed as 'dirty', 'insecure', 'rough') demanding a higher standard of performance from all workers in that industry to remedy the attitude and at the same time increasing the number of potential recruits.

Legislation covering aspects such as Health and Safety, discrimination, rights of employers and employees demanding higher standards of holders of managerial and supervisory posts.
Flex-time.

c) Local

Local government policies (often offshoots of national policies but more defined; an example is the local authority pollution policy affecting standards of performance of engineers and allied employees in a company).

Competition as when a highly efficient retailer opens an outlet in a locality where there has been no one of that size and type before — existing retailers' standards will need revision.

Entry into a new area with a labour force not used to your type or style of operation (e.g. Nissan in Tyne and Wear) will set new standards.

Time for another checkpoint!

Take no more than five minutes and produce a list of external factors you know about from your own experience which might have an effect in setting standards in your own organisation.

Well, we don't know what your list will contain but here are the contents of our list:—

International
- *financial stability/instability*
- *customs and practices*
- *political changes*
- *change of measuring system (metric, decimal, etc.)*
- *attitudes, culture*
- *discovery of new source of raw material*
- *defence requirements*
- *invention*

National
- *trade union regulations, attitudes*
- *changes in education systems*
- *impact of Y.T.S. and other M.S.C. activities*
- *increase in part-time work*
- *changes in employment patterns*
- *deployment of industry to new areas*
- *government involvement (e.g. enterprise zones)*
- *changes in emphasis of different types of occupation*

Local
- *competition (e.g. new firms, new conditions, demands for labour)*
- *population movement, changes*
- *type of work normally mainstay but now defunct*
- *changes in infra-structure*
- *local attitudes*

Standards are thus set by referring to three categories of factor — the task itself, organisational and external factors. It must be remembered that not all factors apply in any situation, nor do they apply equally — you must use those which appear appropriate and relevant at the time.

Who Sets the Standard?

This is not as easy as at first sight appears; here is an example for one organisation which illustrates this point:—

A new employee spent the first few days in the training department where, among other tasks, she was taught how to deal with an order form when it arrived from the customer — the company's standard system. On moving into her department she was told — "Never mind what they told you in the training department — this is how we handle it here". Two standards operating in that company, of course! You have no doubt come across many similar examples; not only do they illustrate that different people in an organisation have different standards but they also illustrate the gap which can exist between functional and operating departments (i.e. the training and similar departments and production and similar departments). Incidentally, it is possible that both sets of standards produce the same or similar results.

Here we go again! Take five or ten minutes to list out your answers to the question — "Who sets the standard?"

Check your replies against ours — as usual, it is most unlikely that our lists will coincide — that's not the purpose of checkpoints — what we are really concerned with is getting you to use your own knowledge, experience and thoughts. Here then is our list with additional information attached:—

a) *the organisation — usually sets overall standards, rules, regulations for general use; may be rigid ignoring necessary variations in different departments or locations.*
b) *the department — similar to the organisation but on a smaller scale.*
c) *the boss — may set his own, may modify the organisation's to suit his requirements.*
d) *the boss's boss — similar to the boss in many ways.*
e) *colleagues — who often produce their own informal ones.*
f) *the jobholder personally — the taxi driver who sets his own standards of courtesy and behaviour.*
g) *the customer — with his own standards which he wishes to apply to you.*
h) *the competitors — who, by varying their standards, can affect yours.*
i) *new technology, methods, systems — producing in their wake rigid rules of operation and removing some individual flexibility.*
j) *new materials — new metals, plastics*
k) *the state — new legislation*
l) *the courts — by interpreting the legislation*
m) *government and local authorities*
n) *public opinion — either via statutory and similar bodies (e.g. Consumer Councils), TV and radio, other media.*

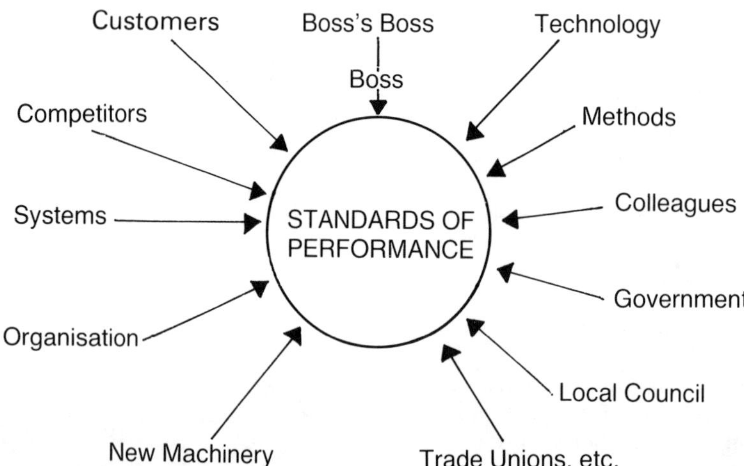

These are just some of the standard setters; you have probably thought of more. Remember that, of course, they do not affect every task nor are they always conscious that they are setting standards but it is essential that you realise that more than one source sets — and modifies — standards and that, in reality, standards are continually being revised.

Thus you need to do two things:—

1. check frequently that the standards to which you are working in your training are still relevant;
2. maintain very close relationships with the activities in the area in which the learner works.

Establishing and Producing Standards

This is the final section of this Component. It is an outline of the steps you take to set and produce relevant standards of performance.

The procedure is:—

a) Analyse the job with which you are concerned into its separate tasks by title only initially.

b) Take each task in turn and conduct a detailed analysis of it separating it into its various stages and noting the key points (e.g. any safety points) plus the standard of performance required (e.g. the degree of accuracy, time involved, financial measures, targets, etc.) for each stage in the task.

Remember that what appears at first sight to be one task may well include others (e.g. wiring a plug may demand previous analysis of the tasks of using wire-strippers, recognising cable colours).

c) Check that the analysis is correct and, in particular, check that the standards of performance are correct and necessary. The checking can be done in a variety of ways — for example, by doing the task yourself, by observing a skilled person doing the task, by discussion with those others involved.

d) Produce the final result in written form using common and understandable language.

e) Ensure that those concerned have copies of the standards required.

f) Set up a simple monitoring system (including self-monitoring where appropriate) to ensure that standards are maintained.

Summary

In this Component we set out to cover the essential points involved in the production of effective standards of performance; we considered in some depth these points:—

a) What is meant by 'Standard of Performance'

b) Why we need to set, maintain and, where necessary, modify standards.

c) The main features of standards bearing in mind not all apply in every situation.

d) The factors you must take into consideration.

e) Who sets standards including the fact that different people and situations will demand different standards.

f) An outline of how to set about producing standards.

You should now be able to examine tasks in some depth and produce standards for them.

Tutor Seen Work

Take three tasks with which you are familiar — one being a task with precise measurement attached, one where the standard is based on opinion or assessment and one other of your own choice.

Produce a task analysis of each with key points and the emphasis on the standards of performance required with some evidence of how you checked your findings, determined that they are relevant and what sort of monitoring is involved.

Component 4:

Sources of Information — Where do you get your Information from?

Key Words

Sources of information; aims and objectives; personnel policy and plans; job specification; age distribution; labour turnover; questionnaires and interviews; external sources.

The difference between success and failure in any walk of life is never very wide and we can all think of past situations when a different decision taken on a certain time would have made all the difference to some of the events that followed. How often have you said to yourself "I only wish I had known about that at the time" or "I should have made sure of knowing about that before I made that stupid decision the other day". If knowing all the facts can be so important at the level of personal decision making then it is even more so for those people whose decisions are going to affect the working lives of others.

All companies are always faced with the problem of having to allocate resources between different departments; every department cannot be satisfied and the one which makes out the best case will, on the whole, be more successful than those departments that have not fully prepared their case. If the training officer is going to be successful in convincing the senior management team that not only is training needed but that funds should be allocated for this purpose then the case must be prepared very carefully using as much up to date information as possible.

Where you get this vital information from is one of the most important steps that have to be decided upon by all those who are involved in assessing the training needs of their organisation.

Deciding on the main sources of information and how to obtain relevant information from them is what this component is all about and I hope that by the time you have worked your way through it you will have a good idea of what the main sources of information are in your own organisation, what you can use to assess training needs and how you can obtain this information.

Where you will look, of course, will depend on the kind of information you are looking for. For instance the information that is required to assess the training needs of a small organisation employing one or two people will be very different from the information required for assessing the training needs of a department within a large organisation and this again will be very different from the information required for assessing the training needs of the organisation as a whole. Also it is not always easy to find the required information and the assessor may have to do a lot of detective work to obtain the required information.

Checkpoint

Let us suppose you have been given the job of gathering information that is going to be used to assess the training needs of your organisation. Make a list of what you consider to be the most likely **sources** of this information.

I do not know how long a list you have got but I should think it is pretty long if you are working in a fairly large organisation or in a department of a large organisation. This list I am going to give you however is much shorter; this is because I do not know what your organisation is like and I want to make my list general enough to include all kinds of organisations. However I think you will find that my more general headings will include most of yours. If not this does not matter as the general principle is the same. My list is as follows:

1) Senior management
2) The Personnel Department
3) Other 'service' departments
4) Middle management and their staff
5) Employees using discussions etc.
6) External sources.

Let us look at these one by one and see what kind of information they can supply us with and how we can obtain this information.

(1) Senior management
Let us begin by assuming that the main aim of the assessment exercise is to identify **How, When** and **Where** investment in training can help the organisation achieve its objectives. Therefore it is probably to further assume that this important information about the organisation's short and long term objectives will be obtained from the organisation's senior management. However beware! There are some serious pitfalls here. As you may remember from some of the Components of Volume No. 1 it may be very difficult to obtain information about the organisation's aims and objectives. First of all they may not be written down in such a way as to be useful to you and it may require some smart detective work to clarify the organisation's objectives. Also the organisation's aims and objectives may not be known to the senior management! Or the senior management may not want to disclose this sort of information to a mere mortal like a lowly training officer!

Nevertheless it is very important that this vital information is obtained as it will form the basis of determining training recommendations and measuring the effectiveness of existing and future training. The training assessor must therefore obtain from senior management any indications of variations in the business such as technical, production or market changes, adjustments to the labour force etc. All these will have implications if they demand new skills etc. When the training assessor has obtained as much as he can of this vital information he will then know what to look for when he begins to obtain information from the other sources.

(2) The Personnel Department
Most large organisations will have a personnel department. However many smaller organisations do not have a separate department but will have someone who is in charge of personnel record keeping; this may

be a specialised job within the organisation or it may be a part of a much wider job specification. Whoever does this job within your organisation must be relentlessly pursued by anyone who is looking for vital information about the way in which the organisation is working.

Before you go any further make sure you know who is in charge of personnel records in your organisation.

Let us now go on to see what kind of useful information can be obtained from this source. In assessing training needs you will have to be familiar with **all** *of your organisation's personnel policies, practices and plans. Recruitment, selection procedures, remuneration, promotion policies etc. are all vital to assessing the training needs of the organisation. I am just going to concentrate on* **four** *such areas of information as an example of what is required of you.*

One of the most important pieces of information that the personnel staff can give you is that of job specifications. This may seem rather obvious but it is not as easy as it looks. In a lot of organisations, and yours may be one of them, there may be no clear definition of jobs and the efforts people make to sort out for themselves who should be doing what can at best cause confusion and disagreements, at worst damaging strikes!

Write down at least **five** reasons why confusion over job specification may cause problems for an organisation.

You could probably have written many more than five but I would argue that the main problem is because people's jobs are understood in different ways by different people. Try this simple check yourself. Write down what you think your job is and then ask one of your colleagues to give his description of what he thinks your job is — are these the same? I would doubt it. Everyone has their own understanding of what their own and other people's jobs are and a job description is an attempt to put these understanding down on paper. You may ask — why bother? Well, one reason is that the different people involved may have conflicting views on what the job is supposed to be. If the written description is clear and specific it can help resolve these conflicts. Another reason is that the person doing the job may never have been encouraged to think it through. If he is involved in the writing of the job description it can help him to clarify his ideas about the job. Another major problem you may be faced with is the kind of document that is produced. These may range from a sketchy half page generalisation to a comprehensive attempt to specify every last detail of the job. Unfortunately all they may have in common is that they tell very little of what the job really is! Regarding job specifications then the golden rule for the training assessor is — make sure the job specification you obtain describes the jobs people actually do!

Another important area of information obtained from the personnel section is about the age distribution of the labour force. The main purpose of an age distribution analysis as it is called is to discover how many employees in the organisation or in the department fall within certain age groupings and to interpret the implications for training of any unbalance in the age structure.

Do an age analysis of your own organisation or department. List the main jobs and write down the ages of the people holding down these jobs. Be discreet in dealing with female employees!

The information you find may prove very interesting. For example an organisation or a department may have a very young labour force in which case both inexperience and staff mobility are likely to create considerable demands on training. However your organisation or department may be staffed largely by older employees with many nearing retirement age. This also can have important implications for training.

Labour turnover is another important source of information. One of the main reasons why some organisations have a high labour turnover is the lack of induction programmes and job training for new staff. Also inadequate training facilities may make new staff frustrated and leave.

If the staff are not correctly trained and find the work so difficult to understand then the labour force may become unstable. A simple method of finding this out is by examining the length of service of those people who leave. But again beware! You must be very careful how you interpret this information as short service may be due to many other factors as well as inadequate training. Also finding out why people leave their jobs in your organisation may be very difficult as people are sometimes reluctant to give the real reasons why they leave.

Make a detailed list of the information you require from your organisation's personnel staff. Take about ten minutes for this activity.

(3) Other departments in the organisation
If your organisation is fairly big, then other departments will have important information to give you. For example the accounts department may be able to provide such details as: Training expenditure in the organisation and the training budgets of each department. The training provision in the organisation expressed in financial terms may be a valuable measure of the scale on which training is taking place. Of course a lot of money spent on training does not automatically result in efficient training so again treat this information with care. The management services section on the organisation and methods section may also be a valuable source of information as they will be in close contact with the kind of work that is going on. They can often suggest where training requirements already exist in the organisation and where future training is likely to be needed.

A lot of very useful information may be obtained then by having informal discussions with members of other departments within the organisation. Sometimes the best place for these may be in the local pub!

(4) Middle management and other staff
Up to now the kind of information you have been obtaining about the training needs of your organisation have been very important but on the whole have been mainly information second-hand, i.e. it has been information from sources which are only indirectly involved with your organisation's main tasks. In order to obtain first-hand information about what goes on within your organisation you must go to these sources who are actively involved in the work i.e. middle management and the other staff.

These are the people who are faced with the day to day problems which your organisation has to overcome in order to survive. They have the kind of knowledge that is vital to any assessment of an organisation's training needs.

I am going to give an example of how you would go about obtaining the kind of information a training manager would require to assess training needs in a medium sized organisation with separate departments. I hope it will help you to obtain the required information in your organisation.

First of all the kind of information you require will be grouped around the following; present training arrangements in the department; the quality of the present training programme; attitudes to training in the department and the future training requirements of the department. Secondly there are two main methods of obtaining this information. Firstly you have to construct a series of questions under each heading and then you will have to interview those people who are directly involved in the day to day jobs. A word of warning; it is no easy task to construct questionnaires and conduct interviews and as these are the two main methods of obtaining most of the information from the sources set out in this component, those who may require help will find valuable information from the books listed at the end of this component. However to start you off I will give some examples of the kind of questions you may use to obtain the information you require.

(a) Present training arrangements
 who is responsible for training?
 what training has this person had for the job?
 what plans are there for training new and existing staff?
 what does this training cover?
 are the training arrangements regarded satisfactory?
 how much is the training costing?
(b) The quality of the training
 are training programmes based on identified needs?
 what are the training standards and how were these established?
 how is training assessment done?
 are good records kept?
 how much resources are allocated for training and are these considered adequate?
(c) Attitude to training
 is everyone well informed about the department's training?
 is everyone aware of the organisation's training policy?
 is it regarded as satisfactory?
 how has the departments training policy been developed?
 what training problems are particular to this department?
(d) Future training needs.
 what training needs have been recognised by the department?
 are there any plans to meet these needs?
 is there a list of priorities?
 have resources been purchased to meet the training needs?

I hope these will help you to set out the questions you want to use in your own organisation but try to make them as clear as possible.

Using the questionnaire as a base, construct your own and go and talk to as many people as possible so that you can get a well rounded picture of what is going on in your department.

I hope you have gathered a lot of useful information!

---

(4) Employees
It always amazes me the number of times training managers fail to consult the very people most of the training is aimed at — the workers. They are the group at the sharp end of the organisation's or departments' work and their experience can be a basis of a fund of information for any training manager looking at the needs of his department or organisation. Some of the information may be communicated in rough and ready styles and language but a patient training manager using individual and group informal interviews will soon get to know what elements are required to change to make the organisation work properly as they see it!

(5) External sources
No organisation can of course ignore what is happening in the external environment. There will be many things happening over which your organisation has no control but may have a very important effect on what goes on inside the organisation. As far as assessing training needs are concerned these can be considerably influenced by the external environment in which the organisation operates. These may include Government policy; the general economic climate; market changes; competitors' labour requirements and the difficulty of recruiting staff. When you are looking for information for assessing training needs, although it is impossible to carry out a detailed investigation into all these factors, you must be aware of them and be able to assess their impact on your organisation's training needs.

Make a list of factors external to your organisation which you think may effect how you are going to assess your organisation's training needs.

If you have worked carefully through this Component you should now be in a position to tap all the major sources of information you require to help you assess the training needs of your organisation. Once you have done this you should now have the information to set the main training priorities for your organisation. This is the subject of the last Component in this Study Unit.

Useful Books

Kane, E. (1984) *Doing Your Own Research* (Marion Boyers)

Component 5:

How do you set about your Training Priorities?

Key Words

Priorities; corporate plan; manpower plan; off-site training; on-site training.

When you have completed this Component you should have a much clearer idea about the following:

a) the problems you run into when you attempt to set priorities;
b) the factors that you have to take into account;
c) the practical tasks you undertake in order to establish what is to have priority;
d) the practical tasks of getting the training under way, once priorities have been established.

What are priorities?

There are two answers to this question: a simple, straightforward one, and a more complex one.

First, the straightforward one. Something is called a priority when it is given first preference, or when it is put at the head of the queue. For example, at a road junction, one stream of traffic is said to have priority over another.

Second, however, comes the important reminder that few situations come ready labelled with a scheme of priorities in the way that road junctions do. For some idea or plan to be given priority often requires that several conflicts have to be resolved.

Few priorities come labelled like road signs. They have to be argued and fought for

An analogy

Take this analogy. Suppose someone asked you, 'what are your priorities for your summer holiday?', you might find yourself hesitant to give an answer. The question does not come with its priorities labelled. Your first reaction might be to say, 'Plenty of sunshine'. But very quickly, you realise that other factors are jostling for first place. 'Must take place during the children's school holiday.' 'Must not cost more than £X.' 'Must be by the sea.' 'Must be near a golf course.' 'Must be where English is spoken.'

This analogy makes one point very clear. There is often no **one right** answer to a question about priorities. Answers depend on the situation, on personal choices, on what people see as practicable and affordable.

If we return from this analogy to the world of the factory or shop or office, we can now see two aspects to the question: what are priorities?

First, a priority is something which management will see goes to the front of the queue, or the top of the agenda.

Secondly, what is to be treated as a priority can be found out only by reference to the organisation's aims and objectives. How can these, in turn, be found out?

Checkpoint

Take about 10 minutes to list what you think are the priorities of your organisation.

When you have completed this task, look at the notes that follow. First, did you find it difficult to work out an answer? If you did, in fact, experience difficulties, it will be useful to ask why. Some suggestions might be along these lines. Is your organisation quite small, and as a result writes down only rarely what its main priorities are? Is the future of the organisation simply taken-for-granted? If the difficulties you found in completing this task led you to ask colleagues for their help, what answers did they give? Were they also in the dark?

Is your organisation a large and complex one? As a result, are there **too many** *statements about priorities? Is it hard to see how the section to which you belong relates to the organisation as a whole? Did you seek the advice of colleagues? Were their reactions like yours?*

You may have found, on the other hand, that you had little difficulty in tracking down an answer to this question. If the priorities of your organisation are clearly written down, you can check a little further by asking how much practical help these statements give in establishing your own training priorities.

Whatever your answer, you have probably made yourself ask a number of questions that will help you to focus more sharply on the rest of this Component.

Factors which have a bearing on deciding training priorities.

The corporate plan. It is common in large organisations for a plan described as a 'corporate' plan to be drawn up. Such a plan, worked out by senior management, outlines what products and/or services are to form the basis of the company's work during the period covered by the plan. To ensure that these products and services are both readily available and of good quality becomes the overall priority of the company. Only in the light of this plan can any training priorities be established.

Example. A car company might make the decision no longer to produce its own gear-boxes, but instead to buy them from another company. Such a decision has implications not only for investment and marketing, but also for training. Training in skills specific to gear-box manufacture may need to be redirected towards other aspects of the company's work, if redundancies are to be avoided.

In small organisations, no plan may exist which actually bears the label 'corporate plan'. Nevertheless, owners and/or managers must have some objectives about what they wish to market, about how they hope to exploit new opportunities, about how they hope to remain viable. This information, whether it exists as a written plan or as a series of ideas in someone's mind, is crucial since, just as in the case of the larger firm, it is otherwise impossible to establish training priorities.

The manpower plan. No matter how many machines a company uses, in the end the corporate plan can be turned into reality only by human beings. This being so, it is common for large organisations to have a **manpower plan.** This sets out, where the company is expanding, what numbers and categories of new employees will be wanted over the period of time for which the corporate plan is to operate.

The manpower plan gives a very important specification of the kinds of skills that new employees may bring with them. It will also give a rough indication of the range of skills for which the organisation may have to accept training responsibility. Some of this training may relate to new employees, some may relate to existing employees.

The result of the corporate plan may be that the manpower has a reduction, not an expansion, built into it. When this happens, the implications for training are likely to be very great, since it may be difficult to take on many new employees.

Example. The organisation, as part of its corporate plan, has decided to co-operate with a Japanese company in the production of electronic equipment. One feature of this co-operation is an increase in the number of electronic engineers who have a working, reading knowledge of scientific Japanese. The current establishment of 100 electronic engineers is expected to rise to 130. The training department can now see these possibilities.

1. Ignore the problem of Japanese for the existing workforce. Explore the possibility of insisting that all future appointments of electronic engineers will be confined to those who have Japanese. (If enquiries show that there is a good supply of such people, then the training responsibility of the organisation is minimal.)
2. If enquiries show that the supply of such people is small, then the organisation has to accept the responsibility for training in Japanese (whether by internal, or external, trainers). The organisation may then, as an inducement to acquiring Japanese, place a ceiling on promotion of both existing and future engineers who are without some proficiency in Japanese.

If the organisation is small, an elaborate manpower plan is unlikely to exist under that name. Nevertheless, the owner/manager must form some notion of what sorts of future employees he hopes to acquire. And it is from this notion that training priorities can be derived.

Skills already available
For the setting of priorities, it is also important to have an up-to-date inventory of the skills and talents already available on the pay roll. Many of these skills will already be known. It is possible, however, that skills, not currently needed but likely to be needed in view of the manpower plan, may well be available amongst the work force, but not recognised, because there has been no systematic checking, or updating of records.

For an aspect of the organisation's affairs with which you are familiar, check out your knowledge of the following:

(1) Do you know what plans the organisation has, for say the next two to five years, for changes in —
the products it makes
the service it provides
the techniques it uses to make these products?

(2) Do you know what plans the organisation has, for say the next two to five years, for likely additional appointments to (or redundancies from) those on the payroll?
How many new employees?
What sorts of employees?
What types and levels of skill will new employees (in the aspect of work with which you are familiar) bring with them on entry?

(3) Do you know what skills are possessed by people already in your section of the organisation?

(4) If you do not know, how can you set about finding out? Remember: without reasonably well-based knowledge under these headings, it is pretty well futile to start thinking about training priorities.

It now becomes worthwhile to look in greater detail at the question of priorities.

If priorities for training are well thought through, then the training plan should have these features.

When it is completed, the organisation will be ready, at a time that has previously and carefully worked out to introduce some new product or process or approach. Employees will have the necessary skills, the appropriate equipment will be available in appropriate buildings, and the organisation generally will have enthusiasm for and commitment to the new arrangements.

Between the starting point and completion point, the organisation will be able to carry on successfully providing its existing products or services. The morale of employees will have been kept as high as possible, and allowance will have been made for possible stress on managers and employees most closely associated with the training programme. The good will of the buying public will have been kept.

The financial demands of the training programme will have been so organised that there are no unforeseen shortages which threaten the success of the plan.

Types of priority

If we now try to set out priorities for the training needed in our organisation, we can list the factors that affect training as follows.

ONE. We need to be very clear what we want the training **for.** There has to be a corporate plan (or something equivalent) that sets out future plans for the organisation.

TWO. We need to be very clear about **who** needs to be trained. There has to be a manpower plan (or something equivalent) that can list the skills needed and the numbers of employees needed to achieve a target.

THREE. We need to set a target date by which a particular cluster of training needs will be met.

FOUR. The setting of an overall target date is related to a further task. It is not wise to set a target date by just guessing or hoping. Setting the date has to come from the task of deciding which training has to come first, which next and so on. One training programme may require six months, another only four weeks, yet another two years!

FIVE. This itemising of the training programme is also linked to the purchasing of equipment or the construction of new buildings. Certain training may be impossible to organise until equipment or buildings are available.

SIX. The priorities need also to include allowance for the absence of some employees. How many absentees can the organisation cope with if it is to continue to provide its products and services during the period of re-training.

SEVEN. Finance. This point needs to be repeated that the training programme's priorities need to be related to a planned allocation of resources.

The Case of Proviprint

It will be useful if we now take an (imaginary) example. The case is that of Proviprint Ltd., a small to medium size company that publishes and prints the Easthampton Evening Gazette, together with three local weekly papers. It is a well-established company, which serves a clear local need, and has a history of good labour relations. Proviprint, which has for a century or so produced its papers by hot-metal process, has taken the decision (in its corporate plan) to move over a period of three years to the use of electronically controlled off-set printing. Its manpower plan has indicated that a sizeable training plan will be needed, together with a scheme for phased redundancies. Existing machinery will need to be replaced, and new machinery will be housed in new buildings, the existing ones being cramped, with poor access to road and parking.

How do Proviprint establish their training priorities? Managers, working with appropriate groups of employees, and union representatives, establish a sequence as follows.

1. The context of training is set.
   i) The company is keen to keep good labour relationships; so the outline of the plan is disclosed and discussed as early as possible.
   ii) Planning for the new building is undertaken at an early stage, since planning permission has to be sought, building contracts tendered for etc.
   iii) Financial plans are outlined. The purchase of new equipment must be as late as possible for financial reasons, but not so late that employees cannot use it to best advantage at the time when the new-style paper is introduced.
2. **Training Priorities**
   Training needs arise from (i) the availability of skills within the work force and (ii) the job descriptions for all those on the payroll. Proviprint, before it can prioritise its training needs, must undertake an effective review of job descriptions (and the numbers needed).
   i) **Priorities for Different Groups of Employees**
   With the new production process, the work of reporters and editors is likely to be different. These changes need to be identified. How much training is needed? How much can be done by using manufacturers' demonstration equipment as distinct from new machinery installed on-site? Operatives and maintenance personnel for the new equipment need also to be trained. How much training will be needed? How long will it take? Longer than that for reporters and editors.
   ii) **Other groups**
   To what extent do other groups face change as a result of the alteration in production methods? Those concerned with distribution? Publicity? Accounts? Analysis may show that changes for these groups are small — or can be kept small. This last point may be important if the organisation is stretched by the training needs of those whose work is radically altered.
   iii) **Types of Training**
   Preparation for the changeover may require different types of training. The practical problems encountered in organising these different types of training will again lead to a scheme of priorities. In a hypothetical case such as the one we are now discussing, it is impossible to say what the detail of such a scheme would be, but it will be useful to look at the possibilities and the constraints.

   (A) **Off-site training**
   Some training may be provided by the manufacturers of the new equipment. Some may be most easily available in a local or regional Further Education College. As priorities are established for these forms of training, two crucial problems have to be faced:

   Problem One: the training may have to be undertaken at times convenient to the **provider** rather than at times convenient to Proviprint. It follows from this that, wherever possible, changes of this sort should be planned well in advance: there is then little risk that the changeover date will be delayed by a bottleneck.

   Problem Two: the employees concerned will not be available for normal duties while they are training. It is important therefore for Proviprint to ensure that the resulting shortage of personnel is of a size that the company can cope with. It will be useful if release for training can be phased to coincide with generally slack periods.

   (B) **On-site training**
   It will be useful to draw a distinction between two types. Some training may require employees to be trained off-the-job. Some may allow them to continue on task, but to receive help e.g. in familiarisation with new equipment.

   With the first type of training, some of the difficulties related to off-site need to be taken into account, but it is likely that the timing of the training can be controlled much more straightforwardly by Proviprint.

   The second type is on-job training. The timing of this must be determined by the arrival of the new equipment, and the point of changeover to new processes.

It now becomes possible to summarise the various factors that need to be taken into account when training priorities are under discussion.

1. The corporate plan (or equivalent) must be clear about what new products and/or services will be wanted by a given date. From this decision, which

will itself have been arrived at only after a good deal of discussion and fact-finding, a plan for priorities can be worked out.

2. A related manpower plan (or equivalent) must be prepared for the changes that are included in the corporate plan.
3. A training programme can then be prepared for the various types that will be needed. The priorities within this can then be worked out by
   a) logic (certain tasks cannot be done until others are completed);
   b) securing co-operation with outside agencies, where these are needed;
   c) sequencing on-site training to fit in with building programme, purchase of new equipment, and minimum disruption to normal work.

It is now worthwhile looking back at the opening words of this Component. You should by now have a clearer idea about the groundwork you have to do before you can even identify the problems you are likely to run into when setting priorities. There is no avoiding the task of getting clear about your organisation's overall priorities. Without these, it is wasteful to try to set training priorities.

You should also feel more confident about listing the factors that you must take into account that are likely to have a bearing on your planning. These factors are summarised immediately above. The diagram with which this Component concludes, has been added so that you can check more easily the order in which the various practical tasks have to be attempted. Read the diagram downwards. The top line marks the point at which an organisation makes a decision to introduce a change in a product or the process by which it is produced. The bottom line marks the point at which the change is, at last, a reality. The section between lists the likely order of priority in which the organisation modifies its programme of training.

Establishing Priorities for Training

DECISION TO INTRODUCE NEW PRODUCT or PROCESS or SERVICE			
(CORPORATE PLAN) This will include Timing Finance Legal Matters Implications for labour relations etc.	MANPOWER PLAN Number of employees affected. Range of skills that will still be needed will cease to be needed will be newly required	RELATED ISSUES Dates for building. Installation of new equipment	TRAINING PROGRAMME Training of long duration Training of short duration Employee groups phased for minimising loss of work Training that can be done without new buildings or equipment Training that needs new buildings or equipment
DATE OF INTRODUCTION OF NEW PRODUCT or PROCESS or SERVICE			

Study Unit 3:

Managing Change

Component 1:

Looking at Change and Innovation

Key Words

Change; innovation; reactive response; proactive approach; external/internal factors; innovators; change agents; barriers to change; personal factors.

Introduction

As the title of this Component suggests, we are going to look at change and innovation in organisations, in order to acquire a general understanding of the main ideas involved and their impact on training. Some of the practical aspects of the discussion will be more fully developed in the following Components of this Study Unit.

It is really unnecessary to point out that we are surrounded by change and innovation. The days when "One man and his dog went to mow a meadow" have gone forever in most societies. Change is ever-present and continuous — it is around us all, and all the time. A popular expression in the high-technology industries is "If it works, it's obsolete". Hopefully not entirely true, but the message is clear!"

We should perhaps establish the way in which most people use the words change and innovation. Change is a more global word which covers all instances of things happening or being done differently for whatever reason. Thus changes will occur when the world's supply of fossil fuels is exhausted, and the event itself can be thought of as a change. Innovation, on the other hand, implies a **planned** change — where deliberate action is being taken to cause change to occur. Thus the development of alternative sources of power (nuclear, wind, wave etc.) is innovatory, as is the introduction of, say, the Youth Training Scheme. Innovation is often seen as a response to changes which have already occurred, or which may occur in the future, but generally the latter.

If we accept these broad statements about change and innovation, then it should be easy to identify a number of implications for training.

Checkpoint

What are the likely effects of change and innovation on training within an organisation?

List a few general points now

Well, I've managed to think of four.

1. The need to ensure that the content of existing

training programmes is constantly under review to reflect changes as they occur.
2. Up-dating (and even re-training) of employees to familiarise them with changes.
3. Introduction of complete new training programmes before major changes are introduced (e.g. computers, automation).
4. A very important, but more general effect is the need to train employees to expect and cope with change, i.e. the need to develop a 'climate' in which change is seen as the normal state of affairs.

Maybe you feel I've stretched things a bit to separate out (2) and (3) since the difference is mainly one of scale, but I was keen to draw a distinction between a **reactive** *response to change and a* **proactive** *forward looking approach, calling for innovation (planned change).*

I suppose I could have added the effects on the trainers themselves, i.e. their attitudes and emotional and work-related responses.

Let us now go on to consider change in its own right.

What is 'Change and Innovation'?

Change and innovation can be looked at from two points of view, i.e. by considering either those **external** factors which produce different ways of doing things, or those **internal** factors within the organisation which set change in motion. This would seem to be a natural distinction which fits in with the Systems Approach referred to and developed elsewhere in this Programme, particularly in Volume One.

External or Internal?

From a training angle we are more likely to be concerned with internal factors, but let us quickly spell out the distinction and identify some of the factors.

External Factors

Factors outside an organisation which lead to change and innovation include new inventions, discoveries and changes in technology, as well as increased knowledge (e.g. the microchip, spin-offs from space research, North Sea gas and oil, modern farming methods); market forces, competition, changing markets (e.g. EEC, exchange rates, labour costs); automation, computers and changing production techniques. Organisations have to respond to these factors, and in some cases (e.g. automation) actually contribute to them. These external factors are fairly obvious and well documented, and their implications for training easily identified.

Apart from the obvious training needs resulting from such external factors there is another consideration. Due to the rapid increase in knowledge and the expansion of knowledge-based industries there is a need to train people to cope with such changes, by becoming more adept at acquiring and processing information and solving problems — rather than simply digesting knowledge supplied by others and then using it in a narrow inflexible way.

Internal Factors

Over the last ten years much interest has been expressed on the question of the optimum size of an organisation. "Small is beautiful" became a popular catch-phrase.

Small organisations can often respond more quickly to the need for change, but larger organisations have greater resources to cope with the problems associated with change (such as risk, market research, advertising, financial backing).

The structure and system of management within an organisation can facilitate or inhibit change and innovation. In the rapidly expanding high technology companies, where change is an everyday feature, structures are usually very 'flat', with few levels of management. This makes change relatively easy to cope with, and encourages innovation.

Investment in research and development is a direct factor in producing change. The company which simply 'rests on its laurels' has no hold on the future in the modern world. Here is a clip from a recent IBM advertisement:

> "At the end of 1958, IBM British Laboratories moved into Hurley House with a staff of 40. Today, nearly 1,700 people work there, some with skills unique to Britain. Hurley has grown because it has been so successful as an IBM **development laboratory.** It now has sole responsibility for a number of important products made and sold throughout the world."

And a statement by British Telecom:

> "Approximately 3% of British Telecom's annual turnover is invested in R and D, last year totalling about £172 million, and 3,700 scientists, engineers technicians and ancillary staff are engaged in this work."

The introduction of new products, as well as continuous development of existing ones, are both necessary for survival.

Changes also take place in work patterns and habits (e.g. hours of work, flexitime, reduction in shift working), management techniques and styles, regulations governing working practices (e.g. Health and Safety).

All these internal factors will have an impact on training requirements, and indicate that training itself will also be the subject of innovation and change.

Is Change Inevitable?

While the rate of change has no doubt increased since the start of the Industrial and Scientific Revolutions, it is wrong to think of change solely as a modern phenomenon.

"We trained hard, but it seemed that every time we were beginning to form into teams, we would be reorganised. I was to learn in later life that we tend to meet any new situation by reorganising, and a wonderful method it can be for creating the illusion of progress while producing confusion, inefficiency and demoralisation."

Gaius Petronius, A.D. 66

No-one seriously advocates change simply for the sake of change. 'The illusion of progress' is the great danger inherent in any attempt to initiate change, where we may be tricked into believing that any change will automatically bring progress. However, progress would be painfully slow if we relied solely on past experience. The application of so-called 'common sense' simply maintains the status quo. It certainly would not allow for jumbo jets or man walking on the moon!

In any case, the rate of increase in scientific and technical knowledge is accelerating so rapidly that yesterday's solutions cannot cope with today's problems. From the training angle, change almost always imposes on the individual a need for learning. The switch from manual to electric typewriters, and then to word processors, is a good example of this need for training.

For your own organisation, list a number of changes which have occurred over the last ten years or so which have led to a need for the training or re-training of individual employees.

Obviously I can't give you a 'model' answer this time, but you may like to check through your list to see which of your items are external or internal, and how many you feel will be common to other organisations.

Identification of Change

As trainers, we need to have our ears to the ground and be sensitive to change in two ways. Firstly, we should be trying to identify changes which are occurring in our organisations, so that we can make suitable responses and suggestions about training requirements. Secondly, we should be looking for areas where there is a need for innovation (for whatever reason) in order to stimulate those innovations via training. Obviously the latter approach is more difficult, and its practicability will depend on the attitude to training within the organisation. The danger is that if we ignore or neglect this area, changes may be introduced without any attention being given to the associated training requirements. I'm sure you can think of examples from your own experience where this has happened.

How Can Change be Encouraged?

If we accept that change is necessary and inevitable, how can it be encouraged within an organisation? Who are the innovators, and how do they operate? On the negative side, what are the barriers to change, and how can they be breached?

In order to stimulate and encourage change:—
- a suitable climate must exist, or be developed
- the need for change must be communicated and accepted
- the philosophy of change must be understood and agreed.

Training has a responsibility and a part to play in this, across the whole spectrum of its activities within an organisation.

Ways of attempting to **introduce** changes will be looked at a little later — at the moment we are considering the cultural background which will facilitate changes. By this we mean the overall atmosphere and attitudes to change within an organisation.

Who are the Innovators?

When looking at change within an organisation, it is often the case that the process of change seems to be channelled through one or more individuals. At the time of writing, recent events in the Coal Industry and the activities of Bob Geldof in raising huge sums for famine relief would support this view. Much attention has been given to attempts to identify and categorise the characteristics of such people. As with the the study of leadership, results are far from clear-cut.

Some years ago the study of creativity was in vogue — trying to identify the features of divergent thinking and the production of novel solutions to problems. Risk-taking has also been considered as a feature of the innovator, as well as the capacity to work in open-ended situations with a high degree of ambiguity. While no-one has quite been able to pin down and analyse the 'missionary zeal' of the true innovator, there are a number of useful leads in the ideas about 'change agents', i.e. those people with a key role to stimulate change and through whose activities innovations are introduced. Later Components of this Study Unit will consider these ideas in more detail, and the role that training can play in raising levels of awareness and associated practical skills.

Try to identify a number of people in your own organisation who seem to stimulate change and innovation. Do they display any common features?

I hope you managed to think of a few, although I would be surprised if you managed to list very many common features.

What are the Barriers to Change?

A vital role for training in any organisation must be to educate people about the existence of barriers to change, why they are there, and what can be done about them.

Identify and list what you see as the barriers to change in your organisation. Explain each one briefly — it will help to clarify your thinking. Suitable areas for consideration might be

a) features of the organisation itself,
b) technological and physical factors,
c) personal factors within individuals.

Barriers to Change

a) Features of the organisation. There would seem to be two inter-linked factors here — the overall philosophy and attitude to change and the structural arrangements for carrying out the organisation's functions.

An organisation with
* rigid procedures,
* an elaborate and bureaucratic hierarchy,
* complex and time-consuming internal communication procedures,
* established them/us, staff/line demarcation boundaries.

will tend to indicate and support a "change over my dead body" philosophy. This is often coupled to a cultural approach which turns a blind eye to the real purposes and goals of the organisation, and instead concentrates on internal procedures and routines. For example, it is interesting to learn that in the early days of the Falklands conflict, the dockyards were only able to convert ships quickly for their new roles by completely disregarding well-established standard procedural routines for undertaking refits. Fortunately in this case the system was capable of adapting to the changed requirements.

Certain management styles may also tend to hinder change. Autocratic or paternalistic managers who are resistant to change can influence the whole organisation; this is less likely to happen with the more relaxed consultative and participative styles.

b) Technological and physical factors. Investment in capital equipment tends to 'freeze' an organisation for some time and create a period of inertia, consolidation and resistance to further change — initially for obvious economic reasons. Technological development tends to occur in spurts, with periods of relative calm and stability in between. The history of, say, aeroplane development or railway technology would support this — pause for a moment and try to find examples of this in your own area.

'Available' technology places limits on the opportunities for change.

At a local level, the physical factors of size, space, manpower, finance etc. all contribute to delimit the extent of possible change.

c) Personal factors. As trainers, we need to be aware of the features of our own organisations and changes in technology which may affect us, but the area which should be of more direct concern is anything to do with the **people** in the organisation and their training needs.

People exhibit a number of barriers to change, based on their psychological makeup and reactions to situations. Most people basically dislike change, because it introduces elements of uncertainty and instability, as well as 'fear of the unknown'.

We tend to identify with those things in our present situation which satisfy our needs, and ignore the often rather vague opportunities which change may provide.

Fears and dislikes may include

* fears that we may be unable to cope — e.g. with automation or more complicated procedures
* fears of possible redundancy or loss of status — coupled to anxiety about the future
* fears of changes in social and interpersonal relationships
* dislike of the need to learn something new or different.

The overriding one is generally fear of the unknown. We should perhaps remember that it has been said that fear is the most powerful human emotion, and the greatest fear is fear of the unknown.

Obviously different people react differently — there are people who relish change and innovation, whereas at the other extreme there are those who are violently opposed to any suggestion of change!

From a training point of view we should be trying to stimulate and increase an awareness of these barriers to change, so that people can adopt a conscious and realistic attitude to change — based on sound knowledge of all the factors involved.

To sum up, in this Component we have considered change and innovation in organisations, their impact on training, and the ways in which we as trainers should respond. It is suggested that we should encourage our trainees to have a positive attitude to change — particularly where associated progress can be clearly identified.

Component 2:

How are Decisions Taken in Organisations?

Key Words and Phrases

Organisational structures; decision making; perception; participation; organisational climate; decision strategies; communication network.

Introduction

Organisations and managers must continually adapt to changing situations and be willing to initiate change if they are to prosper and even survive over time. The very nature of the dynamic complex and at times unpredictable environment in which we live demands this. People change, their tastes and values change, governments and laws change, technologies change and knowledge changes. Unless organisations also change they risk stagnation, decline and even death.

Checkpoint

Take a few minutes to think of any organisation you have known which has ceased to function in the last few years. Why do you think this has happened?

You will probably have listed many factors including technological, physical and personal ones but you probably also listed some features of the structure of the organisation. The previous Component pointed out that an organisation with rigid procedures, an elaborate bureaucratic hierarchy, complex and time consuming internal communication procedures and established staff/line demarcation boundaries would have great difficulty in surviving in the present day business environment.

The organisation that is most able to cope with change is the one which has a structure that is capable of adapting quickly to changing situations.

Central to these organisational structures is its decision making framework. Decision making is so much a part of the daily life of any organisation that most people take it for granted. It is only when things go wrong, when manifestly bad decisions have been taken or the whole process has broken down that people become aware of it. Change, whether externally or internally induced is going to affect the organisation and it is the organisation which has the capability of meeting these changes that will survive. An important part of this capability is the organisation's decision making framework.

This Component will help you to analyse how decisions are taken in your organisation. You can then decide if your organisation is capable of adapting to change. More importantly it will help you decide what steps have to be taken if your organisation is to meet successfully the challenge of external or internal change. Other Components in this Unit will help you in this task. In this Component we will be considering the main questions which you have to apply to your own organisation.

1. How are decisions made and by whom?
2. What kinds of decisions are made and are they appropriate?
3. How are decisions communicated and implemented?

Apply the above questions to your own organisation: Try and answer them in general terms at this stage and keep your answers for future reference.

I hope you answered the questions to your own satisfaction but do not spend too much time on them at this stage.

Now let us look at the questions one by one.
Q.1. — How are decisions made and by whom?

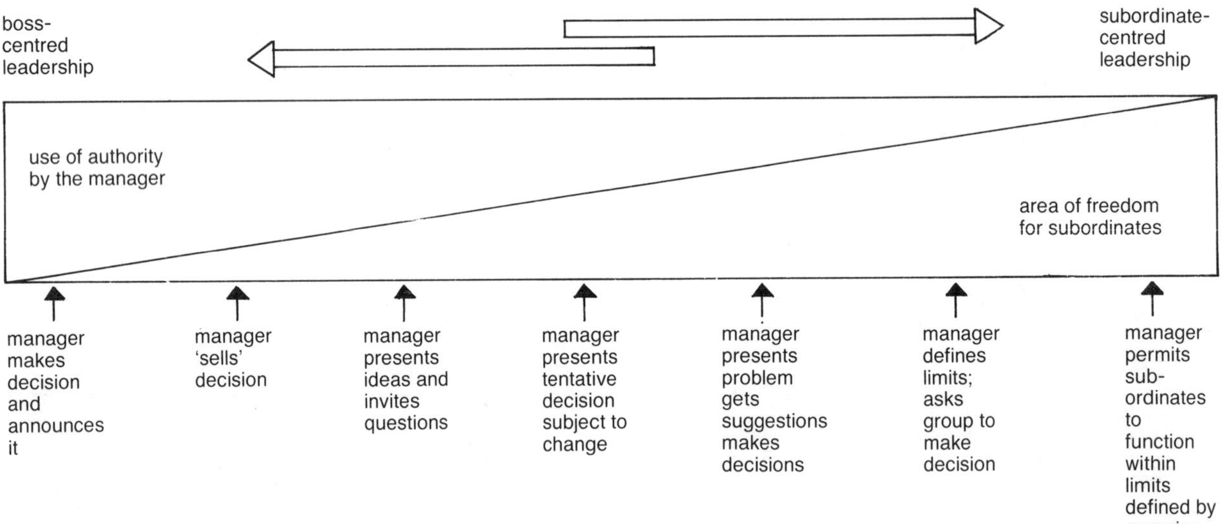

Adapted from Tannenbaum & Schmidt 1958.

Looking at the diagram think of the last major decision you were involved with in your organisation; where would you place it?

I do not know what your answer was but it will illustrate your perception of how the decision was taken and this is what is important to employees within your organisation i.e. their reaction will depend on their perception of what is going on.

What do you see in the above diagram? Depending on how you look at it you will see either an old woman or the portrait of a young attractive lady. Look harder and you will probably now see both. In many situations we see what we expect to see. When teaching problems or analysing data we are often pre-conditioned to organise our perceptions into expected patterns. This mechanism is clearly a powerful one in the process of selective perception of the decision making process in our organisations and how these decisions affect us.

Let's have a closer look at this situation. How would you answer the following questions: Take your time about this.

1. How am I involved in decision making e.g. individually, with another person, as part of a working group, team or department?
2. Do I effectively participate in decision making using appropriate channels?
3. What responsibility for making decisions do I have?
4. Are there decisions that I do not make that I feel I could?
5. Do I involve all affected parties in discussion before making decisions concerning them?
6. Am I possessive of my decisions or do I accept advice gladly?

These questions cover a lot of ground and if you have time to answer them then you should have a good illustration of how you see your own position in the decision making structure of your organisation. Try the questions on your colleagues; you may be surprised at their answers, show them to your boss — he may be astonished!!!

Now let's take one of these questions as a further illustration of the problem. Look at your answer to question two again — are you really satisfied with the amount of participation you have in the decision making process?

Copy the following Chart on a sheet of paper. In the left hand column list your main decision areas. Then tick off in the appropriate column the extent of your participation level.

CHART 1

Participation Levels Decision Areas	Decisional deprivation	Decisional equilibrium	Decisional saturation

Your answers are important because in recent years there has been pressure towards a greater involvement of staff in the decision making process. This is based on the belief that those who are most affected by the decisions should have some part in making these decisions. It may also reduce resistance to any changes that are introduced if the staff have participated in the decisions.

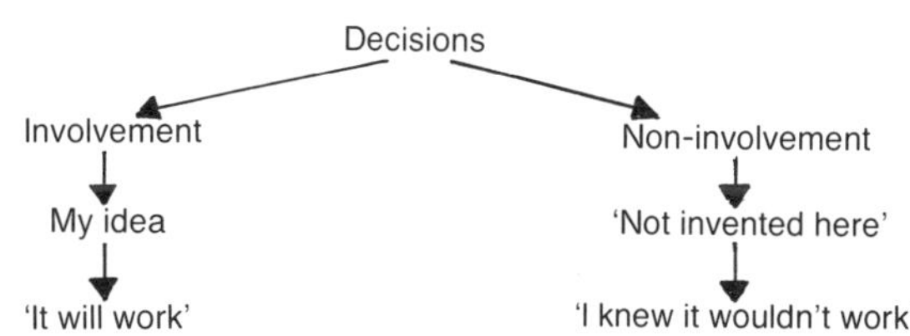

We shall be looking at this in more detail later.

Let's now look at the questions from another angle. Instead of looking at the situation from your own personal point of view, look at it from the organisation as a whole.

Try and answer the following questions; take your time and try and obtain as much information as you can.

1. What procedures of mechanisms for decision making exist within your organisation? e.g. group meetings, department meetings, working committees etc.
2. How will people know that any proposed decisions will be acceptable?

3. What decisions are vested in senior management.
4. What responsibility for making decisions does the senior management delegate to others?
5. How are issues concerning whole organisation policies decided?
6. What encouragement is given to new and junior staff to take part in decisions?
7. How are union representatives consulted about decisions?
8. On what aspects of organisational life are democratic decisions made?

With your answers in mind go back to the diagram on page 94. Where would you place your organisation's approach to decision making? I do not know what your answer was but what you have indicated is what is known as the decision making climate of your organisation.

Let's explore this concept a bit further. In everyday usage the notion of climate is usually felt to be the concern of geographers, meteorologists and holidaymakers! When we think of different regions and countries throughout the world, one significant way in which we form a judgement of them and, perhaps, distinguish between them, is our impression of their climate, their rainfall, humidity levels, temperature, sunshine and so on. Some climates are attractive some are not. In a very similar way, it is possible to form an impression of the internal climate which develops within a company or organisation and within which employees have to operate. Just as geographical climate can be more or less attractive for different individuals, the climate within a company can be supportive, encouraging and motivating, or it can be inhibiting and frustrating to the people who work there and to the tasks that get done. Whilst two companies may share very similar goals and face the same operating conditions, the internal climates generated within each company can often lead to vastly different decision behaviour on the part of the staff. Within one company, strong pressures may exist towards involvement, consultation and sharing, while in the other staff may feel that they are judged heavily on their contribution as individuals and so come to regard sharing activities as a sign of managerial weakness. Creativity, innovation and risk taking may be encouraged in one company whilst in the other, the emphasis is in "doing things by the book". If the climate within a company is not a supportive and encouraging one, then the decision making activities that are essential to its well being and even survival may not happen. Thus an organisation facing change will have a much greater chance of being successful if its decision making climate is perceived as supportive by the staff.

Let's now look at this situation from another angle. Greater participation implies that more than one person is involved in the decision making process, i.e. it implies that a group is involved.

Write down what you think are the main advantages of group decision making.

I do not know what you have written but read the following and compare your own answers with mine. Please remember that what I write may not necessarily fit your organisation so feel free to adapt and amend the answers as you think fit. Again remember we are looking for ways in which you can analyse how decisions are taken in your organisation.

The importance of work groups for managerial decision making lies in the influence they have over the day to day behaviour of the members. Such groups, after all provide the most immediate and the most tangible environment for the individual to work. They are the most likely source of, for example, standard setting, value setting, support, approval, criticism and censure. Group membership commonly provides the setting in which the decision maker translates what ought to be done into what actually gets done.

When considering the potential advantages to the organisation of using groups to make decisions, it is important to distinguish between two things. First, there are these features which in a sense, characterise group decisions only because they are group decisions, and second there are those features which might be achieved if the group works particularly well. Just as an individual decision maker can be more or less effective, dependent upon expertise, practice, skills and so on, a group can also vary in its performance effectiveness. In the same way that individual decision skills can be improved by training, so groups can be made more effective through practice in decision making. This is an important point to keep in mind when introducing change.

Having said all that by way of a preamble, decision making in groups would appear to have the following built in advantages.

1. It reduces the need for communication — the more involved people take part in making the decision, the easier will be the problem of communication after the decision has been taken.
2. It improves coordination — group decision making is, in itself, a coordinating mechanism. Action on implementation can be agreed at the time the decision is taken.
3. It increases commitment — members of the group making a decision want to see it put into effect. Obviously the level of such commitment will depend upon the way the decision is made within the group, but the mere fact of involvement, as was seen when looking at participation, seems to be an important factor in increasing the commitment of implementation.

Advocates of group decision making point to the further range of possible benefits from group decision making which can be obtained under the right circumstances. For maximum effectiveness groups need:

a) competent people as group members
b) training in group decision methods
c) opportunity to practise
d) appropriate leadership by the manager
e) encouragement and positive feedback
f) support from the external system.

Given these conditions, groups can make high quality decisions by producing

1. A wider range of alternative solutions — groups tend to generate and to consider a wider range of alternatives than the individual decision maker makes.
2. More information — in situations where the problem is unstructured, that is, where there is uncertainty over what information might be needed and what form it might take, then groups tend to bring more information to bear on the problem.
3. Increased creativity and risk taking — group situations provide a good vehicle for the generation of creative ideas. Individual ideas can be built on and modified, members may adopt more risky and 'way out' solutions if they get support within the group.

I hope you have absorbed at least some of the above information — go over it again if need be.

Now if you would like to go back to the chart on participation which you filled in on page 95 and try to answer the following questions.

If you have thought carefully about your answers then you should have a pretty good idea of what kind of organisation you work for.

Now let's go on to the second question. To remind ourselves this was "What kinds of decisions are made and are they appropriate?"

We will use the same approach as before. Answer the questions listed below as best you can.

1. What kind of decisions do I make?
2. Do I take sufficiently into account the circumstance in which a decision is made?
3. How do I monitor the quality of my decisions?
4. In what way do I feel the quality of decisions made could be improved?

Again remember that your answers reveal your perception of the situation. This is very important as people will act and react to situations depending on their perceptions. If you have time try the questions on your colleagues.

Using the same approach as we did with the previous questions, let's look at the situation from your organisation's point of view. Again take your time answering the questions as some may take time and a lot of information may be required.

1. Are decisions taken quickly and under pressure which preclude seeking advice and prior discussions?
2. Is there plenty of time given to consider salient factors and to involve required discussion?
3. Does the process sacrifice elegant (simple and effective) solutions in order to placate involved and affected parties?
4. Are there decisions which are the sole province of particular people or groups?
5. Are there decisions which are always about to be made and involve discussion which is of itself so interesting as to allay the desire for a conclusion?
6. Where it is deemed better not to make a decision?
7. Decisions taken as the result of a third party's intervention?
8. Decisions are taken by one area of the organisation but without reference to or knowledge of others?
9. Are decisions taken as deliberate mechanisms for change?
10. Decisions are taken and then conveniently forgotten?

Once you have got all your information together combine this with your answers to the first set of questions. You will by now be gathering together a lot of useful information on the decision making processes in your organisation.

This is sometimes called the organisation's decision making 'style'.

Using the information you have gathered so far, how many styles of decision making can you identify.

How many did you get? One or two? four? six? Compare your answers with mine.

---

1. 'Tell' or Autocratic decisions
   This style is acceptable for routine matters which do not deeply concern people one way or the other. It will also be accepted more easily where the decision taker has a considerable track record of success where he is acknowledged to be an expert or where he has 'charisma'. Though people may grumble, they may also grudgingly accept that the decision taken at a much higher level must sometimes simply be handed down without opportunity for consultation.
2. 'Sell' or Persuasive decision making
   This differs from the autocratic style in that the manager uses his powers of advocacy to explain and justify the decision to his staff, subsequent to the decision being taken. It is not open to negotiation. This can be perceived as dishonest, in so far as the staff are manipulated by slick 'sales talk' into accepting a 'fait accompli'. It would indeed be dishonest if such a decision was called 'consultation', but if it is presented as what it really is, and not fudged, it is an acceptable type of decision making in the right circumstances and we all use it in our daily lives. The secret of persuading people effectively without consulting them is to try to demonstrate understanding and respect for their points of view.
3. 'Consult' or Consultative decision making
   This method combines the advantages of obtaining the ideas, suggestions and commitment of those involved with vesting decision making responsibility in one person who should be able to assure consistency of decision making and conformity to established guidelines. It combines motivation with effectiveness.
4. 'Share Decisions' or Co-determinate decision making
   This is where the accountable person is willing to let some one else share in the decision, accept it and shares the responsibility with others. The approach runs the risk of inconsistency and while having the virtue of 'collective responsibility' it may thereby avoid individual responsibility. It is the only method available when no one party has clear decision taking authority. Negotiation and management by 'committee' are examples of this approach.

a) In not more than two paragraphs write down your perception of the decision taking process in your organisation.
b) Compare your views with some colleagues.

Can you come to a consensus view?

Let's now go on to look at the final question I set out at the beginning of this component; you remember? It was; How are decisions communicated and implemented?

They say the road to hell is paved with good intentions and the road to managerial and organisational ruin is paved with decisions that are not implemented — or worse still which have been implemented half heartedly. There are still managers who are sufficiently foolish or immodest to believe that what ever they have decided will automatically be done. The wise head knows better. A common managerial error is to overlook the need to communicate solution details successfully to others — and to gain their commitment to follow through with all the necessary action.

All organisations grow in size, one seemingly inevitable feature is the shift from a relatively homogeneous structure to one that is much more differentiated. In order to capitalise on the use of resources most organisations divide up their activities into specialist functions. Departments or sub units may be formed, for instance based round a particular product, or more commonly, a particular stage in the production or commercial process so, even in a medium sized company, we may find sales and production departments, quality control, packing and despatch, maintenance, personnel, finance and other specialist activities. The economic benefits of such specialisation are easy to understand and allows the development of skills and expertise, leading to more efficient use of resources, and corresponding economics of scale. The coordination of such specialised actions so as to capitalise on such benefits is, of course, a major management activity, cooperation between specialist departments and, indeed, between all sub groupings within the total organisation, is a fundamental requirement for the effective functioning of the organisation.

However this specialisation does carry its problems. The more sub units there are the more complex the communication networks become. Have a look at the illustrations below. Do they ring a bell?

The adoption of the appropriate communication network within an organisation is of vital importance to the implementation of decision making. Deciding which kind of communication network to use might well become one of the key areas of a manager's responsibility. Some possible communication patterns are set out below. Do any of them fit your situation.

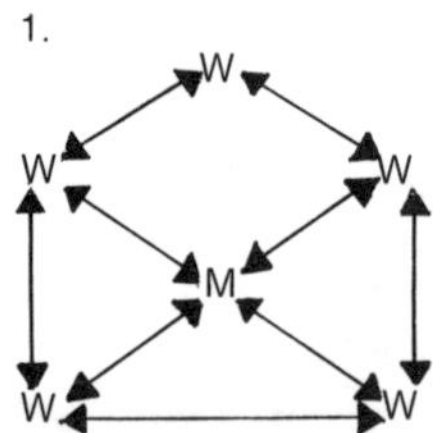

This pattern depicts an organisation in which there are strong two way communications between all participants.

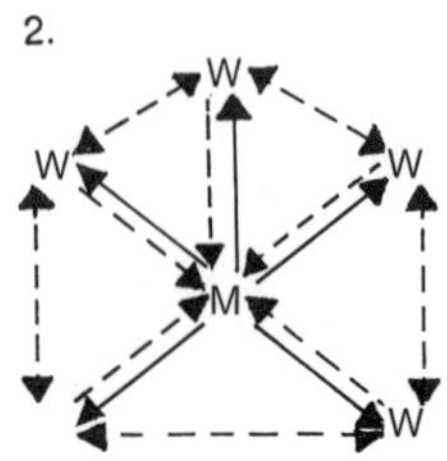

This pattern depicts an organisation in which there is a strong one-way communication from manager to worker but relatively weak upwards over lateral communication.

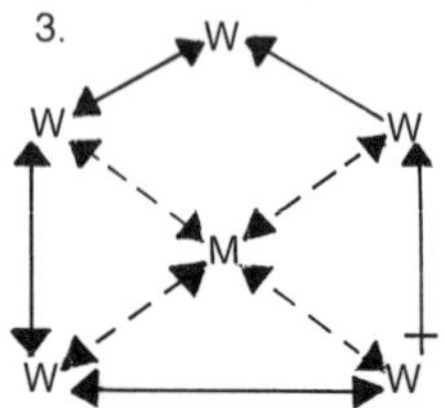

In this pattern there is relatively little communication between manager and worker but there are strong channels between workers themselves.

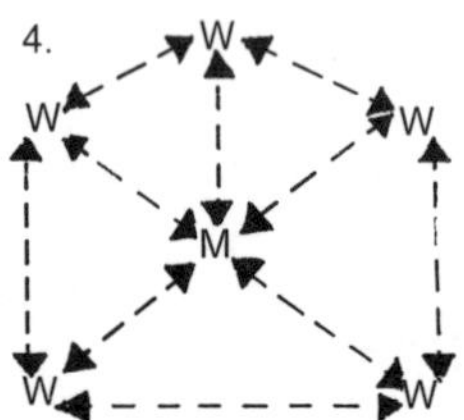

In this pattern there is relatively little communication between the various members of the organisation.

Key: M Manager
W Worker
——— strong channel
– – – – weak channel

Of course networks are much more complex than this — especially in large organisations. The more people involved in the linkage, the greater the degree of potential distortion and the less chance of two way communication.

Design a communication network based on the information you have so far obtained for your organisation.

Now compare your diagram with these set out in the text — which one does it resemble most? Let us hope it is the first one and not the last!!

Let us now go back to the question. Using the same methods as before to help you answer the question have a look at the following questions and take time to answer them. Then try them out on some colleagues.

a) How am I informed of decisions that affect me?
b) Do I learn of decisions soon enough?
c) Am I supported when I make decisions and supportive of the decisions of others?
d) Who informs me of decisions regarding section, departmental or organisational decisions?

I do not know what your answers are or what kind of answers you got from your colleagues but if you have been taking note of what they are saying you should by now have a clear picture of the different perspectives of how decisions are communicated in your organisation.

Now use the same approach with the following questions so that you may be able to obtain a wider and more objective picture of how your organisation communicates and implements decisions. Finding answers may take some time.

a) Is it always clear, e.g. through a printed or verbal statement, that a decision has been made?
b) What means are there in the organisation of informing people of decisions?
c) What procedures has the organisation got for questioning, monitoring or reversing decisions?
d) Is the communication of certain decisions delegated to particular people and methods?
e) Are all relevant people always informed of the decisions that are taken?
f) What is done to ensure the implementation of decisions?

You should now have a pretty good idea what kind of communication process is involved in decision making in your organisation — I hope you will make good use of this information!

Let us now turn back to the beginning of this Component. Remember I asked you to apply the three questions to your organisation. Would you now like to compare the answers you gave then to the information you have obtained by working your way through this Component. Unless you are very perceptive — you may be — and at the heart of the decision making process I shall be surprised if you cannot give very different answers now. You should have a fairly clear idea of the decision making processes in your organisation.

You may ask so what? What good will this do me? Well as a shrewd training officer you may well appreciate the importance of the information you now have. You may have developed a very good training programme but unless you are able to put the programme into effect then it will not be of much use to your organisation. The first step in this process is being able to exploit the decision making process of your organisation. For example who has the most influence with top management? Whose decisions are always implemented? Whose always fail? Your knowledge of the decision making process is of vital importance to you in introducing your training programme. Good luck!

In the next Component we will be looking at some of the skills that are required in order to introduce change into organisations.

Component 3:

How can you Change the Way in which your Organisation Works?

Key Words

Reacting to change; planned change; change agent skills; managing conflict; managing change; strategies for change.

The author would like to thank the following for permission to use copyright material:—
Harper & Row – *Effective School Management* – Everard K. B. and Morris G
Gower Publishing Group – *Evaluation of Management Education, Training and Development* – Easterby-Smith, B. (1986)
The Open University Press – *Management and Education course E321*
Pavic Publications, Sheffield – *Managing Organisational Change* – Elliot-Kemp, J.

Introduction

If you have worked through the first two Components of this Study Unit you should by now, have a general understanding of the process of change and a very clear idea of how your organisation arrives at and carries out its decisions. We saw in the last Component that this was very important to you as a trainer, in order to introduce and implement any change in your organisation. This Component will now take you further along this road by looking at the knowledge and skills you require to bring about change in your organisation.

We have been talking about the process of change for some time so let's take a closer look at this beast. You saw in the first Component of this Unit that organisations can change because of either external factors e.g. New inventions or Internal factors, a change in management personnel say.

How an organisation reacts to these External or Internal pressures for change can be very important.

Checkpoint

Write down as many ways as you can think of how organisations can react to either external or internal pressures.

I don't know how many you have written down but compare your answers with mine.

Response Category	Description
Drift	*Unplanned change; allowing changes to happen without any sense of direction, purpose or policy. (At the mercy of the winds and currents).*
Defensive Innovation	*The preservation of old goals in new circumstances. (Trying to put back the clock or stem the tide).*
Innovation without Change	*Adopting the trappings and rhetoric of innovation, but with token or non-implementation. The lack of implementation may be due to misunderstanding of the nature of the innovation, to staff resistance, or to the fact that the prime reason for adoption is the educational equivalent of 'keeping up with the Joneses'.*
Crisis Management	*This may be thought of in terms of a 'fire fighting' approach, involving a purely reactive stance to changes in the environment when they have reached crisis level. (All organisations have to face 'fire fighting' at times. The art of management is to minimise the amount).*
Planned Change	*Directional or goal-based change which is a conscious, rational response to a felt need. The change is thus the consequence of diagnostic and decision-making processes, and will be subject to evaluation in the light of the needs analysis.*

How did you get on? I hope you got more than I did!

Now although unplanned change may be interesting to look at, especially to the outsider who is not involved himself — it may not be so interesting for those in the thick of it! What you and I are really interested in is planned change. Planned change is a direct response to someone's (your) perception of a performance gap in some part of the organisation. A new training or staff development programme has to be introduced to overcome this gap and the best way to do this is to plan the process **not** to let it happen. Kurt Lewin, a noted American psychologist, recommends that any planned change effort be viewed as a three stage process; unfreezing, changing and refreezing. This can be shown in diagrammatic form as follows:

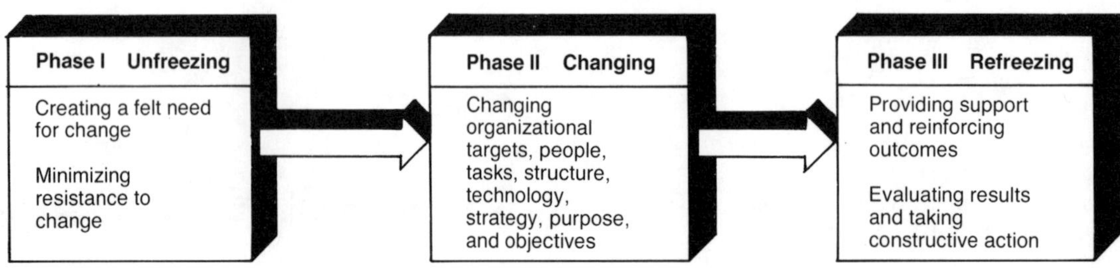

The three steps in the change process. Source: Adapted from John R. Schermerhorn, Jr., James G. Hunt and Richard N. Osborn, Managing Organizational Behavior (New York: Wiley, 1982), p. 495.

The Unfreezing Phase

Unfreezing is the stage of preparing a situation for change. It involves disconfirming existing attitudes and behaviors to create a felt need for something new. Unfreezing is facilitated by environmental pressures, declining performance, the recognition of a problem, and awareness of opportunity or a better way, among other things. Conflict is an important unfreezing force in organisations. The stress it involves often helps people break old habits and recognise alternative ways of thinking about or doing things.

The Changing Phase

The changing phase involves the actual modification in organisational targets for change, including purpose, strategy, people, task, structure, and/or technology. Lewin feels that many change agents enter the changing phase prematurely, are too quick to change things, and therefore end up creating resistance to change in a situation that is not adequately unfrozen. When managers implement change before felt needs for change exist in the minds of the people involved, there is an increased likelihood that the change attempts will fail.

The Refreezing Phase

The final stage in the planned-change process is refreezing. Designed to maintain the momentum of a change, refreezing efforts include positively reinforcing desired outcomes and providing extra emotional and resource support when difficulties are encountered. Evaluation and feedback are key elements in this final step. They provide data on the costs and benefits of a change, and offer opportunities to make constructive modifications in the change over time. Improper refreezing results in changes that are easily abandoned or incompletely implemented.

Now that we have made clear what kind of change process we are interested in let us now look at the organisation itself. We saw in the previous Component how important knowledge of the decision making process was for the successful introduction of change. Let us now look at what other organisational characteristics are important for the change process, i.e. what kind of organisation is most successful at planning its changes in the face of external and internal pressures. This is very important for you as you may be working in an organisation which may not be very helpful in bringing about change.

Make a list of the main characteristics of the organisation which plans and copes with changes effectively. I suppose we should really say — the main characteristics that an effective organisation **should** have because very few organisations have all the characteristics all the time. Well how many have you listed? Let's see how your list compares with mine.

1. *All successful and effective organisations are learning organisations which have developed a whole list of routines to cope with changes. They experiment more with changes and encourage more tries.*
2. *Effective organisations tend to be purposeful and have clear aims. Their managers, departments and their individual members work towards explicit aims and have a clear sense of direction. The development of purpose is a continuing activity providing a focus and a framework for understanding the whole organisation and linking it together.*
3. *The structure of the organisation is determined by work requirements, not by authority, power or conformity. Form follows function. Different departments may be differently organised, according to the nature of their work. Procedures may not be standardised; people can do things their way if it works. Power to do things is dispersed to where it is needed.*
4. *Authority is delegated, decisions are made near to where the requisite information is and communications are frank, open and relatively undistorted. Collaboration is rewarded, where it is in the organisation's best interests and competition is minimised except where it occurs because people are competing with each other to contribute to the organisation's success.*
5. *In the effective organisation each individual's identity and freedom are respected and everybody's work is valued. This individual autonomy coexists with some central direction by management and this crucial mix of freedom and autonomy which is the hallmark of the effective company. Also there are good feedback mechanisms so that everyone knows what is going on.*
   — Note the subtlety of the current NISSAN adverts on Television where they emphasise that everyone in the company is treated in the same way.
6. *The successful organisation is always tracking the changing demands of the environment and making appropriate responses.*

The successful organisation tracking changes!

Rate the conditions in your organisation along the six dimensions mentioned above: learning, purpose, structure, Management process, Treatment of people and environment.,

Do this using a five point scale (1 = favourable, 5 = unfavourable)

How does **your** *organisation rate?*

Now pick out the three least favourable conditions. What practical things can **you** do to make the conditions in your organisation more conducive to change?

You may have answered the above question by saying that you do not have the required skills at this stage to make the required changes. Well, let's see what kinds of skills are required by people who are involved in changing their organisations, i.e. the people who are called CHANGE AGENTS.

Observation of people who are more successful than others at managing complex organisations in which major changes have to be implemented shows that they tend to have a distinctive mix of knowledge, skills, personal attitudes and values and the capacity to orchestrate these as they make a list of personal decisions that are at the heart of organisation management.

Spend up to thirty minutes in making a personal inventory of the knowledge skills and qualities which you consider to be important for anyone who is involved in introducing change into an organisation. I would suggest you write the headings on three sheets of paper and produce a list under each heading. You will then be able to compare your list with those I will give you as you work through this Component. You can then create your own synthesis of the two collections, your own list modified and combined with some of my ideas. When you have finished your lists work your way through the following pages and then come back and see if you have to revise your own list.

We can show the relationship of the knowledge skills and qualities required by the following diagram.

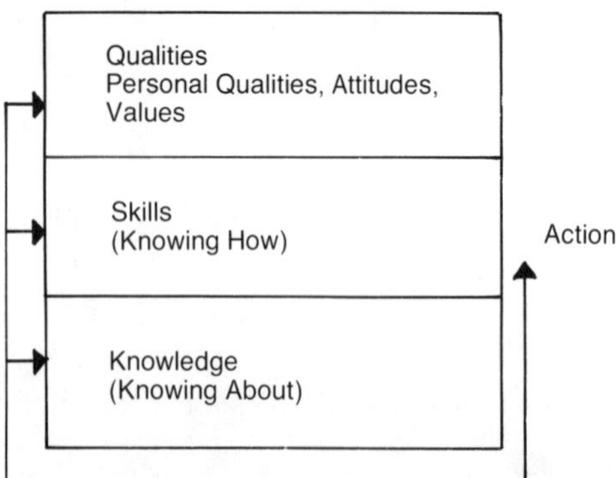

By setting out the framework in this way we can remind ourselves that knowledge, or 'knowing about' is of little use unless we possess the skills to apply it and furthermore although having requisite skills and techniques is important to the change agent his long term effectiveness will depend on key factors concerned with his personal qualities, values and attitudes and which will affect his performance of skills through his ability to improve existing skills and learn new required skills.

Valerie Stewart, a British psychologist and business consultant has listed the following characteristics of people who are good at managing change:

1. They know clearly what they want to achieve;
2. They can translate desires into practical action;
3. They can see proposed changes not only from their own viewpoint but also from that of others;
4. They don't mind being out on a limb;
5. They show irreverence for tradition but respect for experience;
6. They plan flexibly, matching constancy of ends against a repertoire of available means;
7. They are not discouraged by setbacks;
8. They harness circumstances to enable change to be implemented;
9. They clearly explain change;
10. They involve their staff in the management of change and protect their security;
11. They don't pile one change on top of another, but await assimilation;
12. They present change as a rational decision;
13. They make change personally rewarding for people, wherever possible;
14. They share maximum information about possible outcomes;
15. They show that change is 'related to business';
16. They have a history of successful change behind them.

Take each statement in the list and try and place them in the appropriate box in the framework on the previous page.

Which box had the most statements?

Let's now take a closer look at the knowledge skills and qualities required by the change agent. These can then be incorporated into your own list later on if you wish.

Knowledge

First of all any change agent will require what may be called 'situational' knowledge. This includes all the information the change agent will need in order to work effectively in a particular situation. For example:

(a) The purposes and policies of the organisation as stated in official policy documents and as interpreted by those who work there.

(b) The names, titles, roles, functions and personal characteristics of people who work there.

(c) The ways in which people, tasks and jobs are allotted or coordinated.

(d) The basic rules, regulations, procedures and customs of the organisation.

All the knowledge is a foundation for understanding the organisation and the ways people behave there.

The change agent will also require what is called "professional knowledge". This is the kind of knowledge that is required if the change agent is to do this job well.

(a) Knowledge of psychology and sociology relevant to human learning and development.

(b) Understanding of organisation theory and group dynamics, including theory of leadership, followership and human motivation.

(c) Knowledge of the work which the organisation is involved in — this is more than just 'knowing about' the work, it must involve the knowledge which will enable the change agent to take part.

(d) Knowledge of the considerable theoretical and perceptive literature that has been written in the field of planned organisational change. This field is wide but a good public library will carry most of the better known works. Also I have listed some references at the end of this component.

Skills

The skills that a change agent requires may be broken down into three major areas.

1. Updating skills — This area is concerned with 'topping up' the change agent's fund of professional and situational knowledge so that he is completely up to date and well informed. This is by no means an easy task when the growth of knowledge is rapid and there are so many resources of this knowledge. The change agent must be concerned with issues such as
   (a) Do I keep abreast of new developments in all aspects of the professional knowledge outlined previously?
   (b) Am I up to date with all those aspects of the organisation and environment where I work?
   (c) Am I fostering and encouraging sufficient informal communication with people who can help me keep up to date in both professional and situational terms?
2. Then there are the skills required to diagnose and evaluate the strengths and weaknesses of the organisation and the people who work there and set up training programmes for item. The change agent must be able to use Interviews, questionnaires etc. as well as being a good planner.
3. Thirdly there are the interpersonal skills. These include the skills of communication,, listening, reasoning, the ability to inspire and motivate others as well as being able to give and take criticism without causing offence. The change agent must be capable of conflict management as organisational and interpersonal conflict are linked and he must have the skills to be able to help others develop skills of confronting conflict, reconciling disagreements and resolving differences.

   It could be argued that this is probably the major skill that the change agent should possess. Some people accept change eagerly, quickly and with enthusiasm, while others are more cautious, reluctant and hesitant. In some circumstances individuals and groups may reject change altogether and in some cases resistance to change may grow in these individuals and groups who had initially accepted the change. Whatever the reasons for the resistance, conflict is bound to result and the ability to cope successfully with conflict is among the most important skills a change agent can possess.

Coping with conflict

Think of the last time you were in a conflict situation. How did you resolve the problem? Was the solution satisfactory?

Let's now take a closer look at the management of conflict. A model developed by K. W. Thomas provides a good framework for learning various conflict management behaviours. In the following diagram the model describes the behaviours of each party in a conflict situation along two behavioural dimensions.

1. Assertiveness - the extent to which the individual attempts to satisfy his own concerns.
2. Cooperativeness - the extent to which the individual attempts to satisfy the other person's concerns.

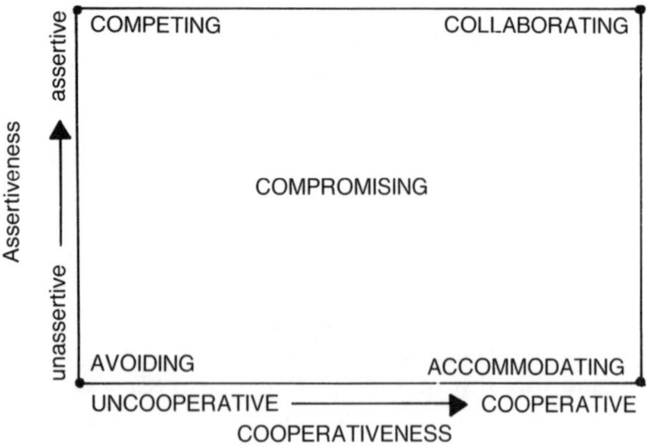

The two dimensions define five distinct styles for coping with conflict — competition, collaboration, avoidance, accommodation and compromise.

Study these five distinct styles of coping with conflict. Which one do you most often use?
What about your colleagues? Which ones do they use?

I do not know what your answers are, but if you know yourself and your colleagues you should have a pretty good idea how most of them could deal with conflict.

However, much more important to you is which one to use in your organisation.

Go back to your answer to the Checkpoint before last, With hindsight which of the above approaches would you have used? Set out your reasons why.

Nothing is inherently right or wrong with any of these conflict management styles. To be effective at managing conflict one should be able to use any of these styles and know when each style is appropriate depending on the situation and parties involved. Each of us has access to a variety of conflict management styles but we tend to prefer certain ones and to use them to the exclusion of other styles that could be more effective in given situations — with adverse consequences. Any change agent must develop the skills to execute any of the styles then he can diagnose conflict situations, choose the appropriate way to deal with whatever comes up. I hope you will obtain these skills.

This area is very important to the change agent for long term effectiveness. Here we have all the factors which influence skills performance and encourage or inhibit personal development. I will only give some examples of these but they should be enough to illustrate what I mean. These qualities include drive, vision, strong will, courage and emotional resilience as well as empathy, positive regard and a high degree of self awareness. The latter is very important as in many ways the change agent's feelings, respect and trust in others depends on his belief and trust in himself.

If you are like me you will probably by now have a sinking feeling and be wondering how on earth is one person going to have all these knowledge skills and qualities! Don't despair! — you probably will have many of these already. You would not be holding down the job you've got if you didn't. However, what about a little test to see how you rate?

Look at the following lists and using a five point scale — 5 high, 1 low, give yourself a rating of each one. Beware of self-delusion!!

Knowledge required for managing change — How much of this knowledge do you think you have? Rating

1. People and their motivational systems — What makes them tick.
2. Organisations as social systems — what makes them healthy and effective, able to achieve objectives.
3. The environment surrounding the organisation — the systems that impinge on and make demands of it.
4. Managerial styles and their effects on work.
5. One's own personal managerial style and proclivities.
6. Organisational processes such as decision-making, planning, control, communication, conflict management and reward systems.
7. The process of change.
8. Educational and training methods and theory.

Skills required for managing change — How many of the following skills have you got and how much of each?

1. Analysing large complex systems.
2. Collecting and processing large amounts of information and simplifying it for action.
3. Goal-setting and planning.

4. Getting counsensus decisions.
5. Conflict management.
6. Empathy.
7. Political behaviour.
8. Public relations.
9. Consulting and counselling.
10. Training and teaching.

Personality characteristics required for managing change.

1. A strong sense of personal ethics which helps to ensure consistent behaviour.
2. Something of an intellectual by both training and temperament.
3. A strong penchant towards optimism.
4. Enjoyment of the intrinsic rewards of effectiveness, without the need for public approval.
5. High willingness to take calculated risks and live with the consequences without experiencing undue stress.
6. A capacity to accept conflict and enjoyment in managing it.
7. A soft voice and low-key manner.
8. A high degree of self-awareness — knowledge of self.
9. A high tolerance of ambiguity and complexity.
10. A tendency to avoid polarising issues into black and white, right and wrong.
11. High ability to listen.

I do not know how you got on but you now have a base from which you can start a change process in yourself **in order to give you a greater capacity to manage change.**

Remember the list of knowledge skills and qualities I asked you to write down at the beginning of this section — now go back to these and see if you are able to revise them in any way. Use these as a basis for your own self-rating exercises and come back to them from time to time. It will help keep you on your toes.

Right? Let's be optimistic and assume that you now possess many of the knowledge, skills and personal qualities that are required by the successful change agent. You are now faced with the next important task — what strategies can be used to introduce your proposed programme of change into the organisation? Well, a number of strategies have been identified but the most common description is that given by Chin and Beune in 1976. They identified three major groups of strategies and we shall look at each of these in turn. It will then be up to you to decide which of these, or a combination of the three, you can use in your organisation. I cannot take that decision for you, only you can do that.

1. Change agents using an **Empirical—Rational Strategy** attempt to bring about change through persuasion backed by Special Knowledge and rational argument. Use of this strategy assumes that rational people will be guided by reason and self interest in deciding whether or not to support a change. Expert power is mobilised to convince others that the cost benefit value of a proposed change is high and that the change will leave people better off than before. When successful, this strategy helps unfreeze and refreeze a change situation. It may also result in a long lasting and internalised change. From the point of view of the change agent empirical-rational strategies are probably the easiest to use and involve him in the least effort. It is, however, a deceptively simple approach, especially in relation to changes which require people to change their behaviour and these are examples of this approach being taken and not being very successful. Now let us apply this strategy to your situation. Here is what it might mean in practice. You believe that people are rational and guided by reason in their actions and decision making once a specific course of action is demonstrated to be in a person's self interest, you assume that reason and rationality will cause the person to adopt it. Thus you approach change with the objective of communicating through information and facts the essential 'desirability' of the change from the perspective of the person whose behaviour you seek to influence. If this logic is effectively communicated you are sure that the persons will adopt the proposed change.

Looking at your own organisation list the main reasons why you think this approach would be successful. Then list the main reasons why this would not be the case.

Are you surprised?

---

2. Change agents using a NORMATIVE REEDUCATIVE STRATEGY identifies or

establishes values and assumptions form which support focuses on the building of essential foundations in personal values, group norms and shared goals to support change in all of its phrases. Change agents using these strategies emphasise such characteristics.

1. Emphasis is on the client system and his (or its) involvement in working out programmes of change and improvement for himself (or itself).
2. It is not assumed that the client's problem is necessarily one which may be solved by more adequate technical information. It is recognised that the problem may lie in the attitudes, values, norms and internal and external relationships of the client system and that alteration or re-education of these may be necessary to solve the problem.
3. A change agent works collaboratively with the client in an attempt to solve the client's problem(s).
4. Non-conscious elements which impede the solution of problems are brought into the open and examined.
5. The change agent and client use methods and concepts drawn from the behavioural sciences to deal with problems.

These strategies for change present the change agent with a much more difficult, complex and time consuming task than the Empirical Rational Strategies. This might be one reason why they are seldom used, but given the high level of involvement the strategy is likely to result in a long looking and internalised change. From your point of view this strategy would be along the following lines.

"You believe that people have complex motivations, you feel that people behave as they do as a result of sociocultural norms and commitments. You also recognise that changes in these norms involve changes in attitudes, values, skills and significant relationships, NOT just changes in knowledge information of intellectual rationales for actions and practice. Thus when seeking to change others you are sensitive to the supporting or inhibiting effects of any group pressures and norms that may be operating. In working with people you try to find out their side of things and to identify their feelings and expectations".

Do the same exercise as before listing the reasons for and against your use of this approach.

---

3. Change agents using a POWER COERCIVE STRATEGY emphasise political and economic sanctions and the use of rewards and punishments as primary inducements to change. In the Empirical-Rational approaches it is the knowledge which is seen as a major ingredient of power, with men of knowledge regarded as legitimate sources of power and a desirable flow of influence or power is seen as passing from those who know to those who do not through processes of education and of dissemination of knowledge. Normative reeducative strategies do not deny the importance of knowledge as a source of power but they mainly emphasise collaborative relationships not coercive tactics. In using a Power Coercive Strategy the change agent acts unilaterally to 'command' change through the formal authority of his position, induce change via an offer of special rewards, or bring about change via threats of punishments. Most people comply with this strategy out of fear of punishment or for rewards. This compliance with the change agents is usually temporary and continues only so long as the opportunity for rewards and punishments remains obvious. For this reason, power coercive is most useful as an unfreezing device that helps people break old patterns of behaviour and gain initial impetus to try new ones.

Again thinking about Strategy as part of your style as a change agent it would go something like this. You believe that people who run things are basically motivated by self interest and what situations offer in terms of potential personal gains or losses. Since you feel people change only in response to such motives you tend to find out where their vested interests lie and then put pressure on. If you have formal authority you use it; if not, you resort to whatever possible rewards and punishments you have access to and do not hesitate to threaten others with these weapons. Once you find a weakness you exploit it and are always ready to work 'politically' and by building supporting alliances wherever possible.

Again do the same exercise listing the reasons for and against using this strategy in your own situation.

I think we have now reached the stage where it is likely to be possible for you to work out **what the best strategy for your own organisation is.** It need not necessarily be any one of the above, in fact I would be very surprised if it were, but I would hope it would be a strategy which was based on a combination of the above.

Looking at your own organisation set out a basic strategy to introduce the changes you want. Take your time over this taking into account what kind of organisation you are working in, the kind of people you have to deal with and your own skills.

The next two Components of this Unit now take you through further stages of achieving the changes in your organisation which you consider to be so important whether it be the introduction of a staff development programme in one department or an organisation wide training scheme. Good luck!

Component 4:

How do you Set Up a Programme of Change?

Key Words

 **Programme of change; current situation; the problem; alternative solutions; preferred solution; justification; task-process model; consultation and involvement; change agent; modifications.**

Introduction

In the first three Components of this Study Unit we have been considering the background to change in organisations. As the issues are so complex and interrelated, it is necessary to acquire a good understanding of the background, before going on to deal with more practical matters. Components Four and Five are now going on to suggest practical procedures for introducing a programme of change. The two keywords **programme** and **change** when combined give us the kernel of the present discussion, and in this Component we are going to focus on how to set up a programme of change. The next Component will deal with the actual implementation of the programme, although as we shall see, the two stages are not entirely separate.

By definition, a programme of change implies a systematic procedure, devised and made explicit, for producing change, i.e. for doing things in some different way. It would seem to exclude ad hoc tinkering or spur-of-the-moment intuitive actions which produce unplanned changes in organisations. The word change is being used, rather than innovation, because it gives a wider-ranging impression and includes modifications to existing procedures which may not be readily thought of as innovations. However, the majority of change programmes are undoubtedly innovatory.

As trainers our main concern, as always, is in the implications for training of any change programme. In some cases the change programme may deal specifically with training — and possibly nothing else. However, we also need to be aware of and sensitive to all changes and their sources, since it is our responsibility to identify and spell out their training implications. So the examples we shall look at from time to time will not be based solely on training.

Where Do I Start?

As with most things, the obvious place to start is where you are now! In other words, you should identify 'how things are at the moment' and look at the present position.

"I'm reviewing the situation."

This survey should be developed into a formal account spelling out in detail the features of the current situation. Some of these features will no doubt turn out to be much more important than others, but it may be useful to consider a comprehensive check-list of items, so that you are less likely to overlook anything important.

Features of current situation
The degree of detail and background information to be included will depend on the 'target audience', i.e. who is likely to see the report. As the topic is 'Setting up a Programme of Change' presumably you will be expecting to present the report to people in your organisation occupying positions where they can influence decisions and events. So the first part of the report will be a descriptive factual account of 'How we are now', probably in outline only but intended to remind readers of the background to, and framework of, the current ways of doing things. While you don't want to 'teach Grandmother to suck eggs' you do want to remind people of all **relevant** features of the existing system.

Obviously the changes to be considered and proposed later on in the report will colour the decisions as to which features are relevant, but if in doubt there should be no harm in including some redundant information. In any case, it will probably help to orientate the reader.

Checkpoint

Imagine you were proposing fundamental changes in the way in which your organisation undertakes training (e.g. a move away from formal classroom instruction given to groups of employees towards individualised computer-based training with tutorial support), which of the following do you think you would want to include in your 'Features of the current situation — a descriptive account'. Add any other factual items you would probably want to include.

Details of Company/Organisation
a) overall policy
b) size
c) number of employees
d) location (single site or spread out)
e) product range/nature of business
f) activities/operations
g) research and development
h) performance
i) financial position
j) competition
k)

Organisation
a) overall structure e.g. 'wiring diagram'
b) areas of responsibility
c)

Training
a) how organised and managed
b) present methods of working and arrangements
c) staffing
d) numbers and costs
e)

Well, there can be no universal answer to this question, but I hope it made you think and you found it a worthwhile exercise. You can always refer to the above list again when you need to. You may have wanted to include features covering problem areas, recent changes, rate of change etc. Fair enough, but I would suggest these are 'highlighted' by being dealt with separately in the next section of the report.

Recent changes
Is the current situation static or dynamic? Have there been any recent changes relevant to the topic of the report? If so, is the rate of change accelerating/decelerating or static?

Again, at this stage in the report, this should be a factual account of the state of affairs, and should not include opinions, evaluative comments or inferences. It is designed to 'set the scene' and provide the background for the subsequent discussion. However, at some stage you will need to delve into the general 'climate' within the organisation regarding change. What is the underlying philosophy, 'culture' and individual attitudes to change. How is morale likely to change and be affected? This leads inevitably into considerations of vested interests (departments, groups, unions etc.) and likely positive or negative feelings towards change. Who has most to gain/lose if any proposed changes are introduced?

It is a matter of personal judgement as to where exactly to put this information in the report — if at all!

Think about your own organisation. Go through the points raised under this heading (Recent changes). What would you want to include in a report? Make some brief notes to clarify your thinking.

Your answer to this must be a matter of personal judgement.

The Problem

Having established the background (under details of company, organisation, training, recent changes — or other suitable headings) the next step is to outline the problem(s) in the current situation. After all, if there is 'No problem' then presumably there would be no need to set up a programme of change! (Or maybe you would want to argue that in that case there is an urgent need for change — to overcome complacency if nothing else! What we need to beware of, however, is the 'selling' of a solution to a non-existent or manufactured problem.)

Obviously there are a number of ways of tackling this section. Let's begin by considering a few questions.

What exactly is the problem?
What is likely to happen if you continue as you are now, i.e. if there is no change or you maintain the current rate of change?
What needs to be changed, and **why?**
What can be changed — what is realistic?

So you are starting to examine and tease out the specific details of the problem, i.e. whatever it is that is preventing the organisation from operating as efficiently and purposefully as it might.

You will remember from Component One in this Study Unit that a distinction can be made between external and internal factors which lead to different ways of doing things. Similarly, problems may be due to external or internal factors — or various combinations of the two! Let's try and list some typical problem areas which might be of interest to the present discussion:—

Out-of-date equipment
Old-fashioned ways of doing things
High wastage of materials
Poor quality control
Over-manning
Competitors more cost-effective
Top-heavy management structure
Over-administration
High staff turnover
Shortage of people with the necessary skills
Over-production
Lack of initiative
Resistance to change
Poor morale
Lack of investment
Too rapid expansion
Makeshift buildings and accommodation
Poor internal communications

As a trainer, select about five of the above which would seem to be problems that could be partially solved by improved training or retraining. Then place those you have selected in rank order of importance from the training point of view.

No doubt your answer reflects your own interests and ideas about training, but I expect most people would include some of the following:—
Old-fashioned ways of doing things
High wastage of materials
Poor quality control
High staff turnover
Shortage of skilled people
Lack of initiative
Resistance to change
Poor internal communication

Ranking them is a useful exercise, but again a matter of personal judgement.

It is interesting to notice that these problem areas tend to fall into two categories — those where the problem seems to be more a technical one (e.g. old-fashioned methods, high wastage of materials) and those which seem to be more to do with people directly (e.g. high staff turnover, lack of initiative, resistance to change).

Don't worry about this important distinction for the time being — we shall return to it later.

For the moment, then, we are simply concerned with describing the existing problem area in as much detail as seems necesssary. Naturally, we will have concentrated on those problems where training would be likely to play an important part in any proposed solution.

What do you see as the major problem in your organisation where change is urgently needed? Try to discuss your ideas with a colleague or friend, to see if they agree with you. Do other people in the organisation respond differently to the above question? If so, can you suggest why?

Alternative Procedures/Solutions

Having identified the problem, the next step is to list and discuss a number of alternative ways of tackling, and hopefully, overcoming the problem. At the very least this should be a brief list of alternative courses of action, starting from the baseline of 'doing nothing' and becoming more wide-ranging. These options may need to be briefly outlined and examined, and the likely outcomes of each suggested.

Notice it is at this point that we are starting to move away from objective, factual information describing things as they are, into the speculative and subjective field of 'futurology'. The crystal ball is now very much in evidence!

Nevertheless, if you have done your homework, the likely outcomes should sound plausible and be based on realistic evidence and assessment.

The preferred solution

Now we come to the 'crunch point'. This is where we try to **justify** the choice of one of the alternative ways of tackling the problem, saying why we prefer it to the others, and then developing the changes and procedures that will be required in order to implement it — in other words giving in detail the proposed programme of change, step by step.

A Government document which outlines the recommended procedures for preparing study reports lists ten sub-headings under "Discussion of Proposed System" but regards "Justification" as a separate later main heading, before going on to "Conclusion and Recommendations". You may find it more satisfactory to weave arguments on justification into the general development, particularly when discussing the preferred solution. To avoid breaking up the main thrust of the argument, detailed technical specifications, if appropriate, can always be given in separate annexes.

Taking the problem identified by you in the previous Checkpoint, go through the stages of outlining a number of alternative solutions, choosing a preferred solution and explaining and justifying your choice. You may like to discuss this with someone in your organisation - or maybe someone 'outside'. Your TTP tutor will always be willing to discuss your ideas with you, or look at anything you produce.

It is at this stage that we really begin to see the implications and ramifications of the proposed changes. We must be sensitive to the fact that if we introduce changes into one part of an organisation, bells ring and lights flash all over the system — often in places that we never thought were wired for sound or light! This should lead us on to the realisation that we are going to have to gain the commitment of other people if the changes are going to be successfully implemented. In fact we will almost certainly have already consulted various other people about the plans, and discussed with them any proposed changes. Plans drawn up intuitively in isolation seldom see the light of day!

You may be familiar with the task-process model (sometimes called task-maintenance), but it is worth reminding ourselves of it again at this point.

Task and Process

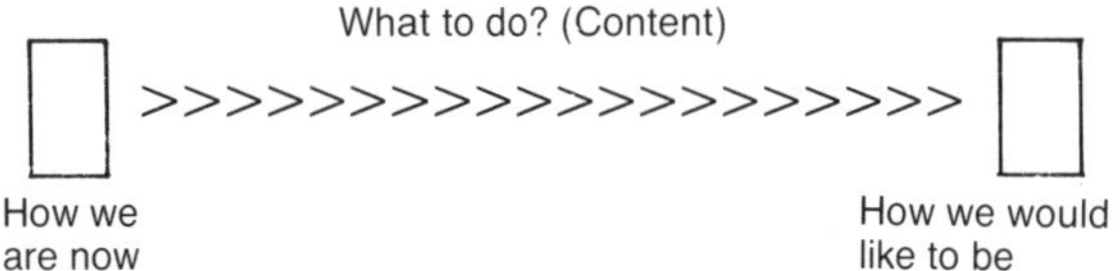

Whenever we decide to do anything, we are starting from "where we are now", i.e. the present position/situation. We have some idea, however vague, of "how we would like to be", i.e. where we hope to get to; our aims, goals or objectives. The problem is in getting from one to the other successfully! The gap between the two determines exactly **what** we will have to do to get from A to B, e.g. build a new factory, introduce a new training scheme, take on 50 extra staff, improve safety records, increase output, improve morale. This can be called the CONTENT of what is required.

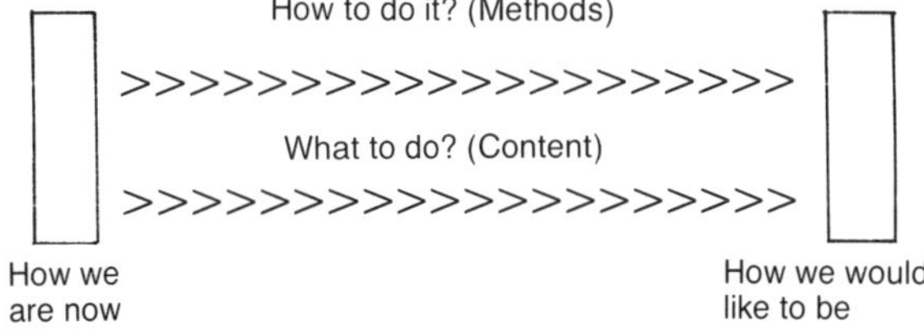

At the same time we will need to consider the details of **how** we are going to go about achieving the content, in other words the METHODS we intend to employ to reach the goal. How do we intend to go about building a new factory, introducing a new training scheme etc?

If you are familiar with network (critical path) analysis you will see that "how we are now" and "how we would like to be" are the same as **events** signalling the start and finish, whereas content and methods are the **activities** required to link the two events — which take up time and require the use of other resources.

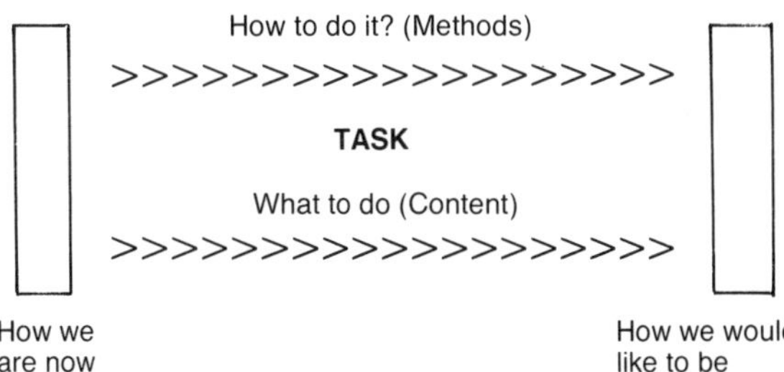

The two activities of content and methods can be combined and then thought of as the TASK to be undertaken — "what" and "how". The danger is that the planning may tend to concentrate on this task, to the exclusion of other important considerations. If you think about the planning stage for a moment, you will probably realise that this 'engineering' or technical approach to the task seems very logical and sequential and, when developed, provides us with a neat set of stages to be discussed. Unfortunately it fails (so far) to take into account one vital consideration. I hope you have spotted what it is — it's the **people** who are or will be involved.

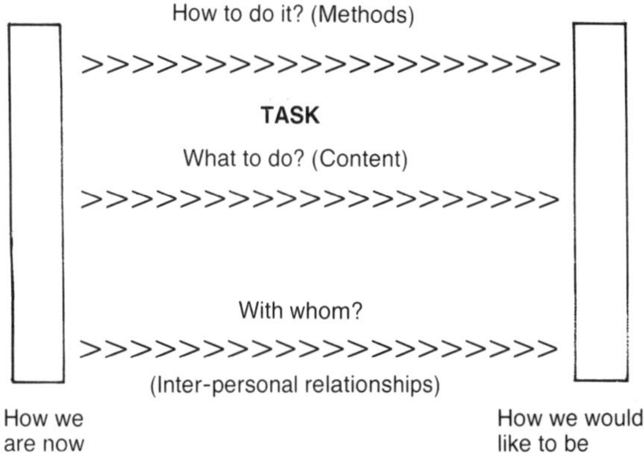

In order to implement any programme of change (i.e. the TASK) we must work with and through people. It is people who cause changes to occur, and without the commitment, involvement and participation of the people likely to be affected, any programme of change is doomed to failure. People can encourage and facilitate change or they can hinder and sabotage any attempt to change — in all kinds of subtle (and often not so subtle!) ways. In addition to the task itself, we must therefore consider "with whom?" i.e. **all** the people likely to be involved or affected in any way. What are the relationships between these people likely to be?

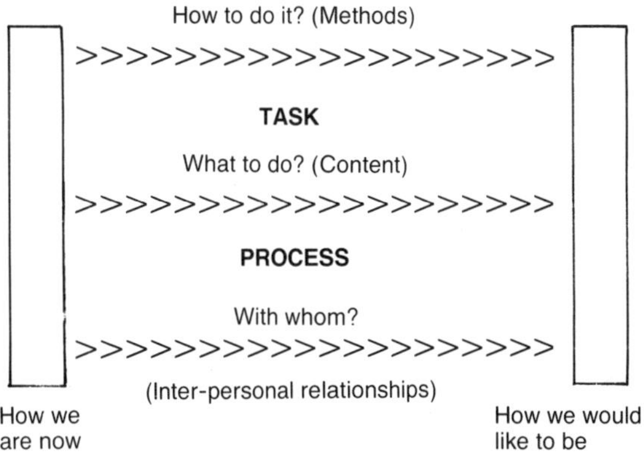

This side of the change programme can be called the PROCESS through which people are actively involved when undertaking the task; the way in which they actually perform and interact. The process deals with the maintenance of inter-personal relationships within the various groups and between the various people involved. **It underpins the task** — if the process is inadequate or not working properly then the task will not be completed.

Taking the problem you identified and developed in the previous checkpoints, make a list of those **people** you think would be involved directly, and those you think would possibly be involved indirectly.

Does the extent of the list surprise you? Did you include anyone from outside the organisation? If not, should you have done? Obviously only you can answer these questions!

Consultation and discussion

So, having established what you regard as the preferred solution, if you have not already done so you must now start involving other people. Not just bouncing ideas off them, but getting them to co-operate in planning and setting up the programme of change.

The precise nature of this involvement and participation will, of course, depend a lot on the circumstances, and it is difficult to give precise guidance, but the key to success lies in this vital stage. Whatever strategy is being proposed must be fully accepted and supported and be the result of the widest consultation. Individuals must, if necessary, be brought together to form productive working groups. This takes time and considerable skill and expertise in group dynamics. If a catalyst or **change agent** is being proposed he must be identified and approval sought.

There seem to be a number of roles or functions which change agents perform, but these are not mutually exclusive. A change agent is often seen as a catalyst, someone who interacts with other people to put pressure on the system and disturb the 'status quo' in order to instigate change. Sometimes a change agent is a specialist, who comes in with a 'bag of tools' and ideas about possible solutions to problems, but again someone who needs to work with and through people. An extension of this role is to think of someone who can bring together the necessary resources (diagnostic skills, finance, expertise, management techniques, people, physical resources etc.) to produce effective problem-solving. Finally, a more diffuse and fundamental role is that of a facilitator of change — someone who helps the people in the organisation to produce change, by showing them how to go about the various stages of problem-solving and development of change. Obviously the position of a change agent in an organisation (insider or outsider, early or late appointment, line or staff, status) is a matter for debate.

The inevitable outcome of all this deliberation will be the need to modify the proposed programme! In the best Boy Scout tradition "Be prepared" and remain flexible. After all, you are the one who is proposing change anyway — so you should be ready and willing to change your own ideas, however cherished they may be.

It takes stamina, conviction and persistence to survive this stage — to gain the participation of other people and end up with a generally acceptable change programme. Many proposed changes fail to survive this exposure to 'public' scrutiny.

The Change Programme

Let us assume, however, that the proposed programme of change has been modified by agreement and endorsed by the interested parties. It now exists as a formal change programme, spelling out in detail the preferred solution. This is a convenient point at which to take stock, before going on in the next Component to consider how we should go about putting the change programme into action.

Summary

In this Component we have developed the stages in **setting up** a programme of change. The Checkpoints have been designed to help you to build up a programme step by step as the stages were introduced and discussed.

Starting from explaining the details of the current situation, including a factual account of recent changes, we went on to presenting an outline of the problem (in consultation with other people). Then we considered alternative procedures/solutions before homing in on a preferred solution. Finally we discussed the paramount need to identify and involve all the people likely to be affected by the change programme. It was then suggested that such consultation would inevitably lead to modifications in the programme.

Component 5:

How do you put the Change Programme into Action?

Key Words

Implications; implementation; consultation and involvement; project manager; changes in training.

Introduction

At the stage reached at the end of the previous Component, we had an **agreed formal** change programme which spelled out in detail the preferred solution. If we have not already included this in the programme, we must now consider and document how we intend to **implement** it. Any proposal for change in an organisation will have wide-ranging **implications** which must be carefully and clearly identified and then taken into account.

Checkpoint

List a number of headings/areas within an organisation and its various activities which may be affected by a comprehensive change programme (e.g. to introduce completely different methods of production or operating). If appropriate, use the example you generated in the previous Component concerning your own organisation.

I hope you managed to draw up a pretty long list which included most of the following:—

1. *The organisation itself and its management structure (existing 'chain of command' and management structure may be inappropriate or inadequate and unable to cope effectively with the new methods).*
2. *Administration is certain to be affected — how the organisation goes about its business.*
3. *Staffing requirements. Obviously a major factor. Changes may require extra or fewer employees, as well as the changes in the jobs to be undertaken. There may be a need for extensive re-deployment.*
4. *Finance. Certain to raise its ugly head at some stage!*
5. *Resources. A major item in any extensive change programme, whether it is simply accommodation, communications etc. or expensive equipment and fittings.*
6. *Time. Maybe you didn't list this as a separate item, but it's probably worth doing so. Apart from the requirement for a 'time-scale' for the programme, the implications in terms of man-hours required to introduce the changes must be considered. Things just don't happen — people need, and must be allocated, the time to cause them to happen. Many proposed change programmes founder because key people are not given the necessary time to implement them.*
7. *Training. Again, this is a vital area which is often neglected, for a variety of reasons. We shall be returning to the training implications in a moment, so let's stop the list here.*

What we have been attempting to do in this Introduction is to remind ourselves of the likely **implications** of introducing any proposed change programme within an organisation. As the Checkpoint asked a very open-ended question, your answer will probably be somewhat different from the above, but this should not matter as long as you now feel more aware of the various issues. Discussion of these may need to be incorporated into your formal change programme.

Implementation

Having thought about the implications, we can move on to plan the actual introduction of the programme. We are not yet 'out of the wood'; a number of questions and problems still need to be considered! As we are trying to be systematic in our overall approach, it should help if we show the process diagramatically as a reminder of where we have come from and where we are at.

Setting Up a Programme of Change

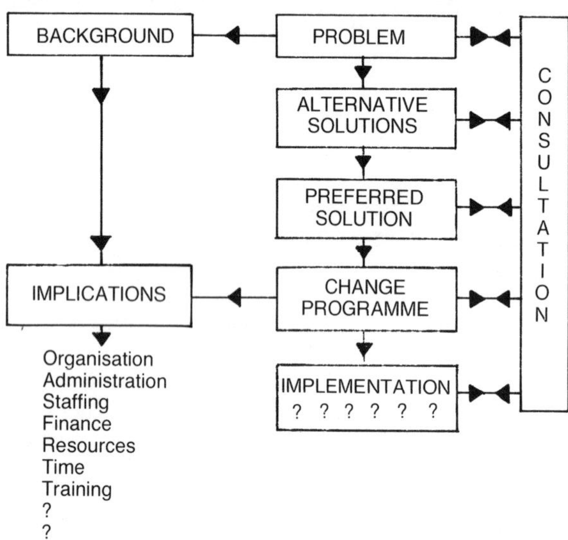

So far we have dealt with the various stages indicated on the diagram up to the production of the change programme itself and the consideration of its likely implications on the organisation as a whole.

The process of **planning the implementation** requires a number of decisions to be made, in response to a series of basic questions, e.g.

1. What is the time-scale for the programme?
2. Would a phased introduction be better than a 'big bang'?
3. How do we get the resources we need, and at the right time?
4. How do we publicise the project and inform the people affected?
5. How do we cultivate the right climate for change?
6. What needs to be done concerning training/re-training?
7. Have we thought about the constraints which might interfere with the proposed changes, and how to overcome them?
8. Would it help to draw up a flow chart or network diagram (showing events and activities as in critical path analysis)?

Write down, say, three other questions to add to the above list. Again, refer to your own example(s) and experience. This is designed to help you clarify your thinking and increase your understanding of the types of decisions which have to be made.

All these questions and the associated decisions point once more to the need for wide consultation and the involvement of all interested parties — however time-consuming and frustrating these activities may seem to be. If you plough a lonely furrow you are likely to end up out on a limb!

The result of these considerations may well be some form of **action plan** detailing the stages and timing of the implementation, and allocating responsibilities. This would then form the blueprint governing the implementation stage, i.e. how to actually put the change programme into action. Since 'circumstances alter cases' we don't propose to spell this out in more detail, but the discussion so far should indicate clearly what may have to be included.

Management of Implementation

It is around this point that you may come to the conclusion that the actual process of implementation can probably best be managed by the formal identification of a 'leader', project manager, change agent, catalyst or some such person. Someone who is sensitive to what is likely to be happening, who can keep a finger on the pulse and who at the same time can control and manage the implementation.

It is also often advisable, depending on the scale of the project, to set up an advisory working group or steering committee in order to provide representation and accountability.

Ready, steady, go!

Once the change programme is actually set in motion, it is important that suitable documentation and recording procedures are introduced from the start — both for reporting purposes and future guidance. There will undoubtedly be unplanned and unforeseen events occurring, and resulting actions and decisions that will have to be taken. The best change programmes allow for such contingencies in the planning.

Does It Really Work?

I daresay you are beginning to feel that this is all very well, but it is talking in very general terms and only providing outline guidance. However, the **actions** to be taken can be extracted from the discussion so far to form a check list, if required. A suggested list of main headings for consideration and action would be:—

1. Describe the current situation
2. Identify the problem
3. List and consider alternative solutions
4. Select and justify the preferred solution
5. Consult and involve all affected personnel
6. Negotiate and modify proposed change programme
7. Consider implications throughout the organisation
8. Plan detailed procedures for implementation, including documentation and recording
9. Repeat 5 and 6!
10. Implement change programme
11. Monitor and evaluate

Perhaps we should look at a real example in the field of training and match it against these guidelines. But before we do that here is a Checkpoint to re-orientate your thinking.

As a trainer, list about half a dozen **changes** in the field of training which you have noticed or been involved in, or which you feel may be likely to happen in the near future.

At a general level, the greatest changes in patterns of training over the last ten years or so have been associated with changes in industry and commerce themselves. Traditional patterns associated with lengthy apprenticeships and career progression within relatively stable environments have virtually disappeared. New schemes such as the MSC's Youth Training Scheme for initial occupational training have been introduced, requiring very different methods and techniques of training. Also, the need for continuous re-training and updating have led to fundamental changes in the provision of training.

At a more mundane and specific level, you may have listed some of the following:—

1. *New training programme/syllabus.*
2. *Change to continuous assessment (or other changes in assessment, e.g. profiling).*
3. *Changes in size of classroom groups for instruction.*
4. *Changes in classroom teaching methods (e.g. from direct 'telling' instruction towards interactive group-based learning).*
5. *Change to team teaching (group of trainers accepting joint responsibility for an area of training and working as a team).*
6. *Introduction of Computer-Based Training.*
7. *Introduction of self-instructional methods.*
8. *Use of open/distance learning (e.g. the fact that* **you** *are using these TTP materials!).*
9. *Introduction of residential components on training courses.*
10. *Need to compress/expand training.*

etc. etc.

Now, if you match your list, item by item, against the procedural 'model; developed in these two Components, and summarised before the above Checkpoint, it should be obvious that in many cases the full set of recommended stages in the development of the change programme will not be necessary, or at least some of the stages will not need to be given very much thought and attention. The main criterion would seem to be **the extent to which you will need to cultivate the support of other people in the organisation in order to implement the proposed change(s).**

Let us then look at a real example.

Example — Basic Numeracy/ Computational Skills

This example is based on a real change programme, although some of the background details have been altered to make it more appropriate to the present situation. However, all the major events, decisions and results took place as quoted.

A large organisation with a strong commitment to training was finding that many newly recruited trainees had poor standards of numeracy. At the same time the wide range of abilities and aptitudes among the trainees was causing problems in normal classroom group instruction. Trainers and trainees were frustrated and there was a high wastage rate amongst the trainees. Trainers were encouraged to discuss the situation and propose ways of tackling the problem. This resulted in the identification of the following alternative solutions:—

1. Better screening and selection procedures.
2. Grouping of trainees into 'streams' based on ability.
3. Provision of self-instructional materials (covering basic numeracy) for use by less-able trainees.
4. Smaller groups for instruction with more time spent on tutorial help.
5. Lower the standards of the aims and objectives of training to a more realistic level.

As a trainer, which of the above five alternative solutions would you favour? Why?

Let's go through these alternatives in turn:—

1. *This would seem to be a useful idea if it could be implemented, i.e. if suitable (valid, reliable and acceptable) selection procedures could be developed and used. However, in this real-life case the recruiting of trainees had already taken place and was out of the hands of the trainers.*
2. *In several cases the size of the total group was too small to allow further division. Also streaming into high and low ability groups for* **normal** *classroom instruction was not generally regarded as a good idea.*
3. *This was felt to be the preferred solution, subject to a number of provisos. It will be developed later.*
4. *Probably the ideal solution, but the expense and staffing requirements ruled it out.*
5. *This would only produce a 'knock-on' effect throughout the whole training system and was not really felt to be a realistic solution.*

Having decided that the preferred solution would be the provision and use of self-instructional materials, it was felt initially that owing to cost, these materials could only be provided for those most at risk in the existing system, i.e. the 'less-able' trainees. A comprehensive testing programme was agreed and set up to find ways of identifying these less-able trainees on entry to the organisation. This proved reasonably successful. The trainers administered the testing programme themselves with support as necessary, and a steering group was formed with representatives from all sections and people involved. Information about the scheme was produced and distributed, and consultation encouraged.

Concurrent with the testing programme the necessary self-instructional materials were being obtained/developed and tried out. The precise requirements and objectives of each training course had to be established and 'packages' of appropriate sets of materials established. Numerous decisions had to be taken on a day-to-day basis resulting from both practical considerations and consultation with all those involved. This resulted in considerable changes to the original change programme!

Look back to the first Checkpoint in this Component (immediately after the Introduction). Go through the seven items listed in the answer. From what has been discussed in this example so far, are any of the seven items unlikely to have been unaffected by this change programme?

No, they were all affected:—

1. *In particular, the steering group had to cut across existing boundaries between sections/departments.*
2. *New ways of administering were needed — particularly for trainees' timetables, monitoring progress etc.*
3. *A special unit was set up to manage the project.*
4. *Extra finance had to be provided (or transferred from elsewhere in the overall training budget).*
5. *Mainly the provision of special accommodation, materials and tests, along with computer support.*
6. *Time. Some provision was made for the extra time required — partly covered in (3) above.*
7. *Trainers were trained to supervise and administer the testing programme and also to* **manage** *the classroom use of 'packages' of self-instructional materials.*

The various points listed in this Component under Implementation (see p. 122) were also addressed. A phased introduction was agreed, based on where the 'greatest needs' appeared to be. A comprehensive network diagram was drawn up and proved invaluable as a management tool.

The implementation of the main thrust of the programme involved the first major change in the programme itself as originally envisaged. The acceptance of a phased introduction, and its reduced initial demand on available resources, made any form of selection or streaming within groups unnecessary. Whole groups of trainees, as originally formed on recruitment, used the materials. This made administration much easier and avoided any of the social stigmas attached to special identification.

However, the testing programme was continued, as most trainers found the information useful and it enabled comparisons to be made at a later stage between the progress of the less-able and more-able trainees.

The change programme was gradually implemented and ran successfully for some years. As might be expected, the degree of enthusiasm varied from person to person, and regular meetings were held to exchange ideas and inform everyone of progress. The majority of trainers using the system became very committed and involved, and the trainees were highly appreciative — once they saw the benefits of self-study and the rate at which they were making progress.

You may be interested to know that the results broadly indicated that the less-able trainees benefitted greatly from the scheme — probably on the basis that what they did learn they learnt thoroughly, and at a suitable pace. Progress and achievement test results for these trainees were all considerably higher than expected. Results for the more-able trainees were much the same as expected — they are probably the ones who will learn effectively whatever methods of instruction are used!

Eventually the changes in the method of instruction (to individualised learning) were absorbed into the 'bloodstream' of the system and accepted as the norm. Having successfully achieved its objectives, the change programme was then wound up and disbanded!

Identify one or two changes that have taken place in your own organisation/training situation.

To what extent do you consider they were successful or unsuccessful?

Outline any reasons why they **were** relatively successful or unsuccessful.

Suggest how the **implementation** of the changes could have been better managed in order to make them more successful.

Show your answers to a friend or colleague and discuss them together. If you wish, also send them to your TTP tutor for comment and discussion.

Having worked through this Component, you should now be able to explain in detail how to implement a programme of change, indicating the implications which may need to be considered and dealt with.

Hopefully, you should also be able to actually implement such a programme!

Component 6:

A Framework for Investigating the Effects of Change in your Organisation

Key Words

The change agent system; the innovation system; the user system; instrumentality; congruence; cost; practicality ethic; organisational cultures.

Acknowledgements
The author would like to thank:—
Open University Press – *The Management of Educational Change* – Roy Bolam (1975)
Penguin Book Ltd – *Understanding Organisations* – Charles Handy (1985)

Introduction

If you have worked your way through the first five Components of this Study Unit you should now have a pretty good idea of how to manage any change that you would like to introduce into your organisation. The final Component of this Unit will present a framework which you may like to use as a basis of studying the effects of changes within your organisation.

Checkpoint

Go back to the first Checkpoint in Component 4 and look again at your answer.

I am sure it covers a wide range of the organisation's activities from the organisation itself and its management structure through finance and resources to staffing requirements and individuals. Looking at all these you are probably thinking the same things as I am: "How on earth am I going to be able to look at the effects of change on all these?"

Well, I hope this Component will enable you to overcome some of the problems by providing an overall framework which you can use to study the effects of change on various sectors of your organisation. If you use the framework systematically then I think it will be as useful for you as it has been for me. It will not provide you with all the answers but I hope it will shed light on quite a lot. The framework I am going to outline is one which has been developed by Ray Bolam of Bristol University. While any model of this kind tends to be over justified its main purpose is to help focus thinking about and understanding change and its effects.

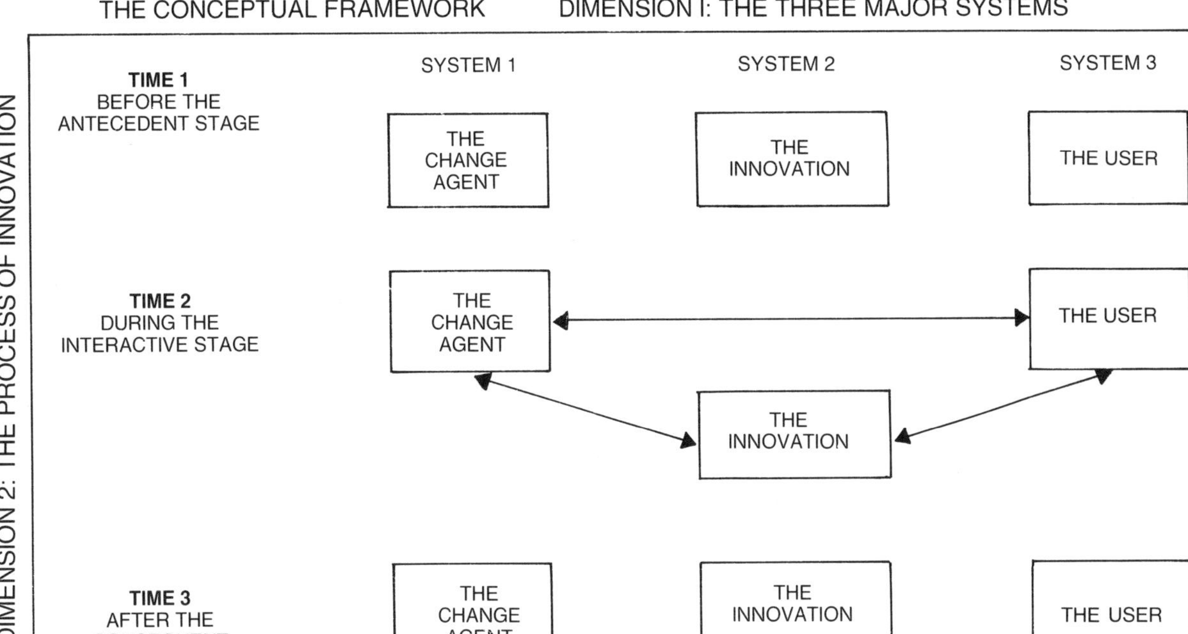

In any change process four major factors can be distinguished (a) **The Change Agent System,** the change advocate, the consultant or the innovator, (b) **The Innovation System** i.e. the change that is being introduced, which may be redefined, and changed as a result of experience and perceptions of the people using it, (c) **The User System.** "This is the system which is either inventing or adopting an innovation or is being aimed at by the change agent, (d) **The Process of Innovation over Time** which involves three stages (i) The Antecedent stage at which point the three systems are said to exist separately, (ii) The Interactive stage, during which the three systems are said to be in interaction with one another and (iii) The Consequent stage by which time the systems may be said to be separate again. Bolam is arguing that the process of change is the interaction of three major systems over time and that the process can be followed using his framework.

Take any change which has been introduced into your organisation over the last few months. Can you distinguish the three major systems that Bolam refers to? Are they quite clear?

I do not know how successful you have been but I hope you will be helped by the next few pages as I go on to describe the three systems to you.

Let's take each of them in turn.

(i) **The Change Agent System**
At this point it may be useful for you to refer back to Component 3 which describes in some detail what

kind of knowledge, skills and attitudes the change agent requires. In Component 3 the change agent is referred to as an individual but Bolam calls the change agent a 'system' because he argues that it can range from one individual to a department in an organisation or an outside firm of consultants.

The system may be internal to the organisation or external to it and it may be influenced by the process of change over time. Bolam argues that perhaps the most important characteristic of the change agent as far as the change is concerned is its authority relationship with the 'user system'. This authority may be based either upon administrative status, professional colleagueship, external consultancy or a combination of all three. Each of these will affect the way in which the change agent will try to influence the User System and as you may remember from Component 3 the change agent may have access to a number of change strategies.

To refresh your memory go back to Component 3 and look again at the three strategies set out. Now try and link each strategy to an authority relationship? How will this affect policy? Take your time to do this exercise, say twenty minutes. Is this long enough? — YES.

I do not know how you got on but you probably decided in the end that it is impossible to connect authority relationships, strategies and policy in any clear cut manner because none will exist in true form in any organisation. However, I would argue that these categories are very useful for the purposes of analysis.

With the help of this section and the change agent section of Component 3 set out the Change Agent system for any change you have been involved in or hoping to introduce. Set out its authority relationship with the organisation, the possible strategies that could be used, the main knowledge, skills and attitudes required and an outline of the main methods you would use to start the change.

You may find this quite a hard exercise and if you cannot manage it at this stage leave it and come back to it again.

Let's now go on to look at the second system.

(ii) **The Innovation System**

this refers to any change that is being introduced into any organisation. It is sometimes easy to forget, especially if you are the change agent, that other people's perceptions of the change may not be the same as yours. Indeed change does not exist in any unchanging objective sense but it is constantly defined, changed and redefined as the result of experience and the differing perceptions of the people who are handling the change. This may have a crucial bearing on the fate of any change as other people's perceptions must be taken into account — this is one of the main skills which the change agent must have at his disposal.

Change has been analysed along a number of sub dimensions with usually two broad purposes in mind: first simply as an analogue aid to understanding; second as an attempt to explain why they succeed or fail. Basically change may be derived from four types of knowledge; basic knowledge; applied research and development knowledge; practice knowledge and user feedback knowledge and come in three broad forms:— Information documents which sets out the main elements of the proposed change, training materials developed for use and "off the shelf" packages developed outside the organisation but which can be brought in and used. Any change will also usually focus upon a particular aspect of the user system; upon for example aims and objectives, values or perspectives, some aspect of the organisation and the administrative system; the role relationships with a section or a department work procedures etc.

Referring to a change you have introduced or are going to introduce are you quite clear as to what it is, what it involves and the possible problems of perceptions that it may encounter?

Obviously you cannot hope to cover all the possible problems that may arise but clear knowledge of as many of the problems as possible will help towards a smooth functioning of the change process.

Let's now look at the third system.

(iii) **The User System**

This is the system which is either inventing or adopting a change or is being aimed at by the change agent. This may be some part of the organisation or the behaviour of groups or individuals within the organisation and it may be useful to look at the user systems under these headings. Firstly those individuals who are likely to respond differently to change. I have found the work of Walter Doyle and Gerald A. Ponder (1986) on 'The Practicality Ethic in Decision Making' very useful when looking at how individuals responded to change. Doyle and Ponder argue that, if we listen to the way in which individuals talk about change proposals, we find that the term 'practical' is frequently used to label them and "thus, labelling represents an evaluative process which is a central ingredient in the initial decision individuals make regarding the implementation of a proposed change."

Underlying any change proposals are certain assumptions about their recipients. Doyle and Ponder pick out three: (a) The Rational Adopter (b) The Stone Age Obstructionist (c) The Pragmatic Sceptic.

The most common image they believe is that of the 'Rational Adopter'. He is a person who fits a highly formalised, rational model of how change ought to be accomplished. First he clarifies his goals and the problems of achieving them. Secondly he collects data about how the problems arise. Thirdly he deliberates about ways of resolving them. Fourthly he evaluates the success of his means in resolving the problems of achieving his ends.

When individuals on the receiving end fail to live up to this model in practice they often become "Stone Age Obstructionists" in the eyes of the change agent. According to Doyle and Ponder it is this view of the individual that has resulted in the attempts to develop change packages which try and neutralise the perceptions and activities of the individual receiver.

Doyle and Ponder argue however that most individuals fall into the category of "Pragmatic Sceptic". They further argue that the "Pragmatic Sceptic" possesses the following interrelated characteristics. First he describes his work in individualistic terms emphasising the uniqueness of his activities. This happens even if he happens to be a member of a team. Second, he "expresses a concern of immediate consequences" rather than long term goals and outcomes. Thirdly, he is much more concerned with the concrete procedures of his work rather than abstract and general principles. These three features — **individualism, immediacy** and **concreteness** characterise the perspective from which the Pragmatic Sceptic views change proposals.

Take a look at the main individuals concerned with any change that has been introduced or is going to be introduced into your organisation or department and list them under the three headings.

I hope you got most of them under the "Pragmatic Sceptic" title and not under the label of "Stone Age Obstructionist"!

Doyle and Ponder further argue that individuals who adopt the "Pragmatic Sceptic" perspective evaluate Change proposals in terms of their "Ecological Validity". They argue that the key concepts employed in such evaluations are those of **Instrumentality, Congruence** and **Cost**. A change proposal must contain **instrumental** content if it is to minimally qualify as practical. This means that it must describe a procedure which makes sense to the individual in terms of his own working practices. Change proposals which do not do this will be seen as not being practical in the situation. Doyle and Ponder conclude that proposals which do not satisfy these points will seldom have any influence on the individual. They also argue that individuals frequently voice complaints that change proposals which are not clearly communicated to them seldom make any practical sense.

However instrumentality is not a sufficient condition of practicality. The extent which procedures contained in the change proposals are **congruent** with the individual's perception of his work situation are also very important. Doyle and Ponder argue that congruence has three aspects.

1. Do the procedures contained in the change proposals fit the way in which the individual conducts his work activities?
2. Have the procedures been demonstrated in work settings which are congruent to the individual's perception of his own and does the spokesman for the proposal have practical experiences of similar work situations?
3. Are the procedures compatible with the self-image which the individual has of himself and in his role relationships with his colleagues?

The final criterion of practicality cited by Doyle and Ponder is that of **cost**. This is seen as the ratio between the amount of investment of time, effort etc. and the amount of return on this investment. This is sometimes known as the "what's in it for me" syndrome!!

I think Doyle and Ponder's "Practicality Ethic" provides a very useful framework for looking at the way in which different individuals are affected by and react to change. I hope you find it just as useful.

Take an example of recent change in your organisation or department. Using some of your colleagues apply the Doyle and Ponder framework to their reactions to the change. Be very careful to whom you show the results of your work!!

The second element within the user system is the organisation itself. The most significant characteristics of organisations have already been set out in Component 1 of Study Unit 1 of this Volume.

Go back to this Component and read through it very quickly making sure you have got the most important points.

I would now like you to combine this knowledge with that set out by a writer on organisations called **Charles Handy.** He describes organisations in terms of their **cultures**. He argues that in all organisations there are deep set beliefs about the way work should be organised, the way authority should be exercised, people rewarded and controlled. How much planning and how far ahead? What combinations of obedience and initiative is looked for in subordinates? Are there rules or procedures or only results. These are all parts of the culture of an organisation. This culture often takes visible form in its buildings, offices, shops or branches; the kinds of people it employs etc. These cultures are founded and built over the years by dominant groups in an organisation but these may have to change over time, as what suits the organisation at one time is not necessarily approporate for ever.

Handy describes four such cultures:

The Club Culture

The best picture to describe this kind of organisation is a spider's web, because the key to the whole organisation sits in the centre, surrounded by ever-widening circles of intimates and influence. The closer you are to the spider the more influence you have. There are other lines in the web — the lines of responsibility, the functions of the organisation — but the intimacy lines are the important ones, for this organisation works like a club, a club built around its head.

The 'organisational idea' in the club culture is that the organisation is there to extend the person of the head or, often, of the founder. If he could do everything himself, he would. It is because he can't that there has to be an organisation at all; therefore the organisation should be an extension of himself, acting on his behalf, a club of like minded people. That can sound like a dictatorship, and some club cultures are dictatorships of the owner or founder, but at their best they are based on trust and communicate by a sort of telepathy with everyone knowing each other's mind. They are very personal cultures for the spiders preserve their freedom of manoeuvre by writing little down preferring to talk to people, to sense their reactions and to infect them with their own enthusiasms or passions. If there are memorandas or minutes of meetings, they go from Gill to Joe or, more often, from set of initials to set of initials, rather than from job title to job title.

These cultures therefore are rich in personality. They abound with almost mythical stories and folklore from the past and can be very exciting places to work in if you belong to the club and share the values and beliefs of the spider. Their great strength is in their ability to respond immediately and intuitively to opportunities or crises because of the very short lines of communication and because of the centralization of power. Their danger lies in the dominance of the character of the central figure. Without a spider the web is dead. If the spider is weak, corrupt, inept or picks the wrong people, the organisation is also weak, corrupt, inept and badly staffed.

These cultures thrive where personality and speed of response are critical, in new business situations, in deals and brokerage transactions, in the artistic and theatrical world, in politics, guerrilla warfare and crisis situations, provided the leader is good — for they talk of leaders rather than managers in these cultures. They are a convenient way of running things — although not necessarily the best — when the core organisation is small (under twenty people perhaps) and closely gathered together so that personal communication is easy; once things get much bigger than that, formality has to be increased and the personal, telepathic, empathetic style is frustrated. The key to success is having the right people, who blend with the core team and can act on their own; therefore a lot of time is spent on selecting the right people and assessing whether they will fit in or not. It is no accident that some of the most successful club cultures have a nepotistic feel to them: they deliberately recruit people like themselves, even from the same family, so that the club remains a club.

The Role Culture

It is all very different in a role culture. Here the best picture is the kind of organisation chart that all these organisations have. It looks like a pyramid of boxes; inside each box is a job title with an individual's name in smaller type below, indicating who is currently the occupant of the box, but of course the box continues even if the individual departs.

The underlying 'organizational idea' is that organisations are sets of roles or job-boxes, joined together in a logical and orderly fashion so that together they discharge the work of the organisation. The organisation is a piece of construction engineering, with role piled on role, and responsibility linked to responsibility. Individuals are 'role occupants' with job descriptions that effectively lay down the requirements of the role of its boundaries. From time to time, the organisation will rearrange the roles and their relationship to each other, as priorities change, and then reallocate the individuals to the roles.

The communications in these cultures are formalized, as are the systems and procedures. The memoranda go from role to role (head of X department to deputy head) and are copied to roles, not individuals. The place abounds in procedures for every eventuality, in rules and handbooks. There are standards, quality controls and evaluation procedures. It is all **managed** rather than led.

Most mature organisations have a lot of the role culture in them, because once an operation has settled down it can be routinized and, as it were, imprinted on the future. All organisations strive for predictability and certainty — for then fewer decisions are needed, everybody can get on with their job, the outcomes can be guaranteed, and the inputs calculated. You know where you will be; it is secure and comfortable even if it is at times too predictable to be exciting.

These role organisations thrive when they are doing a routine, stable and unchanging task, but they find it very hard to cope with change or with individual exceptions. If it's not in the rule book, they really have to wait for the rule book to be rewritten before they can act. Administrative organisations, as in part of the social security system, have to be role cultures and they will prove very frustrating if you turn out to be one of those individual exceptions. On the other hand, if the social security system were administed by a host of club cultures, each responding as they saw fit, social justice would hardly be served. Efficiency and fairness in routine tasks demands a role culture.

The important thing in these cultures is to get the logic of the design right, the flow of work and procedures. People are, in one sense, a less critical factor. They can be trained to fit the role. Indeed role cultures do not want too much independence or initiative. Railways want train drivers to arrive on time, not five minutes early. Role cultures want 'role occupants', not individualists.

The Task Culture

The task culture evolved in response to the need for an organisational form that could respond to change in a less individualistic way than a club culture, and more speedily than a role culture.

The 'organisational idea' of this culture is that a

group or team of talents and resources should be applied to a project, problem or task. In that way each task gets the treatment it requires — it does not have to be standardized across the organisation — and the groups can be changed, disbanded or increased as the task changes. A net, which can pull its cords this way and that and regroup at will, is the picture of this culture.

It is the preferred culture of many competent people, because they work in groups, sharing both skills and responsibilities; they are constantly working on new challenges since every task is different and thus keep themselves developing and enthusiastic. The task culture is usually a warm and friendly culture because it is built around cooperative groups of colleagues without much overt hierarchy. There are plans rather than procedures, and reviews of progress rather than assessment of past performance. It is a forward looking culture for a developing organisation.

These cultures thrive in situations where problem-solving is the job of the organisation. Consultancy, advertising agencies, construction work, parts of journalism and the media, product development groups, surgical teams — any situation beyond the capacity of one person with minions to solve, and which cannot be embodied in procedures, needs a task culture.

The problem is that they are expensive. They use professional, competent people who spend quite a lot of time talking together in search of the right solution. You would not use a task culture to make a wheel because they would want to reinvent it, or at least improve on it, first. It is a questioning culture, which chafes at routines and the daily grind of 'administration' or repetitive chores. A task culture talks of 'co-ordinators' and 'team leaders' rather than managers; it is full of budgets (which are plans) but short on job descriptions; it wants commitment and it rewards success with more assignments. It promises excitement and challenge but not security of employment because it cannot afford to employ people who do not continually meet new challenges successfully. Task cultures, therefore, tend to be full of young energetic people developing and testing talents: people who are self-confident enough not to worry about long-term security — at least until they are a bit older!

The Person Culture

The person culture is very different from the first three. All of the other three cultures put the organisation's purposes first and then, in their different ways, harness the individual to this purpose. The person culture puts the individual first and makes the organisation the resource for the individual's talents. The most obvious examples are doctors who, for their own convenience, group themselves in a practice, barristers in chambers (a very minimal sort of organisation), architects in partnerships, artists in a studio, perhaps professors in faculties or scientists in a research laboratory.

The 'organisational idea' behind this culture is that the individual talent is all-important and must be serviced by some sort of minimal organisation. They do not in fact like to use the word organisation but find all sorts of alternative words (practice, chambers, partnership, faculty, etc.) instead, nor do they talk of managers but of 'secretaries', 'bursars', 'chief clerk' etc.; indeed the 'managers' of these organisations are always lower in status than the professionals. You may have a senior partner in a law office but if you ask for the manager you are likely to be shown into the chief clerk. Stars, loosely grouped in a cluster or constellation, is the image of a person culture.

The individual professionals in these organisations usually have tenure, meaning that the management is not only lower in status but has few if any formal means of control over the professionals. In a university, for these reasons, the heads of department or the dean of a faculty is usually a rotating job, often seen as a necessary chore rather than a mark of distinction.

In other words, a person culture is very difficult to run in any ordinary way. The professionals have to be run on a very light rein: they can be persuaded, not commanded, influenced, cajoled or bargained with, but not managed.

The culture works where the talent of the individual is what matters, which is why you find that the old professions are finding that the problems are too complex for one individual's talents. Architects, city solicitors, even the clergy are grouping themselves into task cultures and submitting themselves to more organisational disciplines.

Handy goes on to argue that few organisations have only one culture — often they have a mix of all four: what makes each organisation different is the mix in each. He further argues that this may depend on certain factors:

1. Size — large size and role enclosures tend to go together.
2. Work flow — the way that work is organised has an important bearing on the culture that can be operated. If it is organised in separate units where a group or an individual can be responsible for the whole job then club, task or person cultures will exist. But if the workflow is sequential or interdependent, in that one piece is tied with another then what is needed is those systems, rules and regulations and the culture is more of a role culture.
3. Environment — Every organisation has to think about the raw material it receives and the products it turns out; whether these are bolts, concrete blocks or educated human beings. If the environment does not give clear signals, if the institution is a monopoly and can therefore set its own aims and standards or if the environment never changes, then the organisation will tend to go for stability and a routine quiet life — a role culture. A changing or demanding environment requires a culture that will respond to change — a task or a club culture.
4. History — Organisations are to some extent stuck with their past, with their reputation, the kinds of people they hired years ago, their site and their

traditions. These can take years if not decades to change.

The cultural mix in any one organisation depends on the relative importance of each of these factors. Often you will find a role culture, topped by a spider's web with task culture project groups round the edges. Some organisations, on the other hand, are really a federation of 'barons', separate club cultures loosely linked together by a role culture each free to run their own empires.

Take a look at your own organisation and see if you can identify what mix of cultures exist.

With the help of Component 1 of Unit 1 and the cultural approach I hope you managed to get a clear idea of what your organisation looks like. This is of vital importance as you will have to combine this knowledge with that of individuals within the organisation or department to see how any change is going to affect the situation. Only you know your organisation and its personnel and therefore only you can answer the question.

Let us now take the other dimension of Bolam's framework - The Process of Innovation Over Time. Remember that earlier in this Component we stressed the importance of seeing any change as a dynamic process which takes place over a period of time during which the change may be redefined and modified as a result of that process. This dimension can be analysed in terms of three major stages; the antecedent, the interactive and the consequent stages. These stages may be somewhat arbitrary but they are useful for analysis purposes.

Time 1: Before: The Antecedent Stage

It is vital to have a clear understanding of the situation before the change process begins. At this stage the three systems — Change Agent, Innovation and User — may be said to exist separately, though each must have a relationship with the other. The characteristics of the systems and their relationships should be analysed in terms of the dimensions outlined above.

Time 2: The Interactive Stage

During the change process the three systems may be said to be in interaction with each other. This period is both the most critical and the most complex as far as understanding the outcome of the change is concerned. The main aim should be to identify and monitor what precisely takes place at this stage. Key questions here relate to the change agent's tactics and the User System's initial response to these and to the innovation.

Time 3: The Consequent Stage

After the completion of the process the three systems may be said to be separate again and an assessment of the impact of the Interactive experience on all three systems can then be made. They will almost certainly be very different. Concentrating on the User System may respond in a variety of ways. First, it may reject the change for some reasons; Secondly, it may resist the change; Thirdly, it may adopt the change; Fourthly it may fully institutionalise the change; Fifthly the User System may become an advocate of the change. Finally account also has to be taken of the terminal relationship between the change agent and the user system which may range from cooperation to total conflict.

Now that you have worked your way through this Component you should have a framework which you can use to investigate some of the key problems, tasks, procedures and effects associated with change in any type of organisation. You can also use it, as I have done, as an organising framework for the Management of Change. The combination of Bolam's framework with the ideas of Doyle and Ponder and Handy establishes a good base on which to analyse how change can be managed and what the effects of any change process are at any time. I hope you will find it as useful as I have done. Good Luck!

Study Unit 4:

Interpersonal Skills in the Management of Training

Component 1:

What are Interpersonal Skills?

Key Words

Conversation; interpersonal skills; trainees; trainer/manager; conducting effective relationships; aims; setting; impression management; formality; other person.

Book List

BACK, K. & K. *Assertiveness at Work: A practical guide to handling awkward situations.* McGraw-Hill, 1982.

TURNER, C. *Developing Interpersonal Skills.* F.E. Staff College, Coombe Lodge, Bristol, 1983.

FENSTERNHEIM, H. and BAER, J. *Don't say Yes when you want to say No.* Futura Press, 1976.

BURGOYNE, J., BOYDELL, T. and PEDLAR, M. *Self-development.* Association of Teachers of Management, Polytechnic of Central London, 1978.

STEWART, A. & V. *Managing the poor performer.* Gower, 1983.

Introduction

Welcome to the Study Unit on Interpersonal Skills in the Management of Training. The focus of this Unit will be how we as managers relate to those people who are involved in training. These people may be providers of records or policy, or they may be prospective trainees.

What we hope this Unit will help you to do while working through it are things like:

* Thinking about the way you actually behave towards others.
* Being more aware of the different people you relate to in the organisation and management of training.
* Checking your own style of relating to others and working out how this could be improved.
* Looking at some ideas to help organise your thinking and practice some skills that will improve your performance.

The area covered by these general aims is far reaching. The central subject matter for the Unit is something that you may feel you know already, namely yourself. But it is worth checking whether simple **familiarity** is the same as **knowing.** We are always developing as persons and professionals. Being aware of how we are developing and taking direct action to promote our development is a good basis for being effective in helping others in their development.

The areas we have selected for your attention are organized around the basic and commonly used process of relating called the **conversation.** This is treated in its broadest sense, from the informal chat through to the planned and formal interview.

The assumption lying behind this unit is that we all have the skills to conduct most conversations, but, while it is clear that some people are much better than others at this process, most of us do it without even thinking about how well we do it. It is an acquired habit rather than a set of developed skills.

What we will be asking you to do in this Unit is not so much the development and application of new knowledge and new skills so much as the honesty to look at what you really know and do already. This can then be used to see how things can be improved.

The only new knowledge we expect you to acquire in this Unit is self-knowledge. If it achieves that, it will be worth every minute you spend on it.

How to follow the Unit:

* Keep a notebook next to you:
 This will allow you (and encourage you) to write things down as they occur to you. Any ideas or reflections on your own behaviour should be noted down before you forget. It will also encourage you to complete each Checkpoint as it comes up. Sometimes this will be in quick succession.
* Think about confidentiality:
 You will be asked to write notes and reflections about yourself and those you work with. You need to keep your notes in a confidential file and possibly not to name people too clearly in the event of their reading your notes by accident. You might need to think of a way to avoid this danger.
* Find a useful colleague:
 If it is possible to find a sympathetic colleague who you can use to help you think out the issues raised in the unit, this will be helpful. They will be able to give you an outsider's view and give you some feedback on how your behaviour affects others. Occasionally we will suggest you complete a task and review it with a colleague. If no-one is available then the best thing is to send a short report of what you have done to us in the form of Tutor Seen Work.
* Try not to block out ideas about yourself which you don't like:
 Often when we discover things about ourselves that surprise us, we tend to reject them and feel threatened. But it is precisely at this moment that we may be learning the most about ourselves. **First think about** the idea or suggestion and ask yourself why you want to reject it. Reject it only when you have really satisfied yourself it does not apply to you. Even if it doesn't apply to you it's worth thinking about why you found it difficult to accept. Does that tell you something about what you **want** or **don't want** to be?

At the end of this Component you should:

* be aware of the need for attention to Interpersonal Skills in the training context.
* be aware of the importance of informal conversation as a basic method for exercising these skills.
* be able to identify the critical requirements needed to make good use of conversations.
* understand how conversations can be used to increase your awareness of the motivations and views of the people involved in training programmes.

I. What are Interpersonal Skills?

A good common-sense answer to this question might be:

The ability we have to get on with people in everyday life as well as in the work situation.

More precisely we might say:

Interpersonal skills are the range of abilities we have which make us more or less effective at doing things like:

- talking clearly and fluently;
- getting our point of view across effectively;
- being able to undertake others' points of view;
- listening effectively;
- being able to use appropriate language with different people;
- checking that .... are understood by others;
- avoiding unnecessary conflicts and misunderstandings;
- being able to handle conflicts with others;
- helping others to do most of the above more effectively;
 etc., etc.

This is not a complete list, of course. It is presented here as an illustration of the kinds of things I mean when I use the technical, umbrella term **interpersonal skills.**

Checkpoint

1) Try adding to this list on a piece of note paper, abilities which you think are not covered in the list I have made.

STOP READING HERE AND REVIEW YOUR LIST.

2) Now try making a new list of skills that are *specific to the management of training*. Use your experience to prompt you.

STOP READING AGAIN AND SPEND A FEW MINUTES MAKING A NEW LIST.

Here are some suggested skills you might have noted:

- *being able to make a good case for training to senior management;*
- *persuading prospective trainees of the value of training;*
- *being able to find out what trainees think/or feel about the relevance/effectiveness/usefulness of the training they do;*
- *being able to tell senior management what is wrong with the training policy (or lack of it) in a non-aggressive way;*
- *giving clear instruction and information to those potentially involved in training so they understand clearly what is intended.*

Again this is not a complete list and is illustrative. You may have noted many more, or some very different abilities that are needed in your own situation — that's a positive start. I'm sure you'd see what relevance this material has to your own work situation. Use my list to expand or add to your own.

II. Why are Interpersonal Skills important for the trainer/manager?

You may already have a clear answer to this question from your own experience in training or as a result of the ideas raised in your mind when doing the last exercise.

It is obvious in some ways that conducting relationships effectively with other people is part and parcel of being a socially mature person. You need interpersonal skills to do this, so these abilities are part of being human.

However, in the training content they are important in additional ways. They can be crucial to the way you do your job. In particular, they can affect how well you set up, maintain and develop training programmes in your work.

Read the following fictional example of a conversation which a trainer/manager might have with someone:

Manager: [Coming into a clerical section and perching himself in the corner of the supervisor's desk.] "Morning Bill, how's things?"

Bill: [Looking up from checking balance sheets] "Oh, . . . hullo Mr Tomlinson."

Manager: "I've been thinking about training for using computers in your section. As you know we now have a company policy on new technology and a training programme worked out. I hear you are interested in computers, you have one at home don't you?"

Bill: "Er . . . yes, that's right Mr Tomlinson. I've had it for several years now . . . ."

Manager: "Well, that's good. I think you ought to go on a basic course for computer skills as soon as it can be set up. OK?"

Bill: "Well . . . I do have an interest in computers, but it is not in business programmes. I did try one or two out and . . ."

Manager: "That's good Bill, I'm sure you will find they are very similar to those we will be introducing. We do need someone to start on this computer business. I think you would be best. You're the only one in the section who seems to have any interest."

Bill: "Yes, er . . . but do we really need computers here? We cope well with the demands and errors are easily checked and made good by hand. You don't think this section is doing a bad job do you?"

Manager: "Well no . . . but it would be more efficient and the company does have this policy on introducing more technology. I think eventually you might be put in charge of introducing it here and then other sections as and when. We will need someone to help choose those who would best benefit by re-training."
"Anyway, I must go, I have a meeting in two minutes: I'll let you know when we are likely to do more on this. O.K.?" [Gets up and leaves the section office.]

Read this with a critical eye. Does it ring any bells in your own experience?

Ask yourself, has the Manager achieved his aim in this conversation?

How would you feel if you were Bill?

Did the manager approach the topic in the most effective way?

Briefly note down your comments on how effective this trainer/manager was.

STOP READING AND MAKE A FEW COMMENTS BEFORE READING ON.

The conversation depicted here may seem a little unreal. This is to emphasise specific points. Or you may feel it is more or less how things often happen in your experience.

Now check your comments against the list below.

Some of the comments you have made will probably include:

- *The aim of the conversation is unclear. Is he telling Bill or 'sounding' him out?*
- *Bill's mind is not necessarily fully focussed on the subject — he is in the middle of a task.*
- *The Manager cuts the conversation short before allowing Bill to respond fully.*

— *The conversation is rushed.*
— *The Manager's physical position could be a little off-putting for Bill.*
— *The Manager uses an informal "chatty" style but Bill seems unused to this.*
— *The Manager knows some personal information about Bill — but makes unwarranted assumptions on the basis of it.*
— *The Manager fails to explore Bill's misgivings.*
— *Talking of 'Company Policy' seems to give the impression that decisions have already been made whatever Bill thinks.*
— *It is not clear that Bill has agreed to anything. It is not clear that the Manager feels this way.*
— *Is Bill being offered promotion or simply additional responsibilities?*
— *The consequences and implications of what is being prepared are left unsaid — will these be redundancies?*
— *The Manager shows little competent knowlege of what computer technology entails.*

So far I have suggested negative comments; there are some potentially redeeming features, I think.
For instance:
— *The Manager has come to Bill, not summoned him to an appointment.*
— *He approaches Bill on Bill's own 'territory'.*
— *He shows some interest in Bill and his life outside work by knowing about his interests.*

You may feel that these points are more than cancelled out by the overall approach. All in all, I would suggest this has been a pretty inept attempt at communicating and relating to a potential trainee.

III. Conducting Conversations

Conversations are the most common way we exercise our interpersonal skills and frequently, we take for granted how we do this. Informal conversations are the most acceptable and obvious way to sound out people about their views, ideas, attitudes and beliefs. More formal conversations are the way we reach agreements, give instructions, convey precise information and so forth.

Just because holding conversations is what we do all the time, it is worth reflecting on what goes into making a conversation; how it is approached, conducted and concluded. This kind of reflection will enable you to be aware of how well you do it and to note your strengths and weaknesses.

Using the fictitious example as a starting point, let us itemise in general terms the kind of things you should note in planning or reviewing the conversations you might have in the training context.

A. The Reasons for Having the Conversation: The Aims

The question that needs asking is, Why am I having this conversation?

The Manager in the example does not **give the impression** of being clear about his aim or intentions. He keeps asking Bill for his views by implication, but wants to push him to an agreement.

> Always signal clear intentions in any conversation.

Make clear statements about the purpose of the interchange,

"I would like to talk to you about how you react to this idea. . . ."

"I want to make clear what we have to do by. . . ."

B. The Situation for the Conversation: The Setting

1. Where should I conduct the conversation?

Probably **not** as the Manager did with Bill, in a busy office, where the other person is distracted by other concerns.

Certainly away from noise and other things that prevent clear hearing and understanding.

> Always ensure a place where the appropriate amount of attention and ability to think is possible.

2. On whose 'territory' should I conduct the conversation?

The Manager decided to use Bill's 'territory', but did not ask his permission. If the desk is Bill's, sitting on it **gives the impression** of being careless about his feelings and his status.

Acknowledging his 'territory' before moving in, allows him to respond freely and to feel he is respected, e.g.

". . . do you mind if I sit here for a minute?"

On the other hand, if you choose your territory, you need to put the other at ease to make him feel welcomed if you want an informal conversation, e.g.

"I'm sorry to have dragged you away from your work, but I would like a serious chat without distractions."

> Always consider the effect of the place you choose on (1) the other person and (2) the way the conversation might go.

3. What is the best physical position for us to be in?

The Manager sitting on Bill's desk is close and talking down to him. It **conveys the impression** of dominance and superiority. It signals the other to adopt a submissive or subordinate role.

Keeping at the same eye level helps to signal a basis of equality.

Sitting down together implies a serious and relatively lengthy discussion.

Standing can imply an intention **not** to stop and get involved.

Standing face-to-face can **give the impression** of confrontation, especially if you stand very close.

Sitting down close but at an angle so you do not "eye-ball" each other, is a good basis for a relaxed but serious conversation.

Infrequent eye contact can **give the impression** of distance or lack of interest in the other.

> Always give some thought to the physical position you use and think of its effect on the conversation.

4. How long should it take?

The conversation between Bill and the Manager was a little rushed and left many things hanging in the air.

This could give Bill **the impression** that he has just been "fitted in" in passing and that little thought has been given to his possible response and the time he might need to think about it.

> Always have a clear idea of how long the conversation is likely to need, and add a little margin for error.

5. How informal should the conversation be?

The manager addresses Bill by his first name, Bill replies more formally. Either Bill is confused as to the formality of the interchange, or this is the normal pattern of relationships, i.e. subordinates express more 'respectful' attitudes to supervisors. Here this difference reduces the level of informality and works against the attempts to be informal by the Manager.

> Always be clear on how formal or informal the conversation should be; adopt appropriate styles of speech etc.

Deciding on levels of formality can be difficult. Insisting on using first names will get in the way if this causes awkwardness in the other. Sometimes a more formal approach is best to begin with, especially if that is the recognised style in the company.

High levels of formality will make it difficult to get to know someone better as a person, or to create a friendly open atmosphere to allow for a free interchange of ideas.

However, mere "chumminess" put on for the occasion **gives the impression** of falseness and raises justified suspicions.

> Start with the style of formality people are used to. Then move the style of the conversation in the direction you want.

Mere "chumminess" . . . raises justified suspicions

C. Getting Inside the Other Person's Shoes: Understanding the Other Person

1. What do I know about the other person?

The Manager, presumably knew about Bill's responsibilities and about his personal interest in computers. He used this (a) to help him decide to approach Bill and (b) as a **way** of approaching him.

It is worth reflecting on how important it is to know the others you work with as **people** as well as professionals. Taking a **real** though **not intrusive** interest in what others do, or are interested in outside the work situation can be a good basis for developing easier relations, which will help you understand them better and allow you to plan your conversations more effectively.

Expressing interest in the concerns of the other, their feelings, their aspirations etc. is a way of expressing respect and interest in them as a person. It helps them to feel that they are taken seriously as people as well as professionals.

Expressing appreciation for skills or abilities that they regard as important also helps in this area when talking about their work.

> Always try to see the other as a full person rather than just an operative. Some personal interest in them helps here.

2. How accurate are my assumptions about the other person?

The problem for the Manager was that his knowledge was limited and his assumptions inaccurate. Bill is not interested in the way he assumed.

It is worth being clear about what you **know** about the person and what you have **assumed.** The assumptions may be true but you should check them out. If you phrase your remarks in an **interrogative** (question) rather than an **assertive** (statement) way, the other has a chance to affirm or deny your assumption, e.g.

"What do you know/feel about computers?"
Rather than:
"I hear you have an interest in computers."

> Always check out your identity and assumptions about the other person.

3. What if the other's response is unexpected or contradictory to my own view?

The Manager more or less ignores Bill's lack of enthusiasm. He is too busy thinking about his point of view and putting this across. He could have made valuable use of the situation (if he had the time) by exploring **why** Bill is reluctant. He might have gained valuable information on (a) Bill's attitude and feelings and (b) some evaluation of the need (or lack of need) of computer technology in the work place, from someone who had specialist knowledge.

In addition, he would have **avoided the impression** that he did not hear or take any interest in Bill's viewpoint.

> Always take the other person's view seriously and explore them non-critically, **especially** when they are unexpected or contradict your own.

1) Write down the three areas of attention you need to consider when conducting conversations across the top of your note-paper.
2) Underneath each area try to write down the kinds of question that you should ask yourself when considering a prospective conversation.

> STOP READING HERE AND TRY TO COMPLETE THE TASK BEFORE GOING ON.

Did you include some or most of the following?

The Aims
Why am I having this conversation?

The Setting
Where should I conduct this conversation?
On whose 'territory' should I conduct the conversation?
What is the best physical condition?
How long should it take?
How informal should it be?

Understanding the Other
What do I know about the other person?
How accurate are my assumptions about him?
What if the other's response is unexpected?

These may have prompted you to add other important questions under each area, if so, do not be slow to add them. This means that you are reflecting on how you might plan conversations or reminding yourself of how you do it already. Making your own **implicit** *knowledge and experience* **explicit** *is an important part of learning in this area, as are new knowledge and ideas.*

D. Impression Management

You may have noticed in the preceding section that every time I mentioned something as **'creating an impression'** or **'giving an impression'** it was in bold type as it is here.

Try from memory to note those things which were mentioned as **creating or giving "an impression".**

> STOP READING HERE AND TRY TO NOTE DOWN AS MANY THINGS AS YOU CAN REMEMBER.

How many did you think of? If you thought of only one or two read the section again. Then stop and repeat this exercise.

They are scattered through a wide area of text, so you may have found it difficult.
Here they are summarised:

	Impression given
— *Not being explicit about aims*	— *Confused.*
— *Being careless as to the space of others*	— *Lack of respect.*
— *Being too close and talking down*	— *Dominating.*
— *Frequent eye contact*	— *Showing interest.*
— *Standing face-to-face*	— *Confrontation.*
— *Rushing the conversation*	— *"Fitted in". Not important.*
— *Forced "chumminess"*	— *Falseness.*
— *Ignoring responses*	— *Not interested.*

Managing the impression you give to others can be very important, and is a theme that was studied throughout the analysis of conducting conversations, which I have already presented.

It's importance lies in the psychological principle drawn from experience, that:

> People tend to develop a positive impression of you if they receive a positive impression of themselves from you.

Being aware of what impression you give of them to others is thus crucial to effective conversations.

Exercise

Try reflecting on your own experience at work or in everyday life and see if you can **substantially extend** the list in the exercise above and the impression they give to others.

Note these behaviours that you think are your habitual style.

If you have a colleague or acquaintance whose views you respect and trust. Plan a conversation with a theme about the aspects of your style of relating to others and the impression it gives . . . have such a conversation.

Tutor Seen Work

If you wish, you can write a report on what you did:
- how you planned the conversation
- how and where it happened
- what was said
- what you learned about your own conversational style

and send it to me for comment.

Component 2:

Using Conversations in the Training Context (I): Preparation, Aims and Setting

Key Words

Conversation; aims; setting; non-verbal communication; planning; conducting and reviewing; conversations, starting; guiding and conducting discussions; abilities; work situation.

After completing this Component you will:

* be able to think more clearly about how to plan conversations.
* be able to reflect on how you use conversations in your management of training.
* be able to develop clear objectives for your more general aims in using conversations and be able to check on how far you have achieved them.
* be aware of how the place where you have the conversation and the physical position and style you adopt can affect how the other person perceives you.

1. Using Conversations in the Training Context

In the last Component I asked you to think about having conversations under the following headings:

* **Aims** of the conversation
* The **setting** of the conversation
* **Understanding** the other person(s).

I hope this has started you thinking about how **you** conduct conversations and if you are getting the best from the time you put into this activity.

Maybe you don't spend much time on informal social contact of this kind and now are asking yourself if it might be a good idea to engage in it more often in your training role.

In either event, this Component will suggest ways of making your use of conversations more effective.

A simple model of conversations

If you completed the task at the end of the last Component, just think of how you completed it. You will have thought about what you want to say, with whom and where (planning). You will have initiated the exchange, steered what was said to the point you wished to raise and closed the conversation on the appropriate note conducting. You may have thought over whether you had achieved what you had intended and whether your relationship with the other person developed as you wanted, and so on (reviewing).

This outline of what we do when talking to others can form the basis of a simple model of conversation:

Here I have represented in diagrammatic form, what we do when using conversations in our social and working lives. I suspect that the more important the expected or intended outcomes of the conversation, the more time we will spend on **planning and reviewing.** Most of the time our attention is on the **effective conducting** of the conversation, actually doing it well.

How we do it

The activity itself is usefully divided for our purposes into a beginning (starting the conversation) a middle (guiding the conversation) and an end (concluding the conversation), like any well told story.

Let's look at an example of someone **starting, guiding and concluding** a conversation:

Starting

John: [Walking into the outer office from his own] "Hullo Pat, I hear your lease has just run out . . . Well your time here might be running out soon if you don't type these letters more accurately in future."

Guiding

Pat: "John . . . you know what trouble I've been having, so why are you being so nasty . . . it's really mean of you, especially when I've tried to be so helpful. I've brought in pot plants to brighten up the office here, . . . I gave you lifts home when your car was in dock **and** I sent that anniversary card to your wife last week when **you** had completely forgotten!"

John: "Er . . . well . . . yes, Pat I was really grateful for that. It got me out of a bad scene at home . . . I do appreciate that . . ."

Pat: "Don't you like the way the office looks now . . . it's a lot more homely and better to work in, isn't it?"

Concluding

John: "Yes, it is . . . ah — keep up the good work Pat. Oh, there's Dave . . . now he's someone I've really got to talk to . . . see you later Pat." (Goes into the office.)

Checkpoint

Briefly write a few comments in answer to the following questions:

1. How well did John start?
2. How well did John guide the conversation?
3. How well did John finish the conversation?

STOP READING HERE UNTIL YOU HAVE WRITTEN YOUR COMMENTS.

Did your comments include any of these?:

On Starting the Conversation

- *John confuses the point of the exchange by raising two potentially emotive topics at once.*
- *The two issues are not connected (except the first might be the potential cause of the second) and one distracts from the other.*
- *If John wants Pat's attention and motivation, he might sound a little more sympathetic.*

Guiding the Conversation

- *John rapidly loses the original point of the conversation.*
- *He allows Pat to distract him with other irrelevant issues.*
- *He begins to sound hesitant and maybe a little guilty about his abrupt start to the conversation.*
- *He manages to sound encouraging about only peripheral aspects of Pat's work.*

Concluding the Conversation

- *John does not bring the conversation back to the main point before leaving.*
- *He leaves abruptly.*
- *He gives the impression that talking to Pat is not important (unless to criticise her?)*

These are the points that occurred to me after a couple of minutes thought. You may have several different points. Do you think you've covered the important aspects of the conversation?

I suspect that many of us would hope we might deal with this simple problem better than John seems to have done. What is clear from this exercise is that **Starting, guiding** and **concluding** conversations do need some attention. John's initial aim was a quite justified demand that his secretary type his letters accurately. Pat's sense of being not understood or appreciated is real also.

Let us assume that:

- John has been complimenting Pat on aspects of her work that are marginal to her job, like making the office "more homely".
- That he feels unsure about his right to demand good standards of work.
- Pat has been wrong-footed by being encouraged to concentrate on minor services and not her typing by John's behaviour.

Tutor Seen Work

Write out an alternative script to John's conversation. Pay special attention to what you think should be his **opening** and **closing** remarks.

Try the final result out on someone you know for their reaction **or** send the script to me as a piece of **Tutor Seen Work** for comment.

2. Using Conversations in Your Work Situation

How do we **plan, conduct,** and **review** our conversations in the training context? The test of the material presented here is its applicability to your own situation and the help it gives to you in working effectively in the training context.

Self-evaluation is difficult in an area of behaviour we perform habitually. You may feel you are a "good conversationalist" or "communicator", or you may be very much aware of your limitations in this area. It is useful to realise that in these matters **people tend to have exaggerated views about their abilities or lack of them.** Thus we tend to think we are **much better** or **much worse** than we are in fact.

Either way, some detailed attention to how you **plan, conduct** and **review** conversation is useful, if only to become more aware of what you do well and what you could improve on.

Planning your Conversation

We have outlined the conducting of conversations in the last component under the headings: **Aims, setting,** and **understanding the other person.**

In planning a conversation some attention should be given to each of these areas.

Being Clear About Your Aims

Briefly make a short list of likely aims that you will have for starting conversations in the context of training in your work situation.

STOP READING HERE AND SPEND A FEW MINUTES NOTING DOWN WHAT YOU CAN.

Here are some aims that I think any trainer in the work place might have:

- *Getting to know the other person better.*
- *Establishing a good (or better) working relationship.*
- *Getting a more accurate view of how the other person sees his work in the company.*
- *Understanding more clearly what training the other person feels they need.*
- *Asking for reactions to aspects of Company Policy.*
- *Asking for agreement to do something, related to training e.g. promoting and supporting or becoming involved in it.*
- *Telling the other person what is going to be required of him.*
- *Checking that the other person is clear what you are intending to do and what their role might be.*

Your list will (hopefully) be more specific to your work situation and probably not as long as this.

You will notice that I have written the list so that the aims start by being very general and become more and more specific towards the end.

My implied suggestion here is that some of the general aims need to be tackled to make the job of achieving the specific, job-related tasks easier. For instance, you **can** simply tell someone what training they are going on without (a) knowing much about them as a person, or (b) having a good working relationship, or (c) learning if they think the training is relevant to their needs or not. But having fulfilled (a)-(c) to a greater or lesser extent will help you to deliver an instruction to go on training in a way which will motivate rather than cause resentment in the other person.

Go back over your list of aims and:
(a) Note which are **general** and which are **specific** conversational aims.
(b) Try re-ordering them to give you an impression of which should come first.
You might need to lay effective ground work before tackling specific and possibly demanding tasks in conversation.

A Note on General Aims and Specific Objectives

The planning is more difficult with general aims than with specific areas. Where do you start when "getting to know someone better" in the context of training? It is not clear what we want to know, or how much better. To some extent the context you work in will answer these questions.

In planning conversations of a general kind, it is useful to set more specific objectives for a particular conversation.

Thus an **Aim**:
"Getting to know the other person better."
can be translated into objectives like:
"Finding out what interests they have outside work,"
or:
"Discuss their views on work conditions or how they like the job."

This kind of planning can be over done of course. This level of conversation is often best done through passing remarks, appropriate topics that come into your head at the time and so on, as when we conduct everyday social conversations.

If your general aims are a background to more specific aims, then this too will indicate the kinds of specific areas of information or impression you want to give or get.
e.g.

An aim: "Getting an impression of how others see their work".

might be a useful background to

a Specific Aim: "finding out if the training needs are relevant"

Check through your own (amended) list of aims:
1. Choose two or three **general aims** and write some appropriate **specific objectives** that will help you achieve that aim. Use your recent experience to prompt you.
2. Write down one or two **specific aims** that are relevant to your own work and then list the more **general aims** you might tackle as a way into **specific aims.**

To get useful critical comments discuss these completed tasks with a trusted colleague or send them in as **Tutor Seen Work** for my comments.

I suspect you will have noticed, that in doing the above tasks, you will have a clearer idea of what is implied in the more generally formulated aims you have written down.

1. Planning the Setting of Conversations

In the first Component we looked at the **Setting** of conversations under the following headings:
— Appropriate place (including "whose territory?")
— Physical position
— The time and timing
— The level of formality

Place Position Time Formality

2. Formal or "Just a Chat"?

The answer to this question determines the rest of the conversation, so we will consider it first. It may be important here to make clear that the term **conversation** is being used as a general term to cover a wide range of interchange between people.

I take it to cover at one extreme an exchange of views about the cricket scores while passing in the corridor through to a formal meeting in a manager's office to appoint, discipline or dismiss someone.

We are looking at the area of human communication that is face-to-face, but ranges from "chats" to interviews.

In planning the setting of our conversation, this gives us a wide range of possibilities.

The level of formality will depend on lots of factors.

Briefly write down a list of things that might determine how formal, or not, a conversation would be:

Stop reading and spend one or two minutes on this.

The following is a suggested list of factors

What the aim of the conversation is, i.e. is it an instruction or an attempt to elicit ideas?

The ethos of the company: i.e. what is the normal style of relationship between subordinates and superiors?

The other person involved: i.e. will this particular person respond to easy chat or rather correct and polite interchanges?

---

1. Look back at the situation between John and Pat (page 146).
2. Write your own brief comments on the following questions:

Question 1
Did John set the right level of formality for the conversation he aimed to have?

Question 2
What can you deduce about the normal style of relations between staff in the company?

Question 3
would it have helped if John had changed his style? How? (If you wrote an alternative script, use that to help you be specific, i.e. what style did you make John adopt?)

Question 4
Was John's approach best suited to dealing with Pat in particular?

Stop reading here and spend a couple of minutes commenting on each question.

The comments that occur to me are as follows:

On Question 1:
If his aim is to get Pat to recognise her poor typing a more formal style, keeping clear of personal issues would help to establish this point without distractions. Maybe a talk in his office — in private, on his own 'territory'?

On Question 2:
The company style seems to be informal, both use first names habitually.

On Question 3:
A shift into more formal address, i.e. "Miss Pritchard" rather than "Pat'? — a bit sudden but might signal to Pat that something is up.

On Question 4:
This is difficult to answer. Knowing Pat has difficult problems in her domestic situation, he can either ignore them altogether and remain focussed on the main aim or he has to acknowledge them in some way, so as not to appear unfeeling. Conversation always takes place in a relationship. The affect of any conversation can change a relationship. Ignoring people's feelings indicates a particular relationship that tries to keep very strictly to professional tasks.

Assuming John does not want this but a more personal working relationship, he might **either** *start with the lease issue and adopt an informal and sympathetic style leading on to a clear demand, gently put, that she look to her typing;* **or** *start formally, get the typing issue clear — check she has understood and then go on to express sympathy and support regarding the lease, so as to end the conversation on a good personal note.*

Did your comments cover most of what I have written? You may have noted other things based on your own experience.

Decisions about formality often determine the kinds of:

place
physical position
and **timing**
of the conversation, we will now turn to these.

3. The place for the Conversation

Think of your usual work situation and write down as long a list as you can of **all** the places where it would be possible and acceptable to have a conversation with another person concerning training or relevant issues. Visualise clearly all the areas in your work place.

Stop reading here and make an extensive list — take 2 or 3 minutes here.

Have you considered **all** of the following or others?
Staff social rooms (common rooms)
General offices
Manager's office
Your office
Corridors between offices
Workshops
Shop-floor space
Open space between buildings
Entrance gates (or foyer)
Car park
Cafeteria (Managers')
Cafeteria (Staff)
Library/records dept.
Union office
Visitors' rooms
Stores.

This wide variety of places can be categorised in different ways.

The following categories might be relevant in considering which place is suitable or not.

1. My 'territory' or the other's 'territory' or neutral 'territory'.
2. Public or private.
3. Busy (noisy) or quiet.
4. Comfortable or sparsely furnished.

1. Check back over your list of places and note what categories they fall into.
2. Are there any other relevant categories you know are important? Note which places fall into them.

---

4. The Time and Timing of the Conversation

How Long?

It is important that you can reasonably achieve the aim of the conversation **within the time** you have planned.

When?

It is important that you can reasonably achieve the aim of the conversation so it occurs **at the time** when the other person is best able to respond.

Always plan with some time in reserve.

General aims need more adequate and lengthy time, but do not require a time when great concentration is needed.

More specific aims may only need limited time span but might require a time when the other is free to concentrate or when the action related to the conversation is near in time.

Sometimes more general aims are best met by a series of short informal chats over a period of time.

5. Physical Position in Conversations

Physical position, expression and movement, can all convey many things about your attitude to the person and the conversation you are having, sometimes, **despite** what you are saying. Such communication is often referred to as "Body Language" or "Non-verbal Communication" (NVC).

A variety of behaviour contributes to this:

Physical position	Standing or sitting, close or distant, relaxed or formal — "settled" or "hovering".
Tone of voice	Emotional or calm, hard or soft, distinct or mumbled.
Gestures	Energetic or slow, stiff or relaxed, aggressive or responsive.
Facial Expression	Smiling or serious, "dead-pan" or responsive, attentive or bored.
Eye contact	Frequent or rare, intense (fixed) or indirect (moving away and look again).

Combinations of all these behaviours can imply many different things — and generalisation is difficult.

i.e. standing close, above a person, talking loudly and gesticulating energetically will likely be experienced as a dominating, aggressive style of approach.

But standing in another's office while they sit is a non-verbal recognition of implied inferiority or politeness — unless we also use a loud voice and gesticulations!!

We will concentrate here on **physical position** for the sake of simplicity and clarity. Other kinds of non-verbal behaviour will be examined in other contexts in other Components.

Think about the following types of conversational situation and how you would approach them in terms of physical position and style of body language. Draw on your own recent experience if possible. Write your comments down.

1. Talking to an interested colleague about a new training policy.
2. Telling an employee that they will be expected to join a training programme.
3. Persuading an employee of the value of training for him.
4. Trying to gauge a trainee's reactions to a training programme he is on at the moment.

> Stop reading here and write a few comments on each situation briefly.

Do your comments cover the situations in a similar vein to the following?

1. Either standing or sitting, but relaxed and at the same height as the other. Probably fairly close and attentive to the other — you don't want to lose his interest!
2. Not too close, probably standing or sitting (if in your office) — keep direct eye contact.
3. Standing or sitting — as long as it is relaxed — (you may be in for a long session!). Same level, responsive and attentive to other's views.
4. Probably sitting if you want some detailed response — again same height, relaxed style, calm and lots of eye contact.

If your comments are substantially different, have another think about the situation. But it is important to realize that there are no clear cut, or right answers here. The exercise is as much about getting you to think of the possible effect of the way you conduct conversations. This is to make you pay attention to thinking what you may usually take for granted. In the end the only answer is to **try out** specific ways of conducting your conversation, using these ideas and your own experience.

Summary

We have considered the Planning of Conversations under the headings of **Aims** and **Setting**. We will look at the **understanding** of the other perosn in the next Component.

To check how far you remember and understand this Component try to write a check list of questions you should ask yourself when planning a conversation:
(a) under the heading of **Aims**
(b) under the heading of **Setting**.

> Stop reading here and try to write out a check list.

If you find this difficult, quickly go back over the Component and see if you have missed anything out.

We can summarise this Component with the following check lists of questions

Planning Checklist 1: Aims

Planning the Aims of the Conversation
* *Do I have a clear idea of why I want this conversation?*
* *Is my aim general or specific?*
* *If it is general, will I need to have more specific objectives for this conversation?*

Planning Checklist 2: Setting

Planning the Setting of the Conversation
* *Should this conversation be formal or informal?*
* *How will I create the right level of formality or informality that I want?*
* *Where is the best place for this conversation? Is it free of distractions? Is it acceptable to the other person?*
* *How much time do I need? will I have enough time for the conversation? What will be the best time to have the conversation?*
* *How should I arrange my physical position in respect of the other person? Should I be relaxed and comfortable or only a little relaxed or does it matter?*

You may have added other points to your list. This does not mean they are wrong. Checklists are useful to draw up and keep to give you a quick ready-made check on points you may forget to cover in the daily rush. Each person has a different point he regards as necessary. The above are only "skeleton models" of checklists which you could adapt to your own use.

I think you will find it useful, if you don't do it already, to make your own checklists as the basis of this Component, on card or in a well bound note book, for your own reference when trying to use the ideas here outlined in your work situation.

Prepare your own Planning Checklists for being clear about AIMS and preparing the SETTING of the conversation you need to have in your role as trainer/ manager.

Component 3:

Using Conversations (II): Understanding the Other Person

Key Words

Knowledge; understanding; empathy; information; opinions; inferences; hunches; your work situation; TIK list; conducting and reviewing conversations; starting, guiding and concluding conversations.

After completing this Component you will:
* have some idea of how to develop your understanding of others in the training context.
* have examined what you know about a particular person who is relevant to your management of training.
* become more aware of how you actually conduct and evaluate the conversations you have in the management of training.
* be able to plan, review and improve the effectiveness of your conversations in your role as a manager of training.

I. Introduction

So far we have looked at using conversations in the training context from the point of view of **planning** and specifically under the more detailed heads of **Aims** and **Setting** (See also Component 1).

The model of using conversation that we looked at also included **Conducting and Reviewing** as well as planning. It is on these other areas that we will spend more time in this Component.

However, one important output of **Planning** has yet to be dealt with which was introduced in Component 1, namely that of **understanding the other person** with whom you are having the conversation.

II. The Importance of How You Understand the Other Person

First let us try to be clear about what various words or terms I am going to use mean.

1. What do we mean by understanding?
This is an everyday word which we all use frequently. But this is a good reason to ask the rather obvious question. The working definition of **understanding** I want to suggest is:

Understanding = knowledge and empathy

It is more than knowing about another person, it is being able to make the effort to see things his way.

2. What do we mean by Knowledge?
Again, this is an everyday word. But it is not easy to define clearly. For some it means information, data and facts. For others it means wisdom, common-sense or knowing how to do something. I will suggest here a definition that covers more than factual information:

Knowledge = Information, inferences and "hunches"

in this case, about the other person.

3. What do we mean by Empathy?
As its simplest and most common meaning, **empathy** is the desire and ability to "step into the other's shoes" as the Chinese say. It requires an interest in the other and the attempts to see things in his way. Understanding is gained by increasing your knowledge of and developing your empathy for, the other person.

> Note: What we are looking at here is not a target to achieve so that at some point we can say we **understand** someone. It is a **process** which is changing all the time. We can always increase our understanding of another. It is always necessary to work on it. Equally, we can lose it and start to "misunderstand" them or understand them less well. Like so much in human relations, this is an ongoing task.

4. Why bother to understand the other person?
You may have your own views on this question already. You may have recognised the value of this in your own experience of life. However, it is worth thinking about its value in the specific area of training.

The attempt to develop your understanding of others in the workplace could:

* give the other a sense of being respected and taken seriously.
* help you to foresee how they might react to specific circumstances or approaches.
* make you more aware of what you say and how you say it and the effect this has on the other person.
* help you to encourage in others a positive view of themselves and their abilities.
* help you avoid creating unnecessary negative feelings in others.
* improve your ability to discover the training needs of others and their view of the job they do.

5. What do I need to understand better?
Time is limited and there is a job to be done, so how far is this business of understanding others in the workplace going to be possible?

Firstly, as a socially competent person you will know that in many ways you are already doing this and have been for some time.

Secondly, with a little reflection on your own situation you will be able to sort out those people who are **relevant** to your managment of training and who you need to know better because of some need you have of them or they of you.

Thirdly, in the attempt to develop understanding of these people, you will very likely change your style of communicating and relating to others in other areas of your work and life.

(The aspects and details of this change in style will be looked at in later Components).

Checkpoint

In order to begin to answer the question about who you need or want to understand better, pause for a few minutes and reflect:—

Think of your work situation and:

1. Make a list of **all** the people who you think you need to, or will need to, work with in your role as manager of training. Make the list as long as possible, don't just note down the obvious ones (use initials if you want to keep the list confidential).
2. Having written the list go back over it and write next to each entry the **reason** you include them on the list, i.e. their role in your training programme etc.

> STOP READING HERE UNTIL YOU HAVE COMPLETED 1

> STOP READING HERE UNTIL YOU HAVE COMPLETED 2

In making my own list of such people, the reasons that I found I had used were the following:—

— *A prospective trainer or needed expert.*
— *A prospective trainee.*
— *A current trainee (actually involved in the programme).*
— *A current trainer (maybe someone I have to work with at the moment).*
— *My immediate superior responsible for the training programme and/or training policy.*
— *The supervisor/manager of a section/branch whose personnel will be coming onto training courses.*
— *The supervisor/manager who will be expected to take on those who have been trained.*
— *Ancillary staff and/or technicians needed to administer and run training programmes, organise materials, keep records, etc., etc.*

You may have noted more specific reasons that are relevant to you and your work situation. Have any of these suggestions reminded you of people you have **not** listed? If so go back to the list and add them. If in doubt, add them to the list and then give your reason next to the name or initials.

III. Developing your Understanding of the Other Person

In the working definition of Understanding, I focussed attention on **two** areas.

The two areas were **Knowledge** and **Empathy**. We need to look at ways of extending both of these in respect to other people.

1. Who do I want to Understand?
Your own motivation in attempting improvement in your understanding will depend on some pressure to get to know another based on things like personal interest, immediate training needs, long term problems, etc.

Look over the list of names you produced earlier and:

1. Choose **one** or **two who you feel you need to know** and **understand** better.
2. Write a note to yourself about **why** you have chosen him, or them. **This is important.**

> STOP READING UNTIL YOU HAVE COMPLETED 1 AND 2

Here are some suggested reasons which you might have used to select particular people:

- *They are people you will need to work with in future.*
- *You think they have useful ideas on training which you would like to hear.*
- *You think (or know) they could do some important task well for you, but you have not approached them yet.*
- *You feel the person is a mystery, you don't know what makes them tick, and it could be helpful if you could find out more about what they are like.*

If you feel the reasons you used were not as specific to the **training context** as these — **don't resist the temptation to go back and choose again for more definite reasons.**

2. What do I know about the other person?
Think carefully about a person you have chosen. What do you know about him? Think of all the things you can recall from memory about him. These things could range from simple facts about his age, marital status and how he likes his tea, to possible guesses about his political views, club memberships and wider social circle. Some areas of his life may be very familiar to you, probably that connected with his job, but not necessarily. Other areas of his life may be a total blank or only sketchily known.

Try to list in **single words** or **short phrases** as many things about the person as you can in a space of five minutes. Take a little longer if you need it.

STOP READING UNTIL YOU HAVE COMPLETED THE LIST.

As an example to compare with your own here is a "Things I know" (T.I.K.) list I made on a colleague of mine.

T.I.K. List for P.W.

Male	Quick thinker
Married	Good negotiator
Aged 39-40	Can be manipulative of others
Two children	Good at managing money and accounts
Address	Very hard worker
Keen sailor	Likes his creature comforts
Roman Catholic	Compares himself with others and finds himself dissatisfied
Ex-sports coach	Good humoured (mostly)
Ambitious	Moody (on occasion)
Very fluent and effective speaker	Energetic
Good organiser	Enjoys acquiring new skills
Tends to take on too much work	Enjoys playing with hi-tech hardware
Drives a saloon, but wants a sports car	

The example may have given you some ideas or reminders of things you do know about the person you have chosen. If so go back to your list and add to it.

3. Is what I know about the other person reliable?
While completing the last exercise it may well have occurred to you that many of the things you noted were not **definite facts** about the other. Or you may have listed **only** those things you felt definite about. My list certainly contains much about which I cannot be definite, but which are based on well-informed guesswork or simply my own opinion.

It is a good exercise to put down in your T.I.K. list as much as you can even if you can't prove it to be absolutely true. This is because much of our picture of other people is strongly affected by things we think about them which may not be simply factual. Our knowledge of them is often shaped by our opinion and judgements about them. It is best to be fully aware of these aspects of our knowing as well as the more obvious facts that are easily verified.

Of course, this means that our knowledge of another is not simply reliable or unreliable — **it is our own view** which may be accurate or mistaken.

IV. The Different Aspects of Knowing the Other Person

Earlier in the Component I suggested that **knowledge** was a combination of three things.

Can you remember the **three** things?

STOP READING AND SEE IF YOU CAN NOTE THEM DOWN

I suggested that knowledge usually consisted of **Information, Inferences and Hunches**

Information
We often call this "hard data", facts which are certain and checkable.

Inferences
These are results of "putting two and two together", drawing conclusions about people from what we know or our interpretation of what the facts mean.

Hunches
These are the product of our own assumptions, opinions and guess-work about the other. They include our personal evaluations of the other person and how we **feel** *about him.*

Go back to your T.I.K. list on the colleague you selected and check each entry. Mark Factual (Information) entries with a 'F'; mark Inferences with an 'I' and Guesses, Evaluation or Opinions with an 'H' for Hunch.

STOP READING AND SPEND A FEW MINUTES CHECKING YOUR LIST

In my own T.I.K. list I would mark the following with an 'F' for Factual Information:

FACTS 'F' LIST	BASIS
Male	From observation
Married	I have met his wife (Though I have not seen the marriage certificate)
Address	I have been to his house
Children	I have met his children
Drives a Saloon, Prefers a Sports Car	Is this a fact or an inference?

I would mark the following with an 'I' for Inferences:

'I' LIST	
Quick-thinker	From observing his behaviour and other reports.
Ex-Sports Coach	From what he has told me.
Ambitious	From what he says and does — is this really a guess or hunch?
Likes Creature Comforts	From his comments on his food and accommodation etc.
Hard-worker	From the amount of work he seems to get through and from others' reports.

I would make the following entries on my T.I.K. list with an 'H' for opinions, guess-work and hunches:

'H' LIST	
Good negotiator	An intuition about the kind of person he is and some observation
Tends to be materialistic	An opinion based on my evaluation of his attitudes and behaviour
Can be manipulative of others	An intuition about the way he operates and a critical evaluation of that
Tends to do too much work	An opinion based on an evaluation of his behaviour

With these examples in mind go back and see if you have an entry you now wish to categorize or put into another category. Are there any which could go into several categories? (See my comments in the 'F' box and the 'I' box).

---

1. Are our Pictures of Others Accurate?

Accurate (factually) but uninformative.

Conveys lively impression of person but can distort the reality.

Information is checkable and more or less definite. **Inferences** and **Hunches** are not directly linked to hard facts and so can be less reliable. By this I mean we can get it wrong **more often** and **without realizing** it. But they do give us a full picture of a real live human in a way that a purely factual description cannot. We need **facts** and **evaluations** to make people real to us.

It is important **to know what you know** about the other person. This includes:—

— knowing what you **don't** know (i.e. lack of information made up for by guesses).
— knowing what you **think** you know (i.e. inferences, based on some facts as you interpret them).
— knowing what you **do** know (i.e. factual information and your views on this).

On the basis of what you have done before, quickly write down a list of things you **don't** know about the person you have been considering.

Concentrate on those aspects of their lives that you might **need** to know because of your likely or actual professional relationship.

STOP READING FOR 3 TO 10 MINUTES TO WRITE THIS NEW LIST

---

2. How do I develop Empathy for the Other Person?

I said at the beginning of the Component that **understanding** was a result of **knowledge** of and **empathy for the other person.**

Can you write down a brief definition of what is meant by empathy?

STOP READING HERE

I said earlier that empathy meant:
- *the ability to "stand in the other's shoes"*
- *taking an interest in the other person*
- *attempting to see things his way.*

---

3. How does one develop this set of skills and attitudes?

There is no easy answer to the question. Empathy is an activity rather than a state. It is based on asking yourself questions such as:—
- how does the other person see me?
- how will they react to this situation?
- how would I feel in their position?

The answers to such questions depend on using your **knowledge** of the person plus careful use of your imagination. It's what we often do when trying to "second-guess" what they might do.

Think about the last time you approached the other person you have been considering.

1. Make some short notes to yourself on:—
   - How he perceived you and your instructions.
   - How he felt or thought about the conversation.

STOP READING AND MAKE SHORT NOTES

Did you find the task easy or difficult?

2. Note down what **information, what inferences,** or what **hunches** you used to think yourself "into their shoes".

V. Conducting and Reviewing Conversations

Up until now and over the last two Components we have been teasing out in detail what you might consider in **planning** a conversation. Now we need to turn to having or **conducting** a conversation.

Can you recall the three aspects of Conducting a conversation we identified earlier in the previous Component?

STOP READING HERE AND SEE IF YOU CAN NOTE DOWN THESE THREE ASPECTS

We suggested a common-sense model of a conversation based on three aspects as follows:—
- *STARTING or initiating the conversation.*
- *GUIDING or steering the conversation.*
- *FINISHING or concluding the conversation.*

Each aspect requires some managing to make the conversation successful and well-performed.

Based on your own extensive experience of having conversations, from interviews to informal chats, can you list some of the important functions of **starting a conversation.**

STOP READING AND NOTE DOWN WHAT YOU THINK FOR 2–3 MINUTES

Here are some of the important functions that occurred to me about starting a conversation.

- Get the other's attention.
- Avoid antagonizing the other.
- Establishing the correct relationship with the other, i.e. formal or friendly.
- Starting a new relationship with the other which you want to develop.
- Preparing the other for the focus or emphasis of the coming conversation.

This is only a limited list of the **kinds** of things involved in starting a conversation, you may have written others which are equally important to you. However, they should all come down to the following general functions:—
- Setting the climate or mood
- Preparing the other for the main part of the conversation
- Trying to gauge the other's feelings, attitudes and thoughts at the time.

Try doing the same exercise, but this time list the important functions of **guiding a conversation.**

STOP READING AND SPEND 2–3 MINUTES NOTING WHAT YOU THINK

Again, here are **some** *of the important functions that I would list, this time for guiding a conversation:—*

- keeping the conversation focussed on what you want to talk about.
- picking up points you want to develop.
- excluding irrelevant or inappropriate topics.
- sorting out what is relevant or irrelevant with the other person.
- checking back to see if you are clear about what the other has said.
- checking that the other is clear about what you want to say.

Again you may have written other things. Is there anything in your list which is a **substantially** different point than the ones I have written? I so, note them for the future. They may indicate specific functions of conversations that are important to you in your situation.

Finally, try to list the things that are important in effective concluding or finishing of a conversation.

STOP READING FOR 2–3 MINUTES AND MAKE NOTES

Here are some of the things that occurred to me, that are important in concluding a conversation.

— leaving the other person feeling O.K. about you and/ or the topic, **if possible**
— making sure the issue is resolved or that you are both **aware** it is **not** resolved
— summarising what has been said and/or concluded
— reminding the other of his agreements
— reminding the other of your agreement with him.

Did you have anything substantially different from this list? Or do you feel you might want to add to yours after reading this list?

---

1. Conversations in Practice

STARTING

This could be prepared for by:
— your clear planning of the aim and setting of the conversation (see above).
— the use of your present knowledge of the other and your own reflection on how to approach them best, based on empathetic self-questions about how they might feel etc. (See above).

GUIDING

This is helped by:

— clear aims and planning for the conversation, knowing what is relevant or not and having some expected outcomes
— being aware of the reactions of the other and modifying your style or aims if necessary
— trying to see the situation from the point of view of the other and building your conversation on that basis.

Modifying your style

FINISHING

This is effectively done on the basis of:
— good timing of the conversation
— being clear about what note to leave the conversation on, i.e. friendly, thoughtful or "take it or leave it"
— a clear statement summarizing what you wanted and have or have not got from the conversation
— being clear about what will follow, i.e. "more discussion of the details later", "the matter is closed" or "it's up to you to come back with some response".

2. Reviewing Conversations

If you have spent some time in preparing for an important conversation or series of conversations, then the investment of time might need to be evaluated. Was it worth all that preparation? Did I achieve what I wanted? Could I have handled it better? — are all questions that it is worth reflecting on after the conversation, if only for a minute or two. Occasionally you may want to recall what you have achieved in specific conversations, both in terms of **content** — i.e. decisions, information etc. and the **performance** — i.e. how well you handled the situation.

However you do this reviewing, I suggest it helps to have some sort of framework to remind you what you might want to look for.

A Framework for a Review

1. A Brief Record of the planning of the conversation, including

BEFORE THE EVENT

- — a statement of the aims
- — the proposed place, time and arrangements
- — notes pertinent to the person and subject that you plan to talk about

↓

2. A Detailed Report of what actually happened and how you felt about it, written as soon after the conversation as possible (as an aid to memory). Covering the following areas:—

↓

AFTER THE EVENT

- — What was said?
- — What you felt?
- — What did you think the other felt?
- — How did he react?

↓

3. An Evaluation of the Conversation based on a checklist, something like the following:—

↓

Planning

- — How far was the plan fulfilled?
- — Was the place, setting and time as planned?
- — If different, was this due to a deliberate change or were you overtaken by events?
- — Was your aim achieved? and How do you know?

↓

Conducting

- — How did you Start the Conversation? Was it effective? How do you know?
- — Did the conversation go the way you wanted? How did you achieve that? or what stopped you?
- — If the conversation changed direction was that because of your decision or the other's decision?
- — How did you react to the other's views? Positively or negatively? In a way helpful to them? or to your own aims? did they surprise you and how?
- — How did you conclude the conversation?
- — What do you think the other person understood, felt like or agreed to at the end of the conversation?
- — How would you rate the effectiveness of the conversation in terms of the actual **planned content** and **your handling of it?**

↓

Reviewing

- — How useful has this review been?
- — Specifically, what aspects of it have been useful?
- — Specifically, which points of it have not been useful?

↓

If you use this review framework in detail on several occasions, it will become quickly clear to you what questions are useful and worth answering in some detail, and what questions are not so useful. It is a good idea to see if you can help your own self-evaluation by adding new questions which you find more useful to your own situation and style.

Having a conversation is an activity done with other people, not something to read about doing. It is a set of skills or abilities we all do more or less well. So far we have looked at how you might reflect on it as a general process and plan to do it more effectively. It is now time to test the usefulness of these ideas by doing it. Having done it we can test our ideas on reviewing by looking at how well we did it.

Task: to Plan, Conduct and Review a Conversation

I suggest you plan, conduct and review an **actual conversation** with the colleague whom you have been considering in detail earlier in the Component:—

1. **The general aim** of the conversation will be to check-out **one or two** assumptions, opinions or guesses that **you have already identified** to see how accurate or mistaken they are.
2. I suggest you use the framework for planning a conversation as discussed above. Use those ideas which seem most useful to you and leaving out what you find less useful.
3. Please try to use the framework for reviewing outlined above to test its effectiveness.
4. The task has been set as a way of helping you transfer learning in the Component to your actual situation. It is also presented to you as a **personal challenge** which you set yourself and through which you can begin to evaluate your interpersonal skills.

I suggest you try it even if you don't feel you want to. The only **real** learning in this area is achieved through **action** and **experience**. Your own interpersonal skills will be most effectively developed on the basis of setting yourself such small challenges and evaluating your performance.

Tutor Seen Work

You might find it useful to send me a copy of your **Record of Planning a Detailed Report of the Conversation** and your responses to the **Evaluation Checklist** plus any other comments you wish to make out the experience, the evaluation or the usefulness of the ideas in this material.

In this way I can provide detailed comment on your actual situation and your own performance.

Component 4:

Using Questions and Listening Skills

Key Words

Open questions; closed questions; listening skills; clarifying, summarizing; active listening; reflective listening; framing questions; empathy; listening behaviour.

After completing this Component you will:

* know how to use open and closed questions effectively
* be able to plan your conversations more precisely by attending to the kind of questions you might use
* have thought about your own listening skills
* be able to mention and evaluate how effectively you listen when managing your training programme.

Introduction

So far we have been looking at interaction or conversation in the training context as a basic activity for a wide set of situations. We have been looking at it as something to be planned and reviewed with some care. We need now to change the focus and look at the performance skills that might help us to conduct conversations effectively. There is much to be said here, but it is probably important to spend time on the really important things. In this Component we will look at the skills of **questioning and listening.**

1. The Use of Questions in Conversation

The reason we want to start conversations with others is usually to convey some message, views, feelings or judgements to another or to get such things from them. In any case it is useful to use questions as a basis for the conversation.

Opening Conversations with Questions — How do I start? For more of us than would care to admit it, starting a conversation is the most difficult thing about the process, especially if it is of some importance. We don't want to get off on the wrong foot, be misunderstood, raise unnecessary barriers and so on.

Opening conversations with questions help to elicit a response from the other from the outset. This helps you to get some indication of the other's mood, attentiveness and so on and requires them at least to begin to shift their attention from what they are doing to what you want to say or ask. **All this is dependent on how you frame the question.**

Checkpoint

Think about how you go about starting conversations in the training context.

Do you always have a particular approach?

Does it vary with the person or the purpose of the conversation?

Do you find it difficult?

STOP READING AND MAKE A FEW NOTES ON YOUR OWN REFLECTIONS IF THEY STRIKE YOU AS NOTEWORTHY

Read these short examples with a critical eye.

I

> Mr Wilkins (Manager): "Ah Tom, I want to have a quick word with you about the firm's training policy. As you know the senior management are concerned about this, and want all supervisors like yourself to become actively involved in identifying areas where training is needed in the different sections. You will be giving some time to this I hope?
>
> Tom (Supervisor): "Er . . . yes Mr Wilkins."

II

> Mr Wilkins: "Tom, can I have a quick word?"
>
> Tom: "What is it, Mr Wilkins?"
>
> Mr Wilkins: "Do you know about the firm's concern about training?"
>
> Tom: "No, but I have heard rumours that there is some way over this."
>
> Mr Wilkins: "That's right. Do you think the senior Management are right to worry about training from where you stand in the company?"
>
> Tom: "Yes, I think so."
>
> Mr Wilkins: "Do you think supervisors like yourself could help us clarify what training we need to focus on?"
>
> Tom: "Yes, I was only talking with Jimmy the supervisor in the next section about this problem the other day . . . etc. etc."
>
> Mr Wilkins: "Thanks for that Tom. This has been very helpful in clearing my mind on this issue. How do you think the other supervisors might react to being actively involved in identifying areas where training is needed?" etc. etc.

What does Mr Wilkins do differently in Examples I and II?

1) List the different skills used.
2) List the advantages and disadvantages.

STOP READING HERE AND MAKE SOME OF YOUR OWN NOTES ON 1 AND 2.

1) Here is a list of points I have made about the skills being used in the two examples. Compare it with your own.

- *In I Wilkins makes his intentions clear and comes to the point rapidly and how he is going to approach the issue.*
- *In II there is a considerable use of questioning which enables Tom to participate and say something of what he thinks and feels.*
- *In II Wilkins expresses some respect for Tom's experience and knowledge.*
- *In I the focus is on being definite and authoritative.*

2) Here are my suggested lists of advantages and disadvantages associated with the two examples.

EXAMPLE I

Advantages	**Disadvantages**
Short and to the point	*Elicits no view about the ideas Tom has*
Very clear about what is intended	*It is not clear what Tom's agreement means, it is just a polite 'yes' and will he just forget about it later. Wilkins makes it very difficult for Tom to say "No" on any grounds or even qualifying his agreement*

EXAMPLE II

Advantages	**Disadvantages**
Wilkins finds out what Tom knows and feels to some extent.	*Takes some thought and time*
Gives Tom a chance to express his views	*Questions tend to be of the Yes/No type. Tom has to take the initiative when he elaborates and this might not always be to the point.*
Gets some idea what Tom's colleagues may be thinking	
Elicits a layout of data from Tom as a possible focus for training.	

In either part of this checkpoint you may have added other points on top of what I have suggested. If there is a considerable difference between the lists you and I have made, go over them and reflect on why that is. It may be that your approach to the same situation is different. If so reflect on why and if it is a better approach (for your situation) or not. As long as you are aware of how your view differs and why, this is the important thing.

2. My position on Conversations with subordinates
I think my position is clear enough, though I have not so far presented an explicit description of what I think is the correct approach to subordinates in the management of training.

I feel example II above is a much better approach (though not perfect) for the following kinds of reasons:

1. It is a more effective way of exchanging information, feelings and judgements.
2. It assumes the other person has something to contribute which is of value.
3. It does not **presume** ideas or opinions in the other without checking them out first.
4. It treats the other person with respect and attention to his own position and special expertise.
5. It underlines the fact that everyone has a useful contribution to make to a particular issue or task and helps them organise their relevant skills to the task.

All of these elements in the style of approach I think are important in interpersonal skills for all managers but are especially important in working as a trainer or co-ordinator of training in the work situation. The principles also apply, it goes without saying, in dealing with upper and senior management as well!

3. Open and Closed Questions
Just asking questions in conversations is not necessarily the cure-all to communication problems and I hope I have not given that impression so far. In all aspects of the exchange of information, feelings and judgements, it is the **kind of questions you ask that determines the range of the response.**

E.g. A standard opening greeting on a Monday morning in an office somewhere in Britain.

"Morning Jill, feeling well today?"

This implies a straight response of "yes" or "no" or "alright" plus a "thank you Mr Brown" or whatever. Indeed it contains an expectation that Jill will say "yes".

What do you think the results would be if she said "No" . . .?

PAUSE A MINUTE AND THINK: HOW WOULD YOU FEEL IF YOU WERE MR BROWN?

It would all depend on

- *The working relationship between Jill and Mr Brown*
- *If Mr Brown was just passing or expressing a* **real** *interest in Jill's response.*

In general such a remark is a form of greeting like "how are you" and expects the response "yes" or "alright thank you".

Anything else, like a long explanation about how she had a bad time with her mother or boyfriend, would demand a change in the interaction towards a more serious and longer conversation or personal matters, which Mr Brown and Jill might find embarrassing, upsetting or unprepared for!

The question is framed to get a **specific** *and* **suggested answer.**

If the greeter **really** wanted to know how Jill was feeling because it was important to him, how could he rephrase the question? Note down one or two alternatives that **you** might use in such a situation.

STOP READING AND MAKE A FEW NOTES

Two of many possibilities come to mind here.
What do you think of them?

1. *The person could* **make more specific** *their motives and interest in the other's feelings.*
   i.e. "What do you feel about . . . your job? Your schedule for today? doing some overtime today?" etc.
2. *They could* **share some information about themselves** *as a prompt to what they expect from the other.*
   i.e. "I've had a really lousy weekend and I'm glad to get back to work . . . how are you feeling today?"

Note, neither question can be answered by a "Yes" or "No". They require some definite response which the other person has the freedom to respond to in their own way. They are constrained by convention or the assumptions in the question to agree or disagree with you.

Closed Questions
Questions carrying the implication of a "Yes" or "No" answer are termed closed questions. They often:

- start with a verb:
  "Do you want to come out today?"
  "Will you be able to do . . . .?"
  "Did you enjoy the . . . .?"

* express a particular view which requires the other person's agreement or disagreement:
  "Will you accept that this is a better . . . ?"
  "Is this the right way forward?"
  "Do you like the proposed plan?"
* contain no request or give any invitation to the other person to explain **why** or **how** they agree or disagree with the questioner.
* elicit only acceptances or rejection of an idea or suggestion but no further information on the other person's views or ideas.

Open Questions
Open questions are a form of question designed to elicit information from the other, but do so in a way that allows the other to:
* say as much or as little as they feel they want to.
* use their own words and ideas, expressed in their way.
* interpret your question as widely or as narrowly as they see fit.
* express their own feelings and opinions and ask their own questions about the topic.

Open questions begin with words like "who", "what", "why", and "how". They avoid the impression of close interrogation and give you the chance to find out in some detail what the other person thinks.

Look over Example II (above) again.
1. note down which questions are **open** and which are **closed.**
2. take the closed questions, re-phrase them as open questions and see if they do the job more effectively.

STOP READING HERE AND MAKE NOTES ON 1 AND 2

1. "Do you know anything about . . . . training?"
"Do you think senior management . . . . stand?"
"Do you think supervisors . . . . focus on?"
are all closed questions. Tom has to say "Yes" and then he has to take the initiative to explain why he said "Yes".

"How do you think other supervisors might react . . . . training is needed?" is the only **open** *question used.*

2. The Closed questions could be re-phrased in the following way:
(a) What do you know about the firm's policy on training?
(b) What do you think should be the main concern in training from your position in the company?
(Leave out all mention of Senior Management lest he wants to say something that is at variance with what he knows they are interested in.)
(c) How do you think supervisors like yourself could help in clarifying what training we need?

I think these are better questions because they ask clearly what the manager wants to know and give the other person a chance to say what he really thinks without implying a set of assumptions that he has to agree with first. This helps him concentrate on the topic, not on the politics of agreeing or disagreeing with you or the Senior Management!

Problems with Open Questions
Providing space for the other person to say what he feels may well lead to several problematic consequences.

They may move off the point of the conversation into more general areas or expressions of feeling.

They may disagree or pour scorn on ideas you support and this may offend or irritate you.

The first problem is answered by:
(1) your **Careful framing of the question**
E.g. "What do you know about the recent courses we have been running on customer relations for the sales assistants?"
rather than
"What do you know about our training facilities."
(2) If you get a response that takes up other issues or expresses emotions and feelings rather than ideas on the topic of conversation, carefully steer the conversation by more questions that focus on the discussion.
E.g. "Yes, I see what you are getting at **but** what about the problems I mentioned before, what do you think about that?"
or "I can see you feel strongly about that. What **ideas** have you got which might solve the problem?"

Occasionally you will, having found out that they feel or think in a particular way, want to find out more.
"Could you say why you feel that way?"
"Why do you say that?"
"That's interesting, would you say more about that idea?"

Developing a conversation using open questions is less easy than it seems. But it is more fruitful in what is produced. In the beginning of this section we talked briefly about the difficulty we often have starting a conversation. Developing it can be difficult as well when the other person tends to be short on conversation. "Yes" and "No" answers don't take you on very easily and it becomes like a question and answer session. Open questions allow you to pick up much more information and this can be used to take the conversation on in a way that you know engages the other because you are talking about his ideas.

The only way to improve this skill is to practice it and try to get some feedback from someone else.

Exercise
Plan a conversation that is part of your day to day work in the training context and get a trusted colleague to sit in on the interchange with the task of noting down the questions you ask and to note down, with you, after the conversation, which questions were **open** and which were **closed.** Evaluate the effectiveness of the interchange and discuss how the questions might have

been better phrased and if open questions were (or could have been) better than the closed questions you used.

Alternatively
Try to note down the questions you typically ask in conversations you regularly have as a manager trainer with trainers or others. Use your own immediate experience as a prompt. Go through the questions you have written down. If you need to, re-formulate them as open questions and deliberately use them in their new form next time and check out how effective they are.

Tutor Seen Work

If you think if would be useful write a short report of this conversation and what you discussed about the way you use questions with your colleague. Send it in to me for additional comment. **Or** write a short self-evaluation of your use of questions and how you think you can improve it.

---

2. Listening Skills

Planning conversations and interviews, learning to frame the right questions and so on all leads up to the effective gaining of information and responding to it. All of this is of limited use if we are inefficient or poor listeners.

> LISTENING SKILLS ARE PROBABLY THE MOST IMPORTANT AREA OF COMPETENCE IN THE INTERPERSONAL SKILLS YOU WILL NEED IN THE CONTENT OF TRAINING.

One of the most flattering things you can say about another person is that he is a good listener. The fact that this is seen as a compliment shows how rare good listeners are. It can be a shock to realise what poor listeners we are. But often such a realisation only comes with the experience of **the difference it makes** when we listen effectively.

Here are some insights from people I have worked with about their listening skills when they have spent some time reflecting on how they listen:

> "I find I listen least when I am most anxious to speak."
>
> "I tend to stop listening when I think I know what the other person is going to say."
>
> "I miss a lot of what is said when I allow my mind to continue thinking about what is preoccupying me at the time."
>
> "I stop listening when I react to words about which I feel strongly, positively or negatively like "progressive", "tory", "Activist" or "expert".
>
> "I often find I have not listened to others when I have jumped to conclusions about what they are saying".
>
> "I find it really difficult to listen when there are disturbing words or sights nearby, or two or more people talking to me at once or when the other person goes on and on".

Picture in your mind a recent conversation with a colleague, trainee, trainer or senior manager. Note down the things you did which hindered your listening. Use the list of comments above as a prompt to your thinking, but include other things that occur to you.

As a help to organising your thoughts on paper the following headings might be useful:

- Things you know you do habitually in conversation (i.e. like interrupting or finishing off the other's sentences — that's what I find I do.
- Things you were aware of doing in this particular exchange you have remembered.
- The effects you think you had on the other person in this conversation — what do you think they felt or understood from what you did?

> STOP READING HERE AND TAKE SOME TIME TO MAKE NOTES. BE AS DETAILED AS YOU FEEL YOU NEED TO BE.

Keep and use these notes as reminders to yourself of what you do that makes your listening less effective. This will be the basis of your own programme of improvement.

1) Good Listening

Empathy and Listening
The value of empathy for the other in any social interchange was presented in Component II. Good listening is both a way of expressing empathy and is based on it. The central difficulty of listening is the requirement to be interested in what the other is saying and conveying that interest. To listen attentively is to give the other person complete attention for the time you are with them. The conveying of this attitude of attention to them makes them feel appreciated, important and gives them status. Likewise the opposite is true of inattentive listening.

> EMPATHY IS THE BASIC ATTITUDE OF GOOD LISTENING. TRYING TO STAND IN THE OTHER PERSON'S SHOES

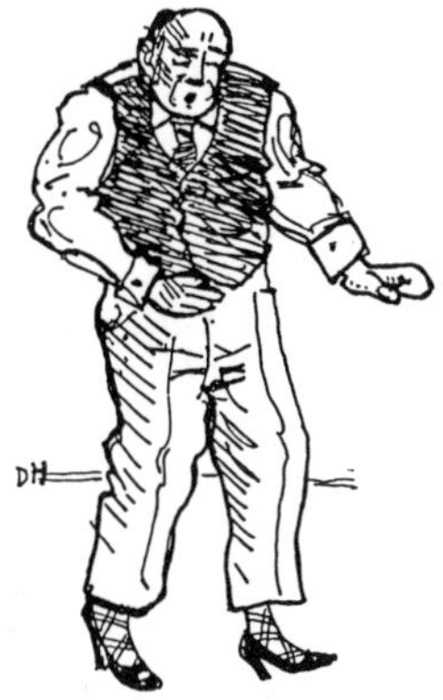

Active Listening
The process of listening is not simply waiting until the other finishes speaking. It is an active process that requires the listener full involvement. It requires you to **pay attention, understand, make clear and respond** to what the other is saying.

Reflective Listening
This is a deeper level of listening that we usually engage in, but which can be appropriate depending on the situation. It requires an active approach and aims to convey your understanding of the feelings of the other person, without necessarily agreeing with them. When the situation is heated or people are becoming upset or personally critical this is a difficult but important level of listening to use.

Listening techniques
All that has been said above implies a basic attitude to the activity of listening that expresses itself in **specific ways** of listening effectively.

As before, recall the kind of exchanges you regularly have with others in the training context. Think about (or re-read) what has been said above about listening. Note down the things **you think you should do** to listen effectively.

STOP READING HERE AND TRY TO LIST IN WORDS OR SHORT PHRASES WHAT YOU SHOULD DO.

Some things you will have noted down will be very specific to your own working situation. But here are some general points that good listening behaviour that I suggest apply to listening in any situation:

Good Listening Behaviours
* Clearing away feelings and thoughts from previous events.
* Giving full attention.
* Checking that you have heard accurately (ask clarifying questions).
* Listening for the main ideas.
* Remembering that we are liable to switch off when we disagree and stopping ourselves doing that.
* Giving encouraging signals.
* Looking at the person (though not too fixedly!)
* Re-stating what you think you have heard if you are not sure about it, or the point is a little complicated.
* Reflecting back to the other the feelings he is expressing, if any. (They might not always be aware of this!)
* Summarizing what has been said at the end (to allow the other to agree to that or to modify it).

For good measure, here are some things to avoid which you may also have noted:

Things to avoid in Good Listening
* Jumping to conclusions.
* Interrupting.
* Talking too much yourself.
* Thinking of what you want to say next.
* Picking up minor points.
* Ignoring what is being said.
* Pretending to understand when you don't.
* Being judgemental about what is being said.
* Defending your own point of view and not being open to others' ideas.

Check your own list with these and see how far you have covered them in your answer.

If your list is larger than mine and covers things you regard as important which I have not mentioned, that's fine. You have a good grasp of the complex process that listening is! Now think about how far you put these into practice!

Exercise
Look back at the notes you made earlier on how well you listen when talking to colleagues in day to day practice. Would you want to add to that list now? Develop a list of (a) what you are good at in listening and (b) what you need to improve on in your own listening skills.

STOP READING HERE AND MAKE NOTES UNDER THESE HEADINGS

From all the listed behaviour above I think I could list five TYPES of listening technique which might make a good check list of the main skills of listening:

1. CLARIFYING: to get additional facts and to help the other explore all the sides of the problem.

This type of technique is basic to the exchange of ideas as it helps **both** *people get clearer what they are talking about. In asking such questions the listener takes active responsibility for getting it right.*

2. RE-STATING: to check you are interpreting what has been said accurately or to show you have listened and understood.

This is similar to clarifying it is a way of expressing clearly to the other that you take what he is saying seriously — try to avoid putting words into their mouths, though — you always need to indicate you are open to correction.

3. ENCOURAGING: using verbal and non-verbal signals to show interest, encouragement to continue, etc.

A fundamental point here is that such signals should be an **actual** *expressing of interest and attention rather than simply a technique to show interest when you don't feel it. Pretence like this is easy to fall into but is rarely undetected by the other who will feel you are being dishonest.*

4. REFLECTING: to show you are aware of and understand how the other feels about what he is saying or to make him aware of the feelings he is expressing to you and to modify his behaviour if he wishes (or to correct your misunderstanding!)

It can be important for the other that you have noticed his feelings on a subject so he feels that this is noted. A studied attempt to ignore the other's feelings in the interest of getting the problem sorted out can make them seem unimportant and you insensitive. Also reflecting back his feelings gives him a chance to recognise he is communicating such feelings and to stop that if he feels it's getting in the way of what ideas he wants to communicate.

5. SUMMARISING: to bring all the discussion into focus in terms of a summary to serve as a basis for more discussion on a new aspect of the problem if necessary.

In a professional context, above all, this is an important skill. It is necessary to be clear what has been said, agreed, and planned and that both parties accept that summary (a kind of verbal "reading through and signing the minutes").

How are all these different types of listening techniques actually done?

For each technique note down what **you** might say with the form of words you might use to exercise that technique in a conversation. (You will find my suggestions on the next row down. If necessary use a ruler to block off that row while thinking of your own suggestions.)

Type of technique

Clarifying	
Re-Stating	**Suggested Answers** "Can you make that clearer?" "Do you mean . . .?) "Is this how you see it . . . ?"
Encouraging	"As I understand it then . . ." "So this is what you want to do and the reasons are . . ."
Reflecting	"I see" "Ah-hah" "Yes, very interesting" "I understand" "Tell me more"
Summarizing	"You feel that . . .?" "It was very upsetting for you" "You felt you were not properly consulted"
	"So these are the key ideas you have expressed . . ." "If I understand how you feel about the situation . . ." "Let's just be clear what we have agreed . . . is that what we decided"?

Clearly, you will not always have the same wording in your answers as in mine, but compare the tone and form of the words and see if they convey the same attitude of openness to the other, active interest and attention.

2. Listening and Questioning

It is obvious from the above that I see questioning as a part of the skills of listening. Thus much of what was said about questions and their form has some bearing on how we actively listen. The advantages and priority given to **open questions** may not **always** apply in listening, however. Opening and developing a conversation is best done from the basis of **open questions.** In active listening and concluding a conversation more specific and often closed questions are both allowable and often better suited to the task (cf. the questions suggested (p. 167) in the Clarifying technique).

Exercise

Practice is vital if you are to use or improve your listening skills. By now you should have some idea of what you need to improve on. Choose one aspect of effective listening from your list of "need to improve on . . ."

For example **Clarifying**

Think about what you need **to do** and **to avoid doing** to improve on this. Make a detailed list of questions to ask yourself.

e.g. Have I let the person finish what he was saying?
Have I been attending to what has been said?
Have I asked for points to be made clear?
Am I sure that I am clear about other points?
Have I listened to what has been said as fully as I can, not allowing my own ideas, feelings or judgements to get in the way?
Are my clarifying questions genuine, not a different form of point scoring etc. etc.

Then use this check list as a way of evaluating how you have conducted a particular conversation. Make a little time after a conversation to check out how far you did exercise the particular listening skill.

Alternatively, involve a sympathetic colleague in the process and get his reflections on how well you listen using a particular skill you both agree needs improving.

Tutor Seen Work

If you think it would be helpful to have another person to comment on what you have done. Write a short report on your own efforts at identifying and improving your listening skills and send it in to me for some comment and feedback.

Component 5:

Assertive Behaviour and the Training Role

Key Words

Assertive; rights; aggressive; manipulative; criticism; negative feelings; appreciation; skills of assertiveness; passive; submissive; unhelpful thinking.

After completing this Component you will:

* Be able to distinguish between aggressive, submissive and assertive behaviours.
* Understand the reasons why assertive behaviour is the most appropriate basis for a professional relationship in the training and managerial role.
* Be aware of the basic attitudes and skills needed to respond assertively in difficult situations.
* Have reviewed your own training situation and prepared to react in a more assertive way to the likely situations where such behaviour is appropriate.

1. The Nature and Importance of Assertive Behaviour

Read through the following examples.

Mike, one of your staff, is being considered for promotion. He has recently been involved in a couple of tricky situations which your boss, Jim thinks he did not handle well. Mike has a good record of success with you over the last two years. You believe he should be promoted. How do you approach the problem?

Your boss comes in and complains about the recent report you wrote which was not detailed enough for the meeting for which it was prepared. He is in a really bad mood and uses the opportunity to suggest that you are not really keen on the project, lacking in loyalty to the company and way over your head in the present job. You actually agree with him about the report but think he is totally wrong about the other things. How do you respond?

A trainee has not completed a project with a group of other trainees which was a central element in the course. He is causing great inconvenience to the others and there is no obvious reason why he alone has not done what was required. When you approach him he says that he has not had the time, he has too much to do, that he is hopeless at the work being required on the course and anyway the others have not helped him. How do you respond?

1. Difficult situations in the training role

In most managerial or administrative roles there are a variety of difficult situations that regularly occur to make life trying, more complicated than it should be and effectively get in the way of the work in hand.

Checkpoint

Is this general statement true for you in your own training role or in other aspects of your job?

If you think so, make a list of the kinds of situations you would describe as difficult or trying. Use the examples above as a prompt.

STOP READING HERE AND TAKE TWO OR THREE MINUTES TO MAKE A SHORT LIST.

Here are my suggested situations

* *Dealing with bad service and facilities*
* *Saying no to people when you have to*
* *Facing personal criticism over your professional behaviour*

* *Dealing with informed criticism of your work*
* *Giving criticism and comments on others' work*
* *Dealing with angry reactions in others*
* *Giving and accepting appreciation and thanks*

You might find it useful to compare this list with yours and note:
1. The difference.
2. If you think that some of my suggestions are strange.

Giving Criticism on Others' Work

Dealing with bad service

The situations outlined above are often difficult because we don't want to offend anybody, or because we get angry and irritated with people. We feel guilty for not responding as they expect us to and so on.

A lot of people, including myself, tend to react to these situations by being either aggressive and angry or submissive and trying to please. We tend to be one or the other in different situations. It seems to be an either/or situation with no middle ground. This Component aims to explore the middle ground, that of ASSERTIVE responses to such situations.

2. What is assertive behaviour?

* Being assertive IS NOT the same as being aggressive.
* It is the most appropriate form of behaviour for any professional role.
* There are THREE different types of behaviour that are commonly to be seen when people are involved in difficult situations where they feel guilty or feel they should be helpful and kind or feel they should not make a nuisance of themselves or feel stupid or incompetent or feel they should not be aggressive or demanding;

They can be SUBMISSIVE (non-assertive). They agree, go along with the situation, tell themselves it does not matter or it isn't worth the fuss.
They can be PASSIVE BUT MANIPULATIVE (non-assertive). They make people feel uncomfortable, though they may accept a service they feel is not good enough or comply to a request they do not want.
They can be AGGRESSIVE (non-assertive). They can get worked up, start fighting, determine that they will win whatever or blame the other for the problem.

* the fourth option is to respond ASSERTIVELY and this involves the following important characteristics:
  — it is the ability to put your ideas, opinions and feelings openly and directly without putting others down or demeaning yourself.
  — it is not aggressive or defensive.
  — it does not assume you can have everything you want all of the time.
  — it assumes that you have definite rights in the situation but also makes clear that you respect the rights of the other(s).
  — it is open to negotiations for a workable compromise.

The above list outlines the values and attitudes that lie behind the idea of assertiveness. BEING assertive is something more difficult.

* the basis for assertiveness lies in:

WHAT YOU SAY
AND
HOW YOU SAY IT

3. Assertiveness: What you say

People behaving assertively are likely to use the following verbal forms:

* 'I' statements like "I think . . .", "I want . . .", "My idea is . . .", I prefer . . ." etc. These indicate that the person is speaking for themselves.
* Statements that are brief and to the point; "I want to get started now . . ." rather than "Do you know what time it is . . . "The boss is expecting us now . . .", rather than "You don't want to be behind do you?"
* Keeping a clear distinction between fact and opinion;
  "My opinion is . . .", "I see it differently . . ." rather than "It is clear that . . ." or "No, it's not that . . .". This recognises that things are not always black and white and that there may be several legitimate ways of viewing things.
* Making constructive suggestions that are not strongly advisory;
  "How about starting here . . .?" rather than "If you want to do it properly you should start here . . ."
* Being constructively critical, stating facts not propounding judgements on peoples' characters; "This job has been completed late . . ." rather than "Why can't you ever get things done on time . . ."
* Making explanations clear;
  ". . . because this month there is nothing to get . . ."; ". . . this will lead to . . ."
* Using expressions that will open discussion on differences;
  "How can we get around that . . .?"; "Shall we . . .?" rather than "It's no use you going on about . . ." or "Will you listen to my point of view for a change. . . ?"

Here are some situations together with a response from someone in your position. See if you can tell which responses are aggressive, which are submissive or manipulative and which are assertive.

Note on this Checkpoint

My suggested answer to each situation is given in the column space immediately before the next situation (i.e. on the line below). You may like to use a ruler or a piece of card to cover the line below while you read and think about the responses illustrated, before checking your answer with mine.

Answer	Situation	Response
	A colleague in a different section has told someone you will help, without telling you, a junior manager drew up his financial returns! You say —	"What a cheek! Why didn't you ask me first? There's no way I can help. I'm far too busy! Why can't he send it out himself?"
Aggressive	A colleague agreed to come to a meeting and then failed to turn up. You write and say —	"Peter, I understood you were coming to the meeting. I would have liked you to be there. What happened?"
Assertive	One of your staff has asked for time off to visit a sick relative. But the department is working overtime to finish an urgent order. You say —	"I hope you won't think I'm mean, but Mr Smith the Manager, will not like you to take time off tomorrow. I'm very sorry."
Manipulative	Your boss wants John, a member of your staff to do a survey for her. You would like Harry, another member of your staff, to do it. You say —	"Well I don't know. John has just started an important project, but perhaps he could be taken off that; Harry won't be so good, but I could always help him out."
Submissive	You are going to do some photocopying when someone, who often asks for you to do her copying says "Can you just run off 30 of these for me?" You say —	"I'm usually happy to help you out, but I don't want to spend time on extra copying this morning."

Assertive	A colleague asks when you will be in your office again so he can arrange a meeting. You say —	"You'll see me when I walk in."
Aggressive	A member of staff tells you he wants to take responsibility for some enquiries. You say —	"what ever for? You know jolly well you're struggling to keep up with the filing — without doing extra work!"
Aggressive	A colleague asks you for a lift home. It's not convenient for you. You are already late. You say —	"I'm about 20 minutes late. I won't be able to take you home. If it helps I can drop you off at the bus stop."
Assertive		

4. Assertiveness; How you say it

We mentioned the attention we should pay to non-verbal behaviour in Component 1. In acting assertively this can be crucial. The following aspects of Non-Verbal Behaviour are important here;

VOICE
Steady and firm, tone middle range and warm.
SPEECH
Fluent, few hesitancies, emphasize key words, even pace.
FACE
Smile when pleased, frown when irritated, otherwise 'open' steady features, no grimaces and relaxed.
EYE CONTACT
Firm without staring fixedly.
BODY POSITION
Open hand movements, inviting, sit upright or relaxed or stand with head held up, avoid slouching or cowering.

Non verbal behaviour can be very important in being assertive because even when you get the words right, you can contradict what you say by the way that you say it.

Example

Don, the manager, comes to you and says, "I would like to hear your views on the new induction scheme for young trainees", then folds his arms firmly across his chest and stares at you fixedly and frowns.

Here Don has used clear language to express his demand, as we would hope in any professional exchange. He does not beat about the bush, or try to approach the point indirectly. But he does give the impression by his stance that he expects you to say something with which he will disagree or which will be 'wrong' in some sense. His stance does not convey an attitude of openness to the ideas he has asked you to share with him.

2. Your Rights and the Rights of Others

By now you may have a good idea why assertive behaviour is important. I have said enough to show how it may make your own role as a trainer or manager more effective. It would be dangerous to see the advice given here as simply a set of techniques to help you to handle others more effectively (that is, getting them to do what you want).

An important aspect of the idea of assertiveness is that it helps you to:

CLAIM YOUR OWN RIGHTS IN A WAY THAT DOES NOT IGNORE, BUT RECOGNISES, THE RIGHTS OF THE OTHER PERSON IN THE SITUATION

In being **submissive** we don't actually claim our rights.

In being **passive but manipulative** we neither claim our rights nor recognise the rights of the other.

In being **aggressive** we claim our own rights but often in a way which ignores or infringes the rights of the other.

1. The idea of rights

There is a lot of talk about rights. We hear people say they have a right to be consulted. At work we have rights spelled out by the management and the union representatives. Often we see rights as associated with confrontation and hostile argument and this may make us reluctant to be 'too demanding' or to see the issue of our own rights as something to be aggressive about.

RIGHTS ARE SIMPLY SOMETHING TO WHICH WE ARE ENTITLED
AND
WHICH WE HAVE THE DUTY TO RESPECT IN OTHERS

This assumes we are clear about what rights we can claim and should respect in others, which is not always so.

It also assumes that our claim to specific rights is based on something that others recognise, or should recognise.

Our rights are based on:

* The law
* Our beliefs and what we value
* The assumptions underlying the idea of assertiveness.

The following list of rights are broadly those I would associate with the idea of assertiveness:

* **You are the ultimate judge of yourself**
  You take final responsibility for your behaviour, thoughts and emotions. When you make decisions it is you, not others, who do it and take the initiative and the consequences.
* **You have the right to express your views and ideas**
  These should be listened to and treated with serious attention even if they are different from everyone else's.
* **You have the right to say no**
  You should be able to say no without feeling guilty or having to justify yourself to them.
* **You have the right to refuse a request**
* **You have the right to be wrong sometimes**
  No one has the right to expect you to be perfect. You don't have to feel guilty when you make mistakes. You also have the right to face the consequences of your error!
* **You have the right to change your mind or admit you don't know.**
* **You have the right not to take responsibility:**
  — for solving other people's problems
  — for other people's feelings, which doesn't mean that you should ignore them or act insensitively towards them.
  — for other people's perceptions of what you say, believe, want etc.
* **You have the right to have others respect your rights.**

Read the following examples.

Can you detect which rights of assertiveness are being denied Jim or which Jim is failing to claim?

A. Jim; "This report will not do, it's very poorly typed."
Bob; "Don't blame me, I'm not responsible for hiring the typist, anyway I'm very busy and you're so pernickety these days!"
Jim; "Sorry Bob, maybe it will do, don't get upset."

B. Jane; "You've really landed me in it this time, haven't you? I don't ask you for a favour very often and now you tell me you have to go home for something or other!"
Jim; "well . . . I suppose I could stay for a little . . . but you should have had this set of invoices organised last week."

C. Jim; "What did you think of my production plan, do you think it overcomes the difficulties we have been having?"
Henry; "Yes, it's all very well worked out, but why do you insist on ignoring the production manager's viewpoint on this? I suggest you think how your plan can be made to fit the company's tradition and style . . . Can't you go along with us, Jim?"

STOP READING HERE AND MAKE SOME NOTES IN ANSWER TO EACH EXAMPLE.

A. Jim does not exert his right to the right standard of service in the face of Bob's aggressive response.
B. Jane tries to get Jim to take responsibility for some of her problems. She succeeds. Jim feels he cannot say no. He does not assert his right not to take responsibility for Jane's problems.
C. Henry ignores Jim's right to express his views, even though they are different from others'. He does not treat the plan on its merits and tries to get Jim to change his views on the basis of vague ideas about "the company's tradition and style."

All these rights of assertiveness are based on the assumption that all people are equally deserving of respect in the work situation and are all responsible for their actions as adults and professionals or skilled workers.

Because of your own values and beliefs, you may be unhappy to agree that all the rights listed above are due to you. You may feel that you cannot claim those rights or should not because your own personal philosophy or religious view contradict what they imply.

Check this list of rights set out above.
Read each one carefully and reflect on:
whether you believe it to be true for you
whether you believe it to be true for others.

One way to think about this is to check your own thinking and behaviour towards yourself and towards others.

Examples:
When I make a mistake, do I tell myself that I should be better or that I am incompetent or that I had better not let anyone else find out? All these are messages to myself that deny the right to make mistakes and take responsibility for the consequences.

When someone I deal with makes a mistake do I blame them by criticizing them personally or giving immediate and negative judgements on their competence for the job they are doing? Or do I move in too quickly and say it doesn't matter or that there's no harm done? Both responses deny the right to make mistakes and to take the responsibility for the consequences.

Take some time to reflect and make notes on each of the rights listed.

Now look at what you have noted down. Have you been as honest with yourself as you can?

---

3. The Skills of Assertiveness

The way we translate the ideas discussed so far into effective professional practice is through identifying and practicing particular skills. Particular situations call for different types of skill.

There is nothing mysterious about these skills. As we go through them you will recognise them in yourself and in others with whom you work. What we all frequently need to do is to make ourselves aware of them and how well and appropriately we use them, as in the earlier components concerning conversations.

In fact, you should look on assertiveness as another set of skills that improves your ability in conducting conversations in the training context.

We can't cover all the necessary skills in the space available so I will try to help you examine the following:

* saying 'no'
* dealing with Bad Service
* dealing with criticism
* dealing with angry reactions.

1) Saying 'no'

saying no to requests is something we all find difficult sometimes. When we do say no or refuse someone, we often feel guilty. Yet it is improtant in the management of training to be able to say no, decline a request or assert your priorities.

We may need to get things done in a short time, prepare to meet urgent orders for your product, get to an important meeting etc. Then the manager or a close colleague makes a sudden demand on our time that will stop us doing what we had planned.

They will say they knew they could rely on us, it will only take a short time, one good turn deserves another, you are the only person who can do it well, you are the only person who understands their problems . . . etc. etc.

Sometimes we are clear enough in our mind what NEEDS to be done and we find it more or less easy to say no without offending them. But often it is much more difficult.

Who do you find it is most difficult to say 'no' to?

* door salesmen?
* a stranger?
* a colleague?
* your boss?
* a lover or spouse?
* your parents?
* your children?

1. Make a few notes to yourself here. You might try ranking them from the most difficult to the least. Don't think too hard or too long, just do it off the top of your head. You may surprise yourself!
2. Now try to think why it is you feel you should not say 'no' to your parents or boss or whatever. Note down all the good reasons you can think of which you use when tempted to say 'no'.

STOP READING HERE AND BRIEFLY COMPLETE TASKS 1 AND 2.

Here is a list of some of the things I often say to myself when I find saying 'no' difficult. Compare them with your own notes.

Saying no will hurt or upset people.
Saying no will lead people to like me less.
Saying no on small things looks petty and inflexible.
Saying no is selfish and uncaring.
If I say no directly, it will make me seem rude.

Some of these reasons may be true sometimes and being aware of them can be a sign of the ability to respond to people. But they are not ALWAYS true. Even if they are true, maybe that is not as important as we think.

ONE OF THE MAIN BARRIERS TO ASSERTIVE SKILLS DEVELOPMENT IS UNHELPFUL THINKING

This is the thinking that is represented in the reasons for not saying 'no' that you and I have listed a few moments ago. It comes from all the conditioning and habits we have been brought up with and carry around with us. You will probably have noticed that few of them refer to the nature of the request and most refer to how others will react to us. (Your list may be better than mine in this respect.)

HOW TO THINK IN A MORE HELPFUL WAY ABOUT REQUESTS
Ask yourself some of these kinds of questions:
- Is the request possible to fulfil?
- Have they the right to ask me to do this?
- How much can people expect of me?
- Should I do it anyway? Is it legal, moral, against my better judgement?

Our answers to these questions to ourself are a more helpful way of assessing when to agree and when to say no, **rather than what others might think.**
In saying 'no' we have to accept these two beliefs:
'I have the right to say no'
'When I refuse a request I do not reject the person'

Saying No: Basic Techniques

1. The broken record

This means simply that in saying no to someone, you simply keep repeating the same message no matter what they say to try to tempt you off it. This can be very difficult, especially if you don't want to convey the impression that you are not rejecting the person.

Example:

Bill: Hi Barbara, are you going to the staff dance?
Barbara: No.
Bill: How about coming with me? I've got no one to go with.
Barbara: No, thanks.
Bill: Oh, come on. You work too hard, and don't go out enough.
Barbara: No, I really don't want to go.
Bill: It will do you good, you know — a bit of fun.
Barbara: I really have not got the time.
Bill: You know people will see you as a dull, frowsy thing if you never join in anything. Why don't you make time for this?
Barbara: I just don't feel like it.

Do you think Barbara has succeeded in being assertive? Has she effectively got across what she wants and closed the conversation?

STOP READING HERE AND NOTE DOWN YOUR ANSWERS TO THIS.

Barbara has stopped asserting her refusal and started to make excuses to justify her position. That is a signal to Bill that she feels the need to defend her refusal and is not so sure about it. This encourages him to continue:

Bill: Quite a few people can't go. It could be a bit of a flop if we all opt out. I don't really fancy it, but I think we ought to go and support it.
Barbara: Well we don't have to go. It's not compulsory.
Bill: Look Barbara I'll be honest with you. Since my wife died last year, I have hardly been out at all. I've not wanted to. But I really want to make an effort this time, and I thought you, as an old friend, might help.
Barbara: Well, if you put it like that . . . .

Barbara has lost touch with her broken record. Bill's chance of getting her to accept or of her getting angry gets higher. Notice he is not being assertive either, but manipulative. He is not being direct with his own request and he is ignoring her right not to do what he wants. The different forms of Bill's manipulation are quite common:—

* *'you work too hard'*
* *'it will do you good'*
* *'people will see you as dull'*
* *'we ought to support it'*
* *'I thought you as an old friend might help'*

All are designed to get Barbara to assume responsibilities that she is not required to, in the interests of getting her to accept.

Other Techniques that can be helpful

*** Ask for more information**

This technique can be used with the broken record and helps to give time before you answer. If someone asks you to run a training course, you should ask for details, time, length, dates before saying yes or no.

*** Ask for more time**

You may need to think about your answer, to reflect on what is involved. No one can demand instant replies to all requests.

*** Don't give excuses**

When you refuse, a polite, but firm 'no' is all that is needed. Like Barbara did at the beginning of the conversation. Excuses only cloud the issue and reduce you to being apologetic, as well as giving potential ammunition to the other to try more manipulation. It is often clear to both parties that excuses are not genuine. You don't have to justify saying no.

*** Don't hang around**

There is a strange feeling that when we have turned down a request we should stay a while. Maybe because we want assurance that the other person will not follow up with a personal rejection. It is a symptom of the guilt we sometimes feel for saying no. You should try to complete a refusal with a polite exit-line unless that is socially inappropriate, and leave. You can always check out the other person's feelings later.

*** Take personal responsibility for saying no**
Say "I don't want to" or "I don't feel like it" rather than "I can't" or "I don't think my wife/boss/husband/friend would approve".

*** Practice saying 'no'**
Some people find great difficulty in saying no and will use other verbal contortions to avoid it. Practice hearing what it sounds like when you say it and adjust the tone and expression to suit it to the different circumstances when you might have to use it.

Exercise
Think of a situation recently in your work situation when you had to say no or wanted to say no.

Write out a short account of what you remember happening and how you felt.

Now check against the points made above and see how far your actions matched the behaviour suggested.

Make a list of those skills you think you are not so good at when saying 'no' and plan to give them some attention.

Tutor Seen Work

You might find it useful to make detailed notes on this, then draw up a plan of action to improve your ability in this area to send in to me for comment. Alternatively, ask a trusted colleague to help you to improve by observation or comment on how you usually operate with others.

Remember they have the right to refuse, **without** rejecting you!

2) Dealing with bad service
It is often a problem in the training context, when dealing with the ancillary staff, or the training providers, trainees or even your boss, to insist that they do what they are contracted to do or specifically employed to do in a satisfactory way. You have a right to expect the accepted standards of work in your company and to ask for this if it is not forthcoming.

We all occasionally produce work that is not up to standard, sometimes more than occasionally! When we do, we have a battery of excuses to pass it off!

'It looks alright to me'
'It's not my responsibility' (this is my favourite one)
'I'm overworked, it's the best I can do'
'It's not down to me to see so-and-so'
'You're holding up my work by complaining'

None of these responses have anything to do with the point that the work or service that has been provided is not good enough. They are distractors to put off the person who is complaining.

The Broken Record (again!)
The basic technique in making an assertive demand of any kind is to state clearly what you feel you have a right to and to politely insist by repeating that demand no matter what the other person says in response. You have to be very clear that it is your right to demand this and to convince yourself beforehand or you might find yourself blustering and becoming aggressive (or submissive) if you are unsure.

Example

Jane: This course programme needs re-drafting for typing right away, it's very late and it's holding up the schedule.

Tom: O.K. I'll see to it when I can.

Jane: I want it ready for typing today, Tom.

Tom: I'm rushed off my feet today; Pam is away, so I can't find the time to do it.

Jane: I guess that makes things difficult, but I want this ready for typing today.

Tom: Can't you make the changes in pen? It would help me.

Jane: No, Tom, I need the programme carefully re-drafted today.

Tom: You know, Mrs Williams, we wouldn't have this trouble if we had been given a word-processor, as promised.

Jane: Well, I can see that must be annoying you, but I want the programme re-drafted today.

Tom: Oh alright, leave it here. I'll try to get it done now.

There are some important things to note in this exchange:

* Jane does not follow up the excuses or complaints, she simply notes them sympathetically. She has the right not to take responsibility for Tom's problems.
* She does nothing but repeat her request with assertion and without aggression.
* She was clear in her own mind that she had the right to ask Tom to do the task in the stated time. She does not waver.
* She remained calm and uncritical. She did not get impatient or comment on Tom's lack of competence or go into all the problems she is having to cope with.

Having avoided all the diversionary offers, Jane makes Tom face the issue of agreeing to do what she asks or refuse. In the interests of good working relations, too many such direct exchanges, where Tom has to comply, with Jane's apparent disregard for his problems, is not desirable and some workable compromises are useful. The above exchange could have been concluded as follows:

Tom: OK I'll re-draft it, it is a bit late. I'll see if I can re-schedule some other work. Will it be alright if I give it to you first thing in the morning?

Jane: That's alright Tom, I can see you are snowed under here. First thing in the morning will do fine, thanks

Make some notes on a recent situation where you had to ask for better work or service, try to recall how you handled it.

Were you apologetic or did you accept the first excuse you were given? (submissive)

Did you try to make the other feel guilty? (manipulative)

Did you criticise the other's competence or personal qualities? (aggressive)

How far do you feel you acted assertively?

Use the examples and discussion above to assess your own abilities.

---

3) Dealing with criticism

Criticism can be the most difficult thing to deal with effectively. It usually makes us defensive, react emotionally, start blaming others or feel inadequate. All this gets in the way of good working and training relations.

It is important to be clear that there are different types of criticism and to be able to recognise them quickly. Two of the most important forms of criticism to distinguish are:

INFORMED CRITICISM OF YOUR PROFESSIONAL COMPETENCE

This is usually well-intended and is usually made in a constructive or supportive way. It is focussed on what you DO and how it effects the other person. It can be given with a genuine attempt to help you reflect on how you do your job, or part of it. Or it can be an expression of irritation from the other. **In either case it is potentially useful to you.**

* remember you have the right to make mistakes, but recognise the right of others to give criticism when you have made them.
* they do not have the right to draw conclusions about your worth as a person because of the mistake.

PERSONAL, PREJUDICIAL CRITICISM AND PUT-DOWNS

These are what we all usually mean by criticism. They are usually hurtful and often intended to be. Trying to be clear whether they are a form of attack or simply the other's inept attempt to deal with you in a difficult situation, is important.

* while it is nice to have others' approval, you have the right to be the final judge of yourself as a person.

INFORMED CRITICISM is often the expression of assertiveness towards you by others;

"Well John, I feel you made heavy weather of that interview, I think you talked too much and occasionally missed what the other chap said."

It should not be treated as a personal attack and given a defensive response.

"Oh yes? Well I'd like to see you do any better!"

It requires an assertive response;

"You're right, I must watch that next time."

or

"I don't agree, I feel I handled it quite well."

PERSONAL CRITICISM is often a form of manipulation or aggression.

"Late again, you are so unreliable, you don't care about anything."

Because the other person has led into the conversation with aggression, there is a strong temptation to react aggressively back;

"What's the matter with you then? Has the boss been at you about that shambles last week?"
or to respond submissively like a child when it's told off;

"All right, I'm sorry. I won't do it again."

1. Dealing with Informed Criticism

It is important to remember that you have a right to make mistakes and so do the people you work with. You also have the right not to feel guilty or to expect others to feel guilty about errors and misjudgements. What you do have a right to do is expect others to learn from mistakes and that they have the right to expect this of you.

In dealing with what you see as informed criticism:

* respond assertively not with aggression or defensiveness;
* accept that criticism which you see as valid;
* do not accept criticism that you think is invalid and show that you recognise it is the other person's view;
* if you think it is needed, assert a contrary statement.

John: "You haven't been very helpful in our committee meetings so far."
Peter: ".."

If Peter feels this is not true how should he respond to John?

Try writing out one or two assertive responses to this criticism.

STOP READING HERE AND COMPLETE THE CHECKPOINT.

I think Peter's response should go along the following lines;

'I don't agree. I feel I have been quite helpful."

A slightly less direct response, which might inform Peter what John is getting at, might be;

"What makes you say that John? I think I have been quite helpful."

Unclear criticism

When the criticism is informed but unclear, it is important to clarify before responding. You need to do this assertively, with an even tone to your voice, looking directly at the other person and conveying some warmth and encouragement.

> **Unhelpful thinking** in this situation often takes the form of:
> "He's at it again, always nit-picking what I do!"
> or
> "Oh no! Another clanger! I never get it right!"
> This needs to be restrained or ignored because it is the stimulus for aggressive or submissive responses.

Your responses here should be aimed at gaining information;

"Can you give me some specific examples of what you mean?"

"I'd like you to tell me what sort of thing you have in mind."

2. Dealing with Personal Criticism and Put-downs

The strategy just outlined above can be a good starting point in dealing with personal criticism.

Asking for information gives you;

* time to clear your mind of any unhelpful thinking;
* may result in some clearer communication;
* directs the conversation off emotional comments and onto information about what has been done or not done;
* allows you to respond without aggression or defensiveness.

Because of these advantages, asking for information and/or clarification is the usual FIRST STAGE in responding to criticism or aggression.

"When did this happen Harry?" "Why do you say that Mary?" "What actually happened?" "Can you give me some specific examples?"	ASKING FOR INFORMATION
"What do you mean by . . .?" "Can I just check. What you are saying is . . . ?" "When you say . . . what were you thinking of?" "So have I got it right; what you are saying is . . . ?"	CLARIFYING AND CHECKING

As before, the manner in which you ask these questions is important. **Speaking slowly** may help to quieten the other and to make the conversation more reflective and less emotional. **Allowing the other person to talk** also helps in this. **Never interrupt** before the other has finished and make sure they have finished before you respond. This gives you time to think and to allow the other to get things off their chest if they are angry.

Making clear where you stand on the issue and

showing some understanding of the other's point of view is the second stage in responding assertively to personal criticism.

"I don't think I have ignored your requests Mary, but I'd like to hear why you feel I have."

Or;

"I see you feel strongly about this Mary, but I really don't agree with what you have just said."

AN EXERCISE TO TEST YOUR ASSERTIVE RESPONSE TO PUT DOWNS

Here is a list of the different types of common put-downs you may meet with as well as an example:

1. INSINUATING

"I expect you have quite a light load in your new job."

2. PATRONISING

"Don't worry your little head about that. We'll look after it."

3. MAKING DECISIONS FOR YOU

"What I'd do is spend less time on this part of your job."

4. SUGGESTING YOU ARE LYING

"Oh come on, you know that's not what he meant."

5. STEREOTYPING YOU

"That's typical of the way all you women in administration think!"

6. NAGGING

"How much longer are we going to have to wait for those invoices?"

7. QUESTIONING YOUR VALUES, JUDGEMENT OR BELIEFS

"You don't really believe that do you?"

"Are you sure you will be on schedule?"

8. MAKING PERSONAL REMARKS

"You are too nice to tell him he's not doing well enough."

9. USING EMOTIVE WORDS

"That was a crazy decision!"

"You were irresponsible in not telling me sooner".

A. Write down your own modified list of put-downs so that it is closer to the things that have been said to you in your own working situation.

B. Next to each example of a put-down or personal criticism write down your own assertive response.

STOP READING NOW AND COMPLETE THE TWO TASKS IN YOUR OWN TIME.

Now compare your responses to the ones suggested below. If they are different it does not mean they are wrong. The responses should be assertive in STATING YOUR POSITION and showing that YOU WILL NOT LET THE CRITICISM SUCCEED.

1. *"What makes you say that?"*
2. *"I'm not worried about it, but I am concerned."*
   "I'm happy to look after it myself thanks."
3. *"I appreciate your concern, Bill, but I'd like to make that decision myself."*
4. *"That certainly is the way I saw it."*
5. *"I don't believe it's typical. It's only the way I'm thinking about THIS problem."*
   "I don't accept it's typical. It's what **I** *feel about it."*
6. *"Why are you asking?"*
   "I understand that you are in a hurry to have it. But I will need to spend at least another day on it."
7. *"Yes, I believe that."*
   "Yes, it will be on schedule."
8. *"I do not see it that way."*
   "I don't agree with you, I am able to do what is needed when I decide to."
9. *"I'm not really happy with the decision now. But I don't think it was crazy,"*
   "I accept it was a mistake not to let you know, but I would not describe it as irresponsible."

It is important to note that being assertive is not the same as denying any criticism that you receive. As in the last two examples here, it is important to assert your own view of your actions even when that is a little negative. You have the right to make mistakes and the right to have them assessed on professional criteria, not personal or emotive responses from others.

Dealing with angry and aggressive reactions

Sometimes we have to deal with someone who is in a very angry mood and convinced that we are to blame. Or they use us as the nearest person on which to express their frustrations.

In dealing assertively with this situation the two stages outlined above, are a powerful and effective way of taking the heat out of the situation. But they may not always be enough. The aggression may continue.

EXAMPLE	TYPE OF RESPONSE	
"You are always ignoring my requests in this department since you took over."	STEREOTYPING/ PERSONAL COMMENT	
"Could you explain what you mean, Peter?"	ASKING FOR INFO.	1. FIRST STAGE
"It's typical of you to give us lower priority!"	MORE PERSONAL COMMENT	
"What makes you say that, Peter?"		
"You just ignore us here . . ."		
" I see you have strong feelings on this Peter, but I don't agree with what you have just said."	SHOWING EMPATHY/ SHOWING WHERE YOU STAND	2. SECOND STAGE
"You wouldn't, would you, you're too nice to get your department to pull its finger out!"	GENERALIZED PERSONAL COMMENT	
"Peter, you really make me annoyed when you make statements like that. You make it more difficult for me to get my staff to make the effort to meet your requests."	EXPRESS NEGATIVE FEELINGS/ MAKE AWARE OF CONSEQUENCES	3. THIRD STAGE
"Oh, alright . . . but we really need that job completed. I'm worried that we'll get very badly behind."	RELUCTANT ASSERTION OF ANXIETY AS REAL BASIS OF THE DEMAND	
"I'll see what we can do to speed it up."	CONCILIATORY CLOSE	

In this example, Peter is only momentarily slowed down by the request for clarity (1) and the response that ignores the personal attack. He has to be faced with a definite statement of where you stand (2) and a follow-up with an expression of how his continued aggression makes you feel that the effect that might have on the job (3).

This last is the THIRD STAGE of assertive response to personal criticism or aggression which may need to be used on occasions. It consists of making quite clear how you feel about the way you are being treated, with some attempt to make clear the effect this has on your ability to do the job in question.

In very difficult cases even this is not enough and you need to move to a FOURTH STAGE. Say, Peter, in our example above, is not prepared to concede your right not to be subjected to his personal criticisms. Instead of grudging assertion he continues with aggression:

> "Your feelings? What about my feelings? It just is not good enough. It's your fault. You always ignore our requests. You never really rate what we do, do you? It's just typical of your department."

Here, you are being drawn back into the general and stereotyped criticisms that he started with. You need to close down the discussion or set it on a new footing, away from the track that Peter seems set on.

Three different approaches can be used in the FOURTH STAGE:

1. Make clear the consequences of further aggression;
   "If you continue to make unwarranted and personal attacks on me and my department, I'll want to take it up officially with the section manager."

   or

   "If you continue in this way, we will deal with your requests strictly according to the book."
2. Simply close down the conversation and say why;
   "I don't feel we are making any progress. Can we meet again tomorrow when we have had time to think about the problem?"

   or

   "I'm not prepared to continue in this way, while you continue to make personal comments on me or my staff, can we . . ."
3. Try to talk about why the issue is so heated;
   "Why are you so upset about all this, Peter? You are coming on so strong I'm finding it difficult to keep the job in mind,"

Can you describe in outline the FOUR stages of assertive response to someone who is being aggressive and/or making personally critical remarks?

STOP READING HERE AND SEE IF YOU CAN COMPLETE THE TASK WITHOUT USING THE TEXT.

The four stages are:

1. *Ask for information or try to clarify the issue.*
2. *Make clear where you stand on the issue and show you know what the other feels about it.*
3. *Express your feelings on the personal criticism as clearly and calmly as you can.*
4. *Make clear the consequences of the other's action, close down the conversation or try to shift the focus onto what is going on the feelings between you rather than the job itself.*

Self appraisal exercise

YOUR RIGHTS OF ASSERTION: A SELF APPRAISAL QUESTIONNAIRE

How do you respond to the following statements? On a separate piece of paper note down the number of the statement and whether you:

Agree Strongly .... AS		
Agree .... A		USE THESE
Are not convinced either way .. NC	}	SYMBOLS
Disagree .... D		IF YOU WISH
Disagree strongly .... DS		

1. I have the right to choose my own priorities.
2. I have the right to be heard when I want to say something.
3. I have the right to say what I am feeling.
4. I have the right to my own physical space, one which no one else may intrude.
5. I have the right to say 'no' to their requests without explaining.
6. I have the right to have an explanation of others' actions when they affect me.
7. I have the right not to express myself if I wish not to.
8. I have the right to to make mistakes without feeling guilty about them.
9. I have the right to ask for what I want.
10. I have the right to spend some time each day as I wish.
11. I have the right to insist I get what I pay for.
12. I have the right to break with tradition or convention if I wish to do so.

Now add up all the AS's, A's, DS's, D's and NC's in four separate totals.

To work out your ATTITUDE TO ASSERTIVENESS score, complete the following calculations;

Multiply the AS total by 5
" " A " " 4
" " NC " " 3
" " D " " 2
" " SD " " 1

Your attitude to assertiveness score is the sum total of all these sub-totals.

IF YOU SCORED MORE THAN 45
You are basically assertive in your attitudes
IF YOU SCORED 30–35
You might review your attitude to see if you really agree with an assertive style.
IF YOU SCORED BELOW 30
You really have little strong affinity with the idea of being assertive. You will need to ask yourself why and if you can work effectively without some change in this area.

It is important to treat this exercise as a simple and crude way of checking out how far the ideal of assertiveness is one you hold or wish to hold. It is in no sense an accurate measure of your personality. Use it to reflect on your own thinking and to try to assess yourself in this matter.

Tutor Seen Work

If you want to develop a clearer picture of your own assertive behaviour and to improve it, I suggest you follow the structured task laid out below. You can do it for yourself alone or in preparation for a discussion with a trusted and supportive colleague or to send to me for comment and feedback.

Developing Personal Assertion

You can develop your assertive behaviour by examining four areas of your activity.

* The things you do to increase assertiveness
* The things you don't do that increase assertiveness
* The things you avoid doing that decrease your assertiveness
* The things that you do that decrease your assertiveness

To help you to organise these reflections on paper, draw a layout on a separate piece of paper as shown below. Make sure you leave enough space below each area to fill in, in as much detail as you wish, your own assessment of your behaviour.

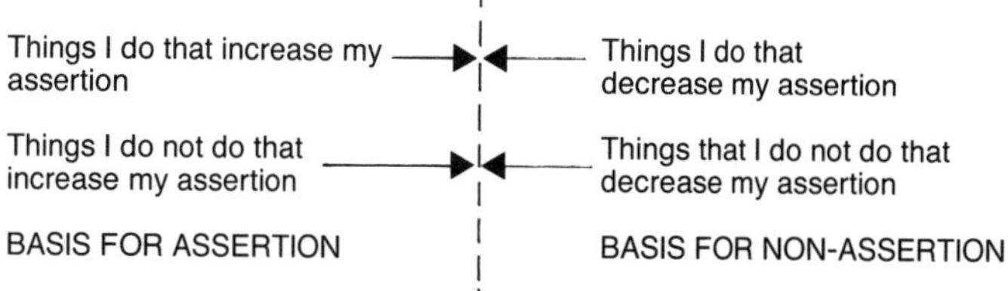

To develop your assertiveness you need to increase the behaviours on the left hand side of the diagram and to decrease the behaviours on the right hand side of the diagram.

In short, can you make a list of:

WHAT IS STOPPING YOU BEING ASSERTIVE
&
WHAT IS HELPING YOU BE ASSERTIVE

From these lists can you draw up a list of:

ACTIONS YOU CAN TAKE TO REDUCE WHAT STOPS YOU

&

ACTIONS YOU CAN TAKE TO INCREASE WHAT HELPS YOU

On the basis of these lists draw up a plan of action as extensive as you wish that you have some chance of implementing in your own professional life, in particular, in your role as a trainer.

The plan of action should be based on clear statements to yourself on:

* THE STEPS YOU WILL TAKE TO IMPROVE THE SITUATION.
  This could include a focus on particular attitudes and actions you find difficult or new to your way of acting.
* THE RESOURCES YOU WILL NEED
  This might include time, people, a framework for checking how well you are doing, extra patience from your colleagues and so on.

Please feel free to send me the results of your thinking for comment and further suggestions. I hope you find the exercise useful and enlightening and a help in improving your training and managing style!

I would be glad to hear about any other aspect of assertive behaviour that you have found difficult.

Component 6:

Making Critical and Evaluative Comments on Trainees' Performance

Key Words

Critical comment; praise; appreciation; specific actions; training situation; manager; submissive; organise; assertive.

When you have completed this Component you will:

* have a good idea why giving critical comments well is important
* have a good idea why expressive appreciation to trainees is important in managing training
* be able to plan how to approach another to give critical or appreciative comment
* be able to help trainees think about their own performance and to take some responsibility for changing it.

I. Giving Effective Criticism

In the management of training, the following situations are likely to confront you at some time or other:

A trainee, having started a course continually turns up late, or is not applying himself to the work as required.

A trainer or instructor is upsetting a group of trainees by his behaviour and is putting them off the training course.

These and other situations require us to confront other people with some critical comments on their behaviour or performance. This is an important aspect of the effective management of training in any firm. However it is often very difficult to do well.

1. Why do we Criticize or Avoid Criticizing?
The objective in giving critical comment is almost always to get the other person to change the way they operate and to improve the training situation.

But we don't do it because we feel we would:
upset the other person
make the other embarrassed
make them angry
seem to be dominating them or setting ourselves up as better people
spoil a good working relationship with them
cause them to like us less
provoke them to look critically at **our** performance.

The result of this kind of thinking usually leads us into avoiding confronting others at all or only when we are forced to.

This is often a sign of a SUBMISSIVE approach to such situations

By contrast, some of us see our role as managers precisely as being able to give out critical comment on other's performance We see it as part of the job to tell people off and we don't want to:

let anyone get away with anything
feel that they can put one over on us
get the impression we are not in charge
let anyone develop bad habits
give the impression we are not on top of things
give the impression we are afraid to upset others and not be popular.

This kind of thinking results in us looking for confrontation and for opportunities to make critical comments to others.

This can often be a sign of an AGGRESSIVE response to such situations.

Checkpoint

When you have been involved in managing the training in your firm and you have been faced with unsatisfactory performance, have you found yourself:

1) Avoiding the issue and delaying or raising the issue apologetically?
or
2) Getting worked up into an angry mood so that you feel able to tell them what's what?
or
3) Operating in any other way, distinct from these two reactions?

Think about a particular situation in your own recent experience where you were faced with difficulties because of someone else's poor performance. If you choose option (3) make some brief notes to yourself on **what** you did and if this is typical of the way you think you act in such situations.

STOP READING NOW AND MAKE SOME NOTES FOR A FEW MINUTES

If you tend to react as in option (1) you are being submissive (non-assertive) in your response.
If you tend to react as in option (2) you are being Aggressive (non-assertive) in your response.
If you have chosen option (3) and made some notes you may have written something like the following.

I don't get worked up and I don't avoid the issue. I say as calmly as I can that this or that behaviour is below standard or unacceptable or I insist that some improvement is necessary for the sake of the job. I try to get the other person to see what is wrong and see if they can identify the reason for it.

If you have some or all of this contained in your notes, then your habitual response is Assertive and likely to be a way of giving criticism that helps to improve the situation. That, after all, is the prime objective.

---

2. Why give Critical Comments to Others?
In deciding how, or it, we should give critical comments on others, when managing training, it is important to be clear why we are giving it.

Which of the following reasons do you think are appropriate for you to give critical comment?

1) To let others know that you are angry and irritated by their behaviour.
2) To let off steam when someone has disappointed or upset you.
3) To frighten them into better work habits.
4) To show you are in charge.
5) To give them another's view on the way they work.
6) To help them think about their behaviour and take a look at what they are doing.
7) To give them guidance in developing good work habits.
8) To stop them being too confident and sure of themselves.
9) To make sure the training or work is done well.
10) To give them an opportunity to become better employees.
11) To help them make up their minds about how to do things better.

STOP READING HERE. CHECK YOU HAVE NOTED DOWN WHAT REASONS YOU AGREE WITH FULLY.

If you have noted any of the following:

1, 2, 3, 4, 8

Count up how many and give yourself a 'X' score.

If you have noted any of the following:

5, 6, 7, 8, 10, 11

Count up how many and give yourself a 'Y' score.

The X score gives you a rough guide to how far you share the assumptions of the X type Manager.

'X' The X-type manager tends to see his and her role as controlling, dominating or based on conflict with subordinates.

The 'Y' score gives you a rough guide to how far you share the assumptions of the Y-type manager.

'Y'

> The Y-type manager tends to see his or her role as being able to get the job done well, by motivating employees. They feel encouragement of good working habits is better than dwelling on bad practice.

Have you come down clearly on one side or the other in your 'X' or 'Y' scores?

It has been found through experience and research that with either form of management style, employees tend to live up to the expectations placed on them. Thus with the 'X' style they respond to criticism and do as they are told, but only **when** they are told. In the case of the 'Y' style they start to look at how they do the job and correct their own mistakes and evaluate themselves. It has been found that the Y style tends to be more effective as a basis for giving criticism.

If your 'X' score was high and 'Y' score was low ask yourself:
"How far is my giving criticism to trainees or employers (i) about getting the job done better and helping them to see how to do it better and how far is it (ii) part of my showing them who is boss?".
If you think it is really about (i) then ask yourself:
Does the way I give critical comment help to get the job done and to get trainees to see how they can do better?"

> STOP READING HERE FOR A MINUTE OR TWO. WRITE A FEW NOTES TO YOURSELF ON THESE QUESTIONS ABOUT WHAT YOU THINK.

---

3. How can I Prepare to give Effective Critical Comment?

If you opted for (2) in the last CHECKPOINT and you had a high 'X' score, it probably means you disagree with the basic approach to management being advocated here. You may have good reasons for this. Nevertheless you may find it helpful to follow the rest of this section to see if it offers any pointers to how you can improve on the way you give criticism.

The 4-stage method of giving effective criticism

> I Identify the behaviour
> II Get a response
> III Encourage suggestions
> IV Summarise the agreement

Effective Criticism

STAGE ONE
Identify the part of the behaviour which is the subject of the critical comment.

- ✲ The criticism **should not be personal** but focussed on the behaviour.
e.g. "I see that you are coming in late".
rather than:
"Why are you so lazy. You always come in late!?"
- ✲ Check your own thinking. Is it helpful rather than an emotional reaction?
- ✲ "Why am I going to talk to . . . about this?"
If the answer is: "He really needs a telling of!" delay talking to him and think about it.
If the answer is: His work is affecting others I need to find out what's going on" etc. etc.; then go ahead.
- ✲ Make the criticism SPECIFIC
e.g. "I see you have been late twice this week, what's the problem?"

↓

STAGE TWO
Get a response or an agreement from the other person to your specific criticism.

- ✲ Here you will need to ask questions to see if the other person sees things the way you do.
This gives you a chance to find out more about their behaviour.
e.g. "Do you agree with me?"
"Isn't that so?"
"What's the problem?"
rather than;
"Can you stop it?"
"Will you improve?"
"When will you pull your socks up"?
- ✲ If you discover new information, you may need to modify your criticism e.g. if the lateness is due to severe difficulties at home you may want to make allowances and offer some support.
- ✲ It may also become clear that the other person has no idea what is expected of them and you might have to concede that you or others have not made this clear before. This gives you the opportunity to establish clear guidelines for behaviour without making the other person feel bad about something that is not their fault.

↓

STAGE THREE
Encourage the other person to come up with suggestions to help the required change in behaviour.

- ✲ Here you may need prompt questions.
e.g."Have you any ideas about how to change?"
"How can you do it differently?"
"What changes can we make?"
- ✲ You may need to help by making some suggestion yourself or at least have some ready if they ask you what to do if they respond non assertively to your question.
It is a good idea to put suggestions in the form:
"would it work if you . . . ?"
or
"how about trying . . . ?"
This gives the other a chance to say if the suggestion is useful.
It also ensures your suggestions are not seen as orders, which the person will simply follow irrespective of how useful they are.
- ✲ Suggestions might include changes that **you** might make to help the situation.

↓

STAGE FOUR
Summarize what has been agreed and make sure you **both** know what is going **to be done.**

- * Having made clear what you think they should **not do** in your criticism, it is important to establish what you have both agreed to **do.**
- * Some definite statement from you about how you will check on the effectiveness of the proposed solution and a **specified time scale,** with the other person, will help them take seriously what you have discussed.
  e.g. "Have we got it clear that you will try to . . . and I will help by . . . ?
  "Shall we review this problem again in . . . weeks and see how things are?"

Using the 4-stage Method and Being Flexible
This process might seem to be a rather complicated way to tell someone off about their behaviour. But what I am suggesting is not that simple. To get someone to see that there is a problem, suggest their own solution and agree to do it is more difficult and more important than simply telling them of!

It is important to remember that there will be times when all the four stages are not really necessary. If the person is simply doing a routine task in the wrong way, they may need simply to be told how to do it correctly and why.

But if you follow the suggested stages in planning what you will say, you will avoid getting aggressive or submissive reactions from the other. This is because you will have avoided giving the impression of being aggressive yourself. What has been outlined here is a simple framework for planning and giving critical comments **Assertively** so **that it helps the other person change.**
In doing it this way you establish your right to expect changes in behaviour and you show that you respect their right not to be criticized personally and to be given clear indications of how they are supposed to operate.

As a quick memory test, see if you can note down each of the four stages in order, with an appropriate question, in your own words.

STOP READING NOW AND WRITE DOWN YOUR RESPONSES

The Stages	**Typical questions:**
I Identify the behaviour	*"I see you have not. . . is that right?*
II Get a response	*"What is the problem?"*
III Encourage suggestions	*"What can you do about this?"*
IV Summarize the agreement	*"Have we got it clear? You will . . . by . . . is that right?"*

Compare your answers with the suggested answer. Now think of a **Specific person** in your work situation whose behaviour needs some critical comment. Re-write your questions from the above response as if you were speaking to them. Remember, keep the comments about their specific behaviour **Specific.** What kind of suggestions do you think they will come up with that you would find acceptable? If what you have written out seems realistic you could try the approach with that person and see how far you get. If you wish to treat this as Tutor Seen Work, please send it to me for my reactions.

II Giving and Accepting Appreciation

1. Introduction
In Component Five we looked at how to deal with criticism. In this component we have looked at how to give critical comment that allows the other to respond assertively. The other side of this is giving and accepting appreciation or praise.

This is just as important as criticism and can be more important on occasion because it is so often neglected. Think about how often you only hear from those above you when something has gone wrong rather than when it goes well. Does it happen often? How far do you give the same impression to those who work for you?

1. How many of these statements do you agree with? Read them through quickly and note down the numbers of those you feel you do go along with. Don't think about it, just react quickly — give a "gut reaction" as they say.

1. It is soft and wet to give employees praise.
2. If you give them praise, they will start relaxing.
3. Saying you appreciate what people have done well will encourage them to repeat good work in future.
4. If you praise people, they will think you want something.
5. People only learn to do better if you point out mistakes.
6. Praising people when they have completed work satisfactorily gives them a clearer idea of the kind of work you expect.
7. Praising people does not serve any useful purpose.
8. Giving praise makes the other person feel valued and shows them that **what** they do **and how** they do it is recognized and valued.

Now check the numbers you have noted down against the following:

a) If you have noted down some or all of 1, 2, 4, 5, 7 and not much else you are clearly suspicious about giving praise.
b) If you have noted down some or all of 3, 6, 8 and little else you clearly recognise the importance of praising people.
c) If you have noted a mixture of the above numbers, you see both sides of the position or you are not sure about it.

2. Look back at your original 'X' and 'Y' scores from earlier in the component.

Do you think your responses to this CHECKPOINT are consistent with your 'X' or 'Y' score?

STOP READING HERE AND CHECK YOUR SCORES AND NOTE DOWN WHAT YOU THINK.

If you had a high 'X' score then you will probably have scored high or (a) here.
If you had a high 'Y' score then you will probably have scored high or (b) here.
If you have scores which are the opposite of this then you have either changed your mind since the beginning of this component or you are less clear about your habitual management style than you thought! Maybe you need to think out what is important here for your future behaviour in managing training.

---

2. So what is so Important about giving Praise?

From the above comments it is probably clear to you that I think appreciation and praise are important. There are two very good reasons for this in the context of managing the training situation at work.

i) Behaving assertively

If you want to be effective and assertive in your work relations, this will involve expressing your ideas, feelings and needs directly and appropriately.

There will be times when you will want to acknowledge what someone has done, or said.

If you have thoughts and feelings about praise as expressed in statements, 1, 2, 4, 5 and 7 above, then you will find this gets in the way and becomes a form of UNHELPFUL THINKING and you may not act assertively.

You may (a) Avoid praising at all
(b) When you express appreciation, you may be aggressive or non-assertive.

Non-Assertive Praise — Examples
This comes in two varieties that are readily recognisable:
HESITANT PRAISE — "I liked, er . . . I mean I thought it was good"
APOLOGETIC PRAISE — "I hope you don't mind me saying this but . . ."
In either case the effect is stilted and unsure and so likely to embarrass the other person or make them suspicious.

Aggressive Praise — Examples
This tends to come in two easily recognisable varieties:
GRUDGING PRAISE — "Well that wasn't at all bad, for you, was it?"
GUSHING PRAISE — "Really good, — magnificent job! In my book that rates as top-notch!" "Keep up the good work! etc.?"
Here the praise comes over as insincere" It also tends to sound like an authoratitive judgement which they are required to accept and does not help them to develop a better self-appreciation of their work.

ii) Learning the Job

The second reason why giving praise appropriately is important is that it makes you a better manager of training. All managerial roles contain some element of helping people **learn how to do their job well.** For a manager involved in training this is even more evident as part of their job.

People don't only learn from their mistakes and having them pointed out, they learn from success. Expressing appreciation for their work gives them a better idea of the standards of the work required and informs them when they have achieved those standards.

3. How can I express Appreciation Effectively?

If you are one of those people who is more than a little suspicious of the idea of giving praise, it may well be that you find it difficult to do it easily. This may well have resulted in some bad experiences when you have tried it in the past. You may have found it embarrassing or you could not find the right words or it was not well received by the other person.

In giving praise and expressing appreciation it is important to think about:
WHAT YOU SAY
AND
HOW YOU SAY IT

What You Say

* **Keep it brief** — just say what you appreciate simply and directly
* **Keep it clear and specific** — talk about particular aspects of the work
  e.g. "I liked the way you completed that difficult order . . . it was a good idea to make the packers double check it

* **Always use "I" statements** — this helps you be direct.
  e.g. "I was impressed by the way you dealt with that difficult customer. You kept your voice calm and you repeated the information they seemed to have misunderstood, that was helpful."

How You Say It
Non-verbal signs are important here. In giving appreciation you are expressing your view of the work and the positive feeling you have about it.

Too much enthusiasm or too much hesitancy can make the other person uncomfortable.

* **Keep an even tone in your voice**
* **Speak clearly and steadily**
* **Maintain relaxed, but direct eye-contact — without staring them down.**

Read this example
Joan is a supervisor for whom you are responsible. You see her dealing with a sales assistant.

Joan (Supervisor)	"Now John, I really don't want you lounging about the shop and generally looking like something the cat brought in. You really must buck up!"
John: (Sales assistant)	"Yes, Joan."
Joan:	"By the way, you did the accounts well yesterday. I liked the way you set out the columns and totals for Mrs Brown. It makes her job that much easier."

Joan asks you later how well you think she handled John — what do you say?

Make some notes on what you would say to Joan to help her develop her skill as a supervisor. It may help to try to write down the **actual words** you might use.

STOP READING NOW AND TAKE SOME TIME TO WRITE OUT YOUR RESPONSE

Helping Joan
Joan has placed a great amount of trust in you and sees you as approachable and helpful. In asking you to comment on her performance she has given you a glorious training opportunity. Does this kind of opportunity often present itself in your work situation? Do you think you handle such situations well?

Let's see what this fictitious example has produced.

Joan's Performance
In general I think Joan **does well** *in* **giving praise** *but she is less adept in giving* **good critical comment.**
In giving criticism she:

* *does not focus on specific behaviour*
* *makes comments about John's person rather than his behaviour*
* *gives no clear indication of the kind of action she wants from John*
* *does not try to give him any ideas on how his behaviour affects the job he is doing*
* *does not encourage him to respond, to see if he agrees with, or even understands what she is saying.*

Do we tell Joan all of these things?

I suggest not. She will probably not remember much and will feel very inadequate. You might say:

"Joan, don't you think John's behaviour might be helped if you told him what was wrong with it, rather than what was wrong with him? Tell him exactly what he is doing wrong and the consequences of that. See if he can come up with ideas as to how he can improve."

In giving praise she:

* *says what she wants to say directly without any extra comment*
* *makes the comment about specific actions*
* *explains the good consequences of the action in its effect on other staff*
* *does not go on and on about it and says it in a matter-of-fact tone.*
* *criticizes first and expresses appreciation last, leaving the conversation on a positive note.*

In responding to Joan we can follow her good practice. After giving the critical comment we might say:

"I liked the way you ended the conversation with John. By giving him a pat on the back for his detailed attention to the job you did not leave him deflated. You made it clear what specific action you liked and how it helped the job for everyone. He will now have a better idea of how to do the job."

Tutor Seen Work

1) Monitor yourself over the next two or three times when you are in the position of commenting on a trainer/supervisor's or a trainee's performance.
2) Review the situations and your own performance. How far did you follow the guidelines set out here? How well did it go?

3) Alternatively, (to give you yourself a flavour of what it is like!) ask a trusted or willing colleague to observe and comment on how well you did in the situation, if that is possible.
4) Write out a short report of what happened (in either case) and add your own personal comments and evaluation and send it in to me for added comments and feed back.

Component 7:

The Marginal Performance Interview

Key Words

Interview; marginal performance; agreement; problem symptoms; summary; reviewing; solutions; responsibility; objectives action; evaluation; appraisal.

When you have completed this Component you will:

* understand the importance of formal approaches to performance appraisal
* understand the Marginal Performance Interview
* be able to plan and conduct an MPI
* have a clear understanding of what to do at different stages of an MPI
* be able to review your own performance in conducting an MPI
* be able to help others improve their performance and evaluate this improvement.

Introduction

Throughout this Study Unit we have been focusing on the art of conversation in managing training and the skills needed to do this effectively. Most of what we have looked at happens informally. But, as we saw back in Component 1, sometimes the situation needs a more formal setting. If the other person's work is seriously defective or their behaviour is creating serious problems in the work situation that are affecting others, a face-to-face interview might well be needed. Such a meeting is often referred to as a 'marginal performance interview'. (MPI, for short).

1. What is the MPI really about?

As when giving effective critical comment, the MPI should never simply be about "telling someone off" or "giving them a piece of your mind". You will already be aware as managers that such feelings are frequently created by people who seem persistently awkward. But this is a form of UNHELPFUL THINKING and gets in the way of your **managerial objectives** (as opposed to your emotional and personal objectives!)

The objectives of an MPI. If you arrange for an MPI as a manager of training the primary objective has to be the CHANGE OF BEHAVIOUR OF THE INTERVIEWEE. This is best achieved by finding a way of helping them deal with the existing problem which they are creating **but also** to help them avoid creating a similar problem in the future.

Example:
If Bill, a trainee, is upsetting Fiona by constant sexual comments, looks and advances so that she is not really able to benefit from a training course and is not turning up as much as she should, simply putting the "frighteners" on him may only stop the behaviour **now.** After the training he may do the same to Fiona in the work situation and impair her performance on the job, or he may affect the work of the female workers to their own detriment and that of the firm. An approach needs to be made that will attempt a **long term change** in such unacceptable behaviour.

The Strategy of an MPI — The interview is likely to achieve its objective if the following basic strategy is followed:

* **Define** the problem
* **Find a practical course of action** to which the other person is committed to try to solve the problem
* **Create the conditions** in which this thinking can happen.

The approach behind the MPI

If you look back at the part of the component dealing with giving critical comment, you will see that the three-part strategy above is part of that process.

It is part of the Y Manager's style that the responsibility for effective work place behaviour is placed firmly with the worker. Some element of trust and respect is required on both sides for the management style to be effective. In the management of training this aspect of the managers' role is even more important. It is well demonstrated in the Marginal Performance Interview method outlined in this section.

2. First Steps in dealing with Marginal or bad Performance.

In general there seem to be two types of people whose behaviour is likely to worry you as a manager of training.

1. The "Impossibles" — a small percentage of people who are completely impossible in their behaviour or work output. Nothing ever seems to resolve this problem. The MPI approach will be a waste of time for them. Get rid of them or put up with them for other reasons.
2. The "Possibles" — a larger group of people (up to 30% in any organisation according to research!) who have the capacity to work well, but who sometimes or constantly fail to reach the standard they are capable of attaining in their work. This group is worth spending time on, but may be the most difficult to deal with in the training context.

Frequently an Organisation will use the training programmes to solve a problem in marginal performance. This does not mean they will send people on the right course or be directed onto relevant forms of training. You could end up acting as nursemaid to the troublesome minority who have been sent for "training" to get them out of somebody else's hair!

For you, in this situation, the MPI might well be a vital tool in sorting out what training is needed and where particular individuals should be directed. This will increase the likelihood of the people being given relevant training and increase their own motivation to get the best out of it.

Checkpoint

1) Reflect on your own experience in your workplace. Can you identify several "Impossibles" and several "Possibles" quickly? Note down their initials.
2) Now note down after each set of initials, some words and phrases that sum up what it is about them that makes you so sure that they are "Impossible" or "Possibles".
3) If you find you are not sure which category to put particular individuals in, what information would you want to add to your present knowledge of them to make a fair judgement?

Spend a few moments making notes for yourself about these people and try to get clear in your own mind what things are important to you when you judge others' performance.

4) Note down what these things are.
5) Apply these criteria to your own performance over the last month — how do you stand up to your own performance appraisal?

STOP READING HERE AND WORK THROUGH THE TASKS

3. What are the causes of Marginal or Bad Performance?

It is important to realise that all behaviour has a cause. Poor performance is often due to a situation where it makes sense to a person to work less well. Some of these causes are due to the individual concerned, but often they may not be. It is important to start out, when considering another person's poor performance, by thinking of the variety of causes that may be operating. The key question you must ask yourself here, and try to answer, is:

"Why is this person not doing what I expect of them"?

Here is a short checklist of types of cause, you should consider:

MANAGEMENT:

e.g. have you given a person a job which they are not able to do?

OUTSIDE EVENTS:

e.g. no room for promotion, or difficult family or social relationships.

PERSONAL CHARACTERISTICS:

e.g. bad health, inability to relate well to others in the work place.

1) Using your own experience, think of some examples of the kind of things that have caused poor work performance in people you know. Can they be easily listed under the three headings above? Are there other types of cause I have missed out?

PAUSE HERE AND MAKE A FEW NOTES ON THESE TASKS BEFORE MOVING ON.

2) have you ever been in a situation when your own performance was not up to scratch? What was the cause of that?

PAUSE HERE AND MAKE A FEW NOTES ON THIS POINT BEFORE READING ON.

4. How to plan and conduct the MPI

If you have recognised or been faced with a clear case of poor performance and you have decided the person is a "possible" then you might decide to plan and conduct an MPI to solve the problems. The work covered in Components 1-3 of this study unit dealt with planning and conducting a conversation in the training context and they are relevant here.

Can you jot down the basic areas of importance in planning and conducting a conversation? See if you can note them down now.

PAUSE FOR A MINUTE OR TWO TO RECALL AND NOTE DOWN WHAT YOU CAN.

In planning I suggested that it was important
to be — clear about **objectives.**
to be — clear about the **setting**
In the planning of the interview itself I suggested you think about

— **Starting** *the conversation easily*
— **Guiding it** *so as to focus on the objectives*
— **Concluding** *it with the right tone when business was concluded.*

5. The MPI Itself. A Step by Step approach

I The Setting

You need:

* to inform the person some time beforehand about the subject of the interview.
* a **definite** time, arranged with the other person.
* to give yourself at least one hour of time free from distractions.
* to use a private room without a telephone (if possible) or with calls blocked.

II Starting the Interview

This will be your way of setting the scene to reach your objectives. These should be clear to you and in your mind at the start.

The general objectives at this stage will always be to get a **mutually agreed description of the problem.** Without this no further stages can be taken. If you resort to imposing your view of what is wrong, the other person will not necessarily understand, or if they do, they might not be motivated to do anything about it, because other things are more important to them.

The steps in this stage of the MPI are:

A — Greeting

Be brief and friendly: no chit chat that could distract from the topic.

e.g. "Morning John, thanks for giving me some of your time. Do sit down."

B — A Statement of the signs of the problem

* You should offer the information you have as "what you have been told" not as the undisputed truth.
  e.g. "it seems, from what I have been told . . ." or "I have had some reports . . ."

* The comments should be descriptive (what happened) not interpretative (what you think about it).
  e.g. ". . . you seem to have upset Fiona with your remarks several times this week".
  rather than "you seem to be behaving in a very uncivilised way to Fiona"
  or "I see your well known boorishness is now affecting the female staff".

> * **If your information turns out to be wrong, stop the interview and check your sources.**
> * **If the person reacts emotionally to what you say, stop the interview and check out what you did. No serious discussion leading to a change in behaviour can be completed in an emotional atmosphere.**
> * **If you explore the emotion with the other person, you are counselling them not conducting an MPI. The former might be important, but you need another time for what you set out to do.**

C — Defining the Problem

If you both agreed on the information, then the causes need to be explored. This is a vital part of the interview process, and it is difficult.

> **The objective here is to get the other person to come up with a usable definition of what they feel is the problem. What they say here will determine how the rest of the session goes.**

The questions must be open and the skill of **reflective listening** (See component 4) needs to be consciously used here.

e.g. "What is the problem do you think?"
"What's the matter?"
"What is the reason for this . . . ?"

The other person's response will need to be followed up with:

e.g. "Why is that?"
"What makes you think this is the problem?"
"Is there more to this?"

If the person gets stuck and seems unable to sort out the problem, some prompt questions might be useful:

e.g. Is it to do with:

1 the pace of work?
2 the load of work?
3 the administration system?
4 the equipment and support services?
5 your working ability?
6 a personal problem?
7 me as your manager?, (this last one is a vital question to get cleared!)

D — Checking for other things

Having got a clear statement about the problem, you need to check back.

e.g. "Have I got it right, you are saying . . . ? and repeat back what you think the other has said. If they agree then make sure you have a complete picture by asking:

e.g. "Are there any other things that we should think about that are causing this problem?"

> **Poor performance is unlikely to be due to one single cause. Here you are attempting to build up as full a picture of what is going on, especially from the point of view of the other person.**

E — The agreed problem

Here again you need to reflect back what you think the other has said. **When you are both happy that you understand what the problem is, this stage of the interview is complete.**

> **It is important that no judgement, advice or suggested solutions are offered by you at all. Your concentration should be on drawing out what the other person thinks.**

If you feel they have misunderstood the problem you should tentatively question their perceptions:

e.g. "Is that really the reason . . . ?"
"Do you always react this way to . . ."

If the other insists on their version you must accept that as their view and move on. To impose your different view means you are simply telling them and attempting to get them to produce a solution will be difficult. Anyway, you could be wrong!

We have now reviewed the steps of the introduction to the MPI. Can you remember the steps in order? See if you can note them down from memory?

> STOP READING AND NOTE DOWN THE STEPS.

The Steps are:
A. Greeting
B. Stating the symptoms of the problem
C. Defining the problem
D. Checking for other causes of the problem
E. Agreeing on what the problem is.

How far do all these things get properly sorted out when you attempt to review someone's performance in an interview?

III Developing the Interview
The real work of the Interview is now begun. You should have a clear statement of the issue and you should both be sure you understand it. **The objective now is to move onto a practical solution.**

The requisite steps are:

A. — Solution seeking
The simplest question is
"What can you do about it?"

> **Notice the "you" in the question: This is to indicate that the responsibility rests with them. Hopefully this will prompt them to produce their own answer.**

Some evasion here is to be expected. Some people like, or expect to be told what to do. If it goes wrong they can blame the person who gave them advice. It removes from them the burden of doing what they say they will and it requires no personal commitment from them.

> **Some prompting may be necessary and because of this AVOID GIVING YOUR OWN SOLUTION!!**

In each case the question demands some specific response from the other in which they are required to say what they would or could do.
Avoid comments in the form:
"If I were you I would . . ."
"What about trying . . .?"
"Will you . . . as soon as possible?"

B — Checking the Solution
Having produced what looks like a solution the other person needs to be given the chance to test how feasible it is.
The key question here might be:
"Will that work?"
This is really designed to check out the practicabilities but also to get the other person to see that it is a real possibility and thus form the basis for them to actively believe in the solution. If the answer to the question is "no" or "not really" you need to return to Step A.

C — Exploring additional alternatives
The question here is:
"Is there anything else you could do?"
This gives you both the chance to develop the details of the proposed solution and make its practicality more obvious. It may be that the other person might see a way in which you could help to allow the solution to be attempted. Agreement on these details takes the other person one further step down the road of being committed to acting on it.

D — Settling on the Solution
The key question here should take the form:
"As I see it, you are saying that the best solution is . . . am I correct?"
This reflects back to the other person what you think they have said. It gives them a chance to correct any misunderstandings on your part.

E — Confirmation
This is a check on the ability of the other person to complete the proposed solution viz:
"Can you do it?"
"Will you be able to try it?"

F — Setting the Time
The key questions here are
"How long will it take?"
"When will you begin?"
This is the last stage of detailed commitment. By agreeing a timetable, a start and a projected finish, the other's agreement is all but complete.

> **In this stage as the others, you must avoid pushing the person into doing things they are not really committed to or letting things remain in a vague and unspecific form. It is a difficult balance to achieve with some people.**

1) Can you briefly note down the steps in this part of the interview and the order they came in?

> STOP READING AND SEE IF YOU CAN REMEMBER THEM AND NOTE THEM DOWN.

The steps for the development of the interview are:
A. Solution Seeking
B. Checking the Solution is feasible
C. Explaining alternatives
D. Deciding on a Solution
E. Confirming what has been agreed
F. Agreeing the timescale.

---

2) In helping the other to come to a solution can you say what you need to **do** and to **avoid**?

> STOP READING HERE AND MAKE NOTES ON THIS.

It is important to:
* *Ask open questions.*
* *Keep giving the other person the responsibility to suggest and develop solutions.*
* *Keep checking you and the other person understand and agree on what is proposed and decided.*

It is important to avoid:
* *Giving your own solutions to the problem.*
* *Telling the other person what they should do.*
* *Pushing them into accepting ideas they do not understand or agree with.*

IV The Conclusion of the Interview
It is important to conclude the Interview by making sure both you and the other person are absolutely clear about what has been decided and are **both** in agreement. This should result in some written statement and the tone should be friendly. This can be achieved through the following steps:

A. - Summarizing
This can be done simply:
e.g. "Are we clear then, the problem is . . . The solution is . . . and you will make sure that happens by . . . ?"

B. - A written record
If this is possible or appropriate, after drafting a record and typing, check it is agreed by you both and confirmed. Alternatively get this completed and agreed at a later date.

C. - Finishing the Interview
It is important that you close on a good note and the other person leaves feeling that the interview has been purposeful and the task ahead is manageable. Expressions of confidence in their ability and the expectation of success are ways of achieving this as well as thanking the other for their time.

D. - Reviewing yourself
It is invaluable to spend a short time immediately after the interview to check how well you feel you have done **and to note this down.** It is a difficult thing to get right and some record of what you did well and what you could improve on will help when you prepare and conduct the next MPI.

We have gone through a fairly long and detailed breakdown of an MPI to give a clear view of the mechanics of the process. It is important not to miss the wood for the trees. As a quick self check see if you can note down the various stages and the steps in each stage, from what you can remember.

STOP READING HERE AND SPEND A FEW MINUTES TRYING TO COMPLETE THE TASK.

I don't expect you got everything down but here is an overview of the whole process to check how much you remembered from first time reading.

The MPI — An Overview
Stage I The Setting

Stage II Starting the Interview
Step A — Greeting
Step B — A Statement about the signs of the problem
Step C — Defining the problem
Step D — Checking for other aspects
Step E — The agreed problem

Step III Developing the Interview
Step A — Seeking solutions
Step B — Checking the solution
Step C — Exploring other possibilities
Step D — Settling on the solution
Step E — Confirming the solution
Step F — Setting a time

Step IV Concluding the Interview
Step A — Summarizing
Step B — A written record
Step C — Finishing the interview
Step D — Reviewing yourself.

If you feel you have remembered very little, now you have compared your answer to this overview, you should go back and re read the section or the MPI especially those sections you forgot.

5. The Interview Process

It is important to note that simply going through each of the stages and steps of the procedure outlined above will not necessarily produce results. It is not a simple mechanical process. At each stage and each step you have to complete what is necessary, as described in the outline. If you fail to get willing co-operation and agreement from the other person at any stage or any lack of understanding you will have to stop the interview or return to earlier stages, backtrack and try again. The following flow chart attempts to make this clear and is offered as a way of helping you conduct the interview and keep a track of what you should be asking yourself as well as the other person.

THE MPI PROCEDURE: A SUMMARY FLOW CHART

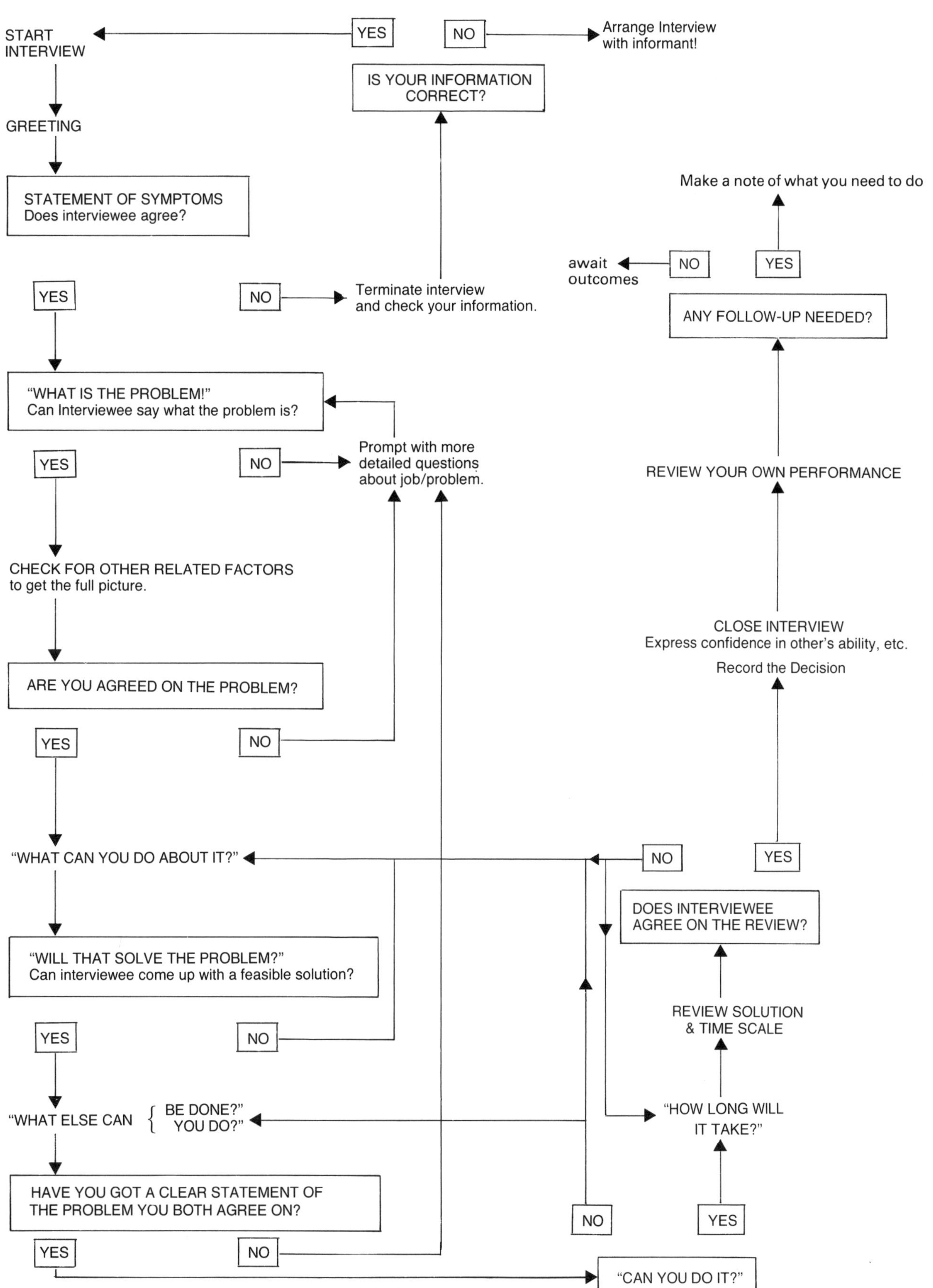

Tutor Seen Work

When you next have to conduct an interview on performance, use the MPI process and the flow chart to guide you through the stages.

Do a detailed review of how it went and how useful you find the process and send in to the tutor for comment and feed back. Alternatively get a trusted colleague to go over the review with you and help you identify how well you did.

Study Unit 5

Analysing Training Materials

Component 1:

How Should I Look at Training Materials?

Key Words

Purpose of analysing; different types; availability; overall approach; selectivity; points of view; direct examination; describing; subjective/objective items; empirical evidence.

What are 'Training Materials' — and how do I look at them?

Introduction

In this Study Unit we are going to consider ways of looking at and analysing the various types of training materials which are available, with a view to deciding whether they are suitable for use. Firstly, we shall attempt to identify the range and availability of such materials, then consider different approaches to analysing them and finally decide how best to describe and evaluate them.

In this first Component we should perhaps begin with a word of caution! It is easy to get carried away with the idea and procedures of analysing training materials — it can become an interesting and absorbing activity which may develop its own 'head of steam' and then carry on regardless. Beware!

Any attempt to analyse training materials should be firmly based on an explicit purpose or goal, which will normally be linked to an established training need. Why am I looking at these materials? If I decide they are suitable for use, can I go ahead and obtain them — and then ensure that they are put into use? What are the implications if I decide I don't like them i.e. have other people already made decisions about them? Can I afford to spend time looking at them in detail, or will I be expected to make a 'snap' decision? And so on.

Checkpoint

No doubt you can think of other equally relevant and important questions, arising from the query "Why do I need to look at these training materials?" Write down any you can think of now.

At this stage, you may have thought of cost factors, availability, ease of use, subject/topic not dealt with adequately elsewhere, etc.

So — first of all establish exactly **why** you want to analyse the training materials in question, and whether the effort is likely to be worthwhile.

What are Training Materials?

You probably already have a fair idea of what you would include in any list of the various **types or categories of training materials.** Write down your own list, and then compare it with mine.

Well, almost anything that can be considered as 'material' that helps in training can be included, although I wouldn't go as far as one elderly teacher who said that his most successful visual teaching aid was the cane, because when he put it on his desk the pupils could see it, and it aided him in his teaching! A piece of chalk is a teaching **aid**, *but what we really mean by* **materials** *are those things which are 'software-based', that is they incorporate knowledge and information of some sort. Thus a tape recorder is excluded, but the recorded tapes (e.g. of a foreign language course) would definitely be included.*

My list would include items such as printed materials (books, manuals, pamphlets, handouts, job aids, worksheets etc.), slides, filmstrips, posters, photographs, films, pre-prepared OHP transparencies, videos, composite packages, computer-based training materials, interactive video materials:- in fact any materials containing information which may be useful for training purposes!

The range of types is therefore wide, but also the content may vary from a short, simple worksheet or set of slides to a comprehensive total package designed to take weeks or months to work through.

What is Available?

Training materials are produced widely and distributed in various ways, but apart from commercially-available and advertised items it is often difficult to find out what is available. This topic will be dealt with more fully later on in this Study Unit, but for the moment:—

* Contacting other trainers can prove fruitful.
* Materials are sometimes reviewed in appropriate journals and magazines.
* Institutes, Associations and Training Boards may be able to help.
* Your TTP Tutor may be able to suggest other sources to you.
* Exhibitions and Conferences often indicate the current 'state of the art'.
* The International Yearbook of the Association for Educational and Training Technology (published by Kogan Page) includes comprehensive lists of producers, along with many useful names and addresses.
* Probably the most fruitful source of information, however, is to build up your own direct contacts and 'old boy' network.

Let us assume for the purposes of this Component that you have now selected and acquired some training materials and wish to examine and analyse them. What should you do?

How Should I Look at Training Materials?

Since basically the whole of this Study Unit is dealing with this question, and is designed to help you to acquire and develop the necessary skills to enable you to analyse training materials in detail, a gradual progressive step-by-step approach is being used. This will run throughout the whole Study Unit. So for the moment we will begin by considering a number of broad questions and principles.

I suppose the first question must be "Am I the best person to do this?". One man's meat may be another man's poison! For example, it is quite possible that you may find yourself looking at some training materials in order to decide whether they may be suitable for direct use by your trainees. Your views and opinions are valuable, but in such a case maybe the trainees themselves should try out the materials as well? In any case two heads are always better than one — a point which will come up again in a moment.

The next point to consider is that **any** approach you decide to adopt in looking at the materials will be selective. You cannot possibly take into account all the different factors which could be considered, and any choice is bound to produce some bias and distortion. The TV programme "Points of View" illustrates this, since it depends for its existence on contrasting different people's reactions to TV programmes, i.e. their own particular points of view.

Beauty is in the eye of the beholder, and your particular stance will colour your choice of what you regard as important and how you see things.

Another good example of this arose recently over the doomed Sinclair electric C5 tricycle. Someone who had bought fifteen of these for hiring out on an hourly/daily basis was very critical of their reliability and the need for frequent repairs and maintenance. He felt that there had been 'a lack of development'. In reply it was claimed that the Lotus Company had spent two years on the development of the C5.

Both these comments were based on sound factual information, but starting from different approaches. This is where the 'two heads' idea may be useful, i.e. asking two people to look at the same materials, but from different stated approaches — with different instructions about what they should be looking at. However, to prevent things getting too out-of-hand, they should both be aware of the common goal or purpose of the analysis!

Let us now consider the different approaches:—

Direct Examination

A natural starting point might be a straightforward direct examination of the materials themselves, looking at their obvious self-evident and 'visible' features only — with an 'open mind' and no pre-conditions laid down.

Spend about ten minutes writing down the advantages and disadvantages of such an approach. If you think hard, you should be able to list about five of each.

I don't propose to give you a list of items to compare with yours, but keep checking to see whether the points you have listed are reflected in the following discussion. Hopefully you will have produced some extra ideas anyway.

Direct examination is generally our first natural approach to most real-life situations. We pick the latest magazine or book off the rack, look at it, examine the list of contents, flip through it etc. before deciding whether to buy it or not.

First impressions are all important but can be dangerous. Just because a paperback is fat and has an attractive glossy cover, it doesn't follow that the contents will be of a high quality. This method, however, is relatively quick, cheap and simple.

This initial direct examination should be completely 'open', with nothing pre-judged (e.g. like looking for favourite authors or publishers) or excluded. Scanning is a useful technique to use as a first step, and permits a global view — the wood rather than the trees.

What, then, are the dangers?

The dangers of this approach tend to be linked together, and arise from the role of the individual undertaking the examination. If the approach is general and lacks any focus, the field is open for the observer's own **subjective** opinions to flourish and control the analysis. Prejudices may bias the results, and could give rise to the well-known 'halo effect', where favourable reaction to one feature colours our assessment of others.

"It may be rubbish, but . . . ."

"Their other materials were OK, so . . . ."

"It's an Open University Set Book on Industrial Relations . . . . ."

"It's got lots of pictures, therefore . . . ."

"It's multi-media, it must be good!"

The **relative** importance of different features (e.g. looks and appearance versus content) may be subject to individual interpretation.

Because the overall process is imprecise, vague statements and comments become the order of the day. Here are a few, taken from recent reviews of educational software printed in computer magazines:—

Best of its kind.

The best around at the moment.

Excellent use of colour and graphics.

Well written.

A lot for your money.

Should prove of genuine value.

I had expected more of this package.

A heavy onslaught of information which the mere casual reader might find overwhelming.

The results are less than riveting.

Well below current standards.

Admittedly, it is rather unfair to take such statements out of context, but the general impression is that they are highly subjective and based on the reviewers' opinions.

What can be done to improve direct examination?

Without moving too far ahead at this stage, let us consider one or two ways in which this type of direct examination may be made more effective and useful. As we are dealing with what is basically a 'soft' subjective approach, we need to be aware of the strengths and weaknesses of such an approach. Raising one's 'level of awareness' is the first point. By this we mean constantly checking with yourself to see that you are consciously trying to examine and analyse the materials in a critical way, based firmly on the original purpose or goal. The next point is to clarify in your own mind exactly what you are attempting to do. You should be collecting and sifting information, considering options and making decisions. Ask yourself a lot of 'Why' and 'What' questions, e.g.

Why this medium?

What is the underlying philosophy and design?

What are the objectives, and do they match my established training needs?

Why this before that?

What is included; what seems to be missing?

No doubt you can think of other questions which you would be asking. Jot them down if you wish.

Remember that the basis of this approach is to be descriptive, analytical and to make judgements. Finally, use the 'two heads' approach if at all possible.

Objectivity

"Never mind the quality, measure the width."

The subjective approach considered so far is mainly concerned with broad considerations of **quality and suitability** and the **overall impression** created by the materials. However, it is also possible to collect certain items of information which are more objective and factual; where different people examining the materials would reach the same conclusions. This type of information is not dependent on the observer's judgement or opinion.

Look at the following ten statements taken from a recent review of a book on educational technology, and try to decide which are subjective and which are objective.

1. The authors' aim in writing this book was, quote "to provide a basic primer for those teachers and students tackling the concepts of educational technology for the first time".
2. This book succeeds in fulfilling its aims.
3. The style is clear and relatively jargon-free.
4. 248 pages.
5. Each chapter is subdivided by subject headings and some chapters have summaries.
6. The early chapters define the subject area and discuss educational strategies.
7. Cost £11.95.
8. At £11.95 it will be too expensive for many teachers and students.
9. The authors leave the best till last.
10. The authors have included a list of organisations involved in educational technology and a good keyword index.

I think you will begin to realise that in practice many such statements are a mixture of subjective and objective information. However, I have slightly doctored the above statements where necessary so that 1, 4, 5, 6 and 7 are objective (1 is objective because the reviewer is simply re-stating something the authors have written), 2, 3, 8 and 9 are subjective — they reflect the reviewer's opinions. 10 is the 'catch question' — it is objective apart from the subjective word 'good'. Sorry about that!

It would obviously be nice if all the information we collected was objective and not the result of personal judgements. But in practice the subjective information often seems more useful to us in making decisions. Look at 2, 3 and 9 above. If we felt that the reviewer was an acknowledged expert authority, I suspect we would attach considerable weight to such statements.

How many times do we perhaps decide to watch a TV programme or read a particular book or article because an expert has recommended it? After all, professional reviewers and critics make their living out of comments which are largely subjective.

Nevertheless, objective information about length, cost, time taken to complete, target audience, aims and objectives, content, assessment, etc. should be a vital consideration in any examination of training materials.

The two most important considerations are to be able to discriminate clearly between the two types of information, subjective and objective, and to be aware of the limitations of personal judgement (for example an invalid perspective, that of the trainer rather than the trainee). There is, of course, a consequent danger in over-stressing objectivity. If we are not careful, much of the 'hard' factual information we collect may turn out to be relatively trivial and unimportant — and I freely admit that that is a subjective statement!

If you feel you would like some more practice in making this distinction between subjective and objective information, read through the following fictitious review, noting down which statements are subjective, objective, or a mixture of both. Numbers have been inserted to make this task easier. This example has been chosen deliberately to show that understanding of the technical content is not a barrier; you should still be able to differentiate between the types of statements.

(1) The package is supplied in two parts, (2) an EPROM and a utilities disc, (3) as well as a comprehensive manual. (4) It is extremely easy to use, (5) being menu-driven, (6) and allowing subsets to be created from a main file. (7) Creating a file mask is not as easy as with some other packages. (8) There is no on-screen editor. (9) Formatting the output is a little tricky. (10) Complex control codes are used to print the fields you want. (11) Once you have got used to the system it is very flexible. (12) It really comes into its own when searching through a file. (13) It is also very easy to create or sort a subset. (14) There is a facility to transfer complete or part files to another file. (15) A particularly friendly aspect is the method employed to browse through a file. (16) This package is a joy to use. (17) At all stages the user is informed what is happening. (18) The approach to the design is clearly most thoughtful. (19) A really powerful tool. (20) The package is reasonably fast.

Items numbered 1, 2, 5, 6, 8, 14 and 17 are clearly objective.

Items numbered 4, 7, 9, 11, 12, 13, 15, 16, 18, 19 and 20 appear to me to be subjective, although most of them do include reference to particular features of the package.

Item 3 states that there is a manual (objective), but the opinion that it is comprehensive is subjective. Similarly, item 10 is objective apart from the use of the word 'complex'.

So far we have been discussing how we would look at training materials by direct examination and analysis, i.e. how to review and describe them. This is often all we are able to do. We act as our own 'guinea pig' and try to visualise how effective we think the training materials are likely to be.

But if we are lucky, we may be able to actually try out the materials — or obtain the results of such trials already undertaken elsewhere.

Empirical evidence
"Suck it and see."

Imagine you are trying to decide whether to buy a particular new car. You can examine it at the dealers — look at it, walk round it, look under the bonnet, sit in it etc. This is similar to our direct examination. To add to your subjective impressions, the handbook will give you certain objective information — length, height, weight, engine capacity etc. However, you wouldn't be too happy if that was the only information you could obtain before making your decision. You would obviously be looking for **empirical evidence** about its practical performance — acceleration, maximum speed, consumption etc., as well as going out for a test-drive yourself. In other words, you would want to 'try it out'.

Similarly, in looking at training materials, we should firstly look for evidence about 'performance'. Have the materials been tried out and tested on representative groups of trainees? If not, can you arrange to try them out? Another clue is to find out how widely the materials have been distributed and used. How popular and successful are they? Subjective reports/impressions from other 'drivers' are often very revealing — they are in a sense empirical in that they are based on practical experience.

To buy, or not to buy?

In the training field we are seldom in the fortunate position of being able to compare similar materials covering exactly the same subject areas and training objectives, leading to the recommended 'best buy' of a 'Which' type report.

Nevertheless, the application of sensible and systematic procedures for looking at and analysing training materials, along the lines indicated in this Component, should enable you to make clear and concise decisions and avoid some of the many pitfalls inherent in making purely subjective judgements.

You should now obtain some training materials in your own area (but preferably something with which you are not very familiar), and produce an analysis of them using the technique of direct examination. When you have done so, go through the analysis and try to decide which items are subjective and which are objective. We will be using the results of this exercise for a different purpose in Component 2, so it is important that you 'have a go' now before proceeding any further with this Study Unit.

Component 2:

Looking at 'In-House' Training Materials

Key Words

In-house; local 'culture'; direct examination; framework for analysis; headings; empirical evidence; performance/reaction; process; product.

Introduction

In Component One we were considering some of the broad principles which should guide any attempt to examine and analyse training materials. We looked at the reasons for attempting any examination, what training materials are — and what is available, problem's of the observer's own point of view, direct examination, subjective and objective statements, empirical evidence. In a sense we were outlining and discussing a straightforward and common-sense approach to looking at training materials in general. We now need to start being more specific, by distinguishing between different categories of training materials and suggesting in much greater detail how to undertake our analysis.

In this Component we are going to focus on **'in-house'** training materials and in the next one (Component Three) we will be looking at **'commercial'** training materials (i.e. those produced by publishers and other organisations and made available on the 'open market'). We shall be drawing out the differences between such materials and suggesting appropriate ways of analysing them.

Looking at 'In-House' Materials

What are they?

The term 'in-house' is used to cover those materials which are produced within a particular organisation and for limited circulation. They may be designed for use in a situation where trainers will be

a) using them themselves, or

b) actively monitoring the use of such materials, and available to iron out any difficulties which may arise.

In larger organisations these trainers may, of course, not be the people who produced the materials.

Checkpoint

Write down any other features you can think of which might apply particularly to 'in-house' materials (compared with 'commercially-published' materials).

Well, it is often the case that in-house materials are produced relatively cheaply using the technology (reprographics, A/V etc.) available within the organisation.

1. The materials may therefore be simple in appearance (e.g. duplicated worksheets) and 'non-glossy'.

2. They may not contain detailed instructions to the trainer/trainee on how the materials should be used.

3. They will be especially relevant to local needs and reflect the overall 'culture' of the organisation.

4. They will either be in use or have been used previously — thus empirical evidence should be available.

5. They may be undergoing development based on the experience of the users.

I don't expect your list will look exactly like the above, but I hope you feel you can agree with the above set of features.

How should I look at them?

As a trainer, you might find yourself in one of three positions regarding in-house materials. You might be:—

a) asked to produce (and maybe tryout) some training materials,

b) looking at some materials and examining/analysing them,

c) involved in trying out materials produced by someone else.

a) is outside the scope of this Component, although hopefully when you have worked through the relevant Volume of this Training Technology Programme (e.g. Volume 1 on the Systematic Approach to Training) it will be well within your capacity!

Let us look at b), and later on c).

Examining in-house materials

Imagine that someone in your organisation has asked you to look at a training package, designed for individual study, and acquired from 'that firm down the road'. The idea put forward is that it might be suitable for use by your trainees. As a first step you have been asked to examine it and produce a report.

Where should you begin?

Look at this diagram:—

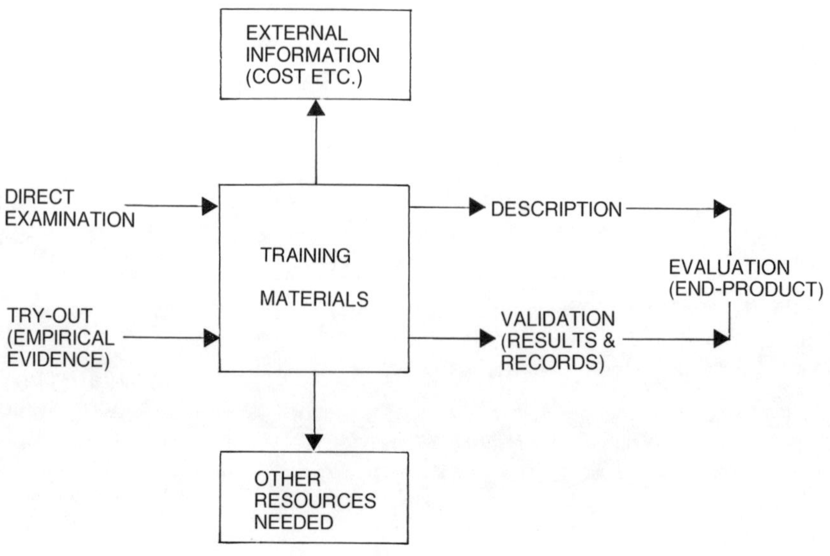

The training materials are shown at the centre, with external information and other resources linked to them. These are 'attacked' from left to right by direct examination or by trying them out (or both) resulting in a final evaluation.

Probably the first natural step is to undertake a direct examination. But with what aim? Again, this should be fairly obvious, bearing in mind the background against which you are working, but do 'spell it out' as a means of ensuring that you keep on the rails. For example:—

> To examine and analyse "X" training package with a view to deciding whether it can be used as it stands for purpose "Y" with "Z" trainees, whether it could be used if modified, or whether it is unsuitable. Examination to take into account cost, ease of use, technical content, appropriateness, likely effectiveness.

In addition to identifying the major decisions to be made, this statement also suggests **a framework** (a set of headings for consideration) to guide the examination.

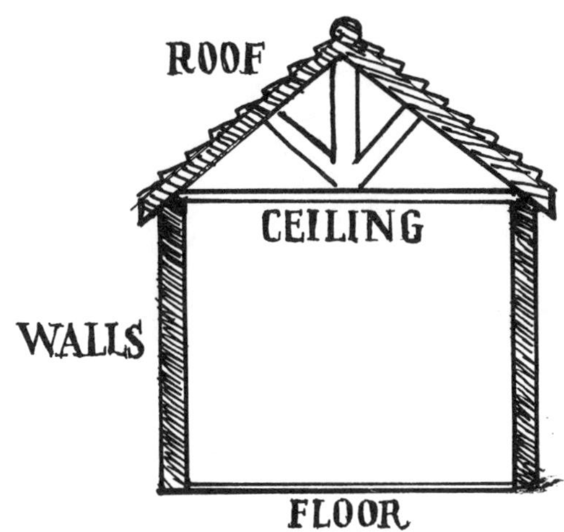

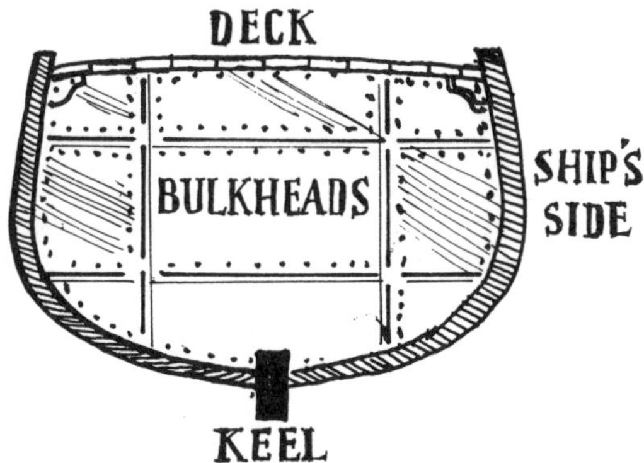

For the moment we are concerned simply with broad headings, as in the diagrams showing only the main features of a structure. The expansion of such a framework into a comprehensive **checklist** will be covered in the next Component (Number Three) of this Study Unit.

If you were producing a framework, what would you want to include in it? Write down your own ideas now — about half-a-dozen **major** headings should be sufficient. (This is not an easy task, but the more time you spend on it now, clarifying and probing your own ideas, the firmer the base you will have established before moving on. Remember at this stage we are only concerned with 'in-house' materials.)

As was suggested in Component One, any choice is selective and highlights some features at the expense of others. Don't expect your list to look exactly like the following one, but I would hope that there is a fair degree of overlap and agreement.

Suggested Framework for analysing 'in-house' training materials.

1. *General background information.*
2. *Description of materials, including their purpose, aims etc.*
3. *Assessment of trainees. (What will be assessed, When and How?)*
4. *Practical issues.*
5. *Empirical evidence (not part of direct examination, but to be included if available).*
6. *Conclusions.*

At this stage it is a matter of deciding on the main headings to use, based on the stated purpose of the analysis. Details can be incorporated under the appropriate headings. In fact I expect you found that the process is a 'chicken and egg' one — the major headings being generated from a longer list of individual items jotted down as they came to mind.

To add some flesh to the framework, here are a few

suggested items which could be included under the above headings.

1. General background information.
   Cost, availability, length, type, overall philosophy and rationale, design.
2. Description of materials.
   Aims and objectives, guidance to trainer/trainee on use of materials, introduction/overview, learning strategies and methods, style, presentation, content, structure, adequacy and appropriateness.
3. Assessment of trainees.
   Type and frequency, formal/informal.
4. Practical issues.
   Ease of use, flexibility, overall 'fit' into training programme, tactical arrangements, documentation, transfer of learning, other resources required.
5. Empirical evidence.
   See next section of this Component.
6. Conclusions.
   To recommend or not?

Remember that for our purposes at the moment such a framework is designed to act as a general guide only.

Not all the individual items will be appropriate to every case, but the 'shopping list' should provide sufficient coverage to prevent the overlooking of any significant detail.

The Checkpoint at the end of Component One asked you to produce an analysis of some training materials. Check your analysis against the framework which **you** have just produced (modified as you think fit in the light of the above list). What items did you concentrate on in your analysis? Were there any important items which you left out?

Well, of course, I don't know what you have discovered, but I hope you found the exercise illuminating and revealing — even if you found you **had** *covered all the items in your framework when doing the analysis! You will now see why the Checkpoint at the end of Component One was deliberately angled to give no particular guidance on which items to include in your 'intuitive' analysis.*

Empirical evidence

"That seemed to go down well."
"No-one complained about it."
"All the comments in the feedback session were favourable."
"Everyone passed the test at the end."
"It seemed to take a very long time."

There are various ways of approaching the analysis of evidence resulting from the actual use by trainees of training materials. If the aims and objectives have been clearly stated, then one obvious approach is to measure the extent to which those aims and objectives are achieved in practice. In other words, how 'valid' are the materials in meeting their claimed purposes?

Evidence from hundreds of 'validation experiments' undertaken in the 1960s and 70s in the hey-day of programmed learning leads us to the conclusion that such evidence may be useful — but other unanticipated results may in reality turn out to be more important. Validation results **are** an important aspect of empirical evidence, but should **not** be taken on their own or simply at face value. Again the best approach is probably to have a general framework for guidance, but to be prepared to **observe** closely what appears to be happening when the materials are put into use, paying particular attention to the more subjective reactions (attitudes and opinions) of trainers and trainees. This clear distinction between information about **performance** (how well/badly the trainees performed) and **reaction** information is an important one. Again, this is a theme which will be looked at in more detail later on in this Study Unit.

Whereas much has been written on assessing the achievement of individuals, and to a lesser extent on assessing courses of instruction, very little information is available on how to assess and evaluate learning materials. Most of the programmed learning validation experiments were based on the use of elaborate and rigorous experimental designs, coupled to complex statistical analysis of the resulting numerical data. On the whole these produced little practical guidance for everyday use.

What we should be concerned about as trainers is to try out materials in as natural a way as possible, accepting that any results obtained will strictly apply to that trial only, and that any conclusions and suggestions about more general use must be treated with caution. Nevertheless, such trials can be used to give empirical evidence and enable us to assess the materials for their possible usefulness.

The overall culture and climate within which the materials are being introduced will often determine their success or failure. For example, if an organisation has a strong commitment to individualised learning and self-assessment, then a package which reflects these strategies will be more likely to succeed. If tried out in an organisation which uses formal instructional methods, with groups of trainees attending courses of fixed length and rigid timetabling, then such a package would almost certainly have less chance of being considered successful.

Make a list of major headings which you feel could be used to guide the acquisition and analysis of empirical evidence derived from trying out some training materials. It may help if you assume that you would be involved in the trial and able to observe what is going on and ask questions.

If you find this task difficult, you may get **some** guidance from the list of headings you produced earlier for analysing the materials themselves.

There would seem to be three main areas of concern

1. Background information about the trial.

2. What happened **during** *the trial (the PROCESS itself).*

3. What were the outcomes (the PRODUCT).

(with the possible addition of

4. Conclusions and recommendations.)

As with the previous exercise, it is necessary to 'flesh out' this outline framework.

1. Background information. You should be looking for details of the **number** of trainees taking part in the trial, and considering whether they were **representative** of the 'target audience', i.e. the trainees for whom the materials were produced or the trainees who are likely to use the materials in your organisation. Were these trainees motivated and interested in taking part? Were the trainees aware that it was a 'trial run', and if so, was that likely to make any difference. (Remember the well-known 'Hawthorne' effect, that people taking part in any experiment may perform better than expected, simply because they feel 'wanted' in some way). Were the administrative and physical conditions set up for the trial suitable and adequate? Were any necessary resources provided? Was adequate time allowed? And so on.

In other words, was the background against which the trial took place a sound one?

2. What happened during the trial? This carries on from the above, and is a largely subjective consideration of the PROCESS of the trial. Apart from looking for any problems in the conduct and administration (e.g. difficulties encountered, complaints from trainers and trainees) the focus here should be on the reactions of the individuals involved. Was interest maintained? Did the 'style' of presentation, layout, language etc. seem appropriate and conducive to learning? This is where careful and perceptive observation skills need to be exercised — but without interfering in the trial itself.

3. What were the outcomes? This is the area most likely to be documented and reported, since it is mainly based on quantifiable information. The results of all assessment procedures should be examined carefully, to see whether the materials are capable of achieving the stated aims and objectives.

In addition the attitudes, opinions and views of the trainers and trainees should be sought. Were there any 'side effects' or unanticipated results? Would similar results be likely to occur in any other trial?

4. Conclusions and recommendations. At this point you would be crossing the threshold from observing, measuring and reporting into the area of judgements and evaluation. How would the materials fit into your overall pattern of training? How do they compare with any previous training materials or methods used? In general, how worthwhile or successful are they likely to be?

Possibly this is a suitable point at which to stop — since evaluation of training materials forms the basis of the final Component in this Study Unit. You should now feel confident that you could construct, develop and apply suitable frameworks for the intrinsic examination of in-house materials and the analysis of empirical evidence about them.

The next Component deals with the analysis of 'commercial' training materials, which is in many ways simply an extension of techniques developed in this Component. By all means attempt an analysis of some 'in-house' materials if you wish, or you may prefer to 'press-on' with Component Three.

Component 3:

How to Draw Up a Framework for Analysis

Key Words

 **Analysis; evaluation; selection; systems approach; description; judgement; framework for analysis; trainer materials; trainee materials.**

Introduction

Faced with a training need (see Units 1 and 2), and having considered materials readily available to you, 'in-house' or perhaps produced by another organisation with similar training needs (Component 2 of this Unit), you may decide to look wider, either to commercially produced materials designed for a broader market or to materials produced or commissioned by an agency interested in training, such as MSC, as are the TTP materials. This will be the focus of Component 3.

If you do decide to consider the whole range of material available on the 'open market' it will be necessary to limit the task, so it will be important to be **selective**:

". . . . it will be important to be selective."

(a) You will need to decide first on criteria for 'short-listing' training material for consideration for adoption by your organisation.
(b) You will need to identify and develop an appropriate method of analysis and presentation which:
(1) is concise yet systematic and comprehensive
(2) presents key facts and figures clearly
(3) is objective—yet considers fully suitability for use in the local context
(4) enables comparisons between materials to be made easily
(5) considers alternative strategies (for example, part adoption; adapting the materials; modification).

The aim of Component 3 is, therefore, to work towards the construction of a framework, or scheme for the analysis of training materials which will help you to meet the above criteria; but we shall also consider the value of the analysis of existing materials as a step towards designing our own 'purpose-built' materials.

Selecting Materials for Analysis

(a) **First questions**

Checkpoint

You have decided to look around to see if training materials exist which you could make use of directly or which have potential and which you could modify. You have, perhaps already looked at 'in house' materials or those produced by other firms or organisations but found them to be too specifically focussed and not quite fitting your requirements.

List as many questions as you can which will help you get clear in your own mind what you are looking for and what are the really important points to consider in drawing up a 'short-list'.

You will probably have listed quite a number of the questions below which are all fairly obvious and have general application. No doubt you have included others which are special to you.

Target audience (who for?)
Where used (how like our own situation?)
Track record? (is it written up anywhere?)
What do the materials consist of? (range?)
Cost?
Who 'wrote' the materials? (status? background?)
Aims/objectives? (knowledge/skills/attitudes?)
Content? (Emphasis?)
Structure? (Sequenced? Modular?)
How easy/difficult to use?
Assessment scheme? (is there one? how does it relate to objectives?) etc.

"Have your training materials got a track record?"

I am assuming that it will have taken you more than just a few minutes to draw up this first list, but it will be something you can add to later in this Component when we move to designing a framework for the analysis of the materials we have selected. It is, in fact, just a start.

(b) 'Short-listing' materials for analysis
Inevitably your choice of materials for analysis will be selective. It may be that this is forced upon you — the materials are not available for careful inspection, they are too expensive to buy merely for analysis purposes, they are so complex that a detailed analysis would be too time-consuming. Your initial sources of information will almost certainly be professional journals, hear-say, a mailing to your firm or the result of a conscious search on your part, involving the contacting of all those advisory bodies or associations connected with your particular industry or area of interest.

This done, you can begin to look at the evidence you have gathered, in the light of the criteria for selection which you have drawn up. Even from a publisher's catalogue, you can often gain enough initial information to help you to decide whether further information is worth seeking or actual inspection or purchase is justified.

Clearly this initial search and selection is difficult and probably time consuming, but it is important. If we are **really** looking wider, we are probably doing so because we can't find any satisfactory 'local model' and our own existing procedures won't do. A partial investigation of the 'open market' is a waste of time, because if we miss something which would actually help to solve our training problem, we shall have to design the materials ourselves, possibly 'reinventing the wheel' at considerable expense and maybe not as efficiently.

". . . reinventing the wheel at considerable expense"

The Analysis of Materials — an Evaluation Exercise

In Volume 6, issues of evaluation were raised, which in turn revived thoughts which had been central to earlier Volumes such as, for example, the Systematic Approach to Training. Although TTP Volumes are designed to stand alone, cross-referencing will often be extremely valuable if you have access to other Volumes.

If you **have** followed the previous Volumes through, you will now be tending to think of training design in a particular way. You may not be totally 'sold' on the Systems Approach, but I hope that, like me, you may feel that there is much to be said for having some idea about:

Where we are going (**objectives**)

Appropriate learning material which will enable

trainees to achieve their objectives (**content**)
In what order things need to be done (**sequence**)
How we'll know whether it's all been worthwhile (**evaluation**)

These considerations are basic to the Systems Approach to training and the relationship between them is reflected in the many models of training design set up by the 'experts' over the years.

For our purposes now it will be sufficient to recognise the model as a help to use in organising our thoughts in the business of training materials analysis. (The emphasis we place on each of the above areas and our interpretation of the approach will be a matter for individual preference, probably influenced by the kind of training we do and context in which we work and the type of materials we are considering. Its appeal is really in its common sense. To quote the famous American authority, Robert Mager (1968*), "If you are not sure where you're going, you're liable to arrive some place else." I find the implications raised by this statement very difficult to avoid when thinking about analysing training materials. After all, training materials analysis is really training design looked at after the event. It's probable and reasonable that we, as trainers, will look at other peoples' courses and materials and apply the same criteria and refer to the same methodology that we have found to be convincing in our own situation, one that is systematic, which knows where it's going and also whether and when it has arrived!

* Mager, R. F., *Developing Attitude Toward Learning*, Fearon.

Try reordering and extending the list you made in the first Checkpoint. Remember, we are beyond the initial selection stage and are beginning to think of detailed analysis. Use the four headings referred to above as 'organisers'. Add others if you need to.
The headings, once again, are:

1. Aims/objectives
2. Content
3. Sequence
4. Evaluation.

I found that I was able to add quite a lot to my original list of 'first questions'. The headings above made me think of several further questions which would be important when it came to a detailed analysis. One or two of the four groups looked a bit thin, particularly in view of our recent thoughts about analysis really being a form of evaluation.
I offer my further points in random order again. Check them against your list and cross out/tick off/add others — now, and as the Component progresses.
What media? (print? audio-visual? computer assisted?)
What knowledge/special skills required of trainer?
How much trainer time required? (in preparation? during the training?)
Does the trainer himself require special training?
What equipment/other resources needed?
Does the firm/organisation using these materials need to be of a particular type or have a particular structure?
Aims of the materials and aims of interests of your firm/organisation? Are they 'congruent'? (do they fit?)
How adaptable are the materials?
Has the material been formally evaluated?
etc. etc.

I'm sure that your reorganised list now begins to look more promising as the beginnings of an approach to clearly presenting an analysis of training materials emerge. We have expanded it and organised it — but are you still left wondering if you have left out something important?

In Derek Rowntree's book — *Educational Technology in Curriculum Development* (2nd Ed 1982) published by Harper and Row, London, I found a helpful list of questions which he himself takes from Henry Brickell (1969).
I have adapted this slightly and list the questions below:

How suitable? (Are objectives, methods and outcomes appropriate?)
How effective? (Does it achieve satisfactory results?)
How big? (How much time, staff, resources needed?)
How complete? (Is extra supporting material needed?)
How complex? (How difficult for trainers/trainees to work with?)
How flexible? (Is there room for adaptation?)
How different? (— from other, or our own, approaches?)
How repeatable? (Will it work elsewhere?)
How compatible? (Will it fit in with the existing training programme?)
How ready? (Could we use it almost immediately?)
How 'samplable'? (Could we try it and abandon it if it didn't work — or is it an all-or-nothing decision?
How expensive? (— both initial and running costs).

Look at your list yet again! You'll find that you haven't done too badly, if you check it against the one above, but still there **are** one or two points (different? compatible? ready? etc.) which we can pick up and, perhaps, degrees of emphasis which we can note. (cost, resources etc.)

Again, don't regard this as final. Other points will occur to you as you work towards deciding on your final framework.

If you have access to other Volumes, you might find it useful now to refer again to Volume 6 — Assessment and Evaluation, in particular, to Study Unit 1 Component 6 and Study Unit 2 Component 6; also Study Unit 7. If you skim these, this will give you further food for thought and help you with your list and maybe suggest other, different ideas about organising the framework further. Here is just one example.

In case you can't turn back to Volume 6, I would like to quote Robert Stake (1967), as I did in that Volume (Unit 2 Component 6) — This section is also culled from Derek Rowntree's book *Curriculum Development in Educational Technology.*

"A full evaluation results in a story . . . it reveals perceptions and judgments . . . it tells of merits and shortcomings. Two main kinds of data are collected:
1. objective descriptions . . .
2. personal judgments . . ."

(in Rowntree, D. (1982) *Curriculum Development in Educational Technology* Harper and Row)

Our present Component is really also about evaluation. Any analysis of training materials which meets the five criteria listed in the Introduction on page 1, is, in effect, evaluating; it **will** tell 'a story' and there should be objective description; it **will** contain judgements and point to merits and shortcomings.

Our aim, as analysis, should therefore be to organise our information so that it makes sense and can be used to help others who need to make judgements and decisions about training materials.

We already have our questions for analysis of training materials arranged in four sections Aims/objectives, Sequence; Content; Evaluation. Stake suggests that it might be useful to organise the evidence of evaluation — in our case, the answers to our analysis questions — into two main sections.

1. **Descriptive** This part is concerned with saying clearly and objectively what the materials are like.
2. **Judgemental** This second section can draw on the **evidence** of Part 1, to enable us, as analysts, to make judgements about the materials themselves and eventually to suggest how they might work in training situations in general and in our own training context in particular.

   It would be especially interesting, of course, to have evidence gained from actually observing the materials in use in a training situation. Component 2 of this package discusses the use of 'empirical evidence' and you may wish to turn back now to look at that section again. Any analysis we might write would be much strengthened by such evidence, particularly if it was the result of observation in several contexts. **Component 4 will be devoted entirely to this important strategy.**

Producing Your Framework for Analysis

So, now to our detailed **framework.** I will start the process, with suggested Headings, Sub-Headings and examples, but of course I can't include everything from your list and I won't include everything from mine. **I'll put in enough to illustrate what I mean and then leave the rest to you to complete.**

The **easiest** thing would be for me to offer a 'blue-print' scheme, but all along I have suggested that the aim of the Component is to enable you to produce your own Framework, based on your own particular needs. What follows and much of what has already been suggested is strongly influenced by one particular scheme of analysis, known as the 'Sussex Scheme' — developed by Dr Michael Eraut and others at Sussex University and used by many authors as a model [for example Open University Course P234/E364]. For further details see Reading List at the end of the Unit.

But the essence is not necessarily to **adopt** an existing scheme, more to think through what **you** need and then **adapt**, borrow, develop, modify, expand, until you find that you have something which is well thought out, rigorous and useful and which, above all, is purpose-built and suits the requirements of **your** situation.

1. Description

(A) Introduction

[for example, quite briefly;]

What do the materials consist of?

What are their aims as stated by the authors/designers?

What is their 'target audience'? (type of trainee? — at what stage in training? etc.)

What is the cost? (— overall or in parts)

etc. etc. Add any other points which you think should be here (refer to your own list). The Introduction should consist of brief, to the point details, the analyst's version of the publisher's pamphlet.

(B) Detailed descriptive analysis of the materials

[for example]

(1) Trainee materials (if any)

(a) What is the **form** of the materials? (range of media? etc).

(b) What is the **content**? (Earlier we thought it important to note the **emphasis**, so: list major topics which occur in the Trainee's Manual or text book; perhaps give a specific example of what you consider to be typical material; possibly actually describe in some detail a key section; produce quantitative evidence to show relative emphasis on particular aspects

(c) What trainee tasks/activities are included? (for example: How varied? etc.)

(d) How is the content sequenced?

(2) Trainer materials

Use any of the points from B(1), as appropriate. Add others:

(for example)

How presented?

Containing any extra material to use with trainees?

What trainer tasks and roles and time requirement are listed?

Is there any indication of further resources which might be needed?

etc.

(3) Structure of the materials
(for example:)
How do trainer/trainee materials fit together?
Content?
etc. etc.

(C) Judgemental analysis
(for example:)
Suggest likely patterns of use.
Suggest ways in which the materials may be modified/supplemented.
Suggest implications for the organisation adopting the materials (such as staff time required before and during use)
etc. etc.

[Much of this section would include the answers to questions of judging such things as the appropriateness of the structure already described or the quality of the activities suggested to bring about appropriate results. In all cases our judgements, if they are to be convincing, must be based on the evidence of the description, by extra specific illustration, or by user reports etc.]

I have started an 'organising' framework for the questions we have raised together in this component and I have fitted one or two of them in as illustrations. The purpose of this Checkpoint is to use the results of your thinking and searching out to reach a final draft of a scheme of analysis which you think would work in your situation.

Tutor Seen Work

Work which you can send to your tutor is usually suggested at the end of each Unit. You may feel that you would like me to look at the result of what you have done in the final Checkpoint, to get my reaction and suggestions. If you would like to do this please send me your Framework now. (You will see that the work suggested at the end of the Unit also includes the possiblity of actually applying the Framework and analysing some materials of interest to you).

Conclusion — The Benefits of the Exercise

In this Component most of the points I have raised have been general but because you have been thinking about your own situation and probably about specific types of material, your points for inclusion in an analysis will probably have been more specific. For example, if the video medium is much used in your training you will tend to have made provision for questions relating to how well the medium is exploited; similarly for tape/slide or print, (with the latter there will be a place for type size, style, layout etc.; with the former there will be a concern with sound quality, visual quality, the linking of the two, etc.).

All the thinking you have done will have been useful, even if you never actually get down to a detailed written analysis. It will have enabled you to identify the key areas to consider, even when you have to scan materials quickly to consider how useful they are in your training context. A check list on the back of a post-card may be all you need — but if you do just this you will know that your list is not random but that it is the fined-down version of a more detailed consideration of key points.

Another possibility is that, having considered everything that is available commercially or locally, the decision is to design and produce your own materials. Component 2 has already looked at the analysis of such materials but the process of working through these two Components will have helped you, we hope, to reconsider most of the issues which are crucial in Course or Materials Design. The ability to ask the right questions in a systematic way is a very useful tool to the designer of materials, both in helping him in the process of design itself and in looking back at the finished product.

Component 4 will take us a stage further in the business of analysis/evaluation — looking at materials in use in a training context.

Component 4:

Observing Training: The Process

Key Words

 **Observation; points of focus; drawing up criteria; methods of recording; observation schedules; objectivity/subjectivity; qualitative/quantitative.**

Introduction

When we examine training materials, we usually suffer from the disadvantage of seeing them 'cold' and out of context. If we are looking at the materials purely out of general interest, as trainers, or as reviewers, we will probably have to **imagine** how they might work in different contexts to consider how widely applicable and how versatile they may be. On the other hand, if we are looking for training materials to meet a particular need in our own organisation we will tend to assess them very much in terms of how suitable they seem to be for our own special context.

One of the most obvious steps to take when one is attempting to solve a training problem is to purchase or develop appropriate materials. Components 2 and 3 have considered ways in which to look objectively and thoroughly at both 'in house' and 'commercial' materials. In these two Components it is suggested that a very good way of evaluating materials of both kinds is to see them in use before the final decision to buy, adopt, adapt or develop is made.

This present Component and the next one focus on two very important aspects of the evaluation of training materials, the observation of the training process and of training materials in use. As with Component 3, we hope that this double Component will enable you to **develop** a methodology which suits **your** purpose rather than to suggest that a particular method can possibly be the right one for every trainer in any context. We hope that this ability to look objectively at training in context and materials in use will add an extra, vital dimension to the method of training materials analysis which you may already have worked out (Component 3). We also think that, even taken alone, without the materials analysis, an observational methodology will be useful to most people who are involved in training at almost any level.

Component 4 is thus entitled 'Observing Training — the process' and Component 5, 'Observing Training — the materials.'

Looking at Training

(a) The Trainer

If we decide to examine the Training Process, we will almost inevitably turn away briefly from the training materials themselves in order to consider what we naturally actually focus on first when we 'sit in' on a training session. Almost inevitably we'll look first at the trainer. Is he any good?

This will be our starting point now, before we look at the influence of the materials on what the trainer does and consider whether materials do exist which are 'trainer proof', and which will help even poor or inexperienced trainers to make a good job of things. We'll also think about other important points of focus, for example the trainees. How to assess how well particular materials help trainers and trainees along will be an important part of Component 5.

Observing what people are doing as a method of discovering the truth about what makes for 'good' training or teaching has occupied many researchers over the years. One of the aims of the Training Technology Programme is to help trainers find practical solutions to their own training problems, a "how to . . ." approach. Most of our authors have tried to avoid too much academic or historical background — we certainly have in this Unit — but at this moment it will be useful, I think, to review the scene of observational methodology, if only briefly. This should help us to appreciate the strengths and weaknesses of some popular approaches and also prevent us from 'reinventing the wheel'.

In the area of observational methodology the overlap between teaching and training clearly exists, although this doesn't mean that most of the 'instruments' for observing teaching in schools transfer readily to the training context — they don't. But to illustrate the sort of connection I mean, I'll quote briefly from an article by M. Galton in the journal *Educational Research* in 1979*. He in turn was quoting an American authority (Nuthall):

> "We have always had a large number of ideas about how teachers should behave, without any evidence that those ideas were right or wrong. Now we have a large number of observation systems for describing how teachers do behave, without any evidence that the things we're observing are the right or wrong things to observe."

If we substitute 'trainers' for 'teachers' in the above passage we may perhaps start our consideration of how to observe training in context with some caution.

Many of us at some time or another have probably seen training being carried out or experienced it, perhaps in a variety of contexts even — at work, away from work (maybe in a voluntary organisation like the scouts or guides) or perhaps in the services. To the casual observer or even to the person actually experiencing it, the training tends to be judged quite simply as good or bad with a number of points on a scale between the two. As Nuthall says, we have our own ideas about what training should be like and the only evidence that these are based on is probably 'gut feel', our own personal reaction to it.

Checkpoint

List some of the qualities which you think good training involves.

Although, as I have said, your ideas will tend to be personal, I'm fairly certain that you'll have listed quite a few of the points I've included in random order below or perhaps others equally important.

- *the objectives are clear*
- *task clearly explained*
- *trainer praises*
- *trainer conveys warmth*
- *the whole group involved*
- *variety of materials used*
- *trainer encourages trainees through facial expression (smiles, nods etc.)*
- *the session has good pace*

etc.

---

*Vol 21 No 2 (Galton M., Systematic Classroom Observation: British Research)

If we are invited to observe training taking place in our own firm or elsewhere it's possible then that we may go along with the sort of criteria we've listed above in mind — a sort of mental check list. We may even write out a list of such things to look for. What is interesting is that most of my list focusses on **the trainer** and hardly at all on the trainee(s) and not at all on the materials. This is not surprising really. If we do have the opportunity of seeing someone doing the sort of job we do ourselves or are about to take on it's natural that we make comparisons between that and the kind of results we hope to achieve or may some time reach. It's very likely that we'll come away from such an experience with a **description** of what the trainer did and of what actually happened and there will probably be some sort of **judgement** about how well we thought he did it.

How useful is this going to be to us in our own training context? Well, it's always good to see other people with a similar job to your own doing that job. You usually feel that you've learned something new yourself which you can incorporate into your own work. Sometimes it may be that nothing you have seen appears to be very much better than the way you do things — in which case, you may feel quite encouraged. Either way, it's a worth-while experience.

Note:

Components 4 and 5 make use of common audio and video case study material. Please read the instructions which follow here in conjunction with the final section of Component 5 entitled Case Study (Components 4 and 5) 'The Training Session'.

1. Listen to/watch the first part of 'The Training Session'. **Switch off at the 'bleeps'.**
   Using the list we made from the previous Checkpoint, identify what you consider to be the key 'good' features of the presentation.

I certainly listed several amongst them, but I highlighted

* **encourage trainees** *through facial expression, smiles etc.*
* **good pace**
* **trainer conveys warmth**

Although you were working from a checklist, was it easy to be objective, or did you find yourself 'judging' subjectively, almost without noticing it?

The Trainer was using notes. To what extent were you focusing on the **materials**, *the 'course' itself, or did your attention rest on the personality of the Trainer as mine did?*

Obviously some of these considerations will be impossible for you if you don't have access to video equipment.

You have seen that I certainly found myself being impressed by the Trainer's personality. His topic was Communication and he was showing very well how to communicate. I tended to forget that the Trainer was following a planned course — some training materials which several other Trainers in the Bank actually use too.

Being objective. Describing what the trainer did is

one thing but making judgements about how well the trainer himself did is quite another. Objectivity in observing others is difficult. In other parts of the Training Technology Programme, particularly in the **Assessment and Evaluation** Volume, the question of objective and subjective judgements has been raised. We know that it's all too easy to let purely personal feelings get in the way of balanced judgement. You don't like the look of the person, or perhaps you are fascinated by the way the person talks, or maybe the room is too hot and you can't concentrate on anything. In all three cases your own feelings may affect your judgement. It is quite alarming to look at some of the research on observing training and teaching, particularly when it sometimes involves important assessment, because it is clear that subjectivity does often play an enormous role. One study involved a sample of sixty student teachers. Fourteen supervisors, working in pairs observed and assessed lessons. There was a very low level of agreement obtained by pairs of supervisors. The researchers (White and McIntyre, 1977) wrote: "Reading some of the . . . reports of pairs alongside one another, it is difficult to believe that the writers had in fact observed the same lesson!" . . .

So, although it is interesting to see other people at work and to compare our own performance with theirs in the way we inevitably all do, it may be more useful to offset this personal, subjective view with something more structured and more objective.

For example, it will probably be very helpful to look at the training process in the context of the trainer's objectives for the session you are observing. It will be very useful to know how this particular session fits in to the programme, what went before and what will follow.

(b) The Trainees

If particular outcomes or behaviours are aimed for, it will be interesting to observe what the **trainees** actually do. We may be spending too much time looking at the trainer. He may sometimes be just a sort of 'enabler' or a master of ceremonies, the person who sees that things go right and that his trainees are actually **doing** things that will enable them to learn. The trainer's 'performance', if that is all we are looking at, may not seem very impressive at all if we only have regard for what **he** is doing, or even worse, what he is saying. If you have experience of training already, you may remember an occasion when you wondered why your trainees didn't seem able to do something which you had thought you'd taught them particularly well. (It's even worse if they **all** can't do whatever it is! Can they **all** be stupid or is it possible that there was something wrong with that very good training session you thought you'd given?) Very often teachers and trainers talk too much. We sometimes feel better if **we** are performing but we forget that for learning to take place it's absolutely vital that we should **let our trainees do something** themselves. When we observe the training process, therefore, an important focus must be the trainees and what **they** are doing.

Summary

So far we have identified two fairly obvious points of focus for our attention when we are observing the training process, the trainer and the trainees. We have listed a number of characteristics of 'good' training, but we have recognised the dangers of a purely subjective focus and particularly the importance of looking at what the trainees are doing and not just thinking about the trainer. Effective training must obviously be a two way process.

We already have two important areas upon which to focus as we observe and as we will want next to consider how best to look at a third dimension, the training materials and the part they play in the interaction of trainee and trainer, it will be useful to suggest methods of recording what actually happened rather than just relying on our own memory or a notebook.

Observing the Training Process

(a) Methods of recording what actually happens in a training session

Up till now we have assumed that if we want to see training in progress the best thing to do is to 'sit in' on a training session to see what happens. Without embarking on a detailed discussion about the relative merits of this method and other possibilities, such as video or audio recording it may be worth making a brief examination of some of the methods commonly used by observers to record 'the truth'.

a. **Sitting in'** Although this seems to be the most obvious and the simplest thing to do, research has shown that the actual presence of an observer changes the situation, sometimes quite markedly. A French researcher (Adda - 1982) writes of what she calls this 'paradox of the observer'. "We must remember", she says, "that this is not a group without an observer, it's a group in which **we** are present"; that is to say, because we are there it is in fact a **different** group. Our presence changes the situation. The trainer and the trainees may now act differently. If you know someone is sitting there watching and even making notes, you do tend to behave differently, depending perhaps on how you see the observer (a threat? Someone to be impressed? Someone to 'play' to?). One could argue that an observer isn't ever likely to see 'typical' training anyway. At the very least the trainer will have to **agree** to the observer being present and the visit will have to be prearranged. It's unlikely that you will even be able just to 'drop in' on some training, out of the blue.

   Where an observer sits or stands in the training area may make a difference. The best way to observe is to try to minimise the difference that you being there makes by simply trying to fade in to the background or becoming part of the furniture — preferably both!

Try to fade into the background and become part of the furniture

b. **Video recording**
One of the advantages of trying to record what is happening when you are actually sitting in on the training is that any other method tends to be much more time consuming. The virtue of video recording is that it does enable you to view as many times as you like, to think about what you see and hear, to stop the tape and return to it later, to look at a particular part of the training process in detail. But, of course, the same objection that we raised in relation to the human observer may loom just as large or even larger with television. Even if the camera is unmanned, it is likely to create a certain feeling of apprehension amongst the participants; it is certain that the camera(s) and operator(s) do change the environment just as the observer did and the training situation is no longer the same.
Another problem with this method which you have probably thought of already is that the camera only sees what it is focussed on. A fixed camera may miss a lot and even a manned camera only looks at what the operator selects — so once again the subjective element can loom large. The fact that the camera is recording i.e. making **a record**, for viewing later on, out of context, may upset some people badly!

c. **Audio recording** on its own is obviously limited, except in rather unusual training circumstances (perhaps some kinds of speech or language training) so nearly always a visual record will be needed to supplement and illustrate. Slides linked with audio tape can form a good record but, again, it can never be a complete one.

Take the three methods I have discussed and consider each as a way of observing training in progress in your own context. Are there other methods you could use? You may find it helpful to use 3 columns to organise your thoughts.

Method	Advantages	Disadvantages

Your preference may well rest on practical constraints which force you to rely on a particular method. For example, the training you want to see takes place in a firm at the other end of the country so a video tape may be the only practicable way of seeing it. Or you don't have access to video and anyway the training can be seen at almost any time just down the road, so 'dropping in' may be easiest and cheapest.

It's possible, however, that, like me, you may think that the best way of overcoming the difficulties of each individual method is to use a combination of methods.

It's hard to record everything you see and hear when you 'sit in'. Perhaps a video recording will help you towards a complete picture and even an audio recording can actually help you to recall clearly what actually happened — the audio prompt sparks off the 'visual' memory.

(b) How to make sense of what we observe

One expert in the observation of training has observed, "Data overload can obscure what is really important." (Strachan, 1983).

The message here for us, looking at other people's training, is to decide very clearly just what it is we want to find out and not to be diverted by other considerations.

In this Component we have been thinking about the training process and, in particular, the interaction between trainer and trainee, what each does and how this brings about learning.

We have considered how this process may best be observed — how to see what actually happens. We have noted that all methods tend to have an element of **subjectivity** in them and that our judgements of what we see tend to be **qualitative;** that is, we are likely to be thinking or saying how good or how bad we think the training, the trainer or the trainees are. We know from research that observers making purely qualitative judgements tend to disagree. It may be that we can add another useful dimension to our observation by **quantifying** what goes on in the training context. **How much** of this or that activity? **How much** trainer talk? **How much** individual work? etc.

How can we make quantitative observations of the training process?

List at random what the trainer actually does, the range of his activities, when he is working with trainees. Your list is bound to depend on your own particular context.

Now compare it with mine.

The context I have chosen is a 'formal' situation. The trainees are probably in a 'classroom'. The trainer is face to face with the group.

In these circumstances the trainer activities might include **Routine** *i.e.* **organising** *the session, preparing trainees for activities, getting activities going etc.* **Presentation** *i.e. presenting information, providing a context for discussion, demonstrating etc.* **Questioning** *i.e. checking how well the material presented has been understood,* **Answering** *questions from the trainees.* **Explaining** *i.e. developing points from the presentation, developing points arising from questions etc.* **Monitoring** *i.e. checking on individual trainees as they work on a task; moving round and helping/advising members of the group.*

This list is just a start. It is certain that there would be other categories of Trainer Activities which would relate to the particular type of training being given and your list will probably include some of these.

If we now take our own list of categories it will be possible to monitor when each activity is happening during a training session, by recording what is actually taking place as time goes by. We could, perhaps, devise a simple grid which would show us, minute by minute just what the trainer was doing at that point. Clearly this would be a somewhat crude recording instrument, as some 'events' may only take a few seconds and be lost to the recorder, but we might still end up with some sort of quantitative record which will show us how much time the trainer spent doing various things.

The grid would therefore look something like the one below:

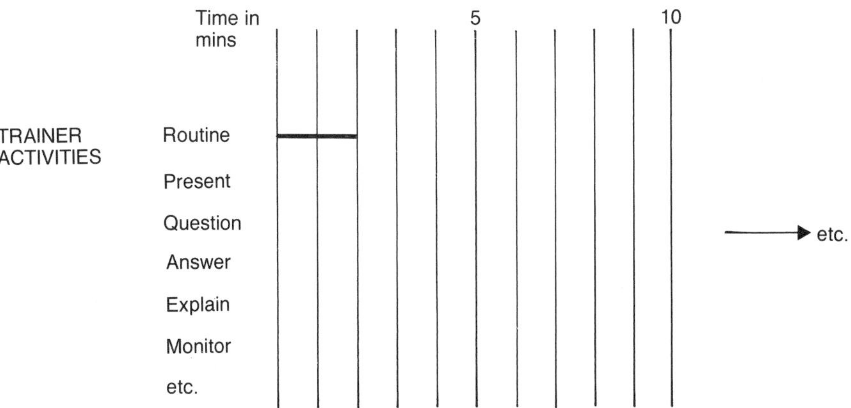

For each minute we could mark a dark line against the type of activity the Trainer was involved in. (Sometimes he might well be involved in more than one activity doing a minute or period so two or more lines would be marked). Let's look at an example:

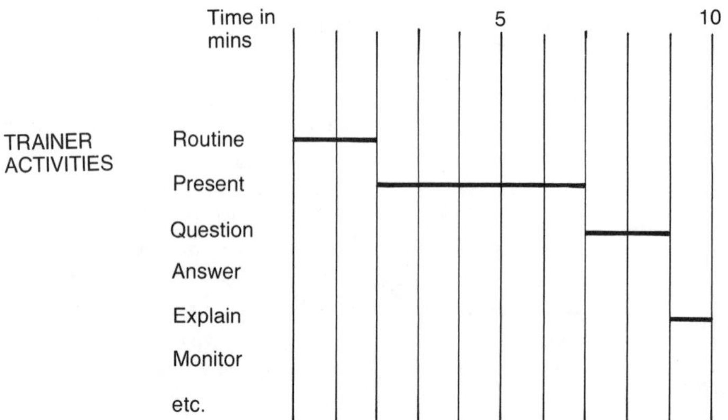

Here we can see that in the first 10 minutes of the training session, the first two minutes were routine activities, greetings perhaps, setting the scene etc. Then there was a brief presentation sequence lasting 5 minutes, followed by a couple of minutes when the Trainer asked questions and in the 10th minute an explanation sequence started.

It's easy to see that we could do the same sort of thing to record what the Trainees are doing too.

So, bearing your own situation in mind, make a list of typical trainee activities which one might record as an observer, in order to see how much time trainees spent on particular activities during a session.

My list relates to the 'formal' type of session I referred to above, so it includes Listening, Questioning, Answering, Writing, Reading, Talking/Discussing etc.

I can now arrange this in the continuation of the grid showing the Trainer activities in order to show what the trainees were doing at the same time.

For example:

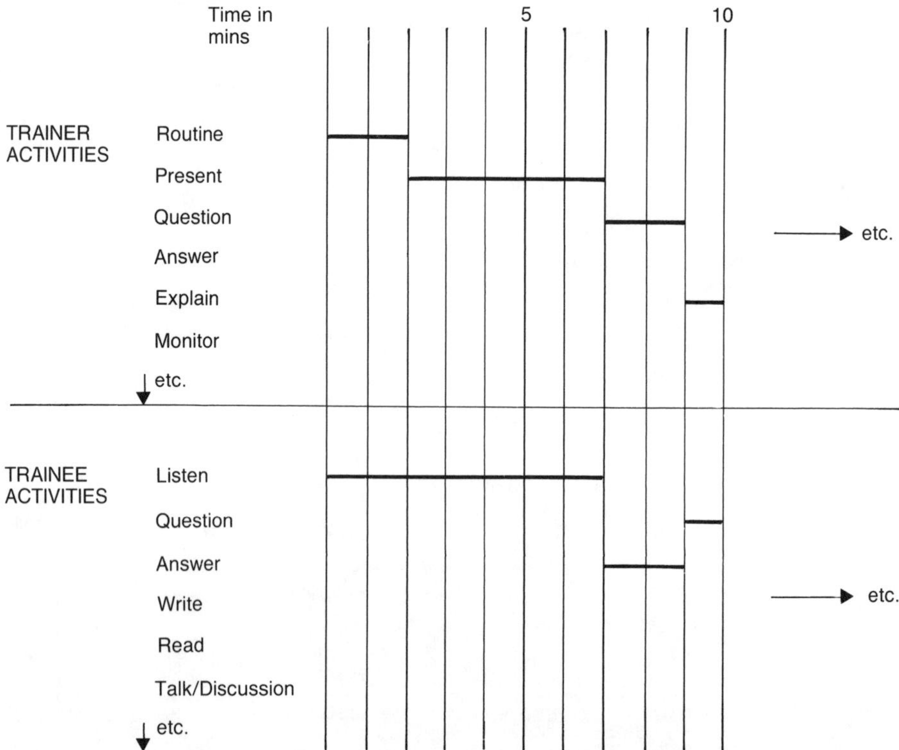

Now we can see that the trainees listened to the Routine and Presentation sections of the Trainer's session, responded to his question and then asked for clarification to elicit an explanation from the Trainer.

I hope that this begins to seem to be a flexible and

useful if rather basic method of helping us to focus on important aspects of the training process. You will already be thinking of other aspects you would wish to record, I feel sure. It is for you to build up a method which will suit you. But beware of over-complication! If you try to record too much, the observation schedule will become impossible to use. As we have said in this Component and in Volume 4 "Beware of information overload".

Beware of information overload

Recording How the Training is Organised
The next Component will look specifically at observing the use of training materials and how they influence the process, but before we leave this present Component which has focussed on the process itself, I would like to suggest one more area for the Observation Schedule. This is **Organisation.** Depending on the type of training, you will probably only need to include a few categories. Perhaps the following will suffice.

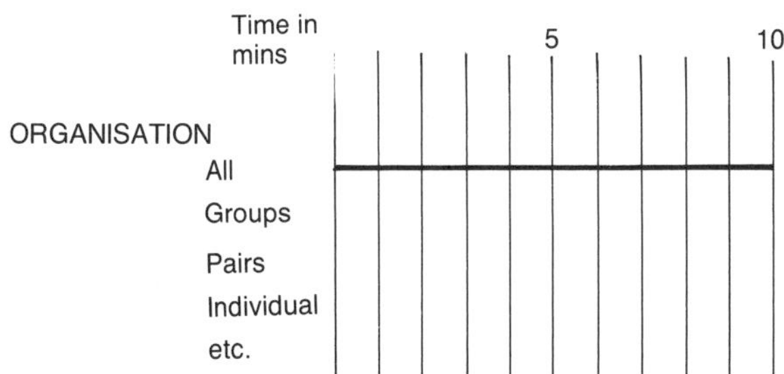

For the session for which I have already started to build up an observation record — the formal training session, for the first ten minutes the group was organised as a 'class', all together. The grid above reflects this. Later, perhaps, the Trainer might set up discussion groups, have trainees working in pairs on a problem or have them engaged in individual work.

Conclusion
In this Component the difficulties of recording accurately what actually happens in a training session are explored. What at first seems to be a simple matter of just sitting in on a session and letting it wash over you to get an impression in one method and it cannot be ignored. A 'gut feel' impression is often supported by other more 'scientific' observations. The unstructured, 'wash over' observation may often be useful in helping us to build up categories of activity to observe more closely. It may help us to focus on what trainers and trainees actually do and how the session is organised; that is, a more structured observation giving some quantitative information. Other methods of recording such as video or audio and slide may be useful too, perhaps ideally in conjunction with actually attending a training session.

The focus of the present Unit is on training materials. Clearly materials are there to influence and assist the success of the training process. The next Component looks specifically at how one might link the observation of the use of materials to the training process and it includes a further practical exercise which draws on our video and audio material.

Component 5:

Observing Training: The Materials

Key Words

 **Observation schedule; performance; process.**

The Introduction

In the last Component we began to draw up a 'schedule' to help us to observe the training process in a systematic way. We made lists of activities to help us to describe what the trainer and trainee actually did and how the sessions were organised. It's very likely that the trainer activities we listed were selected not just as typical trainer activities, but also as examples of what the 'good' trainer does. We all know that some trainers do nothing but 'lecture' to 'listening' trainees. My schedule for observation, and I'm sure, yours too, supposed that there was more to even a 'formal' training session than that. One could argue, therefore, I suppose, that even drawing up a schedule is subjective. It all depends on how we see 'good' training.

However, if we look at what trainers and trainees actually do and add categories or delete them as we observe, particularly if we have a chance to try out our observation schedule, we will begin to see that we are focussing on trainer and trainee **performance.**

When we consider **process** we inevitably convince ourselves that our focus should concentrate on **trainees.** What are they **doing** which enables them to learn? But when we look at trainee activities, we will probably begin to 'home in' on materials. 'Good' training materials will tend to be those with which trainees can learn, **despite** the trainer! Or, one could argue, even **without** the trainer, as with distance learning. This doesn't mean that the human element is not important. The encouragement and enthusiasm the good face-to-face trainer will be able to give to his trainees is often crucial. Indeed, in the first section of our audio/video material for this Unit, we noticed that in the hands of the good trainer, materials sometimes fade into the background. We may hardly be aware that a formal 'course' exists. But it is clearly necessary to note the importance **materials** can play in the training process.

Trainees can learn, despite the trainer!

So don't we need to develop a way of looking at the real life training situation which adds another dimension to the trainer/trainee interaction, that of the materials which, when they are good, can influence learning so powerfully? Perhaps we should now change the emphasis of our observation. As we are trainers or likely to be so, it's all too easy to think, first of all, about what **we** do with materials, how they improve **our** performance, whereas what we should be thinking about equally is how they improve the performance of our **trainees**. It's difficult sometimes to be dispassionate about this, because it sometimes means that we may be 'reduced' to being managers of training. It may be worrying sometimes, perhaps, if we don't seem to be occupying the centre of the stage. Sometimes, indeed, we may decide to take a back seat and to hand over entirely to the materials, as when we show a training video-tape.

What kind of instrument do we need in order to ensure that we can focus on materials just as we have been able to do on Trainer and Trainees, so that we can look objectively at the important business of **the selection of training materials**? We need to be able to take the process of analysis (Components 2 and 3) forward through observing materials in context, seeing how they influence the training taking place. We want to know how the particular materials do or do not influence the **quality** of the training and, in particular, what interrelationship there is between trainer activity, trainee activity, the way training is organised and the actual materials in use.

Oddly enough, observation of materials in action is at its most difficult when the materials are what we have called Trainer Materials (see Component 3), i.e. materials which the Trainer uses to help him to present his message. These could be notes, the plan for the session, material which we as observers or the trainees as learners don't see directly. Often when Trainers are 'performing' very convincingly, we may hardly be aware of the careful plan, the 'cue' cards, or the notes which are structuring the session to make it a confident, spontaneous-looking and highly professional affair. This is why Component 4 (The Process) was an important preliminary to this present one. The consideration of materials and the observation of materials in use are really only of interest when we see them in the context which we prepared in Component 4.

A. Schedule for Observing Training Materials in Use

We have already built up three areas on which to focus when observing training, Trainer, Trainees and Organisation. We now need to add a further dimension, Materials.

Checkpoint

Think now about materials. What do they include? Which media? Which training aids? Make a list of 'the media of training', that is the equipment of the trainer which enables him to present varied materials to the trainees. (The materials can often only be what the trainer can actually present, according to the resources he has available).

I will continue with the example of a 'Formal' training session which I started in Component 4. The equipment for materials for such a session might include Board (black or white); Flipchart; OHP; Slides; Video; Audio; Wall Chart; Worksheet; Text(book); Handouts. The list could be longer. I'm sure that you may also have included Microcomputer; Model; Real objects; Interactive Video etc., depending on your area of work and the level of sophistication of your training programme.

It is now possible to draw up a full observation schedule which, ideally, we can try out in our own training context before using in the observation of training materials elsewhere. You will recall that the focus of Component 4 and of this present one is on that extra dimension which the observation of training materials in use can give us when we are trying to undertake a full detailed analysis of materials. It will not just help us to decide whether to adopt or adapt materials which exist already, produced 'in house' by our own or another organisation or commercially; it will also help us to draw some important conclusions about **how materials should be designed**, so that if we decide to create our own, we can avoid the weaknesses and exploit the strengths which we have noted in the work of others.

One might even say that doing a detailed materials analysis is a very useful preparation for anyone who has to develop training materials. It makes us think clearly and systematically about the whole business of training technology and how best to apply it to our own situation.

The Training Observation Schedule (TROBS)*

If we put the four dimensions to be observed into one schedule, we find that we have an observation instrument which will help us to focus systematically on what we really need to see, materials in use in training. I have put together the categories I decided upon for my formal training session and you will find the complete schedule on the next full page. You will notice that I have added a top line which enables me to note a change of activity by simply putting a tick at the appropriate time-elapsed point. At the bottom, there is a line to enable me to note very briefly the 'content' of the training (for example: note taking/reporting back/simulate telephone conversation etc.). I have left this schedule absolutely blank, in order to let you photocopy it for use in a practical exercise a little later. On the following page, however, you will find an example of the completed full schedule of the first ten minutes of the formal training session which I have used as an example over these two Components, 4 and 5. I hope you will agree that it does help us to see quite clearly the interrelationship of Trainer, Trainees, Organisation and Materials. It also provides us with the quantitative information which may add an

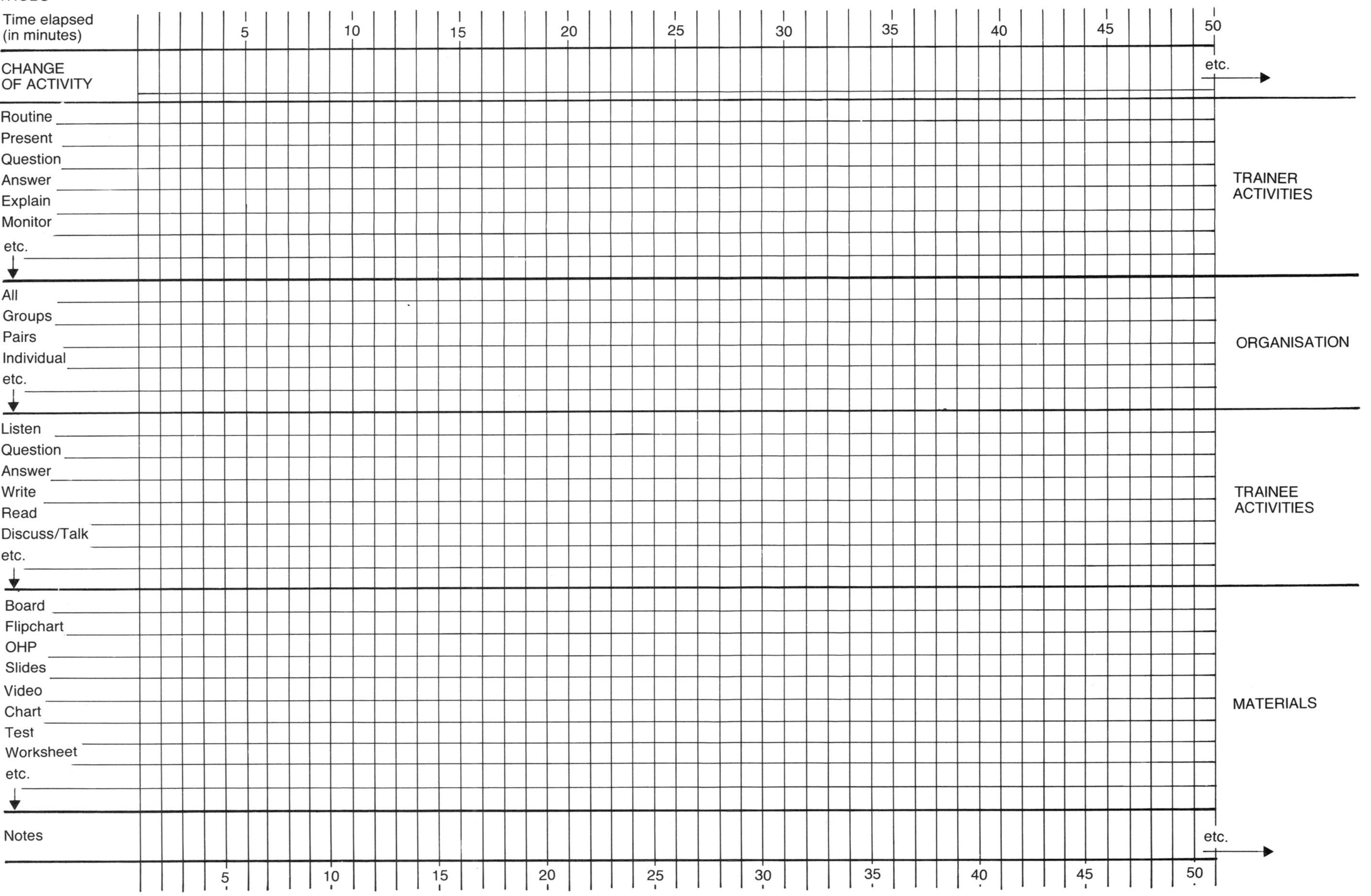
TROBS
Time elapsed (in minutes)
5
10
15
20
25
30
35
40
45
50
etc.
CHANGE OF ACTIVITY
Routine
Present
Question
Answer
Explain
Monitor
etc.
TRAINER ACTIVITIES
All
Groups
Pairs
Individual
etc.
ORGANISATION
Listen
Question
Answer
Write
Read
Discuss/Talk
etc.
TRAINEE ACTIVITIES
Board
Flipchart
OHP
Slides
Video
Chart
Test
Worksheet
etc.
MATERIALS
Notes

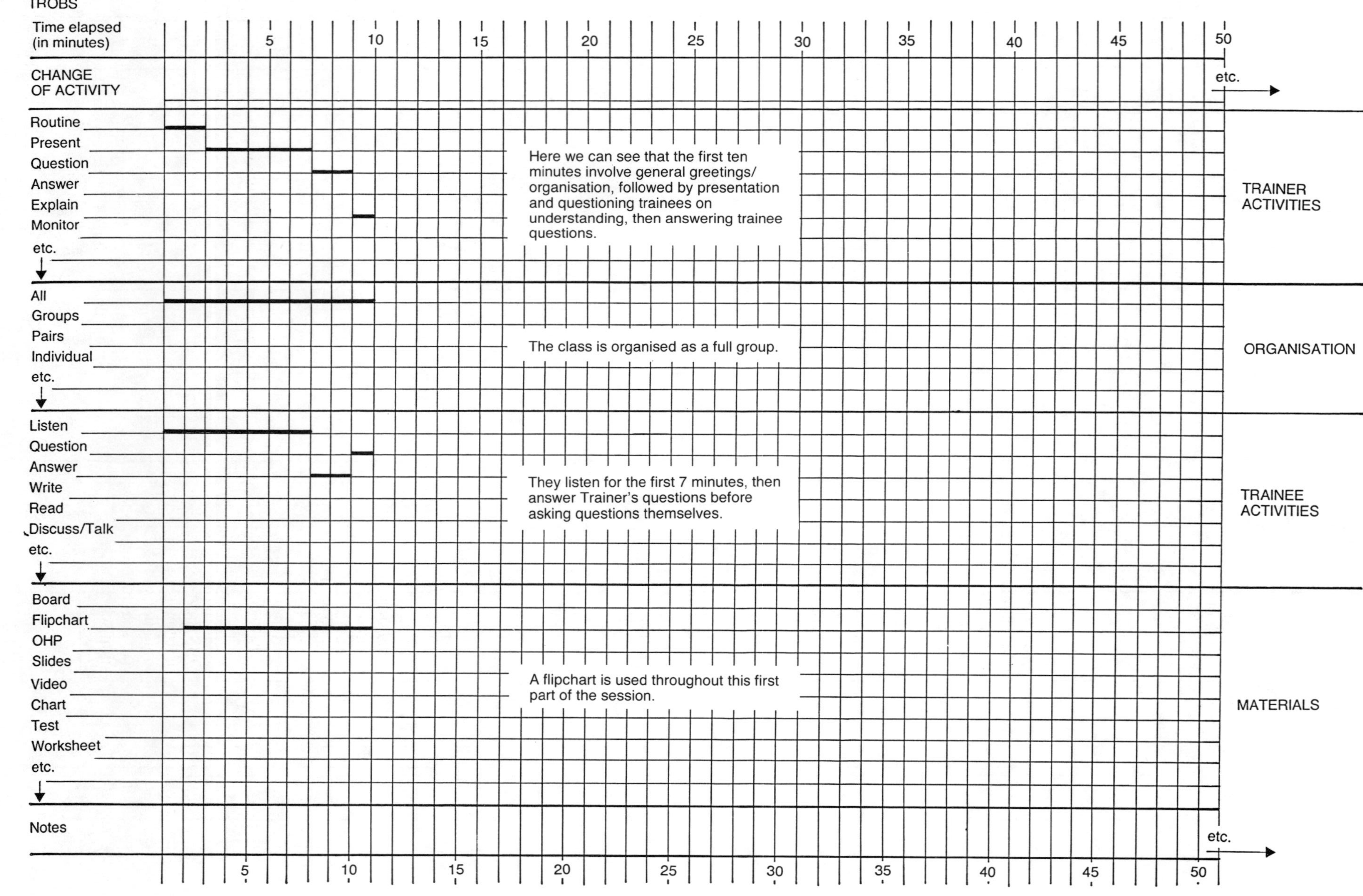
TROBS
Time elapsed (in minutes)
5
10
15
20
25
30
35
40
45
50
CHANGE OF ACTIVITY
etc.
Routine
Present
Question
Answer
Explain
Monitor
etc.
Here we can see that the first ten minutes involve general greetings/ organisation, followed by presentation and questioning trainees on understanding, then answering trainee questions.
TRAINER ACTIVITIES
All
Groups
Pairs
Individual
etc.
The class is organised as a full group.
ORGANISATION
Listen
Question
Answer
Write
Read
Discuss/Talk
etc.
They listen for the first 7 minutes, then answer Trainer's questions before asking questions themselves.
TRAINEE ACTIVITIES
Board
Flipchart
OHP
Slides
Video
Chart
Test
Worksheet
etc.
A flipchart is used throughout this first part of the session.
MATERIALS
Notes
etc.

important dimension to our analysis of materials in use. By simply adding the time spent on each category of each dimension, we can formulate clear statements about, for example, the influence the training materials seemed to have on the particular session.

*In this Component and the last, the building up of the TROBS relies heavily on the work of Nicki Lees and, in particular her instrument for classroom observation described in Report No 15, University of Leicester (School of Education) 1983.

B. Practical application

Introduction

I have suggested that you should try out your observation schedule and then modify it and also decide on how easy or difficult it is to manage. As this may not be easy if you haven't a readily available group to observe or because you think it may be difficult to get someone to agree to let you try, it will probably be helpful now to try out my schedule, focussing on a real-life training session which is recorded both on audio and video tape. I have provided both to enable those without access to video playback to get some flavour of the training session, to see how much of the TROBS they can complete, and to come to some conclusions about the value of audio recording as an aid to the 'observational' part of materials analysis. I hope that those who have access to both audio and video playback will be able to make some comparisons between the audio and video record of events and also to note the strengths and weaknesses of each medium (see Component 4).

Note: Components 4 and 5 make use of common audio and video case study material. Please read the instructions which follow here in conjunction with the final section of this present Component entitled Case Study (Components 4 and 5) *The Training Session.*

Instructions

1. If you haven't completed the second Checkpoint of Component 4, start the audio or video tape at the beginning. The section up to the 'bleeps' will provide you with the **context** for the focus on the training materials. The general theme of the session is **Communication**. You may like to complete the Component 4 Checkpoint now, if you haven't done so already or, alternatively, to refresh your memory about it.
2. At the 'bleeps', stop the tape and ensure that you have ready a blank TROBS sheet. Restart the tape and as you watch and/or listen, fill it in as best you can, depending on the limitations of the recording medium. (With video, it should be possible to complete a full observation schedule).

The main aim of the last Checkpoint was to practise the use of the TROBS, to decide whether you can handle it and eventually to modify it to suit you.

a) **Using the TROBS**
   Was it reasonably easy to use the TROBS? Do you need all the categories? Did you need some categories which weren't there? What about short 'asides' and 'non-verbal' behaviour (smiling, encouraging, etc)?
b) How easy is it to construct a TROBS which will be useful for all types of training session?

My own experience when I tried the TROBS with the video tape was that it **was** *possible to record in all 4 areas without difficulty.*

Your observation just now included a rather special section of the training session (a longish video section) so you certainly didn't need all the categories then. In this section, what else was interesting, apart from the training video itself?

I felt that I wanted to note just how often the trainer actually used encouraging 'signals' and non-verbal behaviour (eye-contact, smiles). I was also interested in the way the trainees reacted, how interested they seemed, and whether **they** *smiled, laughed etc. The TROBS didn't help me here. But I did observe that the trainees* **took notes** *(showing interest) and that is recorded on my TROBS.*

Summary

Components 4 and 5 have raised a number of important issues concerning the observation of training in progress and training materials in use.

- "Look-and-see" methods, sitting in and letting the training session wash over you will tend to lead to a subjective judgement of how good/bad the training or, more likely, the trainer was. In effect, 'gut feel' judgement can be a useful starting point in observing training and it may help us to select important points of focus for more structured observation.
- Even if we identify points of focus, we may be missing a lot of what is **really** important. The very selection of points can be **subjective**.
- More focus on **quantitative** methods may help us to build up a clear picture of what the various participants are actually **doing** and for how long. But some activities may produce an odd quantitative 'picture', as when trainees sit and silently watch a videotape (particularly if an instrument is not 'fine' enough to 'monitor' laughs and smiles etc.).

Conclusion

Although that fairly selective summary seems to suggest no firm conclusion or even, perhaps, that objective observation is both so complicated and unreliable as to be a waste of time, a number of valuable lessons may be learned.

It is clear that no single method of observation will

suffice to cover the range of situations we might wish to observe.

In Component 4, our case study enabled us to see that fairly unstructured methods might be useful in identifying **categories**, and thereafter a structured method might help us to **home in** on particular aspects.

— Structured observation instruments need to use carefully selected categories for observation — and not too many of them.
— Sound and video recording can provide a comprehensive record of events and, though both have limitations, advantages include being able to play and replay sections for careful, detailed analysis and for one to consider real training situations at a distance.
— Short descriptive passages or even short notes need to be used to illustrate significant events or to record impressions which could be missed by some of the other methods.
— If one uses a range of methods of observing and recording, one is more likely to be able to assess with reasonable confidence the contribution of **materials** to the success or otherwise of the training. This is why this present Unit is in the Volume entitled 'The Management of Training'. A vital part of managing training must be the selection or construction of good and appropriate training materials. Careful analysis, which includes thorough, carefully planned and structured observation of the materials in use should contribute vitally to decisions to adopt, to adapt or to reject materials.

Case Study Materials for Components 4 and 5 — 'The Training Session'

a) **Background**

The Trainer is a young yet experienced member of the Bank of Scotland staff. He has been specially selected to work for a time at the Bank's Training Centre in Edinburgh.

The Trainees are newly employed members of the Bank's staff undergoing new entry training at the Centre after having spent a short period in a Branch of the Bank.

The Materials are the Trainer's personal notes, a videotape, and a handout for the trainees for the session on Communication and, in particular, Telephone Techniques.

(Although we may properly think of training materials as something carrying information (see Component 1), it is sometimes the case, as in a formal, lecture-type of session, that the materials actually **become** the 'performance', what the trainer and trainees do. The 'hardware' the trainer used to help him communicate carries information derived from the notes or from the trainer/trainee interaction, so this too can be seen as part of the training materials. This view may help you in your overall analysis of the effectiveness of the materials in action in a 'formal' session.)

b) **Your Own Course Materials**

Your audio and videotapes are a record of what actually happened at the training session. The session was not rehearsed. No sections have been edited out and there was no break in the recording of the session. The Bank of Scotland Videotape used by the Trainer is 'imbedded' in your own audio and video materials.

Note: If you have access to the final Volume in the Programme (Interactive Video in Training) you will find it interesting to refer to two other examples of materials for teaching Telephone Techniques, one in the text and one on the Videotape.

The Trainer's Materials

The final section of this Component consists of the Trainer's notes and the Trainees' handout, authentic and as they were used on the day.

Trainer's Notes

COMMUNICATION

Much of your work in the Bank will involve communicating with customers in some way or another.

What is communication? OHP

— It is the art of being able to convey your meaning to others.

Therefore, What forms of Communication can we use?

— Face to Face
— Telephone
— Letters

Let us now look at these various ways of communication in more detail.

Face to Face Communication

For those of you in Branches and to a lesser extent departmental staff much of your day's work will be dealing with customers at the enquiry counter. If after talking to a customer they don't understand what you mean — it's your fault!

What are some of the problems which can cause difficulty when we try to communicate? PUT SELF IN CUSTOMER'S SHOES!

1) WORDS — Can mean different things to different people.
2) LANGUAGE — Different accents/dialects.
3) PHYSICAL — Age, infirmity.
4) KNOWLEDGE — Never Bluff — limitations yours/theirs.
5) JARGON — Never use technical terms. (Fiche, Forward Postman.)
65) EMOTIONS — Anger, sadness.

So, why do these problems arise?

Every customer is different because of different — OPINIONS — ATTITUDES — EDUCATION — BACKGROUNDS — PRIORITIES — PREJUDICES.

Now we have identified the problems of communication and their causes, let's see how we can overcome them.

1) Recognise that these problems do exist.
2) Be polite and confident — Good Morning/Afternoon etc.
3) Have note pad and pen to take notes.
4) Treat all customers the same — with the utmost respect.

5) Put yourself in the customer's shoes — how does it feel?
A mnemonic to help you.
On Acetate.

L	isten	— listening takes a conscious effort.
I	nterest	— show an interest in your customer.
S	imple words	— are easy to understand.
T	ake notes	— jot down the main points.
E	nquire	— does the customer understand? — do you? — check.
N	ever argue	— win an argument — lose a customer!

Letters
At this stage in your careers you won't be writing letters to customers. You will possibly be concerned with posting the letters out to them.
MAKE SURE ; Correct postage is on and Date is changed on franking machine.
Watch Out for air-mail.
Watch Out for registered/recorded.
Watch Out for any enclosures.
Encourage to read the office mail.

Telephone Techniques

Introduction
One of the first jobs that will bring you into contact with your customers is answering the telephone.

This is a very important job and when we have telephoned Branches and Departments we have noticed, on a number of occasions, that their telephone technique could be greatly improved.

How many of you would feel confident about answering the telephone in the Branch? Compare this to answering the telephone at home with your friend on the line. What is the difference?

In the Branch you do not know the callers or whether you can deal with their request/enquiries — at home you are relaxed and are naturally more confident.

We are now going to spend some time discussing TELEPHONE TECHNIQUE so that when you return to your Branches you will be able to deal with all types of calls correctly.

First of all we must ensure that we have a good telephone manner.

WHY?

Because our customers are of the utmost importance to the Bank and we want to create a good impression over the telephone AT ALL TIMES.

How Should We Sound?
For that reason we must sound:
FRIENDLY
POLITE
INTERESTED — on board
PATIENT
EFFICIENT

Let us now look at how we can convey these points over the telephone.

NEVER let the telephone ring for a long time. What does customer think? 2-4 rings should be sufficient. If you are engaged then ask someone else to answer.

Don't use a false telephone voice, e.g. "I ken what you're talking about" — BE YOURSELF — sound confident on the telephone as this will make the caller confident in the Bank. Also do not sound monotone as this will not impress the caller.

What Should You Say When You Answer the Telephone?
Good Morning/Afternoon. Bank of Scotland . . . . . .
May I help you?

We must then listen to our caller's enquiries and requests. Don't try to retain information in your head. Always organise your desk and have a pen/pencil and notepad beside the telephone so that you may take a note of the caller's name and also purpose of his enquiry as this saves confusion and the risk of the caller repeating himself at a later stage.

NEVER say hello or answer with the Bank's telephone number. Why? Exchange of unnecessary banter wasting the caller's time and patience.

Once you have listened to the caller's enquiry, noting the relevant points you should then try and deal with it as quickly as possible so that the caller is not kept 'hanging on' on the other end.

To speed up enquiries, if we know that it is a customer we can ask certain questions:—

e.g. Do you know your account number?

If there is going to be excessive delay, i.e. 30 seconds-1 minute, ask if you can 'phone back as this seems like an eternity on the other end of the telephone.

This enables us to go about our task more efficiently.

From time to time you may be asked for information which for SECURITY PURPOSES CANNOT be divulged over the telephone.
ASK COURSE FOR EXAMPLES.

1. BALANCES OF ACCOUNTS:— could be anyone. Alternatively offer to send them out a statement, but tell them this will take two days or use Autoteller account balance enquiry facility if applicable. Telephoning back a customer can be dangerous as the caller may be a burglar in the house. For this reason it is not always advisable, but if the customer becomes insistent refer to an official who will decide if it is permissible for you to telephone back with balance — always acquire telephone number independently.

2. CUSTOMERS' ADDRESSES:— never divulge these over the telephone. If someone wishes to send correspondence to your customer tell them that if they send it care of the Bank we would be only too happy to forward it onto our customer on their behalf.

3. ENQUIRIES ABOUT INTERNAL ASPECTS OF THE BRANCH
   e.g. How much cash do we hold?
   When the remittance van arrives?
   How many members of staff are on duty during lunchtimes?

   The reason we would keep this information confidential is SECURITY — protecting your interest, the customers' interests and the Branch's interests.

A good percentage of incoming calls will require to be dealt with by other members of staff and for that reason you will have to transfer the call to the appropriate extension, e.g. change order from customer to teller. Are you going to interrupt the tellers? NO — we can take this information, complete one of these forms (SHOW) recording customer's name and time they will call to pick it up and pass it to the teller. For these reasons it is a good idea to keep a supply of these forms to hand. Know who is in the office, i.e. holidays, illness, etc., also know who deals with what in your office. Have a note of each extension number beside the telephone. Obtain the name of the customer asking him to hold. 'Phone appropriate extension remembering to inform them of the caller's name and purpose of their enquiry so that they do not have to repeat themselves again at a later stage.

What would you do if the person was unable to take the call? Explain circumstances to caller and ask if someone else could help them. If not, ask if it would be convenient for the Bank to call them back, remembering to take a note of their number and make sure this message is conveyed to the appropriate person.

ANY QUESTIONS?

Handout

Show Film
Get course to jot down errors made by bank clerk.

The Telephone

Incoming Calls
Be prepared with PEN and PAPER FOR NOTES.
Answer promptly and politely.
Always say "Good morning/afternoon, Bank of Scotland ...... Branch", don't simply give Branch's telephone number.
NEVER say "Hello" — this could lead to an exchange of "Hellos".
If call is from a coin box — wait for pips to stop then answer.
If call is cut off — don't call back — let caller re-establish contact — otherwise both will get 'engaged' tone.

Dealing with Customers' Enquiries
Jot down relevant details as briefly as possible.

If you are unable to answer a question — pass to senior member of staff.

If asked for confidential information e.g. customer's balance, customer's address, opinions on customers and Branch Security — refer to senior member of staff.

The 'Daily Mail' recently carried out a survey of British Banks and found it extremely easy to obtain particulars of private bank accounts over the telephone.

They stated that they were given a wealth of information about balances, overdraft facilities and signatories but were only armed with the information which appears on the front of any cheque i.e. name, account number and branch.

No particulars about an account can be disclosed over the telephone unless the member of staff is totally satisfied regarding the identity of the caller by asking questions which could not readily be answered by a third party. A list of these questions has been prepared by your branch, make sure you can quickly obtain the list when you answer the telephone.

It should be stressed that complete courtesy should be exercised at all times, even if bullied by the caller, and in cases of doubt the matter should be referred to a senior official.

Calls for the Manager
Get caller's name.

If Manager not available — ask caller if someone else can deal with call.

If caller insists on 'Holding on' — don't forget about him.

If caller wants Manager to call him back — take a note of the name and number and remember to pass on message.

Calls for the Teller
Don't interrupt a teller if he is busy with a customer — take a note of caller's name and number and remember to pass on message.

Outgoing Calls
Keep list by telephone of numbers used regularly.

If asked to get a number for the Manager say to the person you are calling "Good morning/afternoon Mr......., this is the Bank of Scotland, ... Branch. Our Manager, Mr. ...... would like to speak to you; one moment please." Then put the call through.

Telephones are effective only when they are properly used. Whoever answers the telephone represents the Bank of Scotland — and in many cases, creates the initial image of the Bank in the mind of the caller. The impression you create can be a lasting one and therefore it MUST be a GOOD one.

In every telephone conversation, there are SIX important principles:—

1. **Answer Promptly**
— quick service helps build a reputation of efficiency for your branch and for the Bank of Scotland as a whole, so try to answer on the first ring if possible.
2. **Identify Yourself**
— it saves time and gets the conversation off to a good start.
3. **Be Friendly**
— show that you are interested. Be a good listener so the person will not have to repeat what he says.
4. **Be Considerate**
— give the caller your undivided attention. Do NOT try to carry on two conversations at once. Callers should not be made to feel they are competing with people in your office for your attention.
5. **Keep your Promises**
— if you have agreed to call back with more information, or to pass a message on to someone else, do everything you can to keep that promise.
6. **Treat Every Call As An Important Call**
— when customers feel you are giving them personal consideration, they will have more confidence in you and the Bank.

Component 6:

Evaluating Training Materials

Key Words

Analysing; evaluating; judgements; decisions; worthwhileness; headings; check-lists; direct examination; empirical evidence; cost-effectiveness; reactions; culture and environment; comparative studies; purpose of evaluation.

Introduction

The process of **analysing** training materials has been dealt with in considerable detail and tackled from a number of different viewpoints in the previous five Components of this Study Unit. The word **evaluation** has cropped up a number of times, as it has elsewhere in the Volume. No doubt the word is familiar to you as an umbrella term used to 'label' a particular procedure and its associated set of ideas. But what exactly does evaluation mean, and in practical terms what does it involve?

When we start to apply the concept of evaluation to the area of training materials, we are immediately limiting the scope of the term and its associated activities. At the same time we are directing attention at certain aspects of our overall approach to the materials.

Let's begin by reviewing the use of the word evaluation so far in this Study Unit. The following diagram was presented in Component 2, and at the same time reference was made to 'a final evaluation'.

DIAGRAM 1

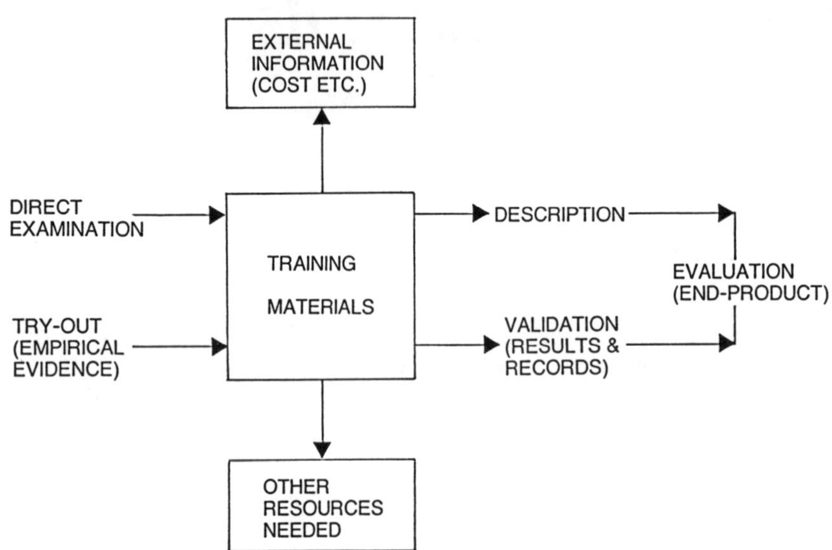

The diagram suggests that evaluation is an end-product which takes into account the results of both direct examination/description and empirical evidence/validation, plus other information about costs, resources etc. Notice the distinction between validation results (Do the materials achieve what is claimed for them — are they **valid?**) and evaluation. A little later on in Component 2 reference is made to analysing the materials for their possible usefulness, and near the end of that Component under Conclusions and recommendations, "At this point you would be crossing the threshold from observing, measuring and reporting into **the area of judgements and evaluation**".

In Component 3 in a reference to the Systems Approach we read "How we'll know whether it's all been worthwhile (Evaluation)" and a little later "A full evaluation results in a story ... it reveals perceptions and **judgements** . . . it tells of merits and shortcomings". The term 'judgemental analysis' crops up further on! Again in Component 3 reference is made to "some sort of judgement about how well . . .".

It has been claimed that evaluation should be an integral part of normal professional conduct, and also that evaluation serves a variety of purposes and cannot be adequately summarised by a single definition.

So what is evaluation and how does it differ from analysis, which has been the major theme of this Study Unit so far?

Checkpoint

Write down your definition/explanation of 'evaluation of training materials'.

Compare your answer with mine:—

Evaluation of training materials refers to the process of making judgements and decisions about the value or worthwhileness of the materials. It involves weighing up **all** *the evidence available and deciding how well the materials have performed, or are likely to perform. It may involve making recommendations about possible use(s) for the materials.*

Your answer will no doubt be different from mine, but I expect you included certain key words, e.g. judgements, decisions, how worthwhile (or similar).

Now write down what you see as the main difference between analysis and evaluation (of training materials).

Well, I would say that evaluation takes up where analysis leaves off! In other words, analysis should refer to any attempt to examine, describe and report on the materials **without including any sort of judgement and avoiding any deliberate bias or particular point of view.**

Analysis and Evaluation

In practice any clear distinction between analysis and evaluation cannot be maintained, since analysis inevitably merges into evaluation. In Component 1 under "How should I look at training materials" it was suggested that any approach you decide to adopt will be selective (i.e. based on some conscious or unconscious **decision** as to what to consider). This theme has persisted throughout the Unit. However, all is not lost, since the aim of any analysis must be to facilitate eventual evaluation. In terms of the sequence of actions, evaluation follows analysis, but any analysis should be based on the information needed for evaluation purposes. Shortly after the diagram in Component 2, the following example was given:—

> To examine and analyse "X" training package with a view to deciding whether it can be used as it stands for purpose "Y" with "Z" trainees, whether it could be used if modified, or whether it is unsuitable. Examination to take into account cost, ease of use, technical content, appropriateness, likely effectiveness.

At the time we were concerned with examination and analysis, but the reason given in the example, i.e. "with a view to deciding ..." forms the basis for an evaluation. Any such analysis therefore provides evidence towards subsequent evaluation.

Diagram 1 also reminds us that evaluation should be based on empirical evidence, if it can be obtained, as well as analysis of the materials themselves. This point is well developed in Components 4 and 5 on Observing Training, although again the emphasis is on the acquisition of the evidence itself rather than on evaluation. It is worth reminding ourselves that analysis on its own, and for its own sake, would seem to be a pointless exercise. The need for an explicit purpose or goal was stressed in the introduction to Component 1. That goal will usually be some form of evaluation.

Evaluation of Training Materials

Evaluation of training materials means making judgements and decisions about them, weighing up good and bad features with a view to deciding how worthwhile or useful they are. This can be done from three different points of view:—

* Evaluating the materials **in use** to decide how effective they were **on that occasion.**
* A broader, longer-term evaluation where we are looking at the materials in use over an extended period.
* Evaluation of the materials themselves in order to make judgements and decisions about possible future use.

Again you will see that these three are not mutually exclusive. For example, you would normally expect the first one to incorporate the third.

So how do we set about evaluation? Well, the seeds have, hopefully, been already sown in this Study Unit. All we apparently need to do is to shift the emphasis forward from analysis and descriptions to judgements and decisions. Or maybe it's not quite as simple as that? As we saw at the beginning, any attempt at analysis involves selection and the possibility of bias — and the same thing arises, only in a more fundamental way, when we attempt to evaluate. The evidence may be there, but judgements are notoriously uncertain and liable to change.

Evaluation is concerned with weighing up the evidence, but on what basis? Which items of evidence are to be considered 'more important' than others? What arguments and criteria are involved? What happens if one factor (e.g. cost) presents a major problem? And so we could go on! What we need to do is to develop, as we have done with analysis so far, a systematic framework and procedure to guide our evaluation.

Go back through Components 1 to 5 and make a list of the **main headings** under which evidence could be collected for evaluation purposes. Don't go into too much detail at this stage. You will probably find it useful to group your headings under the two areas — direct examination and empirical evidence.

I'm sure you found that the same headings kept popping up again and again, as the topics were dealt with in different contexts and at different levels. Here is a compound version which I have drawn up:—

Direct Examination
Objective and subjective information
Criteria
Comparative information ("X" versus "Y" materials)

FRAMEWORK FOR ANALYSIS
Check-list;
"How . . . . . ." list

Empirical Evidence
Validation results— Background
— Process
— Product (Outcomes)
Observing Training— Trainer
— Trainees
Recording — Grids & Schedules
Subjective/Quantitative information

The interesting thing to me is the degree of overlap between the two main areas, and the fact that the same ideas (e.g. subjective/objective, framework for analysis) arise in both.

We should now be able to see the basic structure of the **evidence** which is likely to be available, and on which any evaluation will be based.

Evaluation Check-List

The identification of a number of headings would suggest further development of them into a series of check-lists, as we have done previously in this Study Unit. Check-lists serve three purposes, in that they

* focus attention on those features which are supposedly important
* act as an aide-memoire to provide comprehensive coverage and avoid missing anything out
* provide information for later analysis and evaluation.

Again, the requirements of such analysis and evaluation should govern the design of the check-list itself.

Published check-lists often consist of a series of questions, usually grouped under appropriate headings. Here are a few such questions from a check-list designed to be used for direct examination of training materials:—

Does the unit begin with an introduction?
Is there an overview?
Does the unit contain aims?
Does the unit contain objectives?
Is the content adequate?

How does the final question differ from the first four?

It requires **judgement**, *largely subjective, about the adequacy of the overall content (i.e. some form of evaluation). The first four can be answered objectively 'Yes' or 'No' by direct examination of the materials.*

So beware! Questions in a check-list may appear similar, but may require very different levels of activity and expertise in order to answer them.

Look through the lists of headings and check-lists which you prepared when working through Components 2, 3, 4 and 5. Do they form the basis for providing the comprehensive evidence on which an evaluation should be based?

I hope you feel they do, although I'm sure they will have raised a number of questions in your mind about other issues which have not been fully covered so far.

Other Issues

In addition to information derived from direct examination and actual trials, there are a number of other issues which should be covered in a comprehensive evaluation. Some of these have been touched on already, but they will almost certainly need greater emphasis when conducting an evaluation.

Cost-effectiveness

A major priority in an evaluation may be a concern with the cost-effectiveness of the materials. At first sight, this may look an easy exercise, and it could be — if you were simply concerned with 'value for money' — but the issue is usually clouded with attempts to compare the cost-effectiveness of the materials with other materials or training methods.

For example, in recent years there have been many attempts to compare distance-learning materials with more traditional ways of learning, but as you are not comparing 'like with like' the number of items (variables) which can be brought into the argument are legion — and you end up trying to compare a frying pan with a kettle!

Cost per trainee-hour can probably be easily calculated, and in some cases the subsequent 'effectiveness' of training can be estimated on a costs-saved basis, but it is very easy to find you have wandered off into a minefield!

The costs of production of computer-based training materials, and in particular the much more sophisticated interactive video, are measured in tens of thousands of pounds. Funding of CBT/IV projects has to be 'up-front' i.e. the money has to be made available before the materials have been produced, so how can you try to evaluate their likely cost-effectiveness?

If you were given the responsibility for setting up a CBT/IV project, how would you go about trying to ensure that the results were cost-effective?

The justification of costs is perhaps outside the realms of evaluation, but it would have to be based, as has already been suggested, on estimated trainee throughput (costs per trainee), or maybe by establishing a particular need for the project (e.g.

showing expensive, dangerous or unique experiments).

The best way of ensuring that the results will be cost-effective is by tight control of the project, particularly by the use of the systems approach, with its explicitly-stated aims and objectives and the laying down of criteria for success which can be subsequently measured. Even so it may be very difficult in the early design stages to build in fireproof safeguards against all eventualities. Innovatory projects are often very difficult to evaluate, by the very fact that they are innovatory and cannot be compared with anything similar.

Reactions

When collecting empirical evidence, in addition to the quantifiable data obtained from post-test results, recording schedules, systematic evaluation etc., we should also be concerned with reactions by trainers and trainees. Reference has already been made to this (e.g. reaction versus performance, process versus product, observing training). The focus here from an evaluation angle is to obtain 'gut' reactions to the materials in use. This can best be achieved by 'interviewing' or more usually by the use of a questionnaire. However, as was pointed out in Component 4, "beware of information overload". With longer packages of materials, reactions can often be measured in terms of those who 'vote with their feet' and fail to complete the course!

Culture and Environment

Materials are very dependent on the background environment against which they are used. If they are being used simply as 'bolt-on goodies' or 'icing on the cake' they may be seen in a more critical light than if they are embedded into the system. Materials which work in one place may not work in another. Any evaluation should take into account the context within which the materials may be used.

The choice is yours.

Evaluation may cover the range from a simple comparison between two sets of similar materials, to a full-blooded experimental research study, where trainees are randomly allocated to groups working under standardised conditions, where hopefully the only variable will be the different materials or teaching methods used. The latter will involve the use of sophisticated statistical techniques to analyse and compare the outcomes.

Experience suggests that the most likely outcome of a comparative study will be "no statistically significant difference" and/or the intervention of other confounding variables which interfere with the results obtained. However, if, for example, one method is much cheaper, quicker or more convenient than the other, then "no significant difference" may be a satisfactory outcome to guide the evaluation.

They both got from London to Brighton, but . . ."

The consideration of some/all of these other issues (cost-effectiveness, reactions, culture and environment, comparative studies) will vary in each particular case, but at least the headings (and any others you can think of) should be added to the overall check-list. Selection can then be made as appropriate.

Why Evaluate?

Having had a good look at the various items which may need to be taken into account when evaluating, finally let's consider a more fundamental question.

What do you see as the purpose of evaluating training materials?

Obviously there is no single straightforward answer to this question, but here are a few reasons for conducting an evaluation:—

* *to make* **judgements** *about the effectiveness of the materials (but so what?)*
* *to facilitate* **decisions** *as to whether the materials are*
  - □ *good 'value for money'*
  - □ *suitable for direct use (adoption)*
  - □ *partly suitable for use*
  - □ *suitable for use if modified*
  - □ *suitable for use by "X" trainees but not "Y"*
  - □ *unsuitable for use (rejection)*
  - □ *'better' or 'worse' than other materials/methods*
* *to help you to decide whether to create your own materials, and if you do, to give you an awareness of what the pitfalls may be.*

In other words the 'bottom line' is whether or not to recommend the use of the materials in any way, or whether to try to do better yourself.

Tutor Seen Work

Prepare a comprehensive evaluation of a substantial set/package of training materials. Headings for the report should be derived from your answers to the relevant Checkpoints in this Study Unit.

Sources of Information About Training Materials

Due to the wide-ranging needs of trainers using the TTP, it is impossible to give detailed and specific coverage of sources of information, but here are a few general pointers.

Open Tech Directory
International Yearbook of Educational and Instructional Technology 1984/85 Kogan Page
(contains lists of producers and distributors of training materials, also suppliers of catalogues)

International Yearbook of Educational and Instructional Technology 1986/87 Kogan Page
(contains up-to-date directory of centres of activity)

The Audio-visual and Microcomputer Handbook Kogan Page

Educational Software Directory Rickett Educational Media
Marisnet (via Prestel)

Objectives for Volume 7 Study Unit 5

The objectives for this Study Unit are that students should:

Component One

1. List the various types of categories of training materials.
2. Outline the dangers of direct examination, and indicate ways of improving the approach.

3. Discriminate between objective and subjective statements.
4. Examine and analyse training materials, using a direct approach.
5. List typical items of information to be collected as empirical evidence when trying out training materials.

Component Two

1. Distinguish between 'in-house' and 'commercial' training materials.
2. List the likely features of 'in-house' materials.
3. Construct a suitable framework of headings and sub-headings for the analysis of in-house materials (direct examination and empirical evidence). NB See 4 above.

Component Three

1. List criteria for the selection of suitable material for analysis.
2. Construct an appropriate 'framework' or scheme of analysis for commercially produced materials.
3. Identify those elements of the process of analysis which are also helpful to the designer of materials.

Component Four

1. List criteria against which to judge the effectiveness of training.
2. Define some of the qualities of 'the good trainer'.
3. Be aware of subjective/objective considerations when observing training.
4. Identify a variety of methods of recording what happens in a training session.
5. List the advantages/disadvantages of particular methods of recording.
6. Identify points of focus for the observation of training.

Component Five

1. List criteria for observing materials in use in training.
2. Use the Training Observation Schedule (TROBS) without difficulty in a practice situation.
3. Draw conclusions about how best to combine methods of observation.
4. Use the Case Study materials to reinforce the lessons of Components 4 and 5.

Component Six

1. Distinguish between analysis and evaluation.
2. Define evaluation (of training materials).
3. Construct and use a suitable framework for evaluation.
4. List a number of purposes of evaluation.

Acknowledgements

Grateful thanks are dur to Dr. Michael Eraut for permission to the scheme of analysis developed by himself and others at the University of Sussex, as a basis for material in Component 3.

To Nicki Lees for permission to apply her observation schedule for use in Components 4 and 5.

To Messrs. Harper and Row for permission to draw on material from Derek Rowntree's book — *Educational Technology in Curriculum Development* (2nd Ed. 1982).

Short Bibliography

ERAUT, M., *The Analysis of Curriculum Materials,* University of Sussex Occasional Papers No. 2.

also see

McCORMICK, R. (1981), *Analysing Curriculum Materials,* Open University Press.

LEES, N. J. (1983). *Observing Classroom Procedures,* University of Leicester School of Education Report No. 15.

ROWNTREE, D. (2nd Ed. 1982), *Educational Technology in Curriculum Development,* Harper & Row.

Study Unit 6

Designing and Implementing Training Programmes

Component 1:

What is a Training Programme?

Key Words

Assessing needs; expertise; employment; gender; race; setting aims and objectives; providing resources; selecting training methods; evaluating the programme.

Objectives

As a result of working through this Component you will have a basic awareness of what is required to design and implement a training programme. The intention is to briefly outline the key considerations that you will have to take into account prior to a more detailed examination in subsequent Components.

Introduction

You will want your programme planning to be as efficient and effective as possible. Unfortunately, the pressures of the daily routine often mean that there is too little time and energy to meet with colleagues or to work our the best possible design for a training programme. A much needed tool for trainers is a guide that not only describes what a training programme actually is but which also suggests the broad processes involved in actually designing a training programme. That is the purpose of this Study Unit.

This Component sets the scene for what is to follow. The key features of a training programme are raised and issues to do with devising such a programme briefly described. These issues will be examined in more detail in the subsequent Components.

Finally, this Study Unit suggests a number of processes that have to be repeated time and again. Constant reviews are vital.

1. Assess Needs

One of the first things about a training programme is that it must consider the needs of the trainees if they are to be successful in completing their training. What knowledge skills and attitudes are the trainees going to need to acquire if the training is to be successful? The answer to that question will be provided in part by the nature of the training itself. Consequently you will have to be quite clear about the criteria that you will use if you are to be able to say that someone has been trained. Thus you will be able to make judgement about whether or not someone has been properly trained because they either can or cannot meet those criteria. However, in order to design a training programme that will develop in someone the ability to meet those criteria you will have to know what the needs of the trainees are going to be.

The point will perhaps be made if I provide an example. One of the criteria for judging whether someone can operate a word processor is that they should be able to use a keyboard. So if you are training people to operate a word processor they will need to be trained in using a keyboard. That will become part of the training programme. However, if the people that you are training are already competent typists then the amount of time that you will have to spend on developing keyboard skills is much reduced. Thus the design of a training programme for a group of secretaries will be greatly different from that for people who have never used a typewriter. The needs are different.

What sorts of information are you going to have to acquire if you are to assess the needs of the trainees? It will obviously vary according to the nature of the training but a general list would have to include the following items.

* Level of expertise.
  There is little point in building in to your training programme things that the trainees can already do perfectly well. Alternatively you should be careful about making assumptions about the abilities of the trainees. You will have to find out through interviews, questionnaires and/or application forms just what the level of expertise actually is.
* Employment.
  Are the trainees employed or unemployed? Will the training lead to a different form of employment? Is the training part of current employment and if so what part and what is the degree of congruence? These are all questions that will affect the design of a training programme. The outcomes could be full-time training, part-time training, on the job training, training for redeployment, trainee motivation and so on.
* Gender.
  In an age of equal opportunities this might be thought of as an un-necessary condition. However, in the context of an overall design for a training programme certain factors may need to be considered. It may be necessary to build into the design support for women entering traditionally male areas for the first time in order to forestall possible problems connected with isolation and hostility.

  A fundamental barrier to the advancement of women is that training often takes place in the late teens or twenties when many women are not in employment, and assumes that all workers follow an unbroken career path from teens to sixties. The following positive steps can be taken to overcome this problem.
* Compensatory or special training for mature returners.

  Craft apprenticeship requirements particularly prevent women from entering certain career paths later in life.
* Age limits should not be unduly restrictive and should be examined to see whether they are in breach of the law:
* In employment geared to a traditional male career progression there is often an inherent attitude problem on the part of male-dominated line management. This perpetuates the expectation that women will not undertake necessary training for development. Many women need positive assistance to regard their development as a serious prospect, and should be encouraged to regard opportunities for training as their right.
* Work experience necessary to advancement should not be solely available on all-male shifts.
* If training courses have to be residential, trainees should ideally be told well in advance and child-care facilities provided.
* Race and creed.
  Again it might be assumed that legislation has satisfactorily dealt with the needs of trainees from minority groups. However, if you are involved in developing or negotiating schemes and courses in areas having substantial ethnic minority populations, what steps are you taking to ensure that the schemes are relevant to the needs of these populations? Are you in contact with ethnic minority groups and organisations? Are you aware of the potential they offer and the difficulties they face? Are you able to respond flexibly to them? For example, will your programme design take into account the language difficulties faced by certain groups?
* What can you anticipate from the trainees by way of mood or readiness?
  The trainees will almost certainly have certain expectations of the training programme. In thinking of designing a training programme it would be important to know what those expectations are. There may be certain things that you had accorded a low priority or not even considered at all. It might be possible to arrange the design so that certain expectations are obviously met. Of course certain expectations may quite simply be unrealistic. In that case you could at least build in some time in the programme to explaining what will and what will not be the case, and why. At the very least this will provide the trainees with a feeling of involvement in the programme in the sense that they recognise that their expectations are a matter of concern by you.

That is a good note on which to end this section. Awareness of the needs of the trainees will help you to design a training programme that is appropriate. Deliberately paying attention to those needs will give the trainees the impression that they really do matter. Both are recipes for a successful programme.

Checkpoint

1. Think about the training that you are involved in. To what extent do the attitudes of the trainees act as a stimulus or a constraint in designing a programme?
2. Spend some time on this. Make a list of all the things that you have to know in order to design a training programme. How many of those things are related to the needs of the trainees in some way?
3. What degree of control over the designing of a training programme by outside forces such as examining boards or financial constraints is there?

If you possibly can do it you will find it useful to discuss these questions with colleagues. The important question is "To what extent are the needs of trainees being identified and met or are other issues taking precedence?"

---

2. Set Aims and Objectives for the Training Programme

A training programme will have details of the aims and objectives of the training.

A. Aims.

This is a rather large topic and some time and energy must be devoted to it. It is important to have as clear an idea of the aims of the training programme as possible. Without that kind of clarity no proper programme design can ever emerge. We will take this topic in stages.

Stage One. Institutional Values.
The first step in arriving at a clear set of aims is to understand any prevailing values under which the training programme will have to operate. Institutions often work within a framework of a particular ideology or set of values and this can have implications for the designing of a training programme.

Certain basic questions should be asked.

a) Is there a particular ideology or set of values about training in general?

An example of this might be a belief within the institution in trainee control and negotiation of training programmes. This belief might be based in the idea that training is more effective if the trainees not only understand the criteria by which training can be judged to be successful but also accept these criteria and have a hand in establishing what they should be. For more information on that you may care to refer to Study Unit 5 "Self-Evaluation" in the Package on "Assessment and Evaluation in Training".

There might be prevailing ideas about the most appropriate numbers of trainees to have in any particular group. The judgement about the most appropriate size for a group of trainees might be determined by ideas about efficiency, safety or finance.

b) Are there established views about the acceptability or otherwise of the subject matter of the programme?

An example of this might be the emphasis placed by some institutions on getting trainees to work well together at a particular task rather than simply learn how to perform the task. In other words learning to work well with others might in some cases by regarded as important as learning to do a particular job.

There could be conflict between institutions about the specifics of any particular training programme. This conflict could centre on either what does someone need to know to be competent at a particular task or it could centre on the most appropriate methods to use to make someone competent at a particular task. For example, it would be remarkable if any two courses in vehicle maintenance were exactly alike in what the trainees were taught or in the manner by which they were taught.

There may be other prevailing values which will exert an influence on programme design. These may involve ideas about the way the day should be divided up in terms of time, areas or items that are "out of bounds" to trainees or even matters to do with approved forms of dress. One thing is certain as trainers you will have to be certain that your aims and objectives do not conflict with the overall prevailing values of the institution.

Try and identify the values within your own institution which will have a determining influence on the aims of your training programme.

There is an important point here since believe it or not some institutions appear to want training to happen yet by virtue of their organisation do all that they can to hinder the training process.

Stage Two. A definition.
Your aims will be statements of ideals. They will indicate the position towards which you are striving on the long term and as such are value laden.

Stage Three. Characteristics.
Aims
- refer to the totality of activities;
- act as necessary starting points and therefore while essentially general, should be clear enough to command common understanding and agreement, yet detailed enough to indicate direction of effort and need for modification;
- likely to be continually redefined as they are clarified by subsequent action;
- set limits to more specific objectives;
- relate to evaluation whereby you are able to make judgements about the programme as a whole.

What are your long term ultimate intentions for the training programme? What, in general terms, are you trying to do?

Generate four or five statements of intention which in your view encapsulate the purpose of the training programme.

If you have generated ten or more statements of intention you are probably being too specific. You are actually probably generating objectives.

B. Objectives
What are objectives?
Objectives are statements about what is to be accomplished at each stage of the programme leading to the attainment of the given aims.

The characteristics of objectives are that they —
- are an attempt to describe a specific short term target or particular activity;
- should have a high level of clarity and refer to everyday practice;
- refer to what individuals, or small groups are going to do;
- map out detailed steps in a tactical way;
- require the context of aims to make purpose out of activity;
- should generate opportunity to monitor and assess trainee progress by stating —
  - trainee behaviours or actions
  - criteria for assessing the performance of trainees.

In summary so far the objectives of the training programme will be statements about what is to be accomplished at each stage of the programme. These statements should be as specific as possible: "By the end of this stage you should be able to . . . . " Thus your aims are broken down into specific plans of action as shown in the following example.
Aim: To introduce the trainee to practical word processing.

Objectives: Stage 1 keying in text
By the end of this stage the trainee should be able to —
Start up the equipment
Edit a document
Key-in a short paragraph
Save a document to disk
Print a document.
Stage 2 familiarity with the use of the scroll.
By the end of this stage the trainees should be able to —
Start up the equipment
Edit a document
Use the scrolling function in order to proof-read the exercise
Store the text to memory
Operate the printer
Produce hard copy out-put
Close down the equipment
And so on until all the criteria for the attainment of the aim have been identified and set out.

Aim: For the trainee to be aware of and able to use all the services available through British Telecom.
Objectives: Stage 1. Using the equipment.
By the end of this stage the trainee should be able to:—
Place the earpiece of the instrument in close proximity to his ear.
Have the mouthpiece acceptably close to his mouth.

Who is involved in setting objectives?
Planning sessions where objectives are being set out should involve all those trainers who wish to participate. No-one should be overburdened or underutilized. No one person should feel that THEY have to do everything or that their particular contribution would not be valued. By and large if a team of trainers are working on the same programme then it follows that agreement about the objectives is eminently desirable.

Ideal and practical objectives
Clearly there is little point in creating an unrealistic design for a training programme. The availability of

resources of all kinds (not the least of those resources are yourselves and other trainers) will have an affect on deciding which objectives can be realistically pursued. This is so no matter how desirable the "ideal" objective is. Attention is paid to resources later in this Component and again in a separate Component.

The development of trainers to meet objectives
Those of you who are responsible for designing training programmes which are operated by training teams will have to take into account the important matter of the development of your fellow trainers. Are the trainers themselves receiving the training and the support to enable them to implement the programme and train in accordance with the objectives? The use of certain resources might be the focus of such training and hand in hand with that will be the question of method, or ways of doing the training. The latter issue will also be expanded upon later in this Component and explored in more detail yet again in further Components.

1. Use the example of transforming an aim into objectives given earlier to translate one of the aims that you have identified as a result of the last CHECKPOINT into objectives. Your objectives should have those characteristics described above.
2. What are the practicalities that you know of that will hinder the pursuit of certain of those objectives? Can you do anything to reduce that hindrance? Try to make a list of the things that you could do.
3. In your situation who is involved in setting objectives?
4. What possibilities exist for the development of trainers in your organisation?

The development of trainers is an important issue. It is after all what this and other Study Units are all about. You might care to reflect on the preparation that you received to enable you to be a trainer. Ask your colleagues too if you can.

---

3. Provide Resources

A training programme must consider the resources needed for the training. Once you have decided upon your aims and objectives you are in a position to think about the resources that you will require in order to achieve them. A careful consideration of the availability of resources is an essential step in the design of a training programme. Much will depend upon having the resources to do the job and where a deficiency exists (and in practice there is usually some sort of lacking of resources in some way or another) it is important to be able to identify that deficiency so that your design can be constructed most appropriately.

The use of specific resources will obviously depend upon the type of training that you are involved in. There are, however, some general considerations which will apply to all forms of training. I shall provide brief details of these considerations in a series of sub-sections.

* Staffing.
Important questions here relate to the number of staff available, the balance between full-time and part-time staff, specialist strengths and, as mentioned earlier, staff development needs. Certain trainers may have special skills and interests. As someone involved in designing a training programme your task might be to decide on how they can be used most effectively.

* Accommodation.
In what sort of environment will the training occur? Is the space adequate and is the training area appropriate to the nature of the training? If the training is to be effective then ways of making the best possible use of the available accommodation must be found. Convenience and comfort are both considerations. For example it has been found that learning can be aided if people are in face to face situations. Thus in informal situations the placing of furniture in a circular or horse-shoe pattern can aid active interchange between trainees.

* Equipment: amount and appropriateness.
How much appropriate equipment exists and is it available when it is needed? The non-arrival of audio-visual equipment when required or lack of help in operating the equipment are examples of ineffective usage of resources. Some examples of equipment are:
Books, manuals and other printed material
Films, videos and slides
Radio, cassette player, television, video recorder
Micro-computers
Overhead projector.

* Time.
Time is a resource and it is one that can condition some of the objectives. This would particularly be the case when there is insufficient time for proper planning and certain objectives are missed.

There must of course be proper provision and use of time to actually engage in training. Selecting training strategies (methods of training) will be the subject of the next section of this Component but it is worth noting here that in terms of programme design certain things work better at certain times of the day than at others. This is an important consideration at the planning stage.

For planning to be most effective you will have to predict the time schedule for each aspect of training. This should be specific: introduction, ten minutes; forming groups and giving instructions, five minutes; working on the task, forty minutes; etc.

On a larger scale, review the schedule to see that sufficient time is available for what is planned, for each part of the training.

Provide for "fillers". Is more time available than the work will consume? Avoid planning so much that the participants feel hurried.

* Finance: amount available, effective use.
Is the amount of money available adequate to support all the desired objectives? All the various aspects of resources that have been listed are to some extent contingent upon the available finances.

You may, as part of your designing activities, have to turn the question round and ask, "How can the available money best be used?" "How can I make my programme as cost effective as possible?"

Take a sheet of paper. A4 size should be sufficient. Across the top of the page write out the objectives that you generated at the end of the previous section.

Down the left hand side of the page list the various items of resources that I have described in this section.

You now have the beginnings of a blank matrix which when completed will look like the example given below.

Example

	Start up the equipment	Edit a document	Key in a short paragraph	Save a document to disk	Print a document
Staffing					
Accommodation					
Equipment					
Time					
Finance					

Now try and complete your matrix by filling the blank squares with details of the resources you will require. Don't worry if certain squares remain blank. Certain resource items may not be applicable or may be the same for each objective.

The really worrying thing of course is when one finds that in order to satisfy a particular objective certain resources are required. Yet they just are not available. This is where a review of resources becomes important.

4. Select training strategies or training methods

A training programme must examine the methods that will be used. Obviously as a trainer involved in designing a training programme you will have a lot of knowledge about the content of that training. Equally, effective training skills are required.

There are no 'ideal' training styles, but it is important to achieve some compatibility between trainer and trainee. Two contrasting examples are:

* a learning group wishing to try things for themselves but restrained by a very formal instructional/lecturing style of training.

* a trainer with a style that encourages trainees to try things for themselves faced with a submissive group of learners who require to be told things.

As relationships develop there should be modification in order to incorporate the wishes of both trainer and trainees. The evidence suggests that a flexible training approach is a major asset, and more easily enables trainee attitudes to be kept in view.

The methods used in any educational activity must be suitable to the subject as well as to the trainees in order to secure maximum learning. Examples have been found of trainer using a restricted number of methods and being unwilling to experiment owing to a number of factors such as lack of appropriate expertise and fear of failure. In a mixed group it is not always practicable to serve the needs of all trainees at all times. Yet every training activity should, at some point, provide individual satisfaction.

There should be opportunities for the re-assessment of current practices and for the development of additional expertise and confidence. Exposure to and active engagement with a wide variety of learning and training methods is particularly valuable. On the whole trainees trying things for themselves rather than being told about things appear to bring longer term benefits, although you should recognise the danger of overstressing any one training method. In other words involving the trainees in their own learning is more likely to be more effective than simply telling them.

If the programme is to be satisfactorily implemented trainers need to know what is required and to give it their full support. Any change in training methodology or general approaches which are planned should be fully discussed with trainers. Otherwise there is a likelihood that they will adhere to past practices.

One common fault is for the trainer to attempt too much in the time available. The pacing of the training should take account of the time that individuals actually need to learn new skills. In designing a programme you will have to recognise the trainees existing experience, expertise and attitudes. It is occasionally necessary to allow the trainees to work at their own pace. Similarly your programme design should take into account the fact that certain things are better attempted at certain times of the day than at others. By and large mornings are better for theory and afternoons for activity.

One thing should lead to another. Will the experience of the participants be one of growth and development, or will it seem to them that they are getting a series of unconnected bits?

Your choice of method depends therefore on the type of trainee, the environment and trainer styles as well as upon aims, objectives and content. Yet many trainers and trainees become accustomed to the use of only a small number of training and learning methods.

Some examples of the range available are:

Computer Assisted Learning	Lectures
Case Studies	One-to-one teaching
Demonstrations	Project Work
Discussions	Role-play
Experiments	Seminars
Individual study	Simulations
Investigations	Tutorials
Working with small groups	

Use the list of training methods given above. Which are the ones that you can use with your own training?

Can you add any others?

Now place the methods that you have identified in order of priority so that number one on your list is the method most used and the last on your list is least used.

Are you satisfied with your priorities? Is there anything that you would like to change?

I know that it can be very hard to make changes, especially when things appear to be going well and no one wants change for the sake of it. However, you may be able to think of something that could be done better. Try experimenting with a small change. Nothing too drastic at first, see what happens.

---

5. Evaluating the programme

Your training programme will be evaluated. You will need to know if the programme is effective or not, and why. With that knowledge you will be able to modify the programme so that its strengths are developed and its weaknesses eliminated as far as that is possible. Consequently one of the key features of any training programme must be details of how that programme is to be evaluated.

In order to build into the design of your training programme details of how that programme is to be evaluated there are certain key questions that you will have to ask yourself.

* What will be your criteria for deciding whether the training has been effective?

  These criteria directly reflect the aims and objectives that you detailed at the beginning of your programme. Almost certainly, but by no means exclusively, this will involve a consideration of the knowledge, skills and attitudes that you would expect the training programme to develop in your trainees.

* From where will you get your information for making your evaluation?

  This particular question ties in with another question, "How will you collect your information for evaluation". The sources of your information could (and should in part at least) be the trainees themselves, an examination of the results of their training, your observation of their progress and so on. Further discussion of this will be found in the final Component of this Unit. The point here is that decisions about the source(s) of the information will be one of the factors in determining how you obtain that information.

There is a further question here. If you evaluate as part of the design by obtaining a daily rating of learnings, or by obtaining post-training reaction sheets for each stage of the training or by obtaining an end of programme evaluation then preparation will be needed. Who is going to do it?

* To whom other than yourself may the evaluation be of interest and, if appropriate, how will you inform them of your findings?

  You will want to evaluate the programme for the reasons given. But the trainees should also be in on the evaluation because that is part of their learning. Other groups, such as employers, may also be interested. Again this will be a factor in determining how evaluation is to occur.

* Any provision for follow-up?

  Quite simply what sorts of action will your evaluation inform? For example, the evaluation might have implications for future work.

Evaluation involves

a) collecting information
b) using criteria for making judgements about that information.

It is important to keep the distinction between a) and b) as clear as possible although in practice that can be difficult.

As an exercise write down the sorts of information that you collect at the moment. Now try to write down your criteria for making judgements about that information.

Example:

You may collect information about the ability to mend a puncture.

What are your criteria for affirming that someone can mend a puncture in the best possible way?

Conclusion

In order to summarise the key ideas in this Component here is a checklist of questions for you to consider.

* Which trainee group am I designing for?
* What do I want to achieve:
  — for the trainees?
  — for myself?
  — for anybody else to whom the training may relate?
* What do I know about the trainee group that may be relevant to the design?
* How will I make the work appropriate to that group?
* How much time do I have for the training?
* What will I do to produce the training climate I require?
* How will I order and present the content of the training?
* What materials will the training require?
* Which will be the most appropriate:
  — training procedures;?
  — group structures;?
* How will I arrange the content and method of the training to give a sense of flow and variety?
* Have I allocated time for each stage? Does the total match the time available?
* How will I make the most of the physical setting in which we will be working?
* What are my options if I find I need to energize the group at a certain point or relax and quieten them down?
* How can I evaluate the training?
* How will the evaluation affect future training?

Component 2:

Where do we Start?

Key Ideas

Trainees' aspirations and needs; reactions to the training process; trainee participation; training and learning needs; competencies of trainers.

Objectives

As a result of working through this Component you will be able to identify starting points for designing and implementing a training programme. You will examine three complementary areas: the needs of the trainees, training and learning needs and the demands that are made upon you as trainers.

Introduction

Before any training programme can be implemented and indeed before any training programme can be designed there are certain concerns that have to be considered. These, in broad terms, relate to the needs, expectations and experiences of both the trainees and the trainers. An understanding of these provide the starting point for designing and implementing a training programme. The purpose of this Component is to provide you with a checklist of these concerns which you may use in testing your own readiness to begin the design process. Particular items of concern will be clarified and ways of gaining information about those items will be suggested.

The Trainees

Trainees do not bring blank minds to the programme of training. They have a mixture of expectations, needs and wants on the one hand and experience and knowledge on the other. It is important to dispel false expectations (and in some cases, fears) as early as possible. Where possible training needs, which may not actually be recognised by the trainee at first, should be turned into conscious wants and these can then be related to the aims, content and methods of the training in such a way as to show that there is a reasonable hope that they will be met.

This is not a particularly easy task but it is nevertheless vital. One possible area of difficulty comes through confusing "demands" and "needs". Certain demands may not be compatible with the type of training that is envisaged whilst certain needs may simply reflect the perceptions of the potential trainees and these may not be their real needs. Systematic attempts to analyse real needs seems preferable to either:

the provision of a programme based entirely on explicit demands from the trainees.

OR

the provision of a pre-set and inflexible programme to which the trainees could react by paying attention only to the parts that they find worthwhile and by withdrawing in some way from the other parts.

It may be that the trainees will have already been engaged in activities that are remarkably similar to those that are being planned. Consequently it makes sense to know something of the background of the trainees before the programme design is attempted.

* If all of the trainees have already acquired certain competencies then the programme can be designed accordingly.
* If only a few of the trainees have acquired a particular competency already then it might be possible to move them on to another aspect of the training.
* If it is not possible to move just a few trainees on to another aspect of the training then it may be possible to use their competency as a contribution to the training. They could for example be used temporarily as trainers themselves in such a way as to create more time for other aspects of the programme.

Checkpoint

Utilising the existing talents of the group is a useful training strategy in that it invites that positive participation of the trainees.

Time is a vital resource. Can you think of ways of finding out about and using the existing talents of the trainees in such a way as to be a) of benefit to the entire group of trainees and b) and preserving of your own time?

You may be able to find other resources that can be saved by using the existing talents of the group. The point is to make the training as effective as possible.

Assessing the trainees' aspirations and needs

Your response to the aspirations of trainees is inseparable from your awareness of their needs. How can these two concerns be accommodated so as to design a co-ordinated training programme.

Information about the trainees can be thought of under three broad (and interconnected) headings.

a) Essential factual information

Under this heading would come such items as age; sex; ethnic origin; qualifications; previous training and work experience.

The significance of some of these items has already been indicated in Component One of this Study Unit. However, it is worth spending a little more time on one particular aspect of one of these items at this time in order to understand its relevance to the design of a training programme.

Unless the trainees have an accurate command of the English Language then training will inevitably be less effective than it should be. Among the ethnic minority community there are many whose command of English Language is limited. This may seem strange when so many members of ethnic minority groups are actually born in Britain. But problems of language are more subtle than you might imagine.

On the surface many Asian youngsters appear very fluent in English, but they often lack the sophistication of language that comes through conversing in English with a whole range of people of various ages and backgrounds in formal as well as informal situations. You may find that on your training course there are a number of trainees who spoke Punjabi at home until they entered school. There they learnt English but their use of the language may well have been limited to their school fellows. Very often contact between Asians, particularly Asian women, and others is strictly controlled. We all talk and relate to people differently, depending on who they are and the social situation we find ourselves in. It's a skill that we acquire sub-consciously through day to day contacts. But if our circle of contacts is limited then those skills do not get a chance to develop. The design of a training programme should take account of this, otherwise what happens cannot possibly be thought of as real training at all.

Find out how to contact the following groups in order to begin to assess the training needs of particular groups?:

Area Manpower Board (AMB). This is divided into local groups.

The Training Services Division (TSD) of the Manpower Services Commission.

Community Relations Council (CRC). There are local CRCs in many areas.

One useful address for you to contact for further information is the Campaign for Racial Equality (CRE), Elliot House, 10-12 Allington Street, London, SE1E 5EH. Tel: 01-828 7022

I have provided just one specific example to show why an understanding of the needs of the trainees is an important pre-requisite to designing and implementing a training programme. You may be able to think of other examples.

---

b) Details of a subjective nature requiring personal responses to items concerned with individual strengths, personal qualities, and needs in relation to training aspirations.

These particular details will enable you to find out:

i) whether the trainee's stated training interest was sufficiently firm, realistic and precise to make learning based upon that interest sensible;

ii) whether in a relatively short time and with sound preparation the trainee would acquire skills to cope in a workplace, within a specific occupational area, and then after further training would develop the more complex skills needed for the chosen occupational area;

One straightforward approach to this task is through discussions and interviews with potential trainees. These discussions can give an impression of each applicant's level of literacy, perceived capacity in academic terms, formal learning experience, level of receptiveness, sense of personal value, experience of the world of work.

Whatever approach you decide to use (and other approaches will be described) the process that you are engaged in is one which will:

* check each trainee's interests, aspirations, strengths and needs.
* focus the attitudes and expectations of both trainees and staff.
* introduce new ways of doing things.
* introduce new relationships and learning experiences.

This means that:

i) you need to assess the ways in which the trainee related to a training environment. This includes his ability to work with peers and supervisors and his capacity to cope within a training organisation;

ii) it is important to assess the trainee's capacity to contribute to his own learning. It can be expected that trainees would at times be hostile, passive or afraid in the face of certain activities or styles of training;

iii) it is essential to know the young person's interests, capacities and aptitudes for the activities involving characteristic working environments.

Knowledge of the trainees

Try to answer these questions

1. How much do you know about the work done at previous stages in their training?
2. To what extent are you aware of, and take account of, individual differences in the members of the group?
3. Are you aware of trainees with particular problems and how do you cope with them?
4. Do you "label" trainees prematurely?
5. How far do your reports reflect your knowledge of the trainees?

Do not be too depressed if you find that your answers are a bit skimpy. Think of those questions as being the sorts of things to check up on.

---

c) Specific reactions to the training process

The process of training means that the trainees will be actively involved in their own learning. The important thing is that you will need to know just how well the trainees will react to being given responsibility for their own learning.

First of all, what exactly do I mean when I say that the trainees will be actively involved in their own learning? Quite simply I mean that the trainees will not simply be passively sitting back listening to what you have to say and possibly making notes about it all. They will also, and possibly mainly be actually actively acquiring certain skills or competencies and also certain work related qualities. They will be participating in their own training from the stage of being involved in understanding and accepting the criteria by which the training may be judged to be effective, through the training process itself and up to the stage of making judgements about their own progress.

What does participation involve?

Most first-time trainees have never had the opportunity of participating collectively in the planning and delivery of their learning. They will often lack the confidence, skills and knowledge to set up and maintain participative structures without support. This means that the active commitment of others concerned with their training will be necessary at least in the short term.

Your support must take several forms:

— **logistical:** Schemes must help trainees arrange the times and places to meet. In practice, periodic use can be made of off the job training time, especially if this is in the form of regular day release. Other schemes have set aside time when the trainees visit the scheme to collect their weekly allowance.

— **organisational:** Trainees may need guidance about the conduct of meetings plus help with the production and distribution of agendas and minutes.

— **information:** Unless trainees are made aware of all decisions and discussion relevant to their training then they will be unable to participate fully. Examples exist of this need being met by trainee representatives being allowed to attend parts of scheme staff meetings.

— **encouragement:** The most valuable support that can be given is to show a positive attitude towards participation. Well-developed systems can be devised but unless schemes are willing to act upon trainees' suggestions as far as possible then they are of minimal value. If trainees are not to become disillusioned, they must feel that their contributions are valued and given full consideration. Trainees are not so naive as to assume that all their wishes can be met but they do want to understand how and why decisions come to be made.

In this way you will begin to be able to understand the trainees' needs and be able to plan your programme accordingly. This has a number of real benefits.

Trainees are not children, yet the status of the majority of them as trainees sets them apart from other workers. This difference often means that trainees feel insignificant within workplaces or training schemes. Too often, they lack the opportunity to contribute their ideas and opinions about matters of direct concern to them in their training.

Participation means that when problems do arise, all concerned feel a shared responsibility for resolving them.

An effective system of participation means that communications within the training programme are improved. Everyone involved will gain a clearer understanding of the concerns and views of others. This should mean that necessary change can be introduced smoothly after full consultation, rather than imposed.

Trainee participation also gives trainees a sense of involvement in their training, developing commitment to the training and improving morale. It also allows trainers to ensure that training is truly meeting the needs of trainees.

The implications of this are that it may become apparent that a high level of support and guidance may be required during the early part of a training programme. This may be needed in order to help trainees to acquire confidence and familiarise themselves with new routines and methods of learning, and if it is needed it should become part of the programme design.

It may also become apparent that the trainees have only the vaguest notion of what the training actually involves. Aspirations might be quite unrealistic.

By collecting information under the three broad headings that I have described it is possible to gain insights into six areas.

i) Training aspirations in relation to sex, ethnic origin etc.
ii) Aspirations in relation to some aspects of the educational backgrounds of trainees.
iii) Trainees' expectations of the training environment;
iv) Trainees' knowledge of and attitude towards the world of work.
v) Trainees' conceptions of what will be expected of them.
vi) Trainees' abilities to cope with those expectations.

Without these insights no programme can be devised or implemented.

Can you see how having each of the six areas of insights listed above will affect your programme design?

For each insight make a note to show how having an insight into that particular area will affect your programme design.

Once again it would be worthwhile if you can, to see how your own colleagues react to the six areas of insights. Differences between you might be important to consider.

Identifying training and learning needs

The needs of the trainees must be considered in relation to the demands of the training. Thus any interviews, surveys or questionnaires that are devised in order to establish trainee needs must reflect that nature of the training. Identifying the trainee population can only be sensible in the context of the training.

Thus you will have to identify the knowledge, skills and personal qualities requirements of particular types of training. Priorities will have to be assigned to the knowledge, skills and qualities demanded. For this you may have to attend meetings with managers or even interview them. At the very least your perceptions of training priorities will have to be discussed with management. You may find it useful to work out a job description format that relates to the training methods and programmes used by other training agencies.

Check the frequency with which you engage in the following activities prior to designing a training programme.

	Always	Often	Sometimes	Rarely	Never
1. Identify the knowledge, skills and personal qualities demanded by your area of training.					
2. Establish a priority of knowledge skills and qualities					
3. Consult with management over your established priorities					
4. Devise a job-description format					
5. Examine the training methods and programmes used by other training agencies.					

Are you happy with your results? What, if anything, would you do to change them?

There is one particular procedure that you might find useful in attempting to consider the needs of the trainees in relation to the demands of the training. I will describe the procedure step by step and then provide you with an example. My suggestion is that you try it for yourself. You might be surprised.

1. Think of a goal (or aim or intention) that you have for your training programme. (See Component One for a definition of an aim). Write it down in the middle of a reasonably large piece of paper. A4 will probably do.
2. Draw five circles around your central statement.
3. Into each of the five circles write a specific statement about a particular objective that will lead to the aim. (See Component One for a definition of an objective.)
4. Take each circled statement in turn. On the outside of the circle write down the sorts of questions that you imagine the trainees would ask about that statement.

This should begin to help you to think about the kinds of concerns that the trainees are likely to have about the various elements of your proposed programme. Following from that you will begin to be in a position to think about their needs in relation to the demands of the training. Your own perceptions could at this stage, be clarified by adopting an approach to assessing the trainees aspirations and needs described earlier.

Use the example provided to construct your own diagram. Take as your starting point any particular goal that you have for your training programme. You may well find that on examining the completed diagram the perceived concerns of the trainees suggest a logical or developmental sequence (one concern building upon another) that may be of help in considering the design and implementation of a training programme.

Note: the dotted lines on the example simply remind us that the objective statements are not mutually exclusive but are inter-related and of course all related to the central aim.

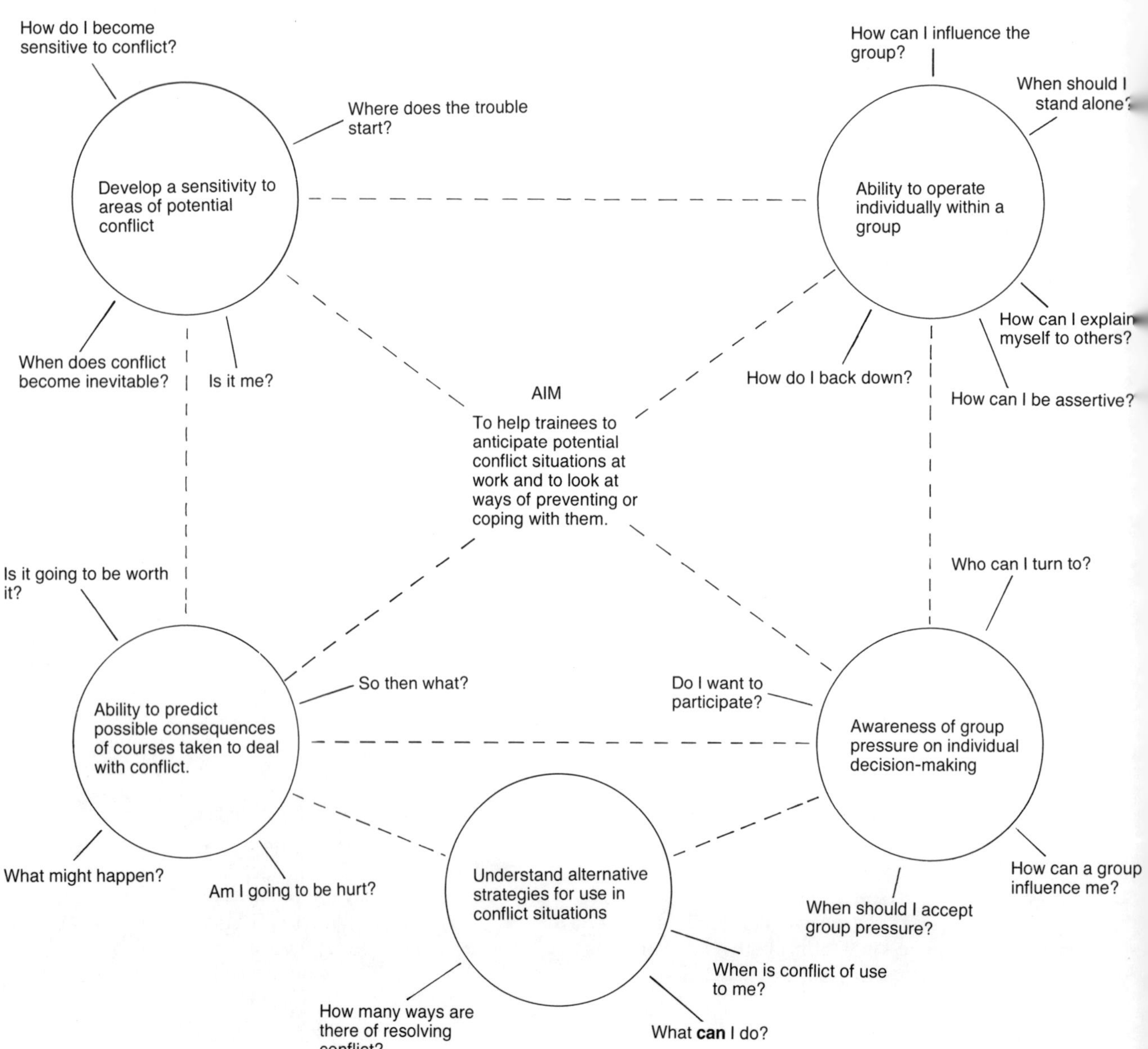

The Trainers

As trainers there are certain things that you can foster that will help you to design and implement a training programme.

In order to design and implement the programme effectively you need to be a good communicator yourself. That means, first and foremost, creating the right atmosphere and a good working relationship. These should be friendly but business like. In creating relationships remember the importance of non-verbal behaviour of all kinds, for example, administrative arrangements, tone of voice and timekeeping.

There are four basic communication skills: speaking, listening, reading and writing. Before, during and after the programme you will have to use them all.

This Unit rests on certain assumptions that the trainer must have:

1. More *knowledge* about the subject, gained through his own experience, than most of the trainees.
2. Average professional *skills* as a programme designer and implementer of training.
3. A preference for structured training, but with the ability to adapt programmes to meet situational requirements. In this area it is especially important for the trainer not to appear as one who knows all the answers (that is, possessing a manual with them in the back!)

We shall devote the rest of this Component to identifying in more detail the kind of competencies that you will need in order to be effective in designing and implementing a training programme.

a) Goals.

A major set of skills relates to the ability to identify the learning goals of the training event very specifically. It cannot be stressed enough that it is important for the trainer to learn ways to be able to clarify his goals for a particular training event or a particular part of a training event, so that these are motivators for the trainees themselves. A closely related set of skills involves helping trainees to clarify their own goals. In designing a programme, then, one begins with establishing, in a highly specific way, the goals of that programme.

Every person should have some understanding of what the programme involves and why they are there.

b) Sensitivity.

A second set of skills in designing training programmes is sensitivity to the trainees' response. You will have to learn to anticipate how trainees are likely to react to particular components of the design. In addition, you must become adept at anticipating the effects of the sequence of the design. You should be able to make some kinds of probability statements about the receptivity of the trainee to particular learning experiences.

Part of this sensitivity involves acquaintanceship with the trainees. How are the same trainees likely to react to a similar kind of activity after they have been together in the same setting for a period of time? Developing sensitivity to the probable responses comes from experience with a variety of learning activities, with a variety of trainees, and with a great deal of trainers' discussion of experiences in similar programmes.

c) Other trainers

A third array of skills involves collaborating with other trainers. In my experience it is more effective and efficient for one trainer to accept responsibility for the initial design of the training programme and to work with other trainers to edit the design to make it more relevant to the training needs of the trainees in light of the goals of the training event. It is expensive to bring together a group of trainers to build a design from basics. It is true that when the trainers create a design themselves, from the beginning, they are more likely to have a sense of investment, involvement, and "ownership" in what is planned. They are likely to approach the implementation of the design with more vigour. It is also true, however, that trainers ordinarily do not have a great deal of time to prepare in such a way. I find it to be useful to have an initial, tentative design which the other trainers will edit rather than build from the beginning.

Another activity which can promote professional development amongst trainers is the study of other trainers' designs. This does

not mean that other designs must be accepted in total. They are almost always to some extent irrelevant to the particular needs of a particular group of trainees. The ability to adapt is important.

d) Other trainees
A fourth step which you can take is seeking out opportunities to work with various groups of trainees. This requires you to be flexible in design and to avoid developing design packages which may be irrelevant to the needs of particular trainees. There are obvious ethical restrictions on you as you seek out trainees as professional ethics require you not to over-represent your qualifications. But within ethical restrictions, you can grow professionally by generating experience in working with a variety of different kinds of groups.

It should be noted however that flexibility is important. This is just not so that you can adapt to the different needs of different groups but also so that you can call upon the widest possible repertoire of training resources and approaches in constructing your design.

e) Personal training experiences
Finally, it is highly useful for you to attend training events occasionally as participants rather than as trainers. The critical point in effectiveness with regard to design and implementation is the human element. The most significant boundary impinging on you is the need to remain healthy: not to deceive yourself about what you are up to. Participating in training as a trainee means living by the same kind of values that you are attempting to teach other people. The major need in your development is to integrate your personal and professional development.

In order to implement training for others we need to be reminded from time to time of what it is like to be trained.

Conclusion

In order to design and implement a training programme you will have to be as clear as you can about the needs of the trainees, the nature of the training in terms of what it is for and the demands that will make and last but no means least, your own needs. This Component should have indicated something of the importance of those concerns and some of the ways in which they might be addressed. The following Checkpoint will ask you to reflect on certain key issues from a personal perspective.

Respond personally to each of the following statements.

	Always	Usually	Sometimes	Rarely	Never
You are fully aware of your goals					
The trainees are aware of the goals of the training					
You are able to predict the reactions of the trainees to particular aspects of the programme					
You collaborate with other trainers in designing programmes					
You work with different groups of trainees					
You occasionally attend training events as a trainee.					

Use the results to draw up a list of ways in which you can better prepare yourself to design and implement a training programme.

Component 3:

Resources

Key Words

Resources are people and things, real and abstract; the learner, the trainer; time, finance, accommodation and equipment as resources; methods and systems; purpose of resources; using them effectively; the people are the essential resource but the others are also important; features of resources.

Objectives

By the end of this Component you will:—

1) understand and appreciate the importance of resources in designing and setting up a training programme
2) have identified the main groups of resources and be able to evaluate them
3) be able to decide which resources are relevant to the programme or course you are planning
4) be able to decide how best to use those resources
5) have identified likely constraints on the use of resources and considered how to overcome them.

Introduction

We all know that the purpose of all training is ultimately to help a learner to change or improve his performance in some way — whether in the sphere of knowledge or skill or attitude. We all also know that you cannot bring about worthwhile change unless you first specify the standards of performance you want the learner to achieve and, just as important, assess as precisely as possible the standard being achieved before the training starts. Finally, we must always remember that failure to reach a pre-set standard may not be due to lack of training but to a host of other causes (such as lack of correct materials, no motivation — to name but two). There's nothing new in this. However, when we come to plan the actual training it is possible to fall into the trap of planning it in isolation — almost in an idealistic way — and assuming a number of things. First, that everything will fall into place ("it'll be all right on the night!"); secondly, that which worked last time will work this time round (it may do — but, it may not). Thirdly, we can confuse efficiency in training with effectiveness. Efficiency is, as you know, doing things right whereas effectiveness is doing the right things. No doubt you have attended courses which have run like clockwork but which have not really interested you or from which you have learned little or nothing — efficiency as against effectiveness.

One area in which efficiency can be confused with effectiveness is in the use of resources; again, you may have participated in a training programme where there has been the biggest range of audio-visual aids possible and at the end you have gained little or nothing. The 'show' (for that is what it is) has only demonstrated the tutor's ability to use all those aids and may well have distracted from the true intent of the training.

On the other hand you have probably attended training sessions where a tutor has brought along a series of slides for use on an overhead projector but the contents run right to the edge of the slide and thus parts are not displayed on the screen. Or the projector has ceased to work and the tutor is lost — doesn't know how to diagnose the fault, possibly repair it, use an alternative method of presentation — or may not even know where the switch is which controls the aid. 'Aid' did we say? 'Hindrance' is more like it! One last example; we might plan a programme and decide to use one of our own staff to provide an input. That person might well be an expert in the subject but just cannot communicate it to others. In all these cases, the training effectiveness is reduced or disappears totally.

When all the potential learners have been assessed, their training needs analysed, training plans and budgets drawn up the problem remaining is one facing all managers repeatedly — whatever the manager decides will be a compromise. All managers — and in this context the trainer is a manager — are faced with the acquiring, disposal and organisation of resources to enable some goal to be reached as effectively as possible. The trainer has to make decisions — judgements among a number of options — and that decision-making activity demands a totally professional approach. The trainer is concerned with balancing the resources available to achieve, as economically as possible, the stated and agreed goal.

In this Component we shall consider in some depth what 'resource' is, what resources are generally available to us; how, when, where and why they could be used. Note the word 'could' and not 'should'; as a trainer you must decide what resources you need, what you have available and how, when, where to use them.

So — What's a Resource?

Well there are many definitions and presently we'll give one but first it is as well if you think about the word a bit and clear your mind about it. Let's get down to business right away with the first Checkpoint.

Checkpoint

Take a few minutes to write down your own definition of 'resource' then have a look at ours.

There are many definitions — depends on which dictionary you consult — but these two suffice:—

1) *A resource is someone or something which can be used by someone in the undertaking of his work (for example, people, finance, tools)*
2) *a resource is an area of support to which one can turn in time of need (for example, advice from another trainer, financial support, other equipment).*

Definitions are useful as starting points but in themselves tell us not a great deal about, for instance, the relative values of different resources, availability, the relevance of resources to the situation under consideration. But, taking these two definitions, we can see immediately that there are a number of general points to be made about all resources. For instance, resources can be divided into two broad categories — human and what might be termed facilities. Again, resources are there to be used — at appropriate times, of course. Let's now take these general points a little further and go into another Checkpoint.

Considering resources in **general terms only** make a list of what you see as the important features of resources. To start you off here is one:— resources must be relevant to the need determined.

Resources must be:—

1) *relevant to the need determined*
2) *understood by the user(s)*
3) *capable of being used efficiently and effectively*
4) *available for use at short notice*
5) *supportive and not take over from the training itself*
6) *maintained efficiently*
7) *re-assessed regularly to see that they are still relevant to the needs and the demands placed upon them*
8) *updated as necessary*
9) *monitored for usage.*

All these points apply to all resources, of course, in management situations away from training; unfortunately these are sometimes forgotten or ignored and the results can be seen in bad results with the failure to achieve the goals set.

Now we have considered a number of general points and seen that they are all essential (though some will be more pertinent than others depending on the actual training situation) if effective use is to be made of the resources. Let us go on a further stage and deal with the two major categories we identified earlier — human resources and facilities — in turn and in some depth.

Resources — The People

'People' sounds much better than 'human resources' which is a clinical way of describing ourselves. In looking at people as a resource remember that we all have our own attitudes, motives, likes and dislikes and so on; thus it can be dangerous or can result in complacency if we assume all people are alike. We realise you will know that but it's worth reminding ourselves of it as so much traditional training assumes only two positions — trainer and learner. One school of thought postulates that there are only two resources in any training situation — the trainer and the learner; this is a rather severe creed and neglects the important (but subsidiary) resource of facilities. On the other hand it does seem that far too many trainers spend more time thinking about the facilities (for example, 'will the video work?') than about the learner yet we train people — not things!

We will divide the people into two main groups with one — the trainer group — further subdivided; here they are:—

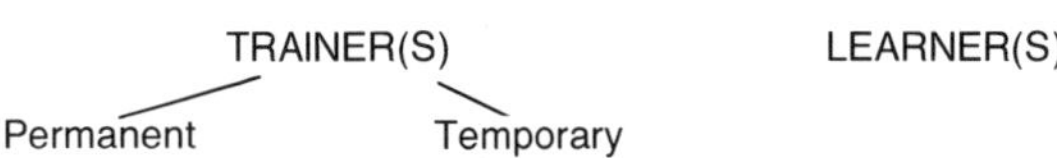

They must be considered separately but it must always be remembered that they co-exist. In what might be termed 'traditional' training it is too often the case that trainer and learner have the same period of time available — that is, the actual training period. The learner(s) turn up at the training place and, though the trainer may have been there beforehand, in effect he only begins to think about the actual training/learning when they meet. Training then begins and it can appear that the trainer is running along well-oiled lines (same examples, same comments, same form of words, same jokes) so much so that it might be better to replace him with a computer system or a well-trained chimpanzee and a tape recorder. And what results? Well, it can be boredom — for both participants (and who will be bored first is anyone's guess — probably the trainer) or it can produce strenuous efforts by the trainer to keep the learner(s) motivated and interested. This is often done by asking questions — sometimes of the group as a whole with then one person being named to answer or sometimes, if there is only one learner, obviously directly. The tactic of group questioning can work well if the learner knows the answer but it demands tremendous concentration by the trainer to ensure that all the group members are covered, that the topic being questioned is sufficient to cover the whole group and if the trainer can, in fact, frame enough relevant questions.

The Trainer

Leaving aside, for the moment, both the temporary trainer and the learner let's have another checkpoint.

The Permanent Trainer

Bearing in mind that, even though we are now trainers, we have experienced, and will continue to experience, many learning situations, make a list of the actions you think a trainer should or could take to ensure he is making the best use of himself. We'll give you a 'free one' for starters, as they say:— 'Prepare'.

Here is our list; compare it with yours and see just how much we can produce together:

1) *Assess own strengths and weaknesses in knowledge, skills and attitudes fairly and (occasionally) write them on paper*
2) *Assess own likes and dislikes similarly*
3) *find out what the learner(s) will have to achieve as a result of the training, to what levels, over what period of time*
4) *Check the learner's existing knowledge, skills and attitudes (difficult often — this last one)*
5) *Check who will support you as the trainer when the learner is in the workplace and ensure you are in harmony*
6) *Try to determine what is likely to motivate the learner (by discussion, for example, with his supervisor)*
7) *Try to find out likely speed of learning of learner*
8) *Devise entry and exit tests (using existing ones as appropriate) to enable you to see if training is effective*
9) *Repeat from learner's point of view — not easy, but a good exercise for the trainer*
10) *Assemble equipment, examples to be used in training and similar items*
11) *Check training area properly laid out but not so pristine that it bears no resemblance to work area*
12) *Check time — for instruction, practice, follow-up, implementation*
13) *Check administrative arrangements — for you and the learner*
14) *Put yourself in the learner's shoes — if you can.*

A long list but all are essential if you are to make proper use of the prime resource of yourself; you cannot expect the learner to become effective in spite of you — it must be because of you! Although the list sounds formidable it is not really so once you have practised training for some time as you can combine some of the actions while others take up very little time. Perhaps the most important one is the last — put yourself in the learner's shoes; think from his point of view

---

The Temporary Trainer

Straightaway let us state who this person is; it is the person, from within the organisation or from outside, who is undertaking training for you (the trainer) on a temporary basis. Perhaps he is the organisation's expert on some topic (for instance, safety with the Safety Officer covering the topic); perhaps you can cover the topic yourself adequately and maybe more professionally than your temporary trainer but your learners see too much of you and would benefit from a change of face, presentation, style, examples and so on. There are very many reasons why you may use a temporary trainer; you can think of more than we have stated here but it's not another Checkpoint! Your temporary trainer can, of course, come from outside the organisation — he might be a 'name' in the field, might have the expertise neither you nor anyone else inside has, you might simply want your learners to experience another angle or opinion to avoid too much bias, it might allow you to sit back and observe your learner(s) — again, there are many reasons. Let us have a further look at the temporary trainer and use a checkpoint to do so.

The choice is between using internal or external trainers on a temporary basis; list the factors you should take into account in considering your choice (but, at this stage, exclude cost).

Fundamentally there are four factors; although you may have discovered others they generally boil down into these:—

1) *the level of expertise in the specific area to be covered*
2) *ability to communicate* **effectively** *(note the word!)*
3) *willingness to act as a trainer*
4) *acceptability to the learner(s)*

Your ability to select is the key point in 1), 2) and 4); you cannot, of course, be sure how willing a person is to act as a temporary trainer. Many people, especially from within an organisation will feel they have something to contribute to your training plans and thus are willing — initially, at least — but in the event their willingness begins to evaporate as the time approaches.

The Temporary Trainer — Internal

In the selection of temporary trainers you must follow the precepts we listed earlier under checkpoint 3; you must start by considering the learner(s), their needs, their levels of attainment and their likely reactions to the trainer.

You may find that, though a temporary trainer from within the organisation has the expertise and the knowledge he can only communicate effectively with one or two levels of people and may not be able to deal properly with, for example, young entrants or senior managers. Factors such as age, experience, attitudes and interest will have a bearing on your choice. In addition you should not overlook the possibility that, before your temporary trainer can be effective, you will have to train him and this will be a precursor to any programme you arrange. Too often trainers have decided to use the internal or external expert and then found that he cannot deal with a group of people, mumbles, becomes authoritative or even dictatorial and perhaps, in extremes, takes fright; probably you have come across situations like this in your own experience. Plan to avoid them. This brings us to a further point; we have dealt, to some extent, as though you will be running a course with a number of people attending it. A great deal of training, as we know, occurs away from the somewhat formal setting of, say, a training room. Learning takes place on the job and may be carried out at irregular times, in brief sessions (almost short spasms!), on an individual basis and may be done more by a form of coaching than anything apparently resembling 'training'. Think of the possible occasions when this occurs — when, for instance, a person is newly promoted into the first level of management or supervision and, after the formal induction (if any), is attached to someone with, as we say, 'more experience'. We want to be sure that that person imparts only the correct information, at the right speed, right level and so on; hence he also needs to be trained. In such situations your ability to select may well be reduced to Hobson's choice and you have to make the best of a bad job — you can still impart basic training skills to the trainer. Similar situations apply when we have to place new employees into departments of a technical or commercial nature. So we have looked briefly at temporary trainers and concentrated on internal ones — including those who act as trainers consciously and participate on courses and those who train in more informal situations. We have, for the present, ignored external trainers, but will come to them presently. To consolidate the points indicated let's have another Checkpoint.

Sit back a bit and think now about using internal temporary trainers; list what you see as the advantages and disadvantages of using them on a training course. At the risk of being thought to be teaching one's grandmother to suck eggs we suggest you split your list into two with the advantages on the left and the disadvantages on the right as one advantage will often beget a possible disadvantage.

Here are some possible advantages and disadvantages, listed as described above:—

Advantages	**Disadvantages**
Knows the organisation	*May be blinkered, knowing one organisation only*
Usually is available	*May not plan until last minute*
Can speak with authority	*May not be available in the event*
Can often refer to actual examples and situations with which the learner(s) is/are familiar	*Status or specialisation may preclude learner(s) asking or arguing (N.B. — not quarrelling)*
Can be briefed fairly easily	*May be inexpert at presentation*
No fees paid	*May not be able to adjust to level of learner(s)*
Status can lend authority	*Examples can be restricted to the organisation when there is a need for others*
May be able to undertake training with little or no notice	*Examples may only show the 'good' side of the organisation so a lack of balance results*
Knows your systems	*Cost may be high* **in reality** *if the time for*
You can work on him over a period to improve performance	

Will probably want to do his best for the sake of the organisation, department, etc.	*preparation, consultation, use of other people's time and similar aspects are taken into account*
Easy to get at for further briefings	*Once used may be difficult to discard without loss of face, some disagreement or other damage*
	May not take kindly to your briefing, especially if he is the expert or senior or similar
	May be difficult for you to brief because of your own lack of knowledge, status, etc.

As you can see, there are many advantages and disadvantages; as you can also see, what may appear as an advantage might also be a potential disadvantage — as, for instance, in the case of the first advantage and disadvantage. As we mentioned at the beginning of this Component, as a trainer you have to exercise management responsibilities and one of those is making decisions. Some of the advantages and disadvantages may not be relevant in some situations, some which appear important in one situation might not be so in another; whatever the case, there is unlikely to be one obvious decision and one only so — it's over to you as the trainer to decide what is best for the learner(s) in the situation you and they face.

The Temporary Trainer — External

Very often organisations resort to the use of an external trainer (perhaps called a training consultant or some similar term) — usually a person who specialises in one or more aspects of training. For instance, you can use a specialist in computer techniques, Industrial Relations, finance, H.G.V. driving. The specialist possesses some special area of knowledge, skill or experience not available within the organisation. A word of caution here — there is sometimes a tendency to use an outsider because it appears easier to find one than to search within the organisation. However, you may well have someone already working in your organisation who can fulfil the same purpose — with some judicious training and help from you.

Let's now think about using external trainers and consider two points:—

1) What you, as the organisation's trainer, should do before employing someone from outside
2) The advantages and disadvantages of using such a person (as we did with the internal temporary trainer).

You — The Trainer

These are the steps you should take:—

1) Establish carefully the needs of the learner(s) in as much depth as possible (noting present level of knowledge, skill, attitude and the target levels)
2) Determine exactly what you want the external trainer to do — often this is more difficult than when you are preparing yourself or an internal trainer as the external trainer is not usually as easily available.
3) Produce a written brief covering, in as precise detail as possible, points such as current attainment levels, objectives, backgrounds of the learner(s), relevant information about the organisation, time available for the session(s), type of training previously undertaken, facilities available, where the external input fits into the overall training pattern — to name but a few)
4) Play devil's advocate; that is, look at the brief from the angle of the outsider and question it (e.g. does it tell you all you, as an outsider, would want to know?). If the brief is not full enough then add to it. Bear in mind that there may be some points you would take for granted — such as location, accessibility, car parking and so on!
5) Brief the external trainer
6) Confirm the broad details (dates, timings, aids required, etc.) in writing so both of you know exactly where you stand.

All this makes work for you, of course, but it will have an advantage to you apart from feeling that you have done all possible to assist the external trainer. That advantage is that it will have made you examine critically your requirements and the way you normally go about arranging training — doubtless you'll see some problem areas where you can improve your own planning, etc.!

Advantages and Disadvantages

Let's now go straight into a further Checkpoint covering these two aspects; here goes.

As with the previous Checkpoint, make two lists covering what you see as the likely advantages and disadvantages of using external trainers.

It may surprise you but there is a reasonable chance that some of the advantages of using internal trainers can appear as potential disadvantages of using external ones; for instance, take the advantage of being able to refer to actual examples (internal trainer). The external trainer may have some very good examples but they may not be relevant to the learner(s) situation and learner(s) do require to be able to see things in the context of the work to be done or the normal environment. However, let's produce our list of advantages and disadvantages for your consideration; here it is:—

Advantages

Generally treats everyone alike so not worried about status

As an external can speak with some authority

Knows more than one organisation

Usually expert at presentation

Can come in to give a 'shot in the arm'

Can be provocative without lasting damage being created

Should have wide range of examples

Ought to be able to show the 'good' and the 'bad' sides to a case without prejudice

Can be discarded without qualms when your purpose has been achieved

Can be changed for another fairly easily without repercussions

Generally will want detailed briefing

Cost known beforehand

Disadvantages

May not know enough about the background to your organisation

Examples may be good but not relevant

May not know the terminology and the 'in' languages of your organisation

May not know the internal politics

May not know your systems

May, in fact, simply have a package for presentation to everyone, everywhere, at all times

Cost

Might be difficult to get hold of for briefings beyond the first

Might be 'here today and gone tomorrow'

Can want you to adapt to his ideas without developing yours

Suspicion of the 'outsider' from the learner(s)

May find it difficult to convince learner(s) that what is being presented will work in organisation

---

As with internal trainers there is no simple obvious decision; you, as the trainer, must weigh up the possible options and decide. However, remember these points in relation to all training assistance:—

1) **You** must do the major preparations — learner(s), trainer(s), etc.
2) **You** decide the format, content, assistance needed
3) **You** must brief the trainer(s) thoroughly
4) **You** are responsible for the training — not the internal or external assistance
5) In general, you probably get what you pay for!

We have spent a long time on people as the major resource and emphasised mainly the trainer(s); for most information about the learner(s) you must, of course, look at other Study Units. If you do not use the resource of people effectively then you can almost forget the other resources; 'almost' is what we wrote — not 'althogether'! So let's now move on to consider the facilities.

The Learner

The learner is a major resource to be used to the full; he has to be understood by you. The learner does not necessarily see things from the points of view of either you or the organisation; very much it is a question of his motivation to learn which is the key point — and a point often overlooked. How then do we use the learner as a resource? Well, here are some steps we can take:—

1) Having set the objectives of the training, look at them from the learner's viewpoint. Think — what's in it for me as a learner? Why should I do it?
2) Decide how you, as the trainer, will use the learner; for example, will you involve him, and if so — how? Will the session be really participative?
3) Get feedback from the learner throughout the training and adjust the speed and style of presentation to suit the learner's achievement to date
4) Use the learner's knowledge, skills and attitudes to help you decide on the level of presentation
5) Get the learner to demonstrate to you what he has learned (this is a form of feedback as mentioned in 3) above)
6) Get the learner to demonstrate to other learners
7) Keep him interested and motivated throughout.

Resources — The Facilities

The facilities — the word 'facilities' sounds good but what does it mean? It means those resources which allow or enable you to conduct training in an effective and worthwhile manner having first established the needs of the learner(s) and the capabilities of the trainer(s).

Facilities can be divided into a number of areas; for our purposes there are five and they are:—

ACCOMMODATION
EQUIPMENT
TIME
FINANCE
METHODS & SYSTEMS

We will take each in turn and consider the essential features of them although we shall not, in this Component, consider Methods & Systems apart from a brief mention as they are covered elsewhere.

Accommodation

Another resource often taken for granted and not evaluated properly — yet how often have you heard (perhaps experienced yourself) tales of poor training accommodation (or very good accommodation, for that matter) and it is the accommodation which has coloured the learner's views of the training. You can probably think of many examples of accommodation which was right, wrong or somewhere in between. Bear in mind that accommodation, whether in the organisation or not, is a cost which has to be met so it ought to be considered in conjunction with the other resources and not just in isolation. Let's see what you think the main features are about accommodation.

Using your own experience, list what you think should be the essential features of training accommodation (and then check to see if your organisation has them).

Probably, like we did, you begin to think that the list is endless; here's ours — how does it compare with yours? It's unlikely we'll agree totally — that's in the nature of the exercise, of course. Our aim was to get you to think as so often we have training accommodation already available and tend not to look at it with a critical and dispassionate eye.

Here we go:—

Accommodation should be:—

1) *relevant to the needs of the learner(s)*
2) *conducive to receiving training*
3) *free from unnecessary distractions*
4) *comfortable (warm but not hot, supportive chairs (not beds), etc.)*
5) *adequate in size to accommodate the trainees without overcrowding or wasting space too much*
6) *accessible to the learner(s) and trainer(s)*
7) *properly laid out to suit the purpose of the training*
8) *properly equipped as far as possible*
9) *an area in which the learner(s) can see the trainer and vice versa — easily*
10) *reflective, as far as possible, of the real situation in which the learner normally works*
11) *reasonably quiet*
12) *available to other users when not required for training.*

We think that last one might have made you think but we have no doubt that you will see the benefits. Obviously all the points we have listed cannot apply to all training accommodation — so much depends on the attitudes to training in the organisation and other factors — but they are there for your consideration and, we hope, action and support.

Equipment

This is rather similar to accommodation in many ways insofar as it is taken for granted or training can be seen as an area on which to off-load old and unwanted machinery and equipment. On the other hand you can come across training departments which have all the latest gadgets and equipment and yet do no dynamic training — you probably think the place is a showroom for a range of manufacturers!

Although it may seem an obvious point to make, it is essential that the equipment does not take over from the actual training; you have probably seen the trainer who has all the gadgets in creation to hand and spent the time moving from one to another so much that you forgot the real purpose of the training! It's a trap we can fall into quite easily.

Another point about equipment is that the machinery used during training must be the same as that the learner(s) will encounter in reality. And a further one is that you must have enough equipment to cover all your learners with the proviso that it is possible, in some cases, to have two learners to one piece; in some cases, also, it can be of value as each can help the other.

Equipment breaks down into two categories; first, that which enables the learner to learn (for example, machinery, documents, materials). Secondly, that which helps the trainer to train. Again, you have probably had experience of using equipment as a learner or as a trainer so let's go on to our next Checkpoint.

List what you think are the essential features of equipment used in training.

Well, as previously, there are many and we shall not coincide but here goes:—

1) *relevant to the needs of the learner*
2) *safe to operate*
3) *where necessary highlighted by the use of colour to emphasise essential points*
4) *reflective of the actual equipment the learner will use in reality*
5) *properly maintained*
6) *subject to the same controls as other equipment in the organisation*
7) *capable of being partially dismantled where necessary for the learner's benefit*
8) *can be operated by the trainer*
9) *fitted with extra safety devices if necessary*
10) *must not replace the trainer*
11) *must be useful in the training — that is, will enhance the training.*

There are others, but these appear to be the main ones. Remember — it is important for us to realise that equipment is an **aid** *to, and not a substitute for, effective training.*

Time

It's pretty obvious to state that time, once spent, cannot be recouped; we all know that. What, however, often escapes the attention of the trainer and the organisation too, for that matter, is that if you do not use the time available to the best effect when training you will have to spend far, far more time later (either in one spell or over a period) trying to remove what you did not do well in the first place before you can implant the correct training. Well then, what are the main features of this resource and how can we use it to the best effect? the first point to raise here is — best effect for whom or for what? It must be the best effect for the learner and the organisation (assuming that what the learner has learned is to be put to use in the organisation, of course).

Let's then consider the main features of time; later we will look at how we can use it effectively — all from the training point of view, naturally enough.

Features

Time must be allocated for training and that allocation ought to be sufficient to enable the learner and the trainer to achieve their common goal. There is little point in trying to cut the time **necessarily** required for the training as some aspect will suffer — perhaps the practice element, perhaps the preparation period or something similar; note the word 'necessarily'. It implies that we have worked out exactly, as far as possible, how much time we will need to achieve the task set. However, there are many occasions (as no doubt you can recall from your own experiences) when time has apparently been wasted; for instance, learners have had to wait for a machine to become available, there has been a lack of materials or insufficient machines or the trainer has cut off a few minutes at the beginning and the end (for some unknown reason) or the time allowed for the training has not matched normal time patterns in the organisation and the trainees have had to hang about. That leads us into the next feature.

PREPARATION
+
PRESENTATION
+
CONSOLIDATION
=
EFFECTIVE USE OF TIME

Time must be planned. There are three elements to the time required in training; first, preparation time, secondly, presentation time and thirdly, consolidation time. In the first you, as the trainer, must prepare (yourself, the learner(s), the other people involved and the facilities required); in general, especially if you are going to run a new training programme or course, you can say that each allocated hour of presentation demands at least three hours of preparation. In general, we stated; it does not apply in all cases — some situations demand more, some less time; experience will show you which is relevant.

Very often we tend to concentrate on the presentation time and forget the other two elements but, for a moment, consider the case of the temporary trainer from inside the organisation and attempt to do a costing of the actual time taken by him in getting ready for the session. You will probably be surprised to find just how much time is actually taken up with preparation. At the other end of the training is the consolidation element — the period during which the learner (under supervision) performs the task, duty or responsibility until he is competent. There is a tendency to disregard this period yet we all know that, for instance, attendance at a course teaching you a new skill does not automatically produce, at the end, a competent qualified person. We need time to consolidate. So you must plan for that and the amount will probably depend on the learner's aptitude, interest, motivation.

The third feature of time is that it must be re-examined periodically to see that it is being used properly; for instance, do you need as much presentation time as you thought you did or as you once did. Probably the answer is 'Yes' — especially if you do monitor its use but if you never ask the question you can become complacent, in a rut and unlikely to question other aspects of training as well!

The fourth feature is that time is not limitless and there are going to be constraints; you can estimate what these are likely to be during your planning stage and try to adjust accordingly. Other demands are going to be made on the time the learner has available during the normal working period and you have to strike a balance. The best way to do this is to have more than one training plan available so you can adapt to the situation; you may decide to amend the consolidation element so that it is prolonged (or concentrated), you may change your training method. Whatever you do you should have considered it in the planning stage so that you are not taken by surprise and have another option ready.

Moving on to using time effectively let's have another Checkpoint here.

You will obviously have had experience of being trained yourself — individually, in a group, on a course, by coaching or whatever. Using that experience make a list of the points to bear in mind when you are planning to run a training programme so that your time and that of the learner is used effectively.

Using the features described earlier you could:—

1) *Survey the tasks you have to do in preparing for training and rank them (a) in order of importance and/or (b) in a sequence to save time*
2) *Allocate your own personal time and note the periods in your work diary*
3) *Try to eliminate potential distractions (e.g. shut off the TV, have telephone calls diverted, change your hours of work a little)*

4) Make a note of what you have achieved per period, with difficulties or points of advantage highlighted
5) Set up and maintain sources of reference so that you can easily refer to information and save time
6) Delegate, if possible
7) Eliminate unnecessary periods; for instance, if you establish a filing system you can bring out, and possibly modify, previous information (notes, examples)
8) Analyse the time allowed for the actual training after the event, make notes of points of wasted time, insufficient time, interruptions and the like to ensure they are minimised in the future
9) Make sure the learner knows clearly the intermediate and final objectives as they affect him
10) Set target times for yourself and the learner(s) — final and intermediate by which you propose to reach specific objectives
11) Examine the time allowed for each part of the programme; it's not unusual to find that insufficient time has been allowed for the skills development part of a programme especially where the trainer is an expert
12) Build 'spare' periods into the programme; that is not to say that you include obvious blank periods but we know that generally we tend to conform to some time pattern in work and hence in training (e.g. a half-hour period) yet the topic being covered does not need quite that amount — so you have a 'spare' period built up (or capable of being built up) during the training. In finance it would be called a 'contingency amount' or, in more common terms, 'something laid aside for a rainy day'. Alternatively, you can consider using different methods of training and thus 'saving' time; for instance, you can use a lecture as against a discussion as the former takes up less time to get points across to the learner(s). We're not saying you should — just that you should consider alternative ways of training to make the most effective use of the time available.

In some cases, particularly in operative training, the use of intermediate targets for the learner(s) is advantageous and you can use work measurement data to achieve this. Fine, but — in what ways will target times be of value to the trainer and the learner?

To the trainer they can:—
1) assist in spotting learning problems
2) identify speeds of learning
3) reduce the need for remedial treatment
4) allow for the use of alternative methods of training
5) allow the building up of 'spare' time

To the learner they can:—
1) make learning seem less difficult
2) make the final target seem more attainable
3) allow frequent and regular checks on progress
4) build confidence

Now we have considered time and its effective use let us move on to the resource of finance.

Finance

Although it may not always be apparent, all training costs money either directly (as in the payment of course fees, hire of rooms, payment of trainers and so on) or indirectly (as in the cost of not having a person in his normal job while undergoing training, notional rents for space occupied, machinery used, etc.). Each organisation will have its own financial and costing systems so we shall not go into depth in this area; suffice it to say that all efforts in any organisation (marketing, production, training — to name a few only) cost money in one way or another. Essentially, as a trainer, you should ensure that one factor above all applies and that is this — the benefits resulting from training must outweigh the costs. Otherwise there is no point in training (and the same applies to other areas of activity, of course).

In any organisation finance is limited and generally departments have to fight for a share of the total. As far as training is concerned three points stand out. The first has already been made — that the benefit must outweigh the cost. The second is that the trainer — you — should endeavour to get the best returns for the money you expend (whether it is direct or indirect outgoings) which means that you should analyse carefully the various training programmes you run to establish if any or all can be run at less financial cost. Of course, we'll all agree with that but, in practice,unfortunately other considerations often take priority (for example, that mystical 'prestige' or having a superb training centre that is in use for only a few hours a week, or going to the 'right' college, or the attitude that 'they've always done us proud so we'll continue to use them (without question)'). To do this comparison efficiently you yourself will have to do some spadework and be sure you are comparing like with like.

The third point about finance in training is that you must have a budget. Why? Because if you don't you will be at the mercy of those departments which have them, you cannot argue from a firm base but, above all, you have no idea of where you are going and may well actually be reacting to the winds of fortune, as it were. This is not the place to go into budgets and how to prepare them but there are some points to be made about them. Let's have a Checkpoint to see what you think they might be.

Name four features of budgets — it's as simple as that!

Here are some points for your consideration:—

1) *budgets mean you must plan ahead — preferably for a year*
2) *budgets allow you to exercise dynamic as opposed to static control of your department, making adjustments as and when necessary*
3) *budgets allow you to make comparisons, year against year, period against period, course against course, departmental costs against departmental costs, etc.*
4) *budgets allow you to anticipate changes and prepare for them*
5) *budgets allow you to establish benefits against costs and argue your case more effectively*
6) *budgets develop a critical ability enabling you to think ahead — hopefully in a rational way.*

So finance is an important resource; one area we have not mentioned is the source(s). In most cases they will be from within the organisation but there may be external finances available from, for instance, governments, the European Economic Community, scholarships, other enterprises. When establishing your budgets you should consider these sources as well as your own.

Methods

this is the last, but by no means the least, of the major resources. Method may be considered as the means by which information and experience can be passed from one person (the trainer) to another (the learner) in the most efficient way and to the best effect. Thus it is essential that the method or methods chosen should be appropriate to that aim — hence should be looked at principally from the angle of the learner. Many of us, as trainers, have our favourite methods which suit us and which work well in the majority of situations but we should beware falling into the trap of using a method because it suits us — the big point is — does it suit the learner? If it does — it is a resource; if it does not —it's a hindrance to effective learning and, after all, that is our main purpose in training — to see that learning is effective!

The choice of method should depend mainly on the learner though other aspects such as the environment in which the learning is to occur must also be taken into account. We cannot do better here than to repeat the list produced in Component 1 of the Study Unit; you, as the trainer, must choose which suits best. Here is the list:—

Computer Assisted Learning
Case Studies
Demonstrations
Discussions
Experiments
Individual study
Investigations
Working with small groups
Lectures
One-to-one teaching
Project Work
Role-play
Seminars
Simulations
Tutorials

Conclusion

In this Component we set out to consider the resources normally available to you as a trainer; obviously we do not know your background or your situation hence we have tried to cover a range of eventualities. You will have to pick out of this Component those parts which directly concern you or might do so in the future.

The most important resource is the people — the trainer(s) and the learner(s) — but there are others, too. For instance, the supervisor of the learner — what about him? And what about the people higher up in the organisation — they are important resources and should be viewed (and used) as such.

All the other resources are, in fact, aids of one sort or another which should enable you as the trainer to conduct your training more effectively and, to be more precise, should enable the learner to learn. After all, that's what training is all about.

Tutor Seen Work

Take a training situation with which you are familiar in your own organisation and examine the resources involved (including the people, if you wish so). Try to analyse them and establish their purpose and use and value in that training.

Component 4:

Planning a Programme

Key Ideas

 **Logistics of the planning process; individual vs group training; 'on-job' training; 'off-job' training; preparation of the learner(s); checking resource availability; joining instructions.**

Objectives

As a result of working through this Component you will:

1) Have developed an outline of the contents of a typical programme
2) Be able to identify the types of information needed to prepare joining instructions
3) Be able to recognise the factors to consider when organising the logistics of a programme
4) Have taken account of individual and group programmes and 'on' and 'off-job' locations when planning a programme

Introduction

The purpose of training is to bring about change; more specifically, the type of change that is reflected in improved individual, group or organisational performance. Naturally, change can't be achieved without first specifying its nature, extent, and the most likely means of achieving it; training being one of several options that may be available. So, in effect a training programme states the change(s) you wish to bring about, and provides a 'route-map' of the 'travel' directions necessary for reaching your destination.

This Component assumes that you possess the knowledge and skill to carry out a training needs analysis and to determine the programme content, objectives, methods and resources. If necessary, you should refer to units 1 and 2 of this Volume which deal more thoroughly with the process.

What follows examines a series of the practical issues and problems which arise when planning the logistics of a training event. Throughout, the intention is to provide guidance in drawing up realistic and workable results.

Programme Content

From a purely mechanistic point of view, the design of a training programme is a straightforward task; if only because most programmes conform to a well recognised and standard pattern. Even if you have never designed a programme before, you will certainly have some idea of the types of information that a programme ought to contain.

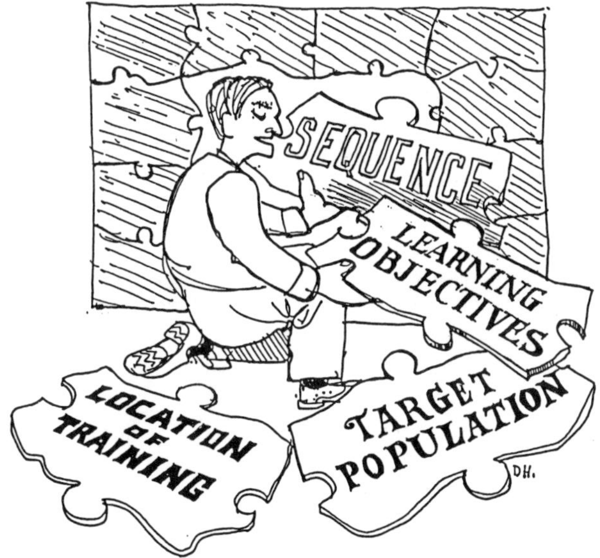

Checkpoint

Think of training programmes you have experienced and try to recall the sorts of information about the 'course' that were spelled out in the details you received.

You may have noted some or all of the following points:

a) *details of who the programme was designed for — the 'TARGET POPULATION'.*
b) *what the participants should have already achieved*
c) *the learning objectives*
d) *the final outcome of the programme; for example, a qualification, increase in pay, improvement in status or position*
e) *the learning content (subjects, topics, or session titles)*
f) *timing and sequencing of the content*
g) *the training location (internal/external and 'on/off job' elements)*
h) *who will carry out the training (full or part-time trainers, internal or external trainers)*
i) *how the programme will be conducted (methods and resources/individual or group programme)*
j) *administrative arrangements*
k) *pre and post-course requirements*
l) *assessment methods.*

The list of items normally included in a programme can be extensive but not difficult to think about or to understand. As with most activities, behind it there is considerable amount of preparation if the programme is to succeed and there's no magic formula for getting it right!

In their book, 'The Evaluation of Management Training', Warr, Bird and Rackham suggest that it is necessary to evaluate each decision commencing with the initial identification of the need for training and continuing through to the selection of methods, facilities, staff and the means to be adopted to judge the results. The message to remember from their approach is that it is important that you 'test', that is, check that as far as possible, you have considered all the influencing factors, at each phase of the design process. With these points in mind, you have the basis for preparing a coherent and successful programme.

Given that you have taken care of the organisation and sequencing of the content and identified methods, staffing and other resources, you can now produce the final outline. This will usually be stated in a form that makes clear the following points:

WHAT is to be covered
WHO is to instruct (and who is the target population)
WHERE the training will take place
WHEN — the timing and sequence
HOW — the methods and other resources required.

The illustration below shows a **possible** layout for a programme taking account of the main features indicated previously.

Time / Day	Mon.	Tues.	Weds.	Thurs.	Fri.
9.00—11.00	Assembly, Introduction: course objects: Admin. (RGB)	I.T.N. Case Study (various)	Presenting a case to Management (MF/RBL)	Producing Job Specifications & Exercise (RBG)	Further Analysis (Practical) (KNW)
11.15—1.00	(RGB) Roles in Training — Outline & clarification of own roles.	ITN Case Study (various)	Analysing Specific Needs (MF)	Devising Learning Objectives (PS)	Introduction to Programme Design (WRL)
2.00—3.45	The Training function. —Introduction (MF)	Presentation of Results. (MF/RBL)	Producing Job Descriptions (MF)	Exercise in Producing Objectives	Course review (Wk. 1) (MTF)
4.00—			The Job		

Once these details are settled the task of organising the event and dealing with the logistics of bringing together each of the elements involved can begin. There are two main elements to consider:

a) Internal organisation — including; Staff, facilities, equipment, materials, timing
b) Informing the learners — the preparation and sending of joining instructions

The last issue is of particular significance and a consideration of the types of information that may need to be made clear can be useful in pointing to the general administrative aspects that will need to be resolved.

Reflect on the types of information you may need to make clear to the learner(s) in terms of basic administration of the programme they are about to commence.

Just what do I need to take with me? I wish someone had told me.

It is not possible to cover every eventuality and some of the items listed will not be relevant to every programme that you might run, but you could have included:

Date and time of starting and finishing
Time(s) of finishing each day
Meal and break arrangements
Where and who to report to
Travel directions
Travel arrangements
Expenses
Pay whilst in training (and how collected)
Pre-course preparation
What to take to the 'course'
Programme (aims, objectives and content)
Accommodation (note that this includes both that required for the course as well as the possibility of residential accommodation for trainees whilst on the course).

What is now required is that each of the items involved are organised and co-ordinated such that they 'dovetail' neatly together ready for the commencement of the programme. So, taking together the points about internal organisation and information needed by the participant(s), let's work out what needs to be attended to.

Organisation

Producing a timetable

As a starting point it's useful to draw up a TIMETABLE of events. There are two distinct but related aspects to this:

a) The internal organisation of the programme itself and how individual needs can be satisfied.
b) Details of and dates by which specific actions related to the organisation of the training event should be completed.

In developing the programme you ought to have already taken into account those points relating to its internal structure and organisation and you should therefore have determined the overall time as well as that needed for each aspect. There are a number of factors that will or should have been considered in deciding on the time needed including:

Flexibility
Number of trainees involved
Likely variations in the rate of learning of different trainees and how their individual needs will be catered for.

Write short notes relating to each of the items listed above, indicating how they might affect the time required.

Your programme should have been drawn up to cater for a specific number of trainees. Thus, the physical space, resources required, methods to be used, and the location of the programme will be influenced by this. Points relating to individual and group training events are dealt with later in this component.

When more than one trainee is involved, it is crucial that you consider how variations in the rates of learning will be catered for. Some parts of the programme will be learned at a faster rate by some trainees than by others but may not influence the overall time required. How will you cater for this?

One possible answer is to build in a degree of flexibility. Instead of programming all the available time, you could leave some time free so that those who need more time can receive it. Those who are well advanced may be catered for by providing opportunities for further practice. This may require you to devise additional exercises. Flexibility in programme design is the important point. Anticipation of these variations will assist in allocating time as well as other resources in a sensible way. No programme will be perfect in terms of the allowed time and the deliberate inclusion of opportunities to be flexible helps you to take account of individual requirements more easily than if you had devised a highly and tightly structured approach.

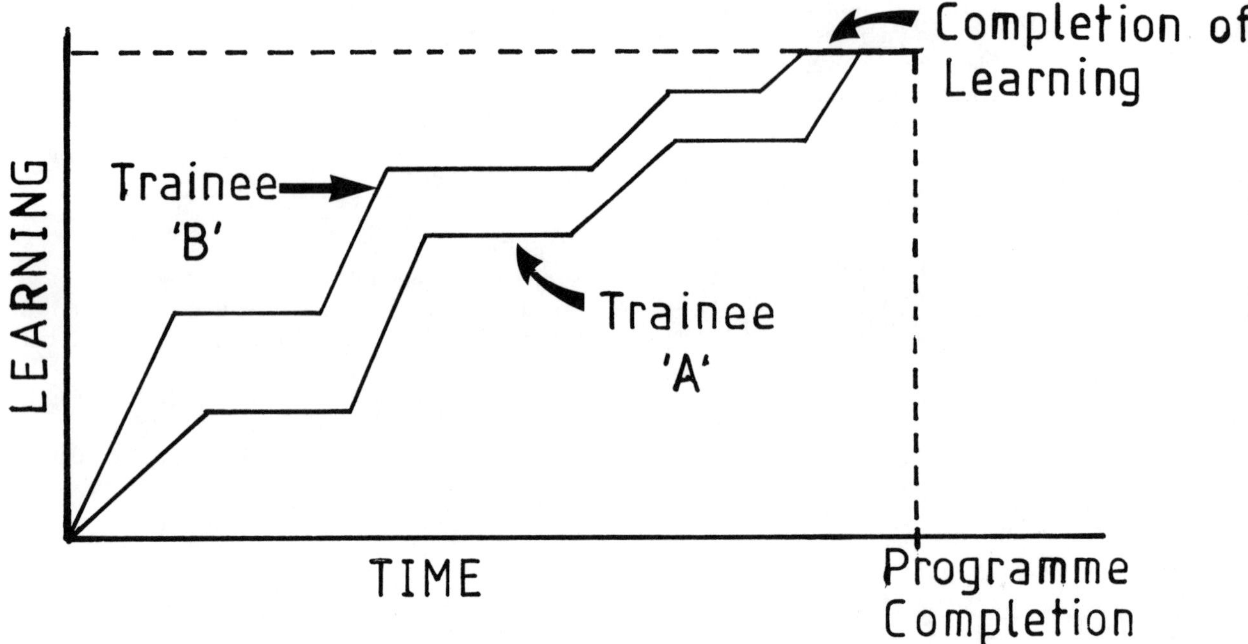

Trainees Learn at Different Rates

Organising the elements within the timetable
Drawing up a timetable of events is no more than what is necessary for good management. There is a series of administrative tasks to be completed before joining instructions can be devised and despatched, and further issues that must be attended to by the time the programme is due to commence. An important point to take account of is that of how soon before the event you will need to make arrangements as well as to inform course members. Let's examine some of these aspects now.

When setting start and finish times/dates, what factors should you consider and what actions might be needed in terms of organisation? When thinking about this, take account of accommodation, tutors/trainers and trainees.

Consider the start and end times and dates and the times of working for each day as well as any evening activities that are planned. What are the implications of this in terms of staffing and the need to forewarn the trainees? In setting dates and times you will need to bear in mind the availability of trainers and trainees and the need to brief them.

Apart from satisfying yourself that each tutor will be available at the time and date required, consider what information they need in order to fully prepare them for their session(s). The most important point here is to ensure that clear learning objectives are provided. Once the details have been attended to, do ensure that what has been agreed is put in writing and confirmed.

Check on what facilities and resources each trainer needs so that these can be arranged to fit in with the times required. Where necessary, you may need to advise tutors if their needs cannot be fulfilled and arrange for adjustment to their intended approach and methods. For example, it may be that several 'syndicate' rooms are required but will not be available. This will need to be taken into account by the tutor and alternatives worked out.

The types of equipment needed by each tutor should be identified and compared to that which is available. It may be necessary to organise for the hire or loan of equipment and sources of supply will need to identified and the necessary arrangements made for delivery, collection and, if necessary, insurance cover.

The location of the training generates further issues. From the point of view of resources and methods, consider how these will be influenced by locating the learning both in an 'on' and 'off' the job setting and whether the programme has been designed for an individual or for a group. The specific requirements, advantages and disadvantages of these are dealt with later. Whatever the case, there may be implications in terms of organisation. It will also be necessary to check on the types of facilities available if the programme is to be operated away from your own premises. It can be vital to check out features such as black-out facilities, power points and the like!

The need for residential accommodation must also be considered. For example, exactly what facilities will be needed, how many are to be catered for, how much are you prepared to pay for this and, if the location of the training event is different from the location of the residential accommodation, how will course members be transported between the different venues?

Start and finish times should be arranged so as to take account of the distances to be travelled by course members. In some cases it may be necessary to arrange accommodation for some trainees for the evening prior to the commencement of the programme. This will need to be established well in advance.

Meals and related issues

Apart from thinking of the specific times to be allowed, you will need to consider the arrangements necessary to ensure that what is needed is available when required. A point that can be easily overlooked is that of special dietary needs. This is worth detailing within the joining instructions; where relevant, remember to ask course members to provide details of any special needs they have beforehand so that appropriate arrangements can be made.

Travel and arrival

Where course members are required to attend at a location other than their normal place of work, you will need to prepare and send out full details relating to travel arrangements. How are people expected to travel, can information be given about train and/or bus times, what can be claimed in terms of travel costs and how will course members be re-imbursed? Do you need to produce a map indicating the location? If so, this will need to be made ready to send out with the joining instructions.

Remember to make appropriate arrangements for the arrival of course members. They need to know who and where to report to. There's nothing worse than to find that no-one is there to meet you and that nothing is known about your arrival. Tell the administrative staff involved. Arm them with all details and ensure that they know who to expect and when.

Pay and expenses

When a programme extends over more than a few days, how will course members receive their pay? In some cases this will have no effect since they may normally be paid by credit transfer to their bank accounts. If this is not the case, what arrangements will need to be made? Remember, you may need to include these details in the joining instructions. The matter of expenses can sometimes cause problems. Think out what it is that you will allow and the rates involved. This should also be clarified when the joining instructions are formulated.

Pre-course preparation

Some programmes may demand course members to carry out some initial work prior to attending the training event and/or that they bring certain items with them. If pre-course reading is necessary, you will need to provide the information/material to be worked on. If materials/items must be brought along to the course ensure that you identify what is required and that adequate information is given to the trainee(s) to enable them to select the necessary items. A point worth remembering here is to provide details of who course members can contact in case of difficulty.

Individual and Group Programmes

The type of programme you intend to operate, whether for an individual or group, and its location, that is, 'off-job' or 'on-job' will inevitably influence the arrangements you will need to make. Let's try to identify the factors that may be at work here.

What factors would you take into account in deciding whether to design a group or individual programme?

There are several possible influences that spring to mind:

a) The nature of the material to be learned.
b) The number who require training.
c) The number of trainees who can be released at any one time.
d) The facilities, finance and other resources you can call upon.

Now think about the types of learning activities that are, in your view, best learned through group situations.

Some learning activities can only be learned when working as a member of a group. Examples include skills such as interviewing, team building exercises, and the development or modification of attitudes. it's not always easy to organise this type of programme because you may have limited numbers of people who require these aspects or can't release people in sufficient numbers to warrant running the programme. So, the decision about group v's individual programme is partially determined by the nature of the learning and partially by economics. Whatever you decide on, remember that there will be implications in terms of both the design of the programme and the staffing, facilities and resources that will be required.

Group programmes can be an effective and economical way of organising training but don't forget that it's not always necessary to use them. In some cases it may be possible to organise part of the programme to operate through the medium of distance learning. Should you intend to use this approach it is important that you recognise the demands it will make on the resources you have available, not least of which are, expertise in producing the learning material; time; facilities, and cost. Even making use of existing material will make demands on your time if only because of the necessity to provide SUPPORT to the learners. Open or distance learning isn't a cheap alternative and can be demanding in terms of the resources needed to make best use of the approach. Nevertheless, it does open up a whole new approach for the organisation of training programmes. Remember too that the matter of SUPPORT is relevant to all learners, not just those learning at a distance.

A little support can be helpful

'On-Job' versus 'Off-Job' Training

The facilities required will clearly vary in each of these cases. You should take this into account when making the arrangements for the course and when deciding on what trainees need to bring with them. At this point it may be useful to consider the relative merits of each of these situations.

Draw up a list of the advantages and disadvantages of training in an 'on-job' setting. (When you have done this do the same thing for an 'off-job' setting and then compare the two lists.) A selection of possible advantages and disadvantages is given below.

On-job

Advantages	**Disadvantages**
Easy to set up	*Can interfere with normal work and may be subject to distracting influences*
Low initial cost	*Abilities of trainers. Trainees may be exposed to bad habits*
Learning occurs in a 'real-life' setting	*Can take longer to learn. May have an effect on costs of scrap, rejects and output. Can result in damage to equipment.*
No problems associated with the transfer of learning from an 'off-job' environment	*Subject to disruption from work pressures*

Off-job

Advantages	**Disadvantages**
Better environment and better quality of instruction	*More costly to establish*
Learning time can be reduced and may be less costly	*Ensuring that the learning content is relevant*
Less disruption	*Problem of transfer of learning*
Easier to control	

Briefing the Learner(s)

One further point, relevant to both 'in-house' and 'external' programmes. Course member(s) should be properly briefed and understand why they have been asked to take the course, what it is about, how it will help them in their job and what arrangements have been made to help them implement the learning on their return to work.

Reflect for a few moments on the points raised in the preceding paragraph. What reasons would you suggest for this being an important issue?

If initial briefing is ignored the learner(s) may become apathetic or antagonistic about the programme. Clearly, in such a state of mind, they would be unlikely to gain maximum benefit from the learning and could even affect other learners. On return to their job they may exhibit resistance to implementing the learning and could portray training as pointless and irrelevant.

Conclusion

By now you should have all the information needed to prepare an effective training event, recognise the importance of issuing clear joining instructions and their place within the planning process.

The message is simple. Identify the various factors involved and ask yourself how they will affect the organisation of the programme. Recognise that training an individual or group has implications and repercussions in terms of the arrangements to be made and identify what must be made clear to the learners at the outset. Above all, be clear about the target population and try to ensure that the learning situations that are devised and the material that is delivered are well matched. Provide clear instructions, both to the trainers and trainees and take account of the type of programme and its location in preparing the facilities and resources required. Finally, remember that you should not 'take it for granted' that everyone knows what is expected — check and confirm at each stage in the planning process.

Component 5:

Running a Programme

Key Ideas

Intervention points; pre, post and in-course activities; learning environment — physical and psychological; management of learning; recognising the signs for change; managing changes to the programme.

Objectives

As a result of working through this Component you will:

1) Have identified the major points where the trainer may need to intervene in the running of a programme.
2) Have listed typical actions that may need to be taken at each point.
3) Have identified a number of the signs and symptoms that may indicate that adjustment or change is required.

Introduction

By the time you come to implement a training programme, most of the hard work should have already taken place. Given that you have taken into account all the relevant factors in the design of the programme, your prime concern will be that of ensuring that the learner(s) learn.

This component focuses attention on some of the issues that arise when running and controlling a programme. It encompasses both the management of administrative duties as well as those that are more usually thought of as being concerned with the management of the learning itself.

There is a wide range of tasks that may need to be carried out in order to ensure that a programme runs successfully. Each forms a significant step in the **creation of an effective learning environment.** Even the most painstakingly designed programme will be of little use if the learning environment is inadequate. In this context, the environment can be thought of as comprising both physical and psychological factors; each may require attention during the course of the programme.

Main Points of Intervention

Few programmes will operate without the trainer having to intervene at some point. It is the trainer's job to recognise when these interventions are necessary, to identify any sources of difficulty, to take appropriate action and, overall, to manage the learning.

I'll soon whip 'em into shape

There are three major occasions when action will be required. These can be itemised in terms of the point in time when they are carried out and could be thought of as follows:

a) Pre-course
b) In-course
and c) Post-course activities

Pre-Course Activities

Here are two distinct aspects. On the one hand they include the organisational arrangements carried out well before the programme commences. Such actions will include:

Administrative arrangements such as sending out joining instructions; checking availability of staff and rooms; meal arrangements; transport; hotel accommodation; preparation of materials learning aids and handouts. Where relevant, ensuring that any pre-course work that trainees are expected to carry out is sent out in adequate time and with instructions on what should be done.

In addition, there are a series of activities that will normally be more likely to take place **immediately** prior to the event; sometimes, within a matter of hours of commencement. It is with this last group that we are concerned here.

Checkpoint

Take the first of the three grouping listed above (i.e., pre-course) and make notes of the tasks you think will need to be taken care of. It may help if you relate your thoughts either to a programme you have already organised and conducted or to one that you have experienced as a learner.

The tasks required will depend on the nature of the programme and the specific circumstances and conditions under which it is being conducted. The checklist below is representative of the types of task you may have to take into account but may need adjustment to meet your particular needs.

Preparation and layout of rooms; checking on physical and environmental conditions; checks on operation and correct set up of equipment/ machines; final safety checks on equipment; availability of safety gear; layout of materials such as paper, pens and other materials to be used by the learner(s); setting out course paperwork.

Wouldn't it be easier if I tried lying down?

These points are all part of creating an environment that is conducive to effective learning. Imagine the thoughts of the learner(s) if, when they arrive at the start of a learning event, none of the points listed above had been taken care of. At the best it would not help to create the right impression; at the worst, it could result in serious damage to the effectiveness of the event!

In contrast, if the training location looks and feels inviting, and demonstrates thought in the way that even apparently small points have been taken care of, then it can only help. Take for example the preparation of a room to be used for an off the job event with a group of learners. The attention given to the task of laying out tables chairs nameplates and materials may seem trivial in the extreme but it can be important. For some learners, especially those less used to being in a more formal learning environment, a layout of neat rows of desks may present a formidable sight. Ask yourself if that form of layout is really necessary; would it be better not to have tables at all; if they are needed, would 'U'-shaped layout be more conducive to establishing the type of setting that is required?

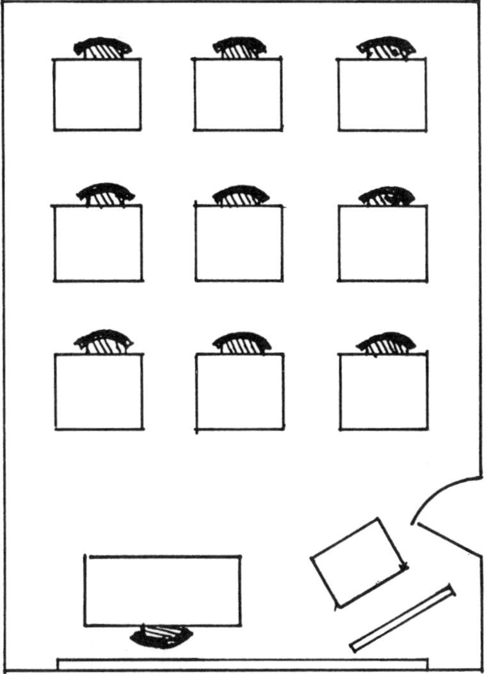

The "School-room" layout

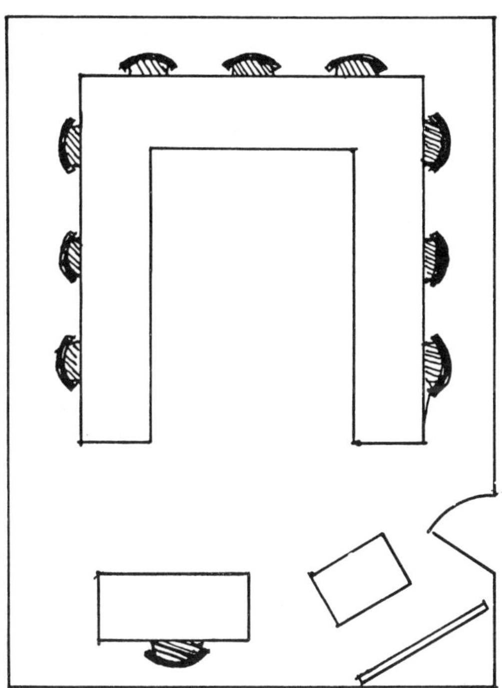

the "Lecture-room" Layout ('U'-shaped)

Visual aids equipment, such as ovehead projectors, need to be properly set up in order to give each learner as good a view as possible and focused ready for use. All the necessary materials, aids, pens for the trainer and so on, must also be easily to hand. Without such care the event is more likely to suggest that what happens is of no importance.

Think also of the physical comfort and safety of the learners. A room that is poorly lit, badly ventilated and affected by excessive external noise will only serve to create distracting influences. Some of these factors may not be entirely within your control but they should have been attended to as far as possible when you selected the location and, of course, may require some attention during the running of the programme.

In-Course Activities

Tutor meetings

Managing the learning event requires that you constantly monitor what is taking place. In some instances there will be several trainers involved at varying times throughout the programme. There is obviously a need for them to meet in order that they may review progress, share views and individual experiences and determine if there is a difficulty which requires action to be taken on. Normal break times will generally provide at least some opportunity for this but, on lengthy programmes it can be useful to hold a more formal review session each day. This provides the chance for each tutor to be kept up to date with events and to determine adjustments to strategies and approach.

Making adjustments

The 'golden rule' is that you should be cautious about making any changes to the programme until you are absolutely certain that they are necessary. Even then, try to avoid wholesale changes, especially to the content and objectives. As a rule, it will be rare for such drastic changes to be required and, if they do prove to be necessary, they clearly indicate a serious fault in the initial design.

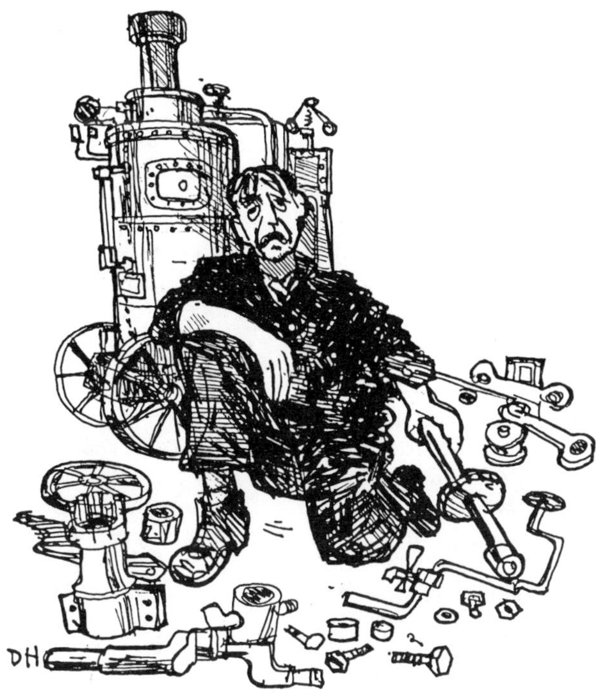

I only wanted to put some grease on this shaft and now I can't put the thing back together again.

Suppose that you recognise that some change/adjustment to a programme is needed. What might you bear in mind with regard to your original design in making such changes?

If changes are decided upon, ALWAYS make them with reference to the original objectives. RECORD the agreed changes and note why they were necessary. This will be useful later, at the end of the programme, when you or the team come to review the course and decide on future design.

Also, be careful not to over-react. It's not unusual to find that what fails to meet the needs of one group, will be precisely what the next finds beneficial. By all means adjust the current programme if that is what is needed but do remember that the current change may not require an adjustment to future events.

More usually, changes will be minor but can encompass a wide range of possibilities. When running a programme it can be useful to bear in mind the likely areas where adjustment may be required. This will at least enable you to know what to look out for.

Think about the possible problems/difficulties that could arise. Make a list of the aspects you think may bring about the need for change or adjustment, remembering that your thoughts should encompass both physical and psychological factors.

You could have included the following points within your list:

the physical setting
failure to take account of individual needs
lack of cohesiveness between course members
composition of syndicate groups
pace of learning
failure to understand
level of instruction

Now let's examine a number of these items in more detail. The headings which follow do not necessarily coincide exactly with the points listed in the last checkpoint, but they do embrace the issues involved and mark possible points of intervention.

Physical factors

There are several possibilities that may need attention. For example, in a location that is not as well ventilated as would be desirable, you may find that extra breaks are necessary so that learners can take a 'breath of fresh air'. Remember too that most people will be unused to sitting for long periods; their jobs will normally involve much more physical activity than will take place on some programmes.

The implications are that you should watch for signs of restlessness. If need be, introduce additional breaks; five minutes may be all that is required and it can make a substantial difference to the effort and enthusiasm that learners bring and apply to the programme. Even action as simple as this can help prevent a programme or individual session from flagging. But, it does require the trainer(s) to be aware, to look for the signs that suggest a break, some other action would be beneficial.

Right, it's time for a break, so we'll go outside and do two circuits of the car park.

Induction/introduction

This represents the starting point for the programme. The intention is that of helping put people at ease, answering any queries and providing them with the information they need about the administration of the programme and the training location. What is included will vary according to the needs of the programme and situation. Nevertheless, it's possible to identify the more common items.

Imagine that you are conducting a programme lasting two days in your own training centre with twelve trainees from different sites who have never attended a programme at that location previously. What points should be covered during the induction session?

You may have listed some of the following:

Introductions — including trainers and trainees; outline of course aims and objectives; course outline; break and meal arrangements; hotel accommodation; travel to and from hotels etc.; course timetable; evening activities; safety regulations, including fire precautions, escape routes and assembly points; facilities available, such as the location of quiet rooms, library, first aid and toilet facilities.

The point about people introducing themselves to each other may seem an obvious one but don't underestimate its significance. Remember, you want to create a cohesive group and this will be less likely to happen if you make no attempt to help them find out about each other or the trainer(s). From your own point of view, even if you already have 'profiles' of the learners, by spending time on this activity, you are beginning to find out more about them as individuals. Such information may be important in deciding how you conduct each 'session' and in helping to understand and take account of the needs of each learner.

It isn't difficult to do this. Try getting people to tell you of their expectations of the event. Better still, why not consider getting the learners to introduce one-another?; this can be a useful way of 'breaking the ice' but it won't happen so easily unless you deliberately intervene.

Structuring and controlling syndicates

At some point, depending upon the type of programme you are running, you may want to arrange for the learners to work on some task as members of a small group or syndicate. The structuring of such groups can be important if the learning experience is to be beneficial to all concerned.

Group structure can be important

Make brief notes on the need for the trainer to deliberately structure groups and, especially, the signs you might look for that may suggest that you need to reorganise them.

Learners bring different experiences to training events. There may be a mixture of experienced and less experienced learners and structuring the groups to make use of this can be useful; learners can learn from each other. It's quite likely that some trainees will be more forthcoming than others and, if not controlled, they may dominate the group. Other learners may feel intimidated and/or annoyed by this and hence derive less benefit from the experience.

A programme may have the objective of developing the ability of trainees to lead others, to communicate and to present arguments, analyses and points of view. If you leave the groups to organise this for themselves, some trainees may be only too happy to leave it all to the more outspoken individuals. Admittedly, there may be times when your aim is to explore the operation of work groups and allowing the group to organise themselves then becomes a legitimate and deliberate action.

Additional signs that a group may need to be restructured are when few ideas are forthcoming or where you notice signs of irritation between group members or there is evidence of frustration. Even then you may not need to step in immediately. Often, the group will impose its own control over difficult members.

You should not leave the groups too much to their own devices. Spend time with them, so that you can guide them when necessary, monitor their performance as a group and identify when it may be necessary to take action.

Pace, achievement of targets and the abilities of trainees

In planning a programme, you should have considered the pace of work that would be suitable for the target population. This should have been translated to arrive at appropriate durations for each session and the targets that were expected to be achieved at each point. But, the act of planning these aspects does not mean that no future adjustment will be required. Learning difficulties can and will arise and you will need to be able to respond to them.

For example, on an advanced course for Direct Trainers, the trainees were expected to present a training session making use of various visual aids equipment. Since this was an advanced programme there was no formal instruction in the use of visual aids. It became apparent that, for one participant, instruction was required in the use of overhead projectors. Whilst the topic has been covered in his initial training, he had never actually used one! The remedy was to find an opportunity within the current programme to help him learn.

Similarly, you may need to intervene to adjust pace and sequence. There is little point in proceeding with new topics if skill or knowledge that are necessary for later parts of the learning have not been acquired. Regular 'testing' or assessment of progress and learning will at least help to identify any major problems. The rate at which people learn varies and it may sometimes be necessary to either speed up or slow down the pace to suit the needs of the trainee(s). It becomes more difficult to do this when dealing with groups as opposed to individuals, for obvious reasons. It may be that the best way of handling this is to have recognised the possibility of the problem in your original design and hence to have made it possible to build in some degree of flexibility.

There are occasions when the planned sequence will need to be changed. For example, suppose that one of the trainers suddenly finds that they cannot take their planned session. How can this be handled? Sometimes this can only be dealt with by altering the sequence but, you should only do so if you can ensure that there will be no ill effects. The need for flexibility in planning the event can be vital and it helps if you have arranged the subject matter such that some changes to the sequence can be accommodated.

Interruptions and personal problems

No matter what special arrangements you might make, there is always the potential for interruptions to the training. Urgent messages, telephone calls and the like are the usual culprits. There's an obvious answer to these irritations. Make sure that when such events occur, messages are left with someone until a convenient point is reached where they can be dealt with without disturbing the learning activity.

There are times when trainers may also need to act as counsellors. This can arise when trainees are experiencing problems which may be presenting learning blocks. Difficulties may be to do with the course material; working within a group; work problems generally and, on occasions, domestic/health problems. Remember that people don't find it easy to switch off from the problems that concern them, especially those that relate to work or domestic issues. They will not always wish to approach you but, when they do, you need to respond positively.

Course reviews

It should go without saying that you ought to have built into the programme opportunities for regular summaries of the work carried out so far and the means to more formally check on progress. The means of assessing learning are covered more fully in Components 6, 7 and 8. You should refer to these for detailed information. The end of course review presents a final opportunity to test the results of the programme. There are dangers here too. It is always possible that the results achieved tend to give a one-sided view of the value of the programme and the manner in which it was carried out. Remember that accurate evaluation may require you to perform a follow-up study, say, some two or three months beyond the end of the 'formal' programme.

Recognising other signs for intervention

How do you recognise when a problem occurs or where you may need to intervene? In some cases the need, as you have already seen, will be self evident: in other cases there will be more subtle indications that all is not well.

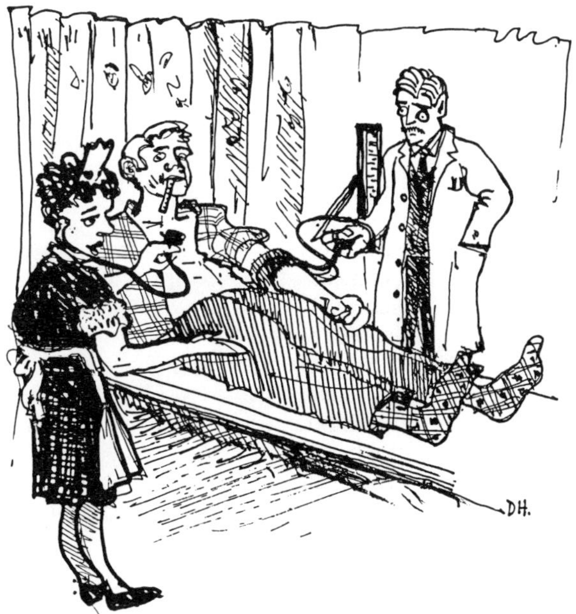

You need to watch out for the signs and symptoms

Other than the points already raised, what might you look out for as possible indicators that there may be a problem with the programme?

Amongst the points to watch, we can cite the following:
The bare minimum of effort being applied to exercises, case studies and feedback sessions and slipshod work coming from people you may otherwise expect a higher standard from.
During normal break times, course members never talk about what they have been doing within the course.
Disruption within the sessions arising out of more 'red-herrings' than usual, unwillingness to venture opinions, or an increase in cynical remarks.
Regular lateness in arriving or returning from breaks.
Failure to complete 'homework' assignments.
Unwillingness to seek help from the trainer(s) and a reluctance to raise personal or work problems.

Of course, these are not the only signs but, what is important is that you are aware of the mood and 'atmosphere'. Sensitivity, without being over sensitive, is what matters.

c) Post-course
The period immediately following the completion of the programme represents an important point in terms of evaluation of results and the opportunity for reflection, appraisal and taking decisions about proposed changes for future programmes.

Spend some time thinking about possible activities that may be appropriate for the trainers immediately following a programme.

Amongst other items, you could include:
Arranging for 'on-job' follow-up as appropriate. Checking with departmental managers on their views about the results achieved. Reviewing the immediate results. Discussions with fellow trainers on specific areas of the programme, including; objectives; content; methods; sequencing; time/timing; appropriateness & adequacy of briefing of trainers; suitability of the training location, and so on. Making adjustments to the programme as necessary.

Conclusion

The range of activities covered is by no means complete. What has been dealt with is meant to represent the typical points at which you may need to intervene, that is, to take action, in running and controlling a training event.

The guiding rule is that you need to be aware of the more likely situations that will occur. Ideally, through anticipation of these events, you will be more prepared to recognise the signs and symptoms that change or adjustment is required and have strategies for dealing with them. Even so, there will always be the unexpected. What matters then is that you take the time to reflect, to check and discuss the situation with others (wherever possible) and avoid the temptation to take action too quickly.

Component 6:

How can we Know if the Training Programme is Achieving its Purpose?

Key Ideas

Evaluation by objectives; interpretive evaluation; establish and monitoring standards; observation; informal monitoring; testing; questionnaires; interviews; structured questions; timing, costs and benefits; writing reports.

Objectives

As a result of working through this Component you will understand different types and methods of evaluation. You will be able to make a match between the different methods of evaluation and the sort of things about training programmes that you might wish to evaluate. The problems and benefits of monitoring standards will be examined and you will become acquainted with some of the issues associated with writing reports.

Introduction

You will obviously want to know if your training programme is achieving its purpose. This means that whilst the programme is operating and certainly once it has come to an end you will want to evaluate its effectiveness. Did it do the job that you wanted it to do? In the light of what you know about the programme and the circumstances under which it operated what adjustments do you wish to make? In this component particular attention will be paid to the means by which you can establish and monitor the standards that your training programme is attempting to achieve. In that way you will be able to judge the effectiveness of your programme and make adjustments to it as they become necessary.

In evaluating your programme, for that is what you will be doing, there are some basic considerations that you will have to take into account before any progress can be made. Your task is to evaluate your training programme. This means that you will have to be clear about your intended learning outcomes in terms of what you expect the trainees to acquire by way of knowledge, skills and attitudes. You will also have to be clear about what you expect from your programme in terms of the process of the training itself. These two sets of considerations will constitute the criteria by which effectiveness can be judged. Without these criteria you will have no standards for making a judgement and consequently you will be unable to evalute your programme. Remember that your starting point for establishing criteria will be the needs of the trainees (See Component Two).

There is a further consideration in judging the effectiveness of your programme. Once you have established your criteria you will have to decide on the most appropriate method for monitoring standards. The method that is chosen must be appropriate for what is to be monitored. A method that may be appropriate to judge the amount of information that a trainee has acquired will probably be different from a method designed to judge a trainee's attitude and both will be different from methods designed to give information about the process of the training.

These considerations are the concern of this Component.

Types of evaluation

I want to concentrate on two types of evaluation. The first type we can call **evaluation by objectives.** In this the objectives that you wish the programme to achieve are specified in advance and the programme is deemed to be successful to the extent that those objectives are achieved. Generally the objectives will refer to the learning that the trainees are expected to engage in usually under the headings of the knowledge, skills and attitudes that you wish the trainees to acquire.

The advantage of **evaluation by objectives** is its straightforwardness. The intended outcomes of the programme can be identified and so too can likely problem areas. A particular drawback is that certain kinds of learning are difficult to specify in advance. This is particularly true of learnings that are to do with attitudes and interests.

The second type of evaluation is **interactive evaluation.** This pays particular attention to the processes of a training programme. Its intention is to present a descriptive and interpretive account of the context of a training programme, the way in which it operates and the experiences of the participants.

The advantage of **interactive evaluation** is that it can provide judgements based on a variety of criteria and not simply those criteria that are associated with objectives that are specified in advance. A particular drawback, however, is that its findings are often less precise than those normally associated with evaluation by objectives.

Both sorts of evaluation have to be considered because taken together they will help you to answer the following questions:

i) What did I intend the training programme to achieve in terms of the development of the trainees knowledge, skills and attitudes?

ii) Did I have any additional objectives for particular individuals in the group (e.g. to encourage a quiet trainee to contribute more)? What were they?

iii) To what extent am I concerned about the nature of the training process (e.g. making it enjoyable, interesting, more personally involving)?

iv) Were the original objectives in any way unrealistic?

v) How much deflection form the original course plan took place? If there were changes, were they necessary and why?

vi) Were the methods used in the training programme effective in helping the trainees to learn? Might a greater use of equipment or other aids have produced improvements?

vii) Did the programme achieve the results thought to be desirable by the trainees themselves?

viii) Was the timetable planned satisfactorily?

ix) Were all the trainers adequately prepared to operate the programme?

Checkpoint

Types of evaluation

Look back at the descriptions of **evaluation by objectives** and **interactive evaluation.**

Some of the nine questions listed above are best answered through **evaluation by objectives** and some are best answered through **interactive evaluation.** Yet others may require both forms of evaluation.

Decide which questions come into which category.

Type of evaluation. (some suggestions)

Types of evaluation	*Question numbers*
Evaluation by objectives	*i iv v vii viii ix*
Interactive evaluation	*ii iii iv v vi vii viii ix*

Establishing standards

In order to know if the training programme is achieving its purpose you will need to establish standards. These standards will be the criteria by which you will judge whether the programme is effective or not.

For example:

* If you wish the trainees to acquire a certain amount of knowledge then you will have to be clear just what that knowledge is and what "acquiring" it actually involves.
* If you have skill objectives then you will have to decide which particular behaviours would indicate that the trainees had acquired those particular skills.
* Attitudinal development would suggest a further set of behaviours.

Each of the three types of objectives will require a particular method of evaluation by objectives and these will be explored in more detail in the next section of this Component. Similarly attention to the processes of the training programme will require different sorts of interactive evaluation. These two will be explored in more detail in the next section.

First of all you should be as clear as possible about the criteria that you have for judging the effectiveness of the programme.

A couple of examples may serve to make the point clear.

Example One. If I wanted to train someone to be a competent angler what knowledge, skills and attitudes (or personal qualities) would I wish to develop?

Knowledge of : which fish eat what
: where different sorts of fish are likely to be found
: different sorts of tackle
: various sorts of fishing regulations

Skills to : construct flies
: cast
: land
: use different sorts of tackle effectively

Qualities of : patience
: stamina
: working alone
: coping with a variety of weather conditions

I would also want the process of training to be enjoyable so that people might be stimulated to fish. This might involve

: providing the opportunity to gain experience
: working with individuals to remedy particular problems
: visiting well known local fishing spots
: using well known local anglers as visiting speakers

I have deliberately chosen four items for each category in order to illustrate what I mean. You will no doubt be able to think of other items that could be included.

Example Two.
Lets consider the case of someone training to be a horticultural worker. What would be my criteria for an effective training programme be in this instance?

Knowledge of

: different types of soil and other growing medium
: necessary weather conditions and soil temperatures
: the effects of different fertilizers and insecticides
: the growing "life" of different types of plants
: the space needed to grow different types of plants
: different types of horticultural equipment
: techniques of harvesting and storing produce.

Skills to

: operate different types of horticultural equipment
: prepare soil and seed beds
: plant out seedlings
: water, weed and hoe
: tie up young plants
: do grafting and budding
: inspect plants for damage
: mix and spray fertilisers and insecticides
: harvest crops of flowers, fruit and vegetables.

Qualities of

: willingness to do dirty jobs
: being punctual and keeping a good attendance record
: enjoying outdoor work
: being interested in nature
: willingness to work in hot greenhouses
: being able to work without constant supervision
: willingness to work irregular hours including some weekends
: being able to make an extra effort at particularly busy times.

I would want the process of training to **involve** the trainees as far as possible in order to develop competent market gardeners. Thus the process would deliberately seek to relate knowledge acquisition to skill development. The emphasis would be on the development of certain skills and qualities rather than on the acquisition of knowledge. Consequently the process of training would have to include

: practical work in a variety of settings (actual "hands on" experience)
: the development of the sense of the worthwhileness of the task
: how to manage one's own time and routines
: flexibility and adaptability
: only the essential lecture and text book-based learning.

Think of your own training programme(s). Using the examples that I have provided draw up your own set of criteria.

If you can it would be very useful if your colleagues on the same training programme as yourself could draw up their sets of criteria. Compare the different sets. At the very least it should give you something to talk about.

The trainees should be part of the process of establishing criteria. That process is part of their learning and it will increase their motivation and commitment to the programme. This notion is explored in the Study Unit on 'Self-Evaluation' in the Volume, **Assessment and Evaluation** in Training.

Monitoring Standards

Once you have established **what** evidence of effectiveness you are looking for you can begin to decide **how** you will collect it. The purpose of this section is to provide a summary of the options that are open to you.

1. Observation.

You and your colleagues will be able to monitor the behaviour of the trainees during the course of the training programme. If it is clear what would constitute progress for the trainees you should be able to observe evidence of it. The behaviour of trainees after a session will indicate a good deal about the way they experienced the learning. After sessions they have enjoyed they are likely to want to stay around and chat; if they have had a negative experience they are more likely to leave quickly. Whether the trainees talk about sessions afterwards, and in what terms, can also indicate what they got out of it.

A little discretion may be necessary.

There will be many clues in the non-verbal behaviour of the trainees to how they experience sessions. Keenness to get into class, bright, expectant expressions, enthusiasm to get started, questions about what work will be coming up next time, etc., are all likely to indicate that the work is being well received.

Apart from yourself and the trainees directly involved, there can be additional sources of feedback in other trainers, other trainees, and where appropriate of trainees. They are likely to be in a position to notice changes in behaviour or attitudes in members of the trainee group, and may be asked to look out for these if that is appropriate, and to give feedback on any developments they notice.

2. Informal monitoring

Casual comments by group members, other trainees, and other trainers are often very useful indicators of what kind of impression is being made by the work done in the group. Whether these comments are positive or otherwise will indicate perceptions that are around outside the group itself. There are limitations in this kind of feedback, because it will be expressed in terms of feelings, impressions or reactions of people who have not been involved in the experience themselves and may not even be in sympathy with the training objectives. The more awareness there is, the more valuable the feedback is likely to be.

3. Testing, a type of formal monitoring

If one wishes to assess whether knowledge has been imparted or skills developed, then this may be checked by testing in some form or another if that is appropriate. Knowledge gained may be measured by oral or written test or by inviting some form of presentation by the trainee. Skill acquisition may be put to some test in real or simulated situations if that is desirable. Observers or closed circuit television may help the analysis and assessment of the skill performance and provide the trainee with valuable feedback. A very useful test of what has been learned can be to invite the trainee to teach somebody else. Having to pass on certain knowledge, or teach a skill one has acquired, is likely to be an excellent test of what one has understood or grasped.

4. Other types of formal monitoring

Other types of formal monitoring could involve the use of questionnaires for trainees and trainers and interviews of various sorts.

i) Questionnaires

Feedback on the programme can be gathered systematically after a session by asking all group members to comment upon:

1 what they think they have learned;
2 what they liked about the session;
3 anything they were not happy with or might want to change.

This feedback can be collected orally or written down. Trainees can even be asked to rate a session on the scales shown below.

Fig. 1. Place a tick in the appropriate space to show how you experienced this session

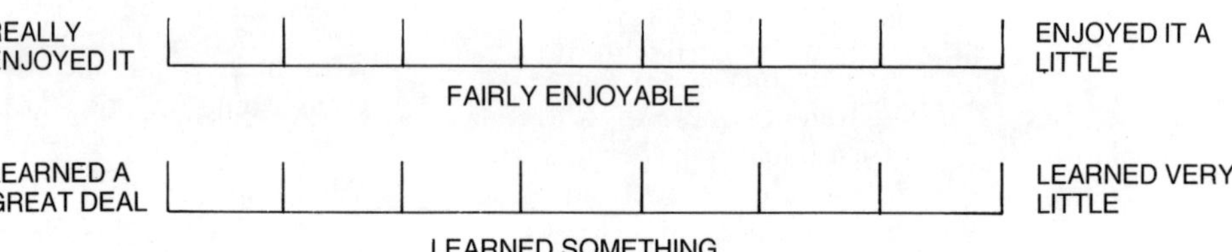

The type of questionnaire illustrated can be fairly easy to construct and to administer. A questionnaire can seem an efficient means of studying whole groups of people, the data will often be easier to analyse than those gathered by interview, and the form itself, if it works, can be used again to gather comparative information. It can also appear less threatening and more controllable than face-to-face interview with a trainee. Because it can be such a controlled method, however, a questionnaire is sometimes found to be less effective than an interview as a way of eliciting the issues that the trainees themselves found important. Questionnaires set limits on what can be found out about a programme because what is not questioned will remain unanswered.

Designing a questionnaire is often a long business, though less so for trainer questionnaires, when pertinent questions and likely responses could be more easily imagined. Even after all members of a planning group have approved a draft questionnaire, a trial with a few trainees (if it was a trainee questionnaire) always reveals the need for amendments. If the questionnaire can be completed anonymously it is likely to encourage a more honest response.

Summarising and analysing questionnaire responses can take a lot of time, even if the task is shared among a group. The analysis of open-ended questions (e.g. "Have you any further comments you wish to make?") inevitably takes the greatest amount of time as categories of response have to be discovered before the responses themselves can be analysed. It is not uncommon, however, to find that the most useful, detailed or surprising information came from just that kind of question.

ii) Interviews

Most people are not very familiar with the actual use of interview as a means of monitoring the effectiveness of a programme and not just to test knowledge. Semi-structured interviews are the most often used device where there is a prepared list of topics but the questions themselves are not precisely standardised. Using the same working and sequence of questions for all of the trainees can be too constraining and artificial as a procedure to follow for long, and again may not tell you things about the training programme that you might need to know.

The interviewing process can present problems:

* Finding a convenient time can be difficult.
* Many trainees (and trainers) are not used to being interviewed (or interviewing) and this can cause a certain amount of stress. Attention must be paid to creating the right sort of atmosphere.
* There is often a feeling that trainees will provide the comments about the training programme that they think they will want to hear. On other occasions the answers come falteringly or uncertainly. Since the usual reason for asking trainees questions is to test their knowledge, it is a justifiable apprehension, but one which it was impossible either to confirm or dismiss. What many interviewers find, however, is that they can ease the difficulty by asking questions to which no 'right' answer exists, by following up uncertain answers with encouragements to the trainee to clarify or elaborate, and by being seen to accept without flinching answers which are critical or self-condemning.

The advantages of using interviews to find out about the effectiveness of the training programme are:

* The trainees see that you are interested in them.
* The trainees can gain a clearer insight into the purposes of the programme.
* The trainees should be involved in judging the effectiveness of the programme since they are probably the most accurate source of information about whether or not the programme is meeting their training needs as they perceive them. And if they have any misconceptions about the programme then you will at least learn what they are and be able to do something about that.

Care must be paid to creating the right atmosphere.

iii) Structured questions.

These can be used during and after any training activity or session as a way of evaluating that session and deepening the trainees' learning.

We can think of learning, particularly learning in which the trainees are actively engaged in learning a skill as occuring in three stages.

1. Experiencing.
   At this stage the trainees are engaged in some activity.
2. Interpreting.
   At this stage the trainees are trying to make sense of the activity, gain some sort of understanding, or

place the activity in the total context of what they are training to do.

3. Applying.
   At this stage the trainees are concerned with how they can apply their understandings to "real life" situations. Possibly they will be making generalisations about the training activity which will enable them to apply their understanding of that activity to a variety of different work situations.

At each stage of the training activity certain questions can be asked.

1. Experiencing.
- What is going on?
- How do you feel about that?
- If you could guess at the answer what would it be?
- Can you say that in another way?
- What happened?
- Were there any surprises?
- Did anything puzzle you?
- What did you observe?
- What were you aware of?

2. Interpreting.
- How did you account for that?
- What does that mean to you?
- How was that significant?
- How was that good/bad?
- What struck you about that?
- How do those fit together?
- How might it have been different?
- Do you see something operating there?

3. Applying.
- What might we draw/pull from that?
- What did you learn/relearn?
- What does that suggest to you about .... in general?
- Does that remind you of anything?
- What principle/law do you see operating?
- Does that remind you of anything? What does that help explain?
- How does this relate to other experiences?
- What do you associate with that?
- So what?
- How could you apply/transfer that?
- What would you like to do with that?
- How could you repeat this again?
- What are the options?
- What might you do to help/hinder yourself?
- How could you make it do it better?
- What would be the consequence of doing/not doing that?
- What modifications can you make work for you?

The advantages of employing this technique are various:

1. if the experience is going as planned, you have a tool for guiding the learning at the pace, depth, breadth, and intensity that you deem appropriate;
2. if the experience is not going as planned, you have a tool for deriving learning from what is occurring, so that something beneficial is gained, regardless of the trainees attitudes and reactions;
3. the greatest advantage is that these questions can be used with virtually any experience in nearly any situation with the vast majority of trainees. They are generalizable, transferable, and guaranteed to evoke learning.

The only word of caution is that you will have to be sensitive to the responses of the trainees and be particularly careful in the way that you ask the questions and listen to the answers.

The questions that I have supplied are obviously very general and will apply to a variety of contexts. You might care to re-write some of them so that they apply to your situation.

Approaches to monitoring

Remember the method that you use to evaluate must be appropriate to the item being evaluted.

Which of the approaches to monitoring are **best** suited to an evaluation by objectives, which are **best** suited to interpretative evaluation and which can be used with both evaluation by objectives and interpretative evaluation?

Approaches to monitoring (some suggestions).

	Objectives	Interpretative
Observation	√	√
Informal monitoring		√
Testing	√	
Questionnaires	√	√
Interviews	√	√
Structured questions	√	√

There is a crucial issue in connection with the time when the monitoring process should take place. Obviously monitoring should be a continuous event. The methods described in the previous section can be used at any time during the programme. They may also be used when the programme has been completed. However, careful judgement must be exercised about just when the evaluation occurs.

Evaluation carried out very soon after a training event will have all the advantages of feedback that comes fresh from the experience, when those involved will be able to use their immediate feeling, thoughts, reactions, impressions, and so on. It will also have some possible limitations simply because it is so instant. Fresh from an experience, you and the trainees may have views and make responses that will subsequently evolve or change. Sometimes participants are 'too close' to an experience fully to assess its value. Immediate impressions have their worth; so does feedback given after participants have had longer to reflect, assess, practice, and test the significance of that experience. Evaluation procedures therefore should take into consideration feedback and assessment data collected at different stages after the event.

..... careful judgement must be exercised about just when the evaluation occurs.

The costs and benefits of monitoring standards.

(i) Costs

Costs can be both short and long term

* The resources required.

  The most obvious resource requirement of course evaluation is staff time. Time must be found to plan, carry out, analyse, interpret, implement, review. In many cases there will be a course team which meets at weekly or monthly intervals. The team's agenda is likely to be long, but there may still be time to plan, supervise and review an evaluation. Nevertheless additional time may have to be found to draft questionnaires, carry out interviews and analyse the results.

  How much time an evaluation requires will depend partly upon how the course is organised and partly upon how modest or ambitious you want to be. To reverse the proposition, what an evaluator decides to investigate is likely to be conditioned by the time available. Except for paper, few other resources are usually required. Some of you may have secretarial help in typing and duplicating questionnaire forms and evaluation reports, but don't worry if you haven't. You should be able to manage quite adequately.

* Criticism of individuals.

  An evaluation can be — and indeed sometimes is — a slow and diffuse business with a threat at the end: "In evaluating the programme you're evaluating yourself and colleagues" is a common view. What was private can become public, what was implicit becomes explicit. Individuals vary in their response to criticism and threats to self-esteem. Establishing the proper climate is therefore essential. A lot of discussion may have to take place.

* Disruption to the organisation.

  Both the findings and the processes of an evaluation can appear to threaten the stability of the organisation. Findings may suggest that programme decision-makers in the past had been wrong, that future decisions could usefully be taken by other groups or individuals, or that the allocation of programme responsibilities and resources should be appraised. The evaluation process itself may give detailed and controversial information to staff whose position in the organisation's hierarchy had previously given them access only to information about their own practice and that of their immediate colleagues. The authority structure of the programme can come under strain, therefore. Naturally this potential 'cost' of evaluation could be judged to be a potential 'benefit'.

Consider your own organisation. Rank order the costs described above so that number one is the most expensive and number three the least expensive. Can you think of additional costs?

What could you do to reduce these costs as far as your own organisation is concerned? Make a list of suggestions and then rank order them so that number one is the **most effective** and the last one is the least effective. Now do the same thing only this time rank according to the suggestions that are most practical to least practical.

Compare your two lists. Are they different and if so why? If they are different then what can you do to make them more alike?

(ii) Benefits.

The benefits, too, can be both short-term and long-term.

* A more formal evaluation can identify areas of the programme which are functioning well and those which are in need of improvement. A more formal and comprehensive evaluation can make available more information from a larger number of sources.
* It can provide sufficient authority for an improvement to be considered or carried out. Strong suspicions might be held about certain weaknesses in the programme, but an evaluation can enable them to be acknowledged or communicated. You will have evidence to support your intuition and will be able to argue for changes from a position of strength.

* The process itself can not only support but **stimulate** programme development. Quite apart from any substantive outcomes, the processes of planning and inquiry can cause useful reflection on the programme and its organisation:
  You are forced to think about what it is you are trying to do.
* It can improve trainee-trainer relations. Talking and listening to trainees can strengthen your understanding of the trainees' experience of the course, and their understanding of your aims and problems.
* It can increase the status of the programme. A focused and public activity with implications for programme and departmental management can improve that standing.
* An evaluation can be a vehicle for the professional development of trainers. An evaluation can develop the skills and knowledge needed for designing, developing and administering programmes for collaborating with other trainers; for negotiating access to sensitive areas of activity; for acting effectively within an organisation; and for introducing deliberate self-appraisal. These are not negligible benefits.

Which particular benefits, from the list provided, might apply to the evaluation of your programmes? What will you need to do to make the most of these benefits?

Writing reports

You may feel that it is appropriate to write a report on your programme based upon your findings. You may even be required to write a report. If your report is going to be seen and possibly used by others then there are certain factors that you should consider. These factors are concerned with the language that you use. The following items indicate some common problems. It is impossible to be perfect in writing reports. All that you can do is be aware of these problems and just go as far as you reasonably can.

* **Undefined statements** say something which, although understood by yourself, may not be understood by your readers. Examples include: words which are not common coinage; words used with specialised connotations which may not be understood by other people; and words which are part of the technical vocabulary of your programme.
* **Mixed statements** say more than one thing at a time. They are often attempts to portray training events in as subtle a way as possible — taking account of the complexity of learning. But they can leave the reader wondering which part of the statement he is supposed to be paying attention to.
  e.g. "..... has breadth but little depth."
* **Non-operational statements,** although apparently based on observation, employ language which cannot readily be used by the reader to conjure up an image of what has been observed. This means that another observer might use the same words to refer to something quite different. It also means that the reader might conjure up a different image of what you are trying to convey.
  e.g. "..... of varying quality."
* **Generalised statements** portray features of the programme as though they apply to the programme in all respects and circumstances. It is rarely possible for one person to make such a statement of a complete programme.
  e.g. "..... generally inhibiting."
* **Interpretative statements** do not pretend to be observations of learning, but point to underlying states. They are the kinds of statements that would require an intimate knowledge of the trainee's learning. In some cases the only person qualified to make such statements would be the trainee himself.
  e.g. "..... stimulates enthusiasm."
* **Value-laden statements** separate 'sheep' from 'goats'; expressing preference for this aspect of the programme — rather than other aspects. They invite bias, in the reader's response. At their worst they declare what is acceptable to the writer — without declaring what sort of person it is acceptable to.
  e.g. "..... makes a constructive and acceptable contribution"

Some statements manage to combine a remarkably wide range of the six characteristics above with the use of remarkably few words. It is an easy criticism to make until we begin to consider the difficulty of avoiding those characteristics. If these are the 'vices', what are the 'virtues'? On these bases objective statements about programmes are those which are:

* **Defined** — everybody who reads them will understand them in the same way;
* **Singular** — they say one thing at a time;
* **Operational** — they conjure up clear images;
* **Specific** — they say in what circumstances the characteristic of the programme has been displayed;
* **Guess-free** — they say what can be concretely known of the programme;
* **Value-neutral** — they do not voice the portrayer's preferences.

These factors, of course, also apply to the compilation of questionnaires and interview schedules.

It is impossible to be perfect . . . . just go as far as you reasonably can.

Conclusion

By way of concluding this Component there is a list of questions that you might care to consider. Check each one in turn and try to arrive at an answer as far as you possibly can.

1. How clear are you about the intended audience for the evaluation information?
2. Who will be affected by the evaluation? How much should they be told about it? How, if at all, should they be involved with it?
3. Who might be interested in helping with the evaluation? How can that assistance be secured (or avoided)?
4. How open-minded are you about what you might find? How open-minded do you appear to others?
5. Who will do the actual drafting of questionnaires, interview schedules, etc.? What opportunities are there to involve trainees in the work of the evaluation?
6. Who will carry out the interviews, adminster the questionnaires, etc.?
7. Who will collate and analyse the information collected?
8. Who will produce the reports (if any)?
9. How much of (a) your time, (b) other people's time is available for the evaluation? Is it enough?
10. Do you have the other resources necessary to carry out an evaluation?
11. How clear are you about what you want to find out? How clear do you need to be?
12. How can you exploit the routinely collected information on trainee flaws and trainee achievement?
13. How will you choose the appropriate methods of collecting the information?
14. How likely is it that action will be considered or taken as a result of the evaluation?
15. How familiar are you with the ways decisions are taken about the training programme?
16. To what extent are you able to influence the processes by which decisions are taken about the training programme?
17. How will you engage the interest and support of other people with the authority to take decisions about the training programme?
18. What support might be needed by other people who wish to change their programmes as a result of the evaluation?

Component 7:

How do you Evaluate the Effects of a particular Training Programme on your Organisation?

Key Words

 **Organisational system; organisational cultures; practicality ethic; situational analysis.**

Acknowledgments
The author would like to thank Penguin Books Ltd for permission to reproduce material from Handy C. (1985) *Understanding Organisations*.

Objectives
(a) Carry out a situational analysis of the organisation before and after a training programme is implemented.
(b) Evaluate the changes.

Introduction
The previous compound in this Study Unit looked at ways of evaluating and reporting training programmes. This component will continue this theme of evaluation but will broaden its scope to look at the effects on the Organisation as a whole. When a training programme is effectively implemented in an organisation and achieves its objectives, more general changes, in the work environment, in the attitudes of people in the organisation and how they behave, and in the structure of the organisation i.e. 'the wiring diagram', will take place. Let us take as an example the organisation I am most familiar with, and you probably will be too, as everyone has been to school; a large secondary school. We can divide any school system into four main areas:

a) What is being taught and why? — the content of the curriculum and how it is organised.
b) How the content is taught — the methods of teaching or the 'teaching styles'.
c) How the process is assessed and evaluated.
d) The structure through which the process takes place in diagrammatic form.

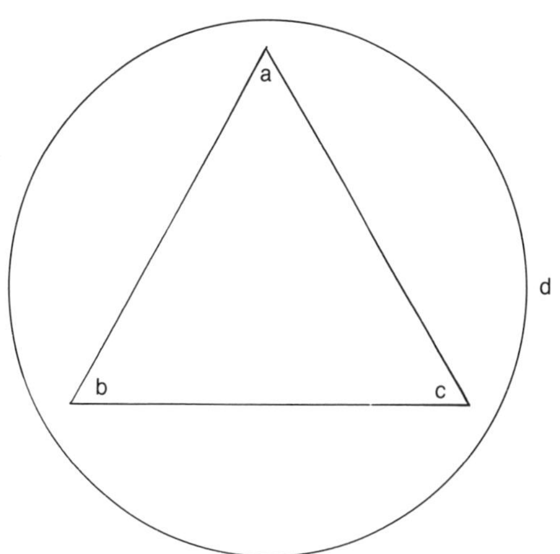

In simple terms we can argue that a change in any part of the system is going to have an effect on the other elements of the system and cause reactive changes; these may be of two kinds.

(1) The System reacts to oppose and cancel the change.
(2) System reacts by accommodating the change re the whole system takes on a different form.

Let us now put this into the situation where a new training programme is put into effect in the firm. The new programme (a) will be either rejected by the people involved or it will affect the whole system and cause changes in (b), (c) or (d), to a greater or lesser extent. The main aim of this Component is to present you with a framework which will help you monitor and evaluate these changes that are introduced when the new training programme is put into effect.

Let us put this situation another way. Leavitt (1965) analyses organisations in terms of people, structure, Technology and Task.

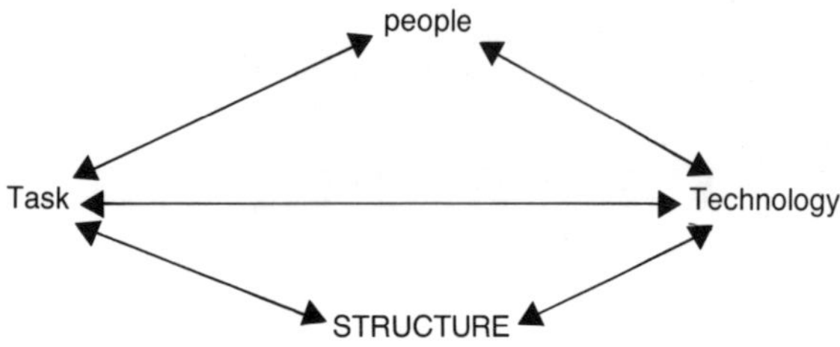

As indicated each term connects with all the others and the system is regarded as so linked that a change in one factor causes reactions in the others. The task is that which is accepted as the task of the organisation and the structure is the way in which the people are related to one another in order to carry out the task. The term technology may be best explained as having the twofold purpose including the techniques, tools and processes used to carry out the work and secondly the rationale of the control of the tools.

Checkpoint

Using the 2 diagrams above as a basis try and represent your organisation in this form.

I do not know what kind of diagram you have got but I am sure you are probably thinking "How on earth am I going to be able to look at the effects of a training programme on all these things?"

Right, let's make a start. Let us suppose that the new training programme is introduced in Time Period **One**. Its effects are then monitored during Time Period **Two** and then evaluated in Time Period **Three**, e.g.

TP1 **TP2** **TP3**

Introduction ⟶ Monitoring Process ⟶ Evaluation

What you have to do is to get a picture of what your organisation is like at Time Period **One**, before the new Training Programme is introduced, and then compare this with what it is like in Time Period **Three** when the Training Programme has been implemented; i.e. what is Diagram One like at Time Period **One** and compare that with what it is like at Time Period **Three**.

What I am suggesting is that you make what is called a structural analysis of your organisation at Time Period **One** before the training programme is introduced, monitor the changes in Time Period **Two** using the methods outlined in Component Six and then do another situational analysis at Time Period **Three** and compare them.

Right; how do we do a situational analysis?

To cover every aspect of your organisation would be an impossible task — for a start I do not know what kind of organisation you work in! What we need is a general framework which can be adopted to make a situational analysis of any organisation. Going back to Diagram (1) I represented a school in terms of what it taught and why, how it was taught, how it was assessed and the structure within which all this took place. Any work organisation can also be represented in the same way. Although each organisation is different with its own history and traditions there are some general aspects of organisations which are the same be they Schools, Hospitals, the local builder or the bank. Diagram (2) took a much more generalised look at how organisations are structured. Some people would argue that the secret of a successful organisation is in the way in which it was structured and many plans have been put forward as the ideal structure. A writer on organisations called Charles Handy developed the idea of organisational cultures. A culture can be defined as "The total of the inherited ideas, beliefs, values and knowledge which constitute the shared bases of social action" and "the total range of ideas and activities of a group of people with shared traditions which are transmitted and reinforced by members of a group." The French have a very different culture from the English although only twenty miles of water separates the two countries. In the same way a bank has a different culture from a steel works and a school works on very different assumptions from an insurance company.

Handy set out four such cultures which he said characterised most organisations. These cultures are founded and built over the years by dominant groups in the organisation but may have to change over time, as what suits the organisation at one time may not necessarily be appropriate for ever.

The Club Culture

The best picture to describe this kind of organization is a spider's web, because the key to the whole organization sits in the centre, surrounded by ever-widening circles of intimates and influence. The closer you are to the spider the more influence you have. There are other lines in the web — the lines of responsibility, the functions of the organization — but the intimacy lines are the important ones, for this organization works like a club, a club built around its head.

The 'organizational idea' in the club culture is that the organization is there to extend the person of the head or, often, of the founder. If he could do everything himself, he would. It is because he can't that there has to be an organization at all; therefore the organization should be an extension of himself, acting on his behalf, a club of like minded people. That can sound like a dictatorship, and some club cultures are dictatorships of the owner or founder, but at their best they are based on trust and communicate by a sort of telepathy with everyone knowing each other's mind. They are very personal cultures for the spiders preserve their freedom of manoeuvre by writing little down, preferring to talk to people, to sense their reactions and to infect them with their own enthusiasms or passions. If there are memoranda or minutes of meetings, they go from Gill to Joe or, more often, from set of initials to set of initials, rather than from job title to job title.

These cultures therefore are rich in personality. They abound with almost mythical stories and folklore from the past and can be very exciting places to work if you belong to the club and share the values and beliefs of the spider. Their great strength is in their ability to respond immediately and intuitively to opportunities or crises because of the very short lines of communication and because of the centralization of power. Their danger lies in the dominance of the character of the central figure. Without a spider the web is dead. If the spider is weak, corrupt, inept or picks the wrong people, the organization is also weak, corrupt, inept and badly staffed.

These cultures thrive where personality and speed of response are critical, in new business situations, in deals and brokerage transactions, in the artistic and theatrical world, in politics, guerrilla warfare and crisis situations, provided the leader is good — for they talk of leaders rather than managers in these cultures. They are a convenient way of running things — although not necessarily the best — when the core organization is small (under twenty people perhaps) and closely gathered together so that personal communication is easy; once things get much bigger than that, formality has to be increased and the personal, telepathic, empathetic style is frustrated. The key to success is having the right people, who blend with the core team and can act on their own; therefore a lot of time is spent on selecting the right people and assessing whether they will fit in or not. It is no accident that some of the most successful club cultures have a nepotistic feel to them: they deliberately recruit people like themselves, even from the same family, so that the club remains a club.

The Role Culture

It is all very different in a role culture. Here the best picture is the kind of organization chart that all these organizations have. It looks like a pyramid of boxes; inside each box is a job title with an individual's name in smaller type below, indicating who is currently the occupant of that box, but of course the box continues even if the individual departs.

The underlying 'organizational idea' is that organizations are sets of roles or job-boxes, joined together in a logical and orderly fashion so that together they discharge the work of the organization. The organization is a piece of construction engineering, with role piled on role, and responsibility linked to responsibility. Individuals are 'role occupants' with job descriptions that effectively lay down the requirements of the role and its boundaries. From time to time, the organization will rearrange the roles and their relationship to each other, as priorities change, and then reallocate the individuals to the roles.

The communications in these cultures are formalized, as are the systems and procedures. The memoranda go from role to role (head of X department to deputy head) and are copied to roles, not individuals. The place abounds in procedures for every eventuality, in rules and handbooks. There are standards, quality controls and evaluation procedures. It is all **managed** rather than led.

Most mature organizations have a lot of the role culture in them, because once an operation has settled down it can be routinized and, as it were, imprinted on the future. All organizations strive for predictability and certainty — for then fewer decisions are needed, everybody can get on with their job, the outcomes can be guaranteed, and the inputs calculated. You know where you will be; it is secure and comfortable even if it is at times too predictable to be exciting.

These role organizations thrive when they are doing a routine, stable and unchanging task, but they find it very hard to cope with change or with individual exceptions. If it's not in the rule book, they really have to wait for the rule book to be rewritten before they can act. Administrative organizations, as in part of the social security system, have to be role cultures and they will prove very frustrating if you turn out to be one of those individual exceptions. On the other hand, if the social security system were administered by a host of club cultures, each responding as they saw fit, social justice would hardly be served. Efficiency and fairness in routine tasks demands a role culture.

The important thing in these cultures is to get the logic of the design right, the flow of work and procedures. People are, in one sense, a less critical factor. They can be trained to fit the role. Indeed role cultures do not want too much independence or initiative. Railways want train drivers to arrive on time, not five minutes early. Role cultures want 'role occupants', not individualists.

The Task Culture

The task culture evolved in response to the need for an organizational form that could respond to change in a less individualistic way than a club culture, and more speedily than a role culture.

The 'organizational idea' of this culture is that a group or team of talents and resources should be applied to a project, problem or task. In that way each task gets the treatment it requires — it does not have to be standardized across the organization — and the groups can be changed, disbanded or increased as the task changes. A net with elastic cords which can pull these cords this way and that and regroup at will, is the picture of this culture.

It is the preferred culture of many competent people, because they work in groups, sharing both skills and responsibilities; they are constantly working on new challenges since every task is different and thus keep themselves developing and enthusiastic. The task culture is usually a warm and friendly culture because it is built around cooperative groups of colleagues without much overt hierarchy. There are plans rather than procedures, and reviews of progress rather than assessment of past performance. It is a forward looking culture for a developing organization.

These cultures thrive in situations where problem-solving is the job of the organization. Consultancy, advertising agencies, construction work, parts of journalism and the media, product development groups, surgical teams — any situation beyond the capacity of one person with minions to solve, and which cannot be emobied in procedures, needs a task culture.

The problem is that they are expensive. They use professional competent people who spend quite a lot of time talking together in search of the right solution. You would not use a task culture to make a wheel because they would want to reinvent it, or at least improve on it, first. It is a questioning culture, which chafes at routines and the daily grind of 'administration' or 'repetitive chores'. A task culture talks of 'co-ordinators' and 'team leaders' rather than managers; it is full of budgets (which are plans) but short on job descriptions; it wants commitment and it rewards success with more assignments. It promises excitement and challenge but not security of employment because it cannot afford to employ people who do not continually meet new challenges successfully. Task cultures, therefore, tend to be full of young energetic people developing and testing talents: people who are self-confident enough not to worry about long-term security — at least until they are a bit older!

The Person Culture

The person culture is very different from the first three. All of the other three cultures put the organization's purposes first and then, in their different ways, harness the individual to this purpose. The person culture puts the individual first and makes the organization the resource for the individual's talents. The most obvious examples are doctors who, for their own convenience, group themselves in a practice, barristers in chambers (a very minimal sort of organization), architects in partnerships, artists in a studio, perhaps professors in faculties or scientists in a research laboratory.

The 'organizational idea' behind this culture is that the individual talent is all-important and must be serviced by some sort of minimal organization. They do not in fact like to use the word organization but find all sorts of alternative words (practice, chambers, partnership, faculty, etc.) instead, nor do they talk of managers but of 'secretaries', 'bursars', 'chief clerk' etc.; indeed the 'managers' of these organizations are always lower in status than the professionals. You may have a senior partner in a law office but if you ask for the manager you are likely to be shown into the chief clerk. Stars, loosely grouped in a cluster or constellation, is the image of a person culture.

The individual professionals in these organisations usually have tenure, meaning that the management is not only lower in status but has few if any formal means of control over the professionals. In a university, for these reasons, the head of department or the dean of a faculty is usually a rotating job, often seen as a necessary chore rather than a mark of distinction.

In other words, a person culture is very difficult to run in any ordinary way. The professionals have to be run on a very light rein; they can be persuaded, not commanded, influenced, cajoled or bargained with, but not managed.

The culture works where the talent of the individual is what matters, which is why you find it in the old professions which are finding that the problems are too complex for one individual's talents. Architects, city solicitors, even the clergy are grouping themselves into task cultures and submitting themselves to more organizational disciplines.

Handy goes on to argue that few organizations have only one culture — often they have a mix of all four: what makes each organisation different is the mix in each. He further argues that this may depend on certain factors:

1. Size — large size and role enclosures tend to go together.
2. Work flow — the way that work is organised has an important bearing on the culture that can be operated. If it is organised in separate units where a group or an individual can be responsible for the whole job then club, task or person cultures will exist. But if the workflow is sequential or interdependent, in that one piece is tied with another then what is needed is those systems, rules and regulations and the culture is more of a role culture.
3. Environment — Every organisation has to think about the raw material it receives and the products it turns out; whether these are bolts, concrete blocks or educated human beings. If the environment does not give clear signals, if the institution is a monopoly and can therefore set its own aims and standards or if the environment never changes, then the organisation will tend to go for stability and a routine quiet life — a role culture. A changing or demanding environment requires a culture that will respond to change — a task or a club culture.
4. History — Organisations are to some extend stuck with their past, with their reputation, the kinds of people they hired years ago, their site and their traditions. These can take years if not decades to change.

The cultural mix in any one organisation depends on the relative importance of each of these factors. Often you will find a role culture, topped by a spider's web with task culture project groups round the edges. Some organisations, on the other hand are really a federation of 'barons', separate club cultures loosely linked together by a role culture each free to run their own empires.

Right, I now think it's time to recap. What we have done so far is to set out in simple diagrammatic form what every organisation contains; we then went on to look at a more detailed way of looking at what the overall structures of the organisation looks like using the ideas of organisational cultures from Charles Handy. You should now have enough information to investigate your own organisation and get a detailed picture of what kind of organisation it is. However, to give you a little further help I have set out below a short list of questions which can also guide your investigations.

(a) **Aims & Objectives**

(1) What are the overall aims of the organisation?
(2) Are those aims clearly defined?
(3) Are they appropriate?
(4) What is the general nature of the work carried out by your organisation?
(5) List the specific objectives of the organisation in terms of the main sections of its work, e.g. profits, market share, services etc.
(6) How clearly are the organisation's objectives understood by its members?
(7) Are the members' objectives clear?
(8) Are all the members quite clear as to what is expected of them?
(9) Are these consistent with the overall objectives of the organisation?
(10) How much job flexibility is there in the main sections of the organisation?
(11) Do all the jobs done by the members give them satisfaction?
(12) Are the organisation's job specifications quite clear?

(b) **Activities**

(1) What are the main actions carried out by your organisation? Classify these in terms of the main sections.
(2) Are all the actions of the organisation consistent with the objectives of
    (a) The organisation
    (b) The members
(3) How much line essay work is being carried out?

(c) **Decisions**

(1) What key decisions have to be made by your organisation in any time period?
 (a) Day
 (b) Week
(2) Who has the authority to make these decisions?
(3) What other members contribute to the key decisions?
(4) Are the guidelines for decision making clearly laid out?
(5) Can those who have to make the decisions in your organisation obtain information easily?
(6) Are **all** the decisions being made by the **right** people in the **right** place at the **right** time?
(7) What evidence can you get to show that the **proper** decisions are **not** being taken?

Remember these are just for your guidance and you may add more questions as you wish.

Now with the use of all the previous ideas try and make as detailed a situational analysis as possible of the structure of your organisation. I think you will find that you will also end up with a lot of detail about the other three variables in the diagram on page 302 — Task, Technology, and People.

Well how did you get on? I hope you now have a good idea of what your organisation looks like.

Probably the most important element in the diagram on page 302 is 'People'. All organisations are made up of members who are related to each other and to the organisation in some way. This, of course, was the basis of handy's ideas on 'culture'. The introduction of something new into an organisation such as a new training programme may upset these relationships and may cause them to change.

How relationships change when something new is added.

Any individual support an organisation if he believes that through the organisation his own personal needs are being met. If not, it won't be long before he loses interest. The effectiveness of a member's input into the organisation is directly related to his own idea of how the organisation helps him to satisfy his own needs. Let me explain further. Each member of an organisation usually has **two** ideas about himself and his organisation; let's call them (A) and (B). (A) is his ideas of the organisation. Of course the member will not think of them as (A) or (B), he may not even be conscious of them at all. What usually happens is something like this; "This firm builds good houses and pays its work force quite well" "I need the money and I think I am a good bricklayer". Thus (A) and (B) appear to coincide, for him. He is therefore happy with the firm so that by helping the organisation he is helping himself.

Now let us suppose that for all sorts of reasons (see earlier Components of this unit) the organisation decides that a new training programme is required in order to make the firm more competitive. How are the members going to react? This will depend on how much their own situation is affected by the training programme and how they will react to it. This in turn will be affected by the kind of people they are. How can we find out? Well, I have found the ideas of two Americans, Walter Doyle and Gerald A. Ponder on 'The Practicality Ethic in Decision Making' very useful when looking at how individuals respond to change. They argue that if we listen to the way in which individuals talk about anything new that is introduced into their lives we find the term 'practical' is frequently used by them. That is, they analyse the change to see how it will affect them. Doyle and Ponder pick out three general types of individuals in organisations when looking at how the people may be affected; (a) The Rational Adopter, (b) The Stone Age Obstructionist, (c) The Pragmatic Sceptic. Doyle and Ponder argue that very few people fitted into the image of the Rational Adopter who carefully weighs up all the pros and cons and then decides. They argue that most people in organisations are either what they call "Stone Age Obstructionists", i.e. those who oppose everything that may change the present situation; no doubt you are quite familiar with them; "I've seen it all before", "It won't work here"; and what they call "Pragmatic Sceptics". These are the people who look at the situation and gauge how it's going to affect them, how the situation is going to change **now** not in the long term, and what is actually going to happen, e.g. "Never mind the crap, just tell me what is really going to happen". Doyle and Ponder further argue that the "Pragmatic Sceptic" will look at a new training programme in terms of three items. First of all a change must be **instrumental**. This means that it must describe a procedure which makes sense to the individual in terms of his own working practices. Any proposals which do not do this will be seen as not being practical. Secondly, the new training programme must be **congruent** to the individual's perception of his situation in the organisation. Doyle and Ponder argue that this term congruence has three aspects.

(1) Does the procedure contained in the change proposals fit the way in which the individual works at the present time?
(2) Have the changes proposed e.g. a new training programme been demonstrated as being successful in similar situations?
(3) To what extent will the proposals change the worker's own self image and his relationships with his colleagues.

Thirdly the final criterion that Doyle and Ponder set out is **cost** — in short the 'what's in it for me' syndrome. If it is going to cost a lot of time and effort and if the perceived returns are not too good then there is little chance that people will view a new training programme with any great enthusiasm.

Now take a close look at everyone who is going to be affected by the introduction of the training programme and try and set out what type of person they are using Doyle and Ponder's categories.

I do not know what your results are but I hope you have not found a preponderance of "Stone Age Obstructionists"; if so, then your training programme will have very little chance!!

If you have carefully worked your way through the last two checkpoints you should now have a very clear picture of what your organisation looks like. This however, is only the first step in trying to find out how the training programme is affecting your organisation. The next step is to take the main elements of the organisation as set out in this Component and monitor the changes that take place as the training programme is implemented. Well, how do you do this? The previous components of this unit will give you the tools to obtain the information. However, you are not finding out information about the training programme but what effect is it having on the organisation as a whole e.g. How are the mix of the cultures changing? What effect is it having on the members of the organisation? Is the task and technology of the organisation changing as a result of your new training programme?

Let us now take a closer look at some of these Questions.

(a) The Organisation Cultures — It is doubtful if all the departments in the organisation have the same culture, each department will probably differ according to the job they do. The departments most affected will be those most closely related to the new Training Programme. When you have established what culture or mix of cultures there are in those departments most closely affected by the new Training Programme monitor the situation and evaluate the changes, e.g. Does the department go from Role to Task, or from People to Role?
(b) People — The introduction of the Training Programme is going to affect different people in different ways with those who are involved being affected most while those who are not may think it a waste of time. The extent to which they will be affected will depend on which Doyle and Ponder category you have put them into. Other elements that could enter into the situation may include gains and losses in self esteem, an increase in anxiety and most important, changes in role.
(c) Task — The introduction of a new Training Programme may have as its objective a change in the main task of the organisation. Changes outside the organisation may have forced it into new fields where the employees may have to be re-trained. Your main aim here is to chart the extent to which the task of the organisation or of a department changes.
(d) Technology — You may remember that this element deals with the way the department or organisation carries out its work. I have no doubt that you will be able to see major changes if the new Training Programme is successful.

A very detailed account of methods of assessment and evaluation is set out in the Study Units of Volume

Four especially Study Unit 7 and I would suggest you try and get hold of them if possible.

The final step in gauging the effects of the new training programme on the organisation is to compare the picture at the end of the implementation of the training programme with what the organisation looked like before it was introduced. To do this you must make another 'situational analysis' of your organisation and then compare them.

Diagram (3)

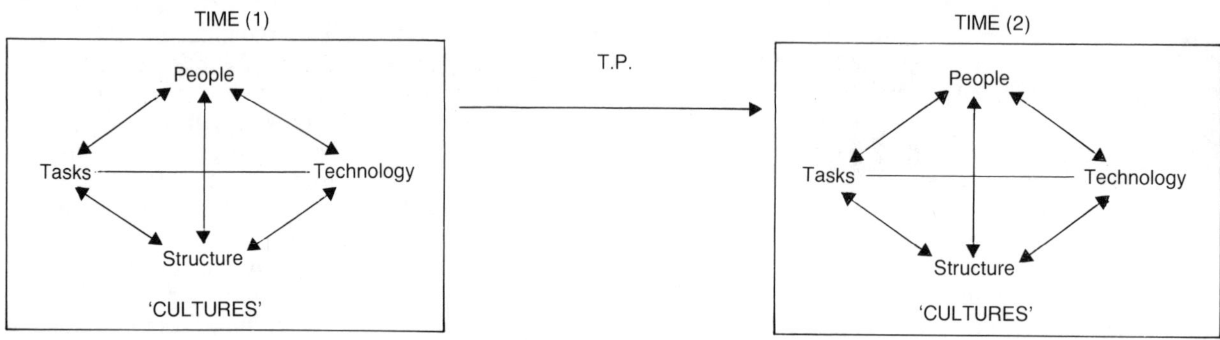

I have no doubt whatsoever that your picture of the firm in time (2) will be different from that in time (1)

What I have done in this Component is to take you through a way of looking at the effects of the introduction of a new training programme into your organisation. What the last Component is going to do is, on the basis of the information you have obtained through working through Components six and seven, look at what conclusions you can draw and more importantly what further action is to be taken.

References

Doyle, W. & Ponder G., 'The Practicality Ethic in Teacher Decision Making', *Interchange,* Vol **8** No 3 (1977), pp 1-12.

Handy, C. B. (1985), *Understanding Organisations,* Penguin.

Leavitt, H. J. (1965), 'Applied Organisational Change in Industry', *Handbook of Organisation* March, J. G. (1965), Raud McNally.

Component 8:

Drawing Conclusions and Planning Future Actions

Key Words

Management of training; context; designing and implementing; evaluating; drawing up conclusions; actions; categories and types of action; action plans; implementing change.

Objectives

Following the implementation of a training programme, to be able to:

* draw up a set of positive conclusions
* list a number of categories and types of possible actions
* produce an appropriate action plan.

Introduction

If you have survived to reach this point in the Volume — "Congratulations!". As this is the final Component in a long Volume, it is a good time to take stock and see where we are, how we arrived here, and where we should head for next. In other words, we need to draw up our conclusions and plan future actions.

Obviously the focus throughout this Volume has been on the management of training rather than on the detail of training itself. Many of the topics have been covered elsewhere in the Training Technology Programme, particularly in the earlier Volumes, but with a different emphasis. Our concern has been with the environment or context within which training takes place and has to be organised and managed; the broad strategy rather than the day-to-day tactical details. In fact the original title for this Volume was going to be "The Training Context".

Checkpoint

Go back to the start of this Volume and quickly skip through the Study Units, reminding yourself of their titles and broad outlines. As you go along, write down a **brief** summary (one or two sentences or short notes) of what you think each of the Study Units was about, e.g. the main topics, ideas, key concepts.

Well, as I see it Study Unit One was about how you go about establishing the overall need for training within an organisation (no surprise!). The emphasis throughout this Study Unit was on the environment — both within the organisation and external to it — along with the training policy and who has the responsibility for training. Study Unit Two dealt with identifying specific training needs, setting standards of performance and deciding training priorities — again in relation to the organisation. Study Unit Three continued the theme by considering the management of innovation and change within the organisation. Study Unit Four looked at interpersonal skills in training, and Study Unit Five considered ways of looking at and analysing training materials. Study Unit Six rounded off the Volume with designing and implementing training programmes.

Before we go on from this brief review, let's look a bit more closely at the relationships between the various topics we have dealt with in the Volume.

The Management of Training

It would seem reasonable to decide that when considering the management of training, the first step would be to establish the need for training — within the context of the firm, company, organisation or whatever. (Of course one outcome might be that we **cannot** establish any need for training; or maybe that we can 'poach' trained people from outside the firm — a not unknown practice!) The next obvious step (SU 2) would be the identification of clear specific training needs. SU 3 followed on logically by dealing with how to manage any changes in training that may need to be introduced as a result of our deliberations. This raises the vital issue of working with and through people, so SU 4 covered the development of interpersonal skills. Before going on to consider how to design and implement training programmes, SU 5 reminded us of the large and growing range of training materials that can be used, and how to analyse and evaluate them. Finally, SU 6 dealt with the actual process of designing, implementing and evaluating training programmes. Thus there is a logical and progressive design behind the topics covered in this Volume, even if at times you may have found it difficult to see the wood for the trees!

Study Unit Six

Let's now take a closer look at this Study Unit, number Six. It has been extended from the normal six Components in order to provide coverage of both designing and implementing training programmes; but keeping within the overall context of the management of training.

Component One was an introductory one, which outlined the key considerations in designing and implementing training programmes. Component Two tackled the question "Where do we start?" in relation to the needs of trainees, trainers, training and learning. Component Three considered in detail the question of resources. Components Four and Five dealt with the practical business of planning and running a training programme. Component Six looked at ways of monitoring, evaluating and reporting on training programmes. (Bear in mind that Volume Four gives comprehensive coverage of **Assessment and Evaluation in Training.**) Component Seven continued this theme, but broadened out to consider the effect of any particular programme on the organisation as a whole.

So now we get to this final Component, number Eight. A medical analogy will give us another view of the 'management' context. When we feel ill, we accept that something is wrong and go to see the doctor. We anticipate a need for some 'treatment'. In response to questioning and prompts, we describe the symptoms and features of the 'complaint'. The doctor may decide to quantify certain aspects and take measurements (e.g. temperature, pulse, blood pressure) to add to the observations and narrative account of events. All this is the equivalent of establishing the overall need for training and the start of the process of identifying specific training needs, and is a further example of a systematic approach to a problem. The doctor then attempts to label (diagnose) the illness — the next stage in the identification of training needs.

At this point the professionalism of the expert should really begin to show, as the doctor tackles the question of "What to do about it", i.e. what treatment (if any) to prescribe.

Diagnosis in many cases may be relatively routine, but the choice of a particular treatment may be difficult and far from routine. Similarly with training programmes, the choice of options may be very wide. The selection of appropriate training was the theme of Components Three and Four dealing with resources and the planning of training programmes. Hopefully the selected treatment is then administered (Component Five on running training programmes), but of course the story doesn't end there. The doctor will need to check (monitor, assess and evaluate) the effects and effectiveness of the treatment, and decide on future action (more/less/different treatment etc.).

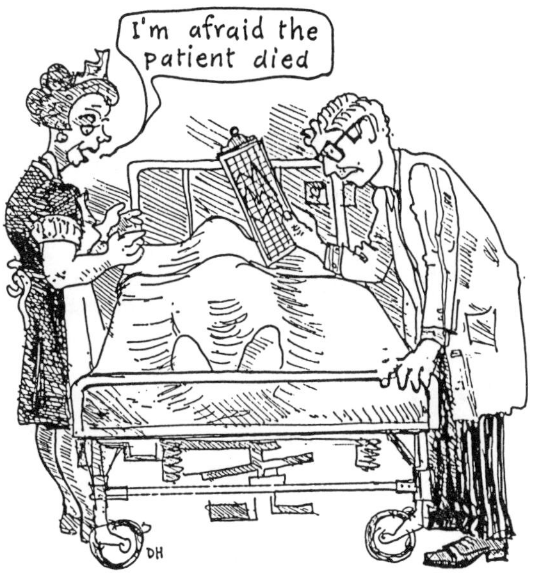

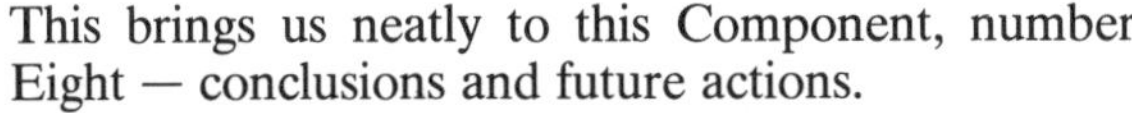

This brings us neatly to this Component, number Eight — conclusions and future actions.

Drawing up Conclusions

Drawing up conclusions should, in the first place, be seen as a means to an end rather than an end in itself, i.e. the conclusions are another management tool. "The patient died" is a valid conclusion, but one would hope it is by no means the end of the matter! At the same time you will be trying to avoid stating the obvious, or teaching grandmother to suck eggs. A good guide is to ask yourself the question "so what?" — if the answer is a blank, then the conclusions are probably not worth stating! Conclusions should lead on to positive proposals for future action.

Categories of Action

When monitoring a training programme and drawing up conclusions, a number of different categories of action may suggest themselves. If evidence is accumulated during the running of a programme that all is not well, we may decide to modify the programme as it goes along — or in extreme cases abandon it altogether before completion. If the trainees are volunteers they may, of course, 'vote with their feet' and quit the programme if it is failing to meet their perceived needs. 'Fine tuning' of a programme during its operation is a quite common occurrence — as when the doctor modifies the patient's medication during treatment. Hopefully the total abandonment of a programme is a rare event — unless there has been a sudden unexpected and dramatic change in training needs.

Most categories of action are, however, proposed after the training programme has been run, based on evaluation and the resulting conclusions. A number of possibilities arise.

We may decide simply to abandon the whole programme, lock, stock and barrel. The harshness of this 'total rejection' has been sometimes disguised under the milder-sounding title of 'discontinuance', but it amounts to the same thing.

List any other **categories of action** you can think of apart from abandonment.

Well, I suppose the opposite extreme is adoption of the complete programme as it stands, without any changes, and the re-running of the programme as and when required. Other categories might be overall modification and revision before re-running, or the rejection/adoption of certain sections of the programme — involving the replacement of any rejected sections by new material.

Thus there would seem to be a number of different categories of action from which choices could be made, on the basis of conclusions arrived at during or following the running of a training programme. Obviously a number of factors will need to be considered, and these have already been covered under evaluation, e.g. comparisons of success/achievement before and after training, or compared with previous training methods; content of training programme in relation to needs; attitudes, interest and motivation.

Types of Action

If the conclusion is that the training programme has only been partially successful, then the details on which the conclusions are based should indicate what type of action needs to be taken. Headings to be considered have already been indicated in this Study Unit, e.g. resources (staff, time, finance, accommodation, equipment), strategies and methods, content of training. Some will no doubt be easier to cope with than others! Also it must be remembered that it is often relatively straightforward to spot that something is wrong or not working effectively, but it may be very difficult to decide on the type of action that will improve things. Back to the medical analogy, where the doctor may need to try out a number of different treatments before finding the best one. Hopefully it is not all trial and error!

So far, then, the conclusions should indicate the appropriate categories and types of action.

From what we have just said under types of action, make up a list of about ten different actions that might be considered when modifying a training programme (e.g. alter/change accommodation).

Here's a list to compare with yours:—

Resources

* *Alter amounts of time given to different sections/topics*
* *Divert finance to bring in (and pay) external trainers*
* *Improve staff/trainee ratio for certain sections*
* *Increase provision of equipment (e.g. projectors)*
* *Alter/change accommodation.*

Strategies and Methods

* *Alter overall strategies (e.g. use team teaching, open/distance learning)*
* *Change/modify methods (e.g. increase the mix of methods; use CBT, simulators, visits; give more 'hands-on' experience)*
* *Alter assessment procedures if suspect*

Content

* *Adjust content to match precise needs*
* *Alter style of presentation to match trainees' abilities, expectations and needs*
* *Increase amount of practice and exercises*

Note that it is often difficult to separate out individual actions, e.g. diverting finance to bring in external trainers will affect finance, staffing and probably time, accommodation, resources in general, methods and content. As was pointed out in Study Unit Three, **any** change tends to produce widespread effects, some of which may be quite unanticipated.

If changes need to be made, apart from a simple adoption or rejection strategy, then we will need to plan for the necessary actions to be taken. One well-tried method of doing this is by the construction and use of action plans.

Action Plans

You may be familiar with the somewhat old-hat method of 'Management by Objectives', where objective statements about performance to be achieved were normally linked to a time-scale e.g. to improve sales by 15% by the end of the year. A similar technique can be used whenever any change is contemplated, and it can best be expressed as a formal written **action plan**. Basically, an action plan is just what the term says. It specifies what actions need to be taken — in sufficient detail to make them explicit, 'objective' and measurable, and it lays down the time-scale and suitable deadlines. The main feature is that it encourages self-discipline, in that it forces you to commit planned actions to paper, resulting in a formal document of intent. The action plan, if appropriate, may then form the basis of a contract which can be checked from time to time to monitor progress.

Headings

An action plan consists of a number of columns running across the page, with suitable headings. These headings can be formulated by asking the basic questions What? How? and When? Thus an action plan for personal development might have the following headings:—

Ideas for improving personal performance
Active steps to be taken to achieve this
Target dates for each step.

Possibly in this case there should also be:—

Assessment of degree of success!

It is quite usual to formulate an action plan in consultation with someone else, and an agreement may be reached as to how and when progress and achievement should be monitored and checked. A 'contract' of this type can act as a powerful spur in ensuring that the plan is followed through, provided that all parties involved feel committed to it.

An action plan can be drawn up for most situations where some future change or action is being actively considered. Thus if changes are to be made either in the way a training programme is to be run, or a training section or department is organised, then you should produce an action plan. The activity itself may indicate the need for other forms of documentation, such as a network diagram, time chart or other diagrammatic representation. It is likely that a number of people will be involved in the various actions identified.

Let's now look at a specimen action plan, remembering that any such plan needs to be tailored to meet the specific requirements.

SPECIMEN ACTION PLAN

BASIC ACTION Steps Necessary to Achieve Action	People Involved and Affected	Resources	Time-Scale **Start** Finish
INCREASE TRAINEE PARTICIPATION			
Motivate, Involve and Re-train Trainers	Trainers + Training Manager + Consultant(s)	Cost of Re-training + Accommodation + Administration	**Now** 2 Months from Now (+2 M)
Revise Lesson Plans	Trainers Supporting Staff	Cost of time & Resources	**+1 M** +3 M from Now
Monitor and Evaluate	Training Manager	(Part of Normal Job)	**+3 M** +5 M
RE-WRITE SECTION "C" OF THE SYLLABUS			
Meetings and Consensus of Trainers Involved	Trainers + Subject Expert + Training Manager	Cost of Time & Resources	**Now** +1 M
Re-write, Edit and Check	As above	As above, plus Administration	**+1 M** +3 M

Here are two more Basic Actions. Complete the other columns for yourself.

Change to Continuous Assessment.

Produce Computer-Based Training Volume to cover Section "A" of the Syllabus.

BASIC ACTION Steps Necessary to Achieve Action	People Involved and Affected	Resources	Time-Scale **Start** Finish
CHANGE TO CONTINUOUS ASSESSMENT			
Motivate, Involve and Re-train Trainers	Trainers + Training Manager + Consultant(s)	Cost of Re-training + Accommodation + Administration	**Now** +2 M
Decide and Plan Ways of Introducing C/A	As above	Mainly Cost and Use of Experts	**+2 M** +4 M
Implement C/A	As above	Administration	**+4 M** +6 M
Monitor and Evaluate	Training Manager	(Part of Normal Job)	**+4 M** +8 M
PRODUCE CBT PACKAGE TO COVER SECTION "A" OF THE SYLLABUS			
Draw up Specification	Trainers + Training Manager + Subject Expert	Mainly Cost of Time	**Now** +2 M
Negotiate with and Select CBT Producer	Training Manager + CBT Prod.	Financial Budget to Cover High Costs	**+2 M** +4 M
Produce CBT Package	As above	As above	**+4 M** +10M
Validate Package	All staff	Equipment and Accommodation	**+10M** +12M
Monitor and Evaluate	Training Manager	(Part of Normal Job)	**+12M** +18M

Of course, each of the steps could be broken down further — it depends how far you feel you need to go in specifying the fine detail. The above tables, due to the restrictions of normal printing, look a bit clumsy. In practice the best way is to take a fairly large sheet of paper (e.g. a flip chart pad) to give more scope in construction and presentation.

You will no doubt have realised that what we have just been doing is applying the methods and techniques of the systems approach which has formed the core of the TTP. The process of managing such changes was dealt with in Components Four and Five of SU 3 of this Volume — you might find it useful to have another quick look through them. Any change should involve a re-cycling through the step-by-step procedures of the systems approach, and validation and evaluation of the revised methods and materials should not be by-passed. By doing this you should be able to identify clearly any improvements over the previous training programme.

Finally

Evaluation and stating conclusions must be seen as the means to an end, and not an end in themselves —

however elegant and satisfying the procedures themselves may become. Any necessary actions must be clearly spelt out and implemented, otherwise we are just wasting our time. Co-operation of all those involved must be actively sought, and the actions themselves monitored and evaluated.

Voluntary Volume Assignment (VPA)

This Volume has been written by a number of authors and each Study Unit contains one or more pieces of Voluntary Tutor Seen Work (TSW). If you have completed all of these, you will have received, in a substantial way, the content of this Volume and you should consider this as completion of the VPA. You may, however, have omitted a number of items of TSW or have received suggestions from your tutor about revising or expanding an item of TSW.

We suggest that you **either** complete one or more of the items of TSW which you previously left aside **and/ or** you revise or expand an item of TSW already submitted.